PARTIES, POLITICS, AND
PUBLIC POLICY IN AMERICA

D1172981

PARTIES, POLITICS, AND PUBLIC POLICY IN AMERICA

ELEVENTH EDITION

MARC J. HETHERINGTON
Vanderbilt University

and

BRUCE A. LARSON
Gettysburg College

CQ PRESS

A DIVISION OF SAGE

WASHINGTON, D.C.

CQ Press
2300 N Street, NW, Suite 800
Washington, DC 20037

Phone: 202-729-1900; toll-free, 1-866-4CQ-PRESS (1-866-427-7737)

Web: www.cqpress.com

Cover design: www.thedesignfarm.com
Composition: C&M Digitals (P) Ltd.

☺ The paper used in this publication exceeds the requirements of the American National Standard for Information Sciences—Permanence of Paper for Printed Library Materials, ANSI Z39.48-1992.

Printed and bound in the United States of America

13   12   11   10   09   1   2   3   4   5

Library of Congress Cataloging-in-Publication Data

Hetherington, Marc J.
 Parties, politics, and public policy in America / Marc J. Hetherington, Bruce A. Larson. — 11th ed.
     p. cm.
 Includes bibliographical references and index.
 ISBN 978-1-60426-458-6 (paper-bound : alk. paper) 1. Political parties—United States.
 I. Larson, Bruce A., II. Title.

 JK2265.H54 2010
 324.273—dc22

                                                                    2009046420

For Mom and Dad, strong partisans
M.J.H.

For Alice and Lily, with all my love
B.A.L.

CONTENTS

3 POLITICAL PARTIES AND THE ELECTORAL PROCESS: NOMINATIONS   71

4   CAMPAIGNS AND CAMPAIGN FINANCE   109

5   THE CONGRESSIONAL PARTY AND THE FORMATION OF PUBLIC POLICY   153

TABLES, FIGURES, AND BOXES

TABLES

FIGURES

BOXES

PREFACE

The American political party system is in flux. For decades, parties were eclipsed by individual candidates, interest groups, and the mass media to such a degree that at times the parties appeared to be mere bystanders to the struggles over power and policy. Recently, however, they have strengthened their position, challenged their competition, and produced a resurgence that most scholars and pundits did not forecast. What is more, the latest scholarship shows that party revival has occurred in the context of a candidate-centered politics heavily influenced by television, personality, celebrity, mass merchandising, image making, interest groups, and the like. The conventional thesis that American parties are suffering from decay and decline is less compelling today than it was in the 1970s or 1980s. In short, there is new life in the parties. More organizationally diffuse and porous than the hierarchical parties of the past, the contemporary parties have adapted to, and are now influential players in, the cacophonous politics that began emerging in the second half of the twentieth century.

In tracking this resurgence in the eleventh edition of *Parties, Politics, and Public Policy in America,* we explore some important questions. In a two-party system that has traditionally rewarded moderation, why have the parties become more ideologically distinct? In a political culture that continues to hold parties in low esteem, why do ordinary Americans follow party cues more closely today than they have in generations? We keep these questions firmly in mind in our consideration of the American party system, from its core characteristics to its functions and roles in elections, nominations, campaign finance, partisanship, and the formation of public policy. This reassessment of the status of parties in the United States allows us to bring into focus the most recent and important changes in the party system.

Party revitalization appears on many levels. When the Bipartisan Campaign Reform Act (BCRA) of 2002 closed the soft money loophole that parties were aggressively exploiting, the parties responded by raising more hard money in the most recent election cycles alone than they had raised in hard and soft money combined in the cycle prior to BCRA. Moreover, in the most competitive congressional contests, the parties have spent millions of hard dollars on independent expenditures to support their own candidates and attack opposition party candidates. Such expenditures allow parties to make a real difference in marginal congressional districts—where control of Congress ultimately is decided. Parties, then, are playing a major role in campaigns in which they have a chance to win, and for a very good reason: they have the money to do so.

On the governing level, interparty conflict in Congress is more intense now than it has been in generations. Major policy differences separate the parties, and voters have no trouble realizing that Republicans in government are more conservative than Democrats and that Democrats are more liberal than Republicans. Research by Keith Poole and Howard Rosenthal shows that seventy or more members of the House in the 1970s typically voted as if they belonged in the other party, but in the 110th Congress (2007–2009) not a single House Democrat had a voting record more conservative than that of the most liberal House Republican. There is almost never any ideological overlap between the parties, and mavericks have declined in number and influence. To be sure, factions such as the Blue Dogs—a coalition of moderate congressional Democrats that flexed its muscle on health care reform legislation in the 111th Congress—continue to exist, and such factions pose significant obstacles to party government in the United States. But on many, if not most, issues, even factions such as the Blue Dogs remain squarely in the partisan fold. The conservative coalition—a band of conservative Democrats and Republicans that was effective between the 1940s and 1970s—belongs to America's past.

In this edition we trace the scholarly explanations for the polarization of the congressional parties as well as the explanations for this trend offered by former members of Congress who served during both weak and strong party eras. In addition to well-known explanations for congressional party polarization that center on changes in the constituencies that elect members of Congress, former members cite important changes in the political culture in Washington, D.C. Since the mid-1990s, the partisan balance in Congress has often been so close that majority control following the next election has been uncertain. Precarious control leads to a team mentality within the party caucuses. Members of Congress also are afforded fewer opportunities to get to know those on the other side of the aisle than in past decades, which has led to significant changes in interparty relations. One nagging result is that members treat those of the other party with considerably less respect than they once did. If the environment in Washington has become poisonous, as many participants and observers contend, no one should be surprised.

The growing ideological divide between the parties in Washington has been institutionalized in leadership selection. Over the past decade or so, strongly ideological members such as Tom DeLay, John Boehner, and Nancy Pelosi have dominated party leadership. When moderation infused the parties, the caucuses generally chose centrists as leaders. Although we cannot predict the impact of heightened, acrimonious partisanship, we can surmise that more ideological leadership, when combined with workable majorities in both houses, will at times culminate in fundamental shifts in public policy.

With partisan and ideological figures now leading the political debate, parties on the electoral level also have become stronger in certain respects. Although many voters still see themselves as independent, a growing number do not act that way. New data show that ordinary Americans view politics in more partisan and ideological terms than in the past. Americans now vote straight party tickets more often, perceive more differences between the parties, provide more reasons for liking and disliking the parties, and evaluate leaders in more partisan terms. This trend exists even though the majority of voters continue to say they dislike and distrust parties and, indeed, favor divided over unified party government. Ironically, citizens are becoming what they say they dislike: partisan and ideological. We link these changes to the information environment produced by the ideological polarization between the congressional parties.

In this edition, we examine what divides partisans in the electorate. Much of the debate about the polarization of the electoral parties has centered on issue differences, but not everyone agrees. Morris Fiorina, for one, demonstrates that Republicans and Democrats do not differ as much as political commentators suggest. Although Fiorina is no doubt largely correct in regard to specific issues, we demonstrate that nonissue differences exist today between ordinary Republicans and Democrats that did not exist a decade or more ago. Specifically, a values chasm has emerged as Republicans and Democrats increasingly approach politics with fundamentally different worldviews. And when strongly held values collide in the electorate, debate becomes more heated, politics more intense, and losing more difficult to accept.

We also capture other important trends, such as the changes in the coalitions of groups that make up the parties. The widening differences between men and women can hardly be exaggerated. As recently as 1980, the "gender gap" between the parties was nonexistent. In the 1996 and 2000 presidential elections, however, women voted more than ten percentage points more Democratic than men did. Although the gender gap shrank slightly in 2004 with the greater emphasis on security concerns, a large difference between the sexes remains. In the 2008 presidential election, women voted seven percentage points more Democratic than men. Current studies also show that the extent of voters' religious observance yields as many clues about their partisanship as it does about their religious affiliation. People who regularly attend church are moving to the Republican Party, and those who do not attend as frequently are disproportionately Democratic. Racial and other minorities continue to provide more support to Democrats than to Republicans. Because Latinos are the fastest growing group in the United States, this trend will have significant future implications, especially as Latino voters diffuse into a larger number of states.

Although significant revisions have been made to this book, its structure and core elements will look familiar to instructors and other readers. We continue to offer a broad treatment of what parties are in the American context, how they compete both nationally and regionally, how the nomination and campaign finance systems work, and how parties and partisanship affect both the masses and the elite. As in the past, the treatment of these topics is designed to provide insights into the party role in the formation of public policy. In addition, we have augmented the traditional elements of the book with enhanced tables and figures, and we have updated all coverage through the 2008 election cycle wherever possible.

Acknowledgments

Marc J. Hetherington especially thanks William J. Keefe, the longtime author of this book. Although this is the first edition that does not include Bill's name on the cover, his profound influence can still be seen in the pages that follow. Even with the marked resurgence of parties in America lately, Bill's original insights about the barriers to disciplined and responsible parties that are inherent in the American political system still hold true. Indeed, being reminded of this fact during a time of party polarization has been the most interesting part of the intellectual journey we have taken for this new edition. Younger scholars should spend some time with the work of those who were socialized when Bill was. Instead of trafficking in the thin gruel of bite-sized facts strung together into a larger work, that generation of scholars spoke about larger ideas of normative import while attempting to engage a larger audience than most political scientists endeavor to do today.

In addition, Hetherington thanks Bruce Larson for joining him on this edition. No one knows more about campaign finance and congressional parties than Bruce, and this book benefits handsomely from his expertise. More than that, the joys of working on a project with one's best friend in the profession are impossible to overstate. It allows for smooth transitions between discussions of the organization of congressional committees and party voting on the one hand to the relative importance of John Entwistle and John Paul Jones to their respective bands on the other.

Hetherington is indebted to Jason Husser and Matt Simpson for their capable and steady research assistance and grateful for the advice from colleagues. Bruce Oppenheimer was, as always, a helpful sounding board about ideas for revisions to the chapter on Congress, and Jonathan Weiler has been a great source of insight on the things that divide partisans in the electorate today. Finally, as is the case with every project that he has taken on in the past fifteen years, Hetherington acknowledges that it never would have been as satisfying without Suzanne Globetti. In addition to being a wonderfully supportive wife, she is the most talented political scientist and editor around.

Bruce Larson thanks his dear friend and professional colleague Marc Hetherington for inviting him to coauthor the eleventh edition of *Parties, Politics, and Public Policy in America.* As anyone familiar with elections, voting behavior, and public opinion scholarship knows, Marc's research regularly sets new standards for the field. Indeed, it is difficult to think of a political scientist during the past decade who has had a more important impact than Marc on the field of mass political behavior, and Larson considers himself extremely fortunate to have the opportunity to work with such a talented scholar. On a personal note, Larson would also like to thank Marc for his extraordinary friendship. He especially looks forward to many future conversations with him about American cultural life in the 1970s, particularly the decade's music, inexpensive beer, and muscle cars. Larson thanks his colleagues and students at Gettysburg College for providing an intellectually stimulating environment in which to teach and do research. Eric Heberlig, a friend and collaborator on other projects, regularly offered valuable insights on congressional parties and congressional campaign finance, and Rob Bohrer provided important insights about political parties from a comparative perspective. Char Weise tendered many keen insights about American parties (especially for an economist). Finally, Larson would like to thank his extraordinary spouse, Alice Carter, and their lovely daughter, Lily, for their love, support, and encouragement throughout this project. As always, Alice's editorial suggestions greatly improved the final product, and Lily's infectious energy and zest for life ensured that every day was filled with absolute delight.

The following individuals deserve our appreciation for the time they took to review this eleventh edition and for the input they provided: Nancy Billica, University of Colorado; Daniel Coffey, University of Akron; Amy McKay, Georgia State University; Anthony Nownes, University of Tennessee; and Steven Tauber, University of South Florida.

The authors acknowledge the support of Brenda Carter, Charisse Kiino, Allison McKay, and Allyson Rudolph from CQ Press, as well as freelance copyeditor Carolyn Goldinger, for all their help. In their various roles, they made this project happen. Brenda coordinated the effort as head of the College business unit, Allison kept us focused on our deadlines and provided a helpful sounding board, and Allyson skillfully shepherded the book through production. Carolyn reorganized some of our efforts and managed to catch our mistakes; we are eternally grateful to her for her very skillful copyediting, her sense of humor, and her appreciation of Al Green. Everyone's talent was indispensable.

1 POLITICAL PARTIES AND THE POLITICAL SYSTEM

THE AMERICAN POLITICAL PARTY SYSTEM is not an insoluble puzzle, but it does have more than its share of mysteries. The main one could be how it has survived in a difficult and complicated environment. The broad explanation is that the party system survives because parties are an inevitable outgrowth of civil society ("factions... sown in the nature of man," thought James Madison[1]); because parties perform functions important to democratic polities ("democracy is unthinkable save in terms of parties," wrote E. E. Schattschneider[2]); and because the American public has never had particularly high expectations of parties or made particularly rigorous demands on them. In truth, their survival has not been contingent on performance.

The term *political party* has roughly the same number of definitions as it has people who observe them. These definitions fall largely into two categories: electoral and ideological. In the electoral camp, Schattschneider defined a party as "first of all an organized attempt to get power."[3] Leon Epstein described a party as "any group, however loosely organized, that seeks to elect governmental officeholders under a given label."[4] In this view, parties form, first and foremost, to win elections. Others define parties in terms of ideology or principles. Edmund Burke defined a party as "a body of men united, for promulgating by their joint endeavors the national interest, upon some particular principle in which they are all agreed."[5] By this definition, groups like the American Green Party, which have little realistic chance of winning an election, are still parties because they campaign on the ideals held by their members and voiced by their leaders.

With good reason, those who study American political parties tend to rely on definitions that emphasize the electoral, not the ideological. Simply put, the

American political system is hardwired to produce two dominant parties. Because they operate in such a large and heterogeneous political environment, American parties tend to downplay ideology, even when party leaders are strongly ideological, as is the case today. By emphasizing either strongly conservative or strongly liberal principles, American parties run the risk of alienating voters in the political center, voters who in a two-party system invariably decide the outcome of competitive elections.[6] Indeed, political commentators today often suggest that the Republicans' decline from holding the presidency and majorities in both houses of Congress between 2003 and 2007 to losing Congress and the presidency in the 2006 and 2008 election cycles resulted from moving too far to the ideological right. Compared with European democracies, which feature a multitude of sternly ideological parties, the major parties in the United States gravitate (or at least they should) toward the political center, emphasizing elections over policies and political advantage over principle. Indeed, it is nearly impossible for a party to implement its ideological preferences unless it has first won an election.

The Activities of Parties

A principal thesis in the scholarship on political parties is that they are indispensable to the functioning of democratic political systems. Scholars have differed sharply in their approaches to the study of parties and in their appraisals of the functions or activities of parties, but they are in striking agreement on the linkage between parties and democracy. Representative of a wide band of analysis, the following statements by V. O. Key Jr. and Schattschneider, respectively, sketch the broad outlines of the argument:

> Governments operated, of course, long before political parties in the modern sense came into existence....The proclamation of the right of men to have a hand in their own governing did not create institutions by which they might exercise that right. Nor did the machinery of popular government come into existence overnight. By a torturous process party systems came into being to implement democratic ideas. As democratic ideas corroded the old foundations of authority, members of the old governing elite reached out to legitimize their positions under the new notions by appealing for popular support. That appeal compelled deference to popular views, but it also required the development of organizations to communicate with and to manage the electorate....In a sense, government, left suspended in mid-air by the erosion of the old justifications for its authority, had to build new foundations in the new environment of a democratic ideology. In short, it had to have machinery to win votes.[7]

> The rise of political parties is indubitably one of the principal distinguishing marks of modern government. The parties, in fact, have played a major role as *makers* of governments, more especially they have been the makers of democratic government.... [Political] parties created democracy and...modern democracy is unthinkable save in terms of the parties....The parties are not...merely appendages of modern government; they are in the center of it and play a determinative and creative role in it.[8]

The contributions of political parties to the maintenance of democratic politics can be judged in a rough way by examining the principal activities in which they engage. Of particular importance are those activities associated with the recruitment and selection of leadership, the representation and integration of interests, and the control and direction of government.

Recruitment and Selection of Leaders

The processes by which political leaders are recruited and elected or appointed to office form the central core of party activity.[9] The party interest also extends to the appointment of administrative and judicial officers, such as cabinet members and judges, once the party has captured the executive branch of government.[10]

Even though their power is far from complete, the parties must participate in recruitment. It is difficult to see how hundreds of thousands of elective offices could be filled in the absence of parties without turning each election into a free-for-all, conspicuous by the presence of numerous candidates holding all varieties of set, shifting, and undisclosed views. Composing a government out of an odd mélange of officials, especially at the national level, would be very difficult. Any form of collective accountability to the voters would vanish. By proposing lists of candidates and campaigning on their behalf, the parties bring certain measures of order, routine, and predictability to the electoral process.

That said, party influence is not a set-in-stone guarantee of success. In 2008 Rep. Albert Wynn (D-Md.) had the endorsement and financial support of the Democratic leadership in the House, but an ensemble of liberal bloggers and Web sites collectively known as netroots helped engineer the victory of Donna Edwards over Wynn in the primary.[11] And party organizations do not necessarily dominate the process by which candidates are recruited or nominated. Some candidates are self-starters and choose to enter primaries without waiting for approval from party leaders. With their personal followings and sources of campaign money, they may pay scant heed to party leaders or party politics. Other candidates are recruited and groomed by political interest groups, which can be particularly lucrative sources of campaign funds. This is not to say that parties are irrelevant to the recruitment and nomination processes; indeed, candidates spend considerable time and energy vying for the endorsements of key activists, leaders, and fund-raisers in the informal party network.[12] But the looseness of the American party system creates conditions under which a party's control over many of the candidates who run under its banner is thin or nonexistent.

So, given all of this, how involved *are* parties in the recruitment of candidates? Sandy Maisel and his collaborators find that party influence is greater than one might guess in a supposedly candidate-centered political system, although it is also far from universal. In 1997 they conducted a study of two hundred congressional districts throughout the country, identifying potential U.S. House candidates in each of the districts. They asked these potential candidates whether they had been contacted by party officials and, if so, by which level of the party? Forty percent of the potential candidates reported having been contacted by at least one party committee, with local party committees by far the most active in the recruitment of candidates. Moreover, those who had been contacted by party committees in 1997 were significantly more likely to run in 1998 than potential candidates who had not been contacted.[13] Maisel's work suggests that parties can, in fact, play an important recruitment role.[14]

Whatever their varying levels of influence, the constant factors in party politics are the pursuit of power, office, and advantage. Yet in serving their own interest in winning office, parties make other contributions to the public at large and to the political system as a whole. They help to educate the voters on issues and mobilize them for political action, provide a link between the people and the government, and simplify the choices to be made in elections. The parties do what voters cannot do by themselves: from the totality of interests and issues in politics, they choose those that will become "the agenda of formal public discourse."[15] In the process of shaping the agenda, they provide a mechanism by which voters not only can make sense out of what government does but also can relate to the government itself.

Representation and Integration of Group Interests

The United States is a complex and heterogeneous nation. An extraordinary variety of political interest groups, organized around particularistic objectives, exists within it. Conflicts between one group and another, between coalitions of groups, and between various groups and the government are inevitable. Because one of the major functions of government is to take sides in private disputes, what it decides and does are of high importance to groups. When at their creative best, parties and their leaders help to keep group conflicts within tolerable limits. Viewed from a wider perspective, the relationship between parties and private organizations is one of bargaining and accommodating—groups need the parties as much as the parties need them. No group can expect to move far toward the attainment of its objectives without coming to terms with the realities of party power, because the parties, through their public officeholders, can advance or obstruct the policy objectives of any group. At the same time, no party can expect to achieve widespread electoral success without significant group support.

Bargaining and compromising are key elements in the strategy of American parties. The doctrinal flexibility of the parties means that almost everything is up for grabs—each party can make at least some effort to satisfy virtually any group's demands. Through their public officials, the parties serve as brokers among the organized interests of American society, weighing the claims of one group against those of another, accepting some programs and modifying or rejecting others.[16] The steady bargaining that takes place between interest groups and party leaders tends to produce settlements that may not be wholly satisfactory to anyone but that the participants can accept at least for a time. Of deeper significance, the legitimacy of government itself depends in part on the capacity of the parties to represent diverse interests and to integrate the claims of competing groups into a broad program of public policy. Their ability to do so is certain to bear on their electoral success.

The thesis that the major parties are especially sensitive to the representation of group interests cannot be advanced without a caveat or two. Parties are far more receptive to the claims of organized interests than those of unorganized interests. The groups that regularly engage the attention of parties and their representatives in government are those whose support (or opposition) can make a difference at the polls. Organized labor, business, agriculture, medicine, and religious groups—all have multiple channels for gaining access to decision makers. Indeed, party politicians are about as likely to solicit the views of these organized interests as they are to wait to hear from them.

Special cause groups—those passionate and uncompromising lobbies concerned with issues such as gun control, abortion, tax rollbacks, equal rights, nuclear power, and the environment—also attempt to exert influence as they judge members on the "correctness" of their positions. For example, the Club for Growth, an antitax group that spends millions of dollars to unseat elected officials it deems insufficiently conservative on fiscal issues, nearly ended the Senate career of Arlen Specter by underwriting conservative GOP challenger Patrick Toomey in the 2004 Pennsylvania Republican primary. (Specter won the primary with just 51 percent of the vote.) In 2009 Toomey, who became Club for Growth's president after his primary defeat, announced that he would challenge Specter again in 2010—this time causing Specter to switch to the Democratic Party.[17]

In contrast to these groups, many millions of Americans are all but shut out of the political system. The political power of agricultural workers, migrants, and general laborers has never been commensurate with their numbers or, for that matter, with their contribution to society. With low participation in elections, weak organization, low status, and poor access to any form of political communication, their voices are often drowned out in the din produced by organized interests.[18] Although no problem of representation in the United States is more important than that of finding ways to move the claims of the unorganized public onto the political agenda, the task is formidable. "All power is organization and all organization is power," says Harvey Fergusson. "A man who has no share in any form of organized power is not independent of organized power. He is at the mercy of it."[19]

Control and Direction of Government

A third major activity of the parties involves the control and direction of government. Parties recruit candidates and organize campaigns to win political power, gain public office, and take control of government. Given the character of the political system and of the parties themselves, however, it is unrealistic to suppose that party management of government will be altogether successful.

First, the same party may not capture all the separate branches of government. Until the Republicans won control of the Senate in 2002, the same party had controlled the presidency and both houses of Congress for fewer than three years since 1980. And, after the Democrats regained control of Congress in 2006, they had to wait another two years to elect a Democratic president, only then unifying party control of government. Divided party control complicates the governing process by forcing presidents to work not only with their own party in Congress but also with elements of the other party. For example, the legislative success of Republican presidents has often depended on gaining the support of conservative Democrats. Party achievements and failures, therefore, are often blurred in the mix of coalition votes. Who was to blame for the enormous budget deficits of the 1980s—the Republican president or the Democratic Congress? Who ought to get credit for the long run of prosperity in the 1990s—the Democratic president or the Republican Congress? With divided party control, it is harder for voters to assign credit and blame to politicians for their decisions.

Second, even though one party may control the legislative and executive branches, its margin of seats in the legislature may be too thin to permit it to govern effectively. Early in their presidencies, both Bill Clinton and George W. Bush had to expend tremendous political capital to move their programs forward despite their respective parties' control of both houses of Congress. This made it harder for them to accomplish other goals later in their presidencies. The Democrats' relatively larger majorities after the 2008 election have the potential to increase the duration of whatever success Barack Obama's agenda might enjoy.

Disagreement within the majority party, moreover, may be so great on certain issues that the party finds it virtually impossible to come together to develop coherent positions. In the 103rd Congress (1993–1995), no version of President Clinton's health care plan could garner a majority among the various factions of House Democrats. Party cohesion can be particularly challenging when the president is not particularly popular, which makes it harder for him to persuade members of his party to advance his programs. When Bush's approval rating fell into the mid-30s in late 2005, moderate Republicans in both the House and Senate refused to back him on drilling for oil in the Arctic National Wildlife Refuge or on cuts in the budget that members of Congress believed fell too heavily on the poor. GOP loyalty to the unpopular Bush diminished further as his second term came to a close. With a month to go before the 2008 elections, and the president's public approval rating hovering in the low 30s, 133 House Republicans joined 95 Democrats to defeat his $700 billion initial emergency bailout measure (HR 3997), which was designed to confront a worsening economic situation caused by a crisis in the banking industry. Majority party coherence may also come less easily when a party expands by picking up seats in regions typically held by the opposition party. Many Democratic challengers who defeated GOP House incumbents in the 2008 elections hail from politically moderate districts. These members' perspective on key policy issues will likely be different from those of liberal Democratic stalwarts such as Barney Frank (D-Mass.) or Maxine Waters (D-Calif.).

Third, midterm elections invariably complicate a president's plans because his party almost always loses seats in both houses. In 1994, after the first two years

Table 1-1   Off-Year Gains and Losses in Congress by the President's Party: 1946–2006

Year	House		Senate	
1946	D	−55	D	−12
1950	D	−29	D	−6
1954	R	−18	R	−1
1958	R	−47	R	−13
1962	D	−4	D	+4
1966	D	−47	D	−3
1970	R	−12	R	+2
1974	R	−48	R	−5
1978	D	−15	D	−3
1982	R	−26	R	0
1986	R	−5	R	−8
1990	R	−8	R	−1
1994	D	−52	D	−8
1998	D	+5	D	0
2002	R	+6	R	+2
2006	R	−31	R	−6

Source: Reprinted with permission of the American Enterprise Institute for Public Policy Research, Washington, D.C.

Note: R = Republican; D = Democrat.

of unified party government since the 1970s, the Democrats lost fifty-two seats in the House and eight in the Senate, creating the first Republican Congress in forty years. In 2006 Republicans lost their congressional majorities, owing to deep midterm losses, during a particularly bleak period in the Bush presidency. Indeed, since 1946 the administration's party has suffered an average loss of twenty-four seats in the House and about three and a half in the Senate at midterm (see Table 1-1). Although congressional districts are now generally drawn to protect incumbents of both parties, which has often reduced the size of recent midterm losses for the president's party, very few events are as predictable in American elections or as dispiriting for administrations as the chilly midterm verdict of the voters.

The upshot of all of this is that although the parties organize governments, they do not wholly control decision-making activities. In large measure they compete with political interest groups bent on securing public policies advantageous to their clienteles. Sometimes certain groups have as much influence on the behavior of legislators and bureaucrats as legislative party leaders, national and subnational party leaders, or the president. Yet to identify the difficulties that confront the parties in seeking to manage the government is not to suggest that the parties' impact on public policy is insubstantial. Not even a casual examination of party platforms, candidates' and officeholders' speeches, or legislative voting can fail to detect the parties' contributions to shaping the direction of government or ignore the differences that separate the parties on public policy matters.

An understanding of American parties begins with the recognition that party politicians value winning elections more than using election outcomes to achieve policy goals. Candidates have interests and commitments in policy questions, but rarely do they rule out bargaining and compromising as ways to achieve a slice of the party "loaf." Politicians tend to be intensely pragmatic and adaptable people. For the most part, they are attracted to a particular party more because of its promise as a mechanism for moving into government than as a mechanism for "governing." A party is a way of organizing activists and supporters to make a bid for office. This is the elemental truth of party politics. The election of one party over another has policy significance, but it is more an unanticipated dividend than a triumph for the idea of responsible party government.

Parties as a "Dependent Variable"

It is critically important to understand that parties are less what they make of themselves than what their environment makes of them.[20] In the language of social science, parties typically are the dependent variable. That is, the party owes its character, form, and relative strength to the impact of four external elements: the legal-political system, the election system, the political culture, and the heterogeneous quality of American life. Some of those characteristics, such as the legal-political system, are relative constants over time, which provide parties with their general character. But other characteristics, such as the election system, can change over time and affect party strength in measurable ways. Indeed, the latest changes have contributed to a reinvigoration of parties. Some of these changes will be discussed later in the chapter.

The Legal-Political System

The Constitution was designed in part to limit the reach of institutions like parties that sought to aggregate power. The Founders, whose intent was to establish a government that could not easily be brought under the control of any one element, provided a system that ensures that American parties are weaker than most of their European counterparts. The Founders' underlying theory was both simple and pervasive: power was to check power, and the ambitions of some men were to check the ambitions of others.[21]

The two main features in this design were federalism and the separation of powers—the first to distribute power among different levels of government, and the second to distribute power among the legislative, executive, and judicial branches. Division of the legislature into two houses, with their memberships elected for different terms and by differing methods, was thought to reduce further the risk that a single faction (or party) might gain ascendancy.

Federalism makes the parties' job more difficult because it decentralizes power: not only are there fifty state government systems, but also fifty state party systems. The ideology of one state party may be sharply different from that of another. Contrast the state Democratic Party of conservative Mississippi with its counterpart in liberal New York or the state Republican Party of conservative Utah with its counterpart in liberal Connecticut.[22]

In addition, within each state all manner of local party organizations exist, sometimes functioning in harmony with state and national party elements and sometimes not. There are states (and localities) in which the party organizations are active and well financed and those in which they are not, those in which factions compete persistently within a party and those in which factional organization is nonexistent, those in which ideology and issues are important and those in which they are not, and those in which the parties seem to consist mainly of the personal followings of individual politicians and those in which party leaders exercise significant influence.[23]

The laws that govern party activity in the states also differ, which shapes party influence. A great variety of state laws govern nominating procedures, ballot form, access to the ballot, campaign finance, and elections. On the whole, northeastern states are most likely to have statutes that foster strong parties, whereas southern states tend to have statutes that weaken them.[24] Strong ("monopolistic") local party organizations have been more prominent and durable in the East than anywhere else.[25] The broad point is that the thrust of federalism is toward fragmentation and parochialism, permitting numerous forms of political organization to thrive and inhibiting the emergence of cohesive and disciplined national parties.

The Election System

The election system is another element that shapes American political parties. Parties and elections are so closely linked that it is difficult to understand much about one without understanding a great deal about the other. Parties are in business to win elections; election systems shape the way parties compete for power and the success they achieve.

The United States has exactly two major parties because of the rules governing the election system. Chief among these rules is the election of House members from single-member districts by plurality vote. Under this arrangement a single candidate is elected in each district, and this candidate needs to receive only one vote more than each of his or her challengers. Third party candidates have little incentive to run because the prospects are poor that they could defeat the candidates of the two major parties. If members of Congress were elected under a proportional representation system, with several members chosen in each district, third party candidates would undoubtedly have a better chance of winning some seats.[26]

Third parties face the same obstacle in presidential elections as in congressional races: only one party can win. For the office of the presidency, the entire nation takes on the cast of a single-member district. Each state's electoral votes are awarded as a unit to the candidate receiving a plurality of the popular vote; all other popular votes are in effect wasted. In 1992 Ross Perot received nearly 20 million popular votes (winning more than 27 percent of the vote in Alaska, Idaho, Kansas, Maine, and Utah), only to be skunked in the Electoral College. If electoral votes were divided in proportion to popular votes in each state, third

Table 1-2   Split Outcomes in Presidential-Gubernatorial Voting: 1964–2008

Year	Gubernatorial elections	Split outcomes	Percentage
1964	25	9	36
1968	21	8	38
1972	18	10	56
1976	14	5	36
1980	13	4	31
1984	13	5	38
1988	12	4	33
1992	12	4	33
1996	11	3	27
2000	11	5	45
2004	11	4	36
2008	11	5	45

Sources: Various issues of *Congressional Quarterly Weekly Report.*

party and independent candidates would make a bigger dent in the electoral vote totals of the major parties, which, in turn, would provide them with more influence. Electoral practices in the United States are hard on third parties—so successful in limiting competition that they force outsiders to think about running for the nomination of a major party.

In addition to ensuring the dominance of two parties, the election system was designed to keep one faction (party) from easily controlling government. For example, a state's election calendar can have a substantial impact on party fortunes. If all elections were held at once, people would tend to vote based on the governing party's performance in the years leading up to the election. Instead, states tend to separate their elections from national elections. In the presidential election year of 2008 only eleven states held gubernatorial elections, and five states currently hold odd-year gubernatorial and state legislative elections. Such arrangements insulate state politics from national politics.

The behavior of voters may also weaken the links between these levels. In those states in which governors are elected at the same time as the president, the party that carries the state in the presidential contest loses at the gubernatorial level more than a third of the time. (See Table 1-2.) It is perhaps not surprising, then, that eighteen states had governors in 2009 who were of the party opposite of how the state voted in the 2008 presidential election. In fact, three states that provided Obama his highest vote percentages (Hawaii, Rhode Island, and Vermont) also elected Republican governors in 2008. Wyoming and Oklahoma were the two states most loyal to John McCain but elected Democratic governors in 2006.

The use of staggered terms for executive and legislative offices also diminishes the probability that one party will control both branches of government at any given time. When the governor is elected for four years and the lower house is elected for two—the common pattern—chances are that the governor's party will lose legislative seats, and sometimes its majority, in the off-year election.

The same is true for the president and Congress. Whatever the virtues of staggered terms and off-year elections, they increase the likelihood of divided control of government, which weakens the influence of parties. Conditions may change between elections, and if things are not great in the state at the time of the off-year election, the governor's party is going to be blamed whether deserved or not.

In addition, reformers did much to weaken party control of politics through the development of the direct primary in the early twentieth century. The primary was introduced to combat the power of party oligarchs who, insulated from popular influences, dominated the selection of nominees in state and local party conventions. In the past, if a party boss tapped a person to run for a seat, that individual received the party's nomination. Primaries challenged the power of party bosses to make such decisions. By empowering voters to choose party nominees, reformers sought to democratize the nominating process. Today, all states employ some form of primary system.

Although the convention method survives for the nomination of presidential and vice-presidential candidates, the reality is that the preconvention struggle has become so decisive that it now governs the selection process. The conventions simply ratify the voters' choices in caucuses or the more popular primaries. In 2008, forty states, including all of the most populous, selected their convention delegates in presidential primaries.

In the past, scholars criticized the direct primary because it appeared to eviscerate party responsibility. First, critics argued that transferring the choice of nominees from party assemblies to the voters increases the probability that candidates with different views on public policy will be brought together in the same party. Whatever their policy orientations, the victors in primary elections then become their party's nominees, perhaps to the embarrassment of other party candidates. Second, observers contended that primaries contribute to a decline in party responsibility. Candidates who win office largely on their own and who have their own distinctive followings within local electorates have less reason to defer to party leaders or to adhere to traditional party positions. Third, the primary is a door to intraparty clashes, and bitter primary fights sometimes render a party incapable of generating a united campaign in the general election.[27] Finally, primaries apparently contributed to the consolidation of one-party politics. In an area where one party ordinarily dominates, its primaries tend to become the arena for political battles. The growth of a second party is inhibited not only by the lack of voter interest in its primaries but also by its inability to attract strong candidates. One-party domination reveals little about the party's organizational strength; indeed, one-party political systems are likely to be characterized more by factionalism and internecine warfare than by unity, harmony, and ideological agreement.

Despite these arguments, it now appears that the direct primary has not done much to undermine party responsibility. In the several decades after their introduction in the early twentieth century, they were the source of significant competition. More recently, however, incumbents have come to enjoy even larger advantages in primaries than they do in general elections.[28] In fact, the direct primary may have contributed to the emergence of more ideologically distinct parties over the past twenty years—a development that party responsibility advocates would applaud. In some jurisdictions the dominant party organization is sufficiently strong that unendorsed candidates have little or no chance of upsetting the organization's slate. Potential challengers may abandon their campaigns once the party leaders or the organization have made their choices known. Other candidacies may not materialize because the prospects for getting the nod from party leaders appear unpromising.

Given this, it is questionable that direct primaries actually undermine the decisions of party leaders, particularly in the case of presidential nominations. Although Barack Obama upset Hillary Clinton, the consensus front-runner for the Democratic nomination in 2008, such a result is not the norm. Only Obama and Jimmy Carter in 1976 won major party nominations as underdogs.[29] And, in the case of Obama, it took his remarkable personal appeal combined with what experts describe as a perfectly run campaign to capture the nomination. Using devices such as front-loading, which concentrates delegate-rich states at the beginning of the primary season, the major parties almost always end up nominating the person that party leaders would have chosen. The informal party network of activists, fund-raisers, party leaders, and allied interest groups work their ways during the "invisible primary"—the campaign for money and endorsements that begins long before the first primary contest.[30]

In addition, those who decide to run for office in the present political environment usually are not free agents who support Republicans on certain issues and Democrats on others. Instead, candidates tend to be drawn from the ranks of ideological activists within each party.[31] Policy outcomes and ideology mean more to this new breed of candidate than they meant to old style party bosses. Moreover, because the people who vote in primaries are more ideological than those who vote in general elections, candidates have an incentive to position themselves toward the ideological poles in campaigns and to vote more ideologically in office in a system where primaries matter.[32]

In sum, election rules matter. In spite of myths to the contrary, election systems are never designed to be neutral and never are neutral. Some election laws and constitutional provisions, such as the single-member district system or the rigorous requirements that minor parties must meet to gain a place on the ballot, provide general support for the two-party system. According to the Federal Election Commission, none of the twenty-four minor party candidates for the presidency in 2008 got on all fifty state ballots, although a few came close.[33] Ralph Nader did the best of the minor party candidates, with 738,775 votes (0.56 percent), while the other twenty-three shared less than 1 million votes.

Some election laws and constitutional provisions, such as staggered terms of office and off-year elections, make party government difficult and sometimes impossible. But the major parties are not always passive witnesses to existing electoral arrangements. At times they seek change because the prospects for party advantage are sufficiently promising to warrant the effort. At other times major parties simply endure the conventional arrangements because of the difficulty of changing them or because the parties recognize their benefits. Either way, it is a good bet that no one understands or appreciates American election systems better than those party leaders responsible for defending party interests and winning elections.

Political Culture and the Parties

A third important element in the environment of American political parties is political culture—"the system of empirical beliefs, expressive symbols, and values which defines the situation in which political action takes place." [34] Decades of studies demonstrate that the American public is highly skeptical of political parties and their activities. Instead of choosing candidates based on party affiliation, almost all Americans believe "the best rule in voting is to pick the best candidate, regardless of party label." Indeed, an overwhelming majority of the public believes that the parties do more to confuse issues than to clarify them and that they often provoke unnecessary conflict.[35] A June 2007 survey provides evidence. *Newsweek* asked a sample of registered voters whether they thought "the two-party system does a pretty good job of addressing issues that are most important to people like you, or not." Only 37 percent thought it did a "pretty good job." [36]

That result may explain why support for cohesive and disciplined parties is extremely limited. Only about one in five persons believes that a legislator "should follow his or her party leaders even if he or she doesn't want to." In surveys of voter attitudes toward control of the presidency and Congress by the same party, a majority typically prefers divided party control.[37] Although Americans are more tightly tied to their parties today than they have been in generations, in October 2008, 48 percent still thought that it is "better if different parties control Congress and the presidency," and only 41 percent thought it is "better if the same party controls Congress and the presidency." [38] Overall, little in this profile of popular attitudes suggests that the public understands or accepts the tenets of a responsible party system.[39]

Virtually all surveys that tap popular understanding and appreciation of political parties indicate that the public has little confidence in them. The Gallup Organization asked in September 2008, "In your view, do the Republican and Democratic parties do an adequate job of representing the American people, or do they do such a poor job that a third major party is needed?" Half the public thought a third party was necessary.[40] This is true even though parties are stronger now than they have been in decades. Adding to the problem, many voters see little or no difference in the governing effectiveness of the parties. Since 1972, the National Election Study has asked Americans, "Which political party do you think would be most likely to get the government to do a better job in dealing with [the nation's most important] problem—the Republicans, the Democrats—or wouldn't there be much difference between them?" A plurality always chooses the "wouldn't be much difference"

Figure 1-1 Percentage of Voters Casting a Split Ticket for President and House: 1952–2008

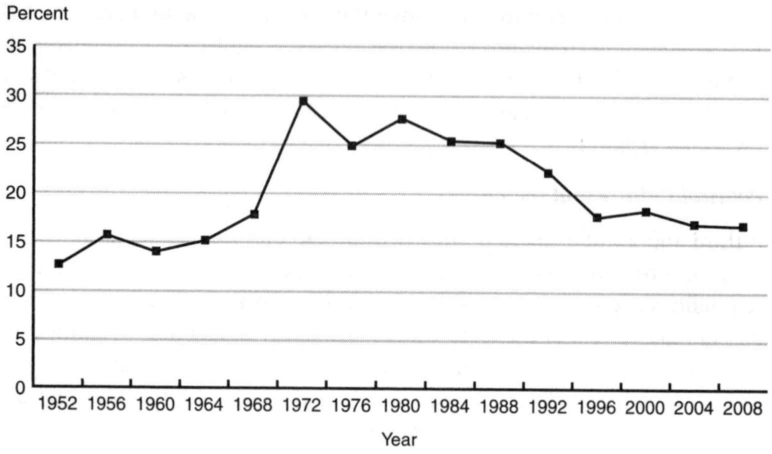

Percent

Year

Source: American National Election Studies, Cumulative File, 1948–2008.

response and, more often than not, a majority does. In short, most people do not see the parties as effective problem solvers.[41]

Despite these *feelings,* the American public has more recently exhibited a marked increase in party-centric *behavior.* A reduction in the occurrence of ticket-splitting (voting for candidates of more than one party in the same election) is an example. Figure 1-1 shows the percentage of people voting for presidential and House candidates of different parties in the same year. In the 1960 Kennedy-Nixon race, occurring during a period when parties were characterized as very strong, only 14 percent of all voters split their tickets. By 1972 the percentage of ticket-splitters had more than doubled to 30 percent. Since then, however, split-ticket voting has decreased with almost every election, and in 2008 only about 16 percent of Americans did so. Political scientist Larry Bartels demonstrates that party identification has become a more important determinant of presidential and congressional voting. In fact, he finds that party affiliation is an even stronger predictor today than it was in the 1950s.[42]

One reason for the resurgence in party voting is that Americans are increasingly likely to see important differences between the parties. (See Figure 1-2.) In the past, many Americans correctly viewed the parties as Tweedledum and Tweedledee. Less than half of the surveyed population (46 percent) perceived important differences in 1972, when the Democrats still had a very conservative southern wing that was significantly more conservative than many liberal northeastern Republicans. Over time, however, conservative Republicans replaced these southern Democrats, and liberal Democrats replaced many of the northeastern Republicans.[43] The public has picked up on these changes. By 2008, about eight in ten Americans perceived important differences between the parties.

Figure 1-2   Percentage of Respondents Who See Important Differences between What
the Parties Stand For: 1960–2008

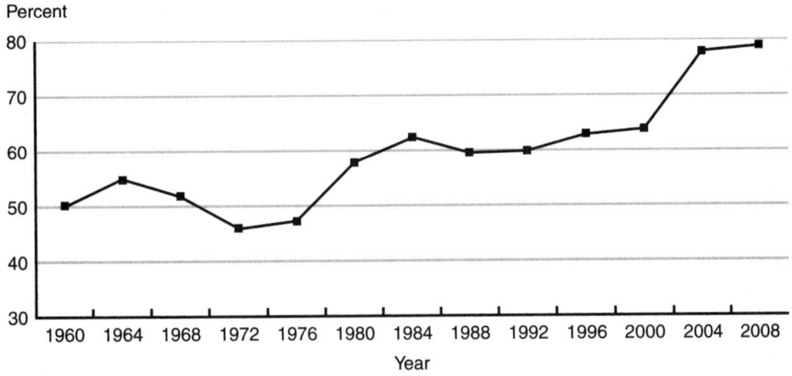

Source: American National Election Studies, Cumulative File, 1948–2008.

Moreover, the differences that people see are ideological in nature. In the last twenty-five years, the American public has become adept at attributing a conservative public policy course to Republicans and a liberal one to Democrats.[44]

Although Americans are behaving in a more party-centric manner, they still do not like parties. In the argot of popular appraisal, political organizations often turn into "machines," party workers emerge as "hacks," political leaders become "bosses," and campaign appeals degenerate into "empty promises" or "sheer demagoguery." No one can deny that some politicians have contributed to this state of affairs by debasing the language of political discourse or by their behavior. But the fact remains that one critical factor of the American political culture is a strong suspicion of the political process and the agencies that try to dominate it—the political parties.

A Heterogeneous Nation

To complete the analysis of the environment of American political parties, it is necessary to say something about the characteristics of the nation as a whole. No array of statistics is required to assert that the United States is a nation of extraordinary diversity. The American community is composed of a great variety of economic and social interests; class configurations; ethnic and religious groups; occupations; regional and subregional interests; and loyalties, values, and beliefs. There are citizens who are deeply attached to inherited patterns and those who are impatient advocates of change, those who care intensely about politics and those who can take it or leave it, and those who elude labeling—active on one occasion and passive on another. There are citizens who think mainly in terms of farm policy, some who seek advantage for urban elements, and others whose lives and political interests revolve around business or professions. Sometimes deep, sometimes shallow, the differences that separate one group from another

Table 1-3 Voting Behavior of Groups in the 2008 Presidential Election

	Democratic	Republican
All	53	46
Race		
White	43	55
Black	95	4
Hispanic	67	31
Asian	62	35
Gender		
Men	49	48
Women	56	43
Age		
Under 30	66	32
60 and over	45	53
Religious Denomination		
Protestants	45	54
Catholics	54	45
Jews	78	21
White "Born-Again"	24	74
Church Attendance		
Attend Church Weekly or More	43	55
Never Attend Church	67	30
Labor Ties		
Union Household	60	37
Income		
Under $50,000	63	36
$50,000 to $100,000	49	49
Over $100,000	49	49

Source: Developed from Mitofsky and Edison Exit Poll Data.

and one region from another make the formation of public policy that suits everyone all but impossible.

The United States remains a heterogeneous nation, but recently party strength has increased because the bases of the two parties' group support have become less diverse. The New Deal coalition, which dominated politics from the 1930s to the 1960s (highlighted in chapter 2) had to balance the interests of groups as disparate as southern whites who supported segregation and African Americans who opposed it. In contrast, parties today are increasingly well sorted by race, population density, religion, and religiosity, making intraparty compromise somewhat less critical, especially on social issues.

Voting behavior in the 2008 presidential election illustrates this point (see Table 1-3). Barack Obama, the Democratic candidate, did particularly well among African Americans, Jews, Hispanics, Asians, those who do not attend church, persons with lower incomes, union members, and younger Americans.[45] Overall, Obama, like most Democratic standard bearers before him, dominated among racial and ethnic minorities. Obama won the votes of nineteen of twenty African

Americans, which is not surprising given that he was the first African American presidential nominee. Although some wondered during the primaries whether Latinos would support an African American candidate, this group cast their ballots by more than two to one for Obama. Obama won non-churchgoers by 37 percentage points. Young people were also particularly attracted to Obama; whereas John Kerry won the under-thirty demographic by 9 points in 2004, Obama won this group by a whopping 34 points.

For John McCain, the Republican candidate, the most distinctive supporters were whites, Protestants (particularly white and "born-again" Christians), those who attend church at least weekly, and those who were sixty-five or older. McCain won among whites and regular churchgoers by 12 percentage points each. He carried white "born-again" voters by a remarkable 50 points, and among older voters he won by 8. Republicans usually do well among those with high incomes. George W. Bush won among voters making over $100,000 per year by 15 points. In 2008, however, Obama and McCain split this group 49 percent to 49 percent.

But neither party excludes any group from its calculations for winning elections. On the contrary, each party expects to do reasonably well among nearly all groups, although efforts to attract one group may undermine efforts to win another. In other words, the nation's heterogeneity can undermine party strength. One reason that Bush increased his vote share from 48 percent in 2000 to 51 percent in 2004 was that his support among Latinos, the nation's fastest growing minority group, grew from 35 percent to 44 percent.[46] Part of his appeal was a promise to work for comprehensive immigration reform that would provide a path to citizenship for some illegal immigrants. White evangelical Christians, however, were overwhelmingly opposed to this version of immigration reform. After Congress failed to enact reform legislation during Bush's second term, McCain largely abandoned the idea during his 2008 campaign despite his staunch support for such reform in the past. Instead, he decided to favor the concerns of white evangelicals who make up the base of the Republican Party and with whom his relationship was strained. Although McCain did solidify his support with evangelicals, winning their votes by nearly three to one, he won only 31 percent of the Latino vote, even worse than Bush's showing in 2000.

Homogeneity can, in turn, have a large impact on party extremity. When parties grow more homogenous, they can take more extreme positions on issues without the risk of alienating conflicting constituencies. The Democrats became a much more liberal party on race after conservative white southerners departed the party in the wake of the civil rights revolution. Republicans today might be tempted to chart a more conservative course on immigration since few Latinos identify with the party. But to win elections on a consistent basis, parties usually do better by building a big tent that includes a range of different groups. The bigger the tent, the more heterogeneous the coalition will be, which, in turn, will require at least some moderation to balance conflicting group interests.

Party Organization

Party organization has two common features in all parts of the United States. First, parties are organized in a series of committees reaching from the precinct level to the national committee. Second, party committee organization parallels the arrangement of electoral districts. With the exception of heavily one-party areas, party committees can be found in virtually all jurisdictions within which important government officials are elected. The presence of party committees, however, reveals little about their activities or their vitality in campaigns.

The organizational structure of American political parties is like a pyramid. At the top is the national committee, and at the bottom are the precinct organizations, with various ward, city, county, and state committees lodged in between. Although it is convenient to view party organization with this pattern, it is misleading in that it suggests that power flows steadily from top to bottom, from major national leaders to local leaders and local rank and file. Subnational committees actually have considerable autonomy, particularly in the crucial matters of selecting and slating candidates for public office (including federal office), raising and spending money, and conducting campaigns. (See Figure 1-3.) Changes in the campaign finance system have, however, made the national committees bigger players than in the past.

The National Committee

The most prestigious and visible of all party committees is the national committee. The people who serve on the national committee of each party are prominent state politicians, chosen in a variety of ways and under a number of constraints. Their official tenure begins when they are accepted at the national convention of each party.

The selection of national committee members is not a simple matter. The Democratic Party, operating under its 1974 charter, has elaborate provisions governing the composition of its national committee, which now includes more than four hundred members. Among its membership are the chair and the highest-ranking official of the opposite gender of each recognized state party; two hundred additional members allotted to the states on the same basis as delegates are apportioned to the national convention; and a number of delegates representing organizations such as the Democratic Governors' Conference, the U.S. Congress, the National Finance Council, the Conference of Democratic Mayors, the National Federation of Democratic Women, the Democratic County Officials Conference, the State Legislative Leaders Caucus, the College Democrats of America, and the Young Democrats of America. As in the case of delegates to the party's national convention, the party's charter stipulates that members of the national committee must be selected "through processes which assure full, timely, and equal opportunity to participate" and with due attention to affirmative action standards. The Republican National Committee (RNC) has a smaller membership than the Democratic National Committee (DNC), with each state and territory

Figure 1-3 Party Organization in the United States: Layers of Committees and Their Chairs

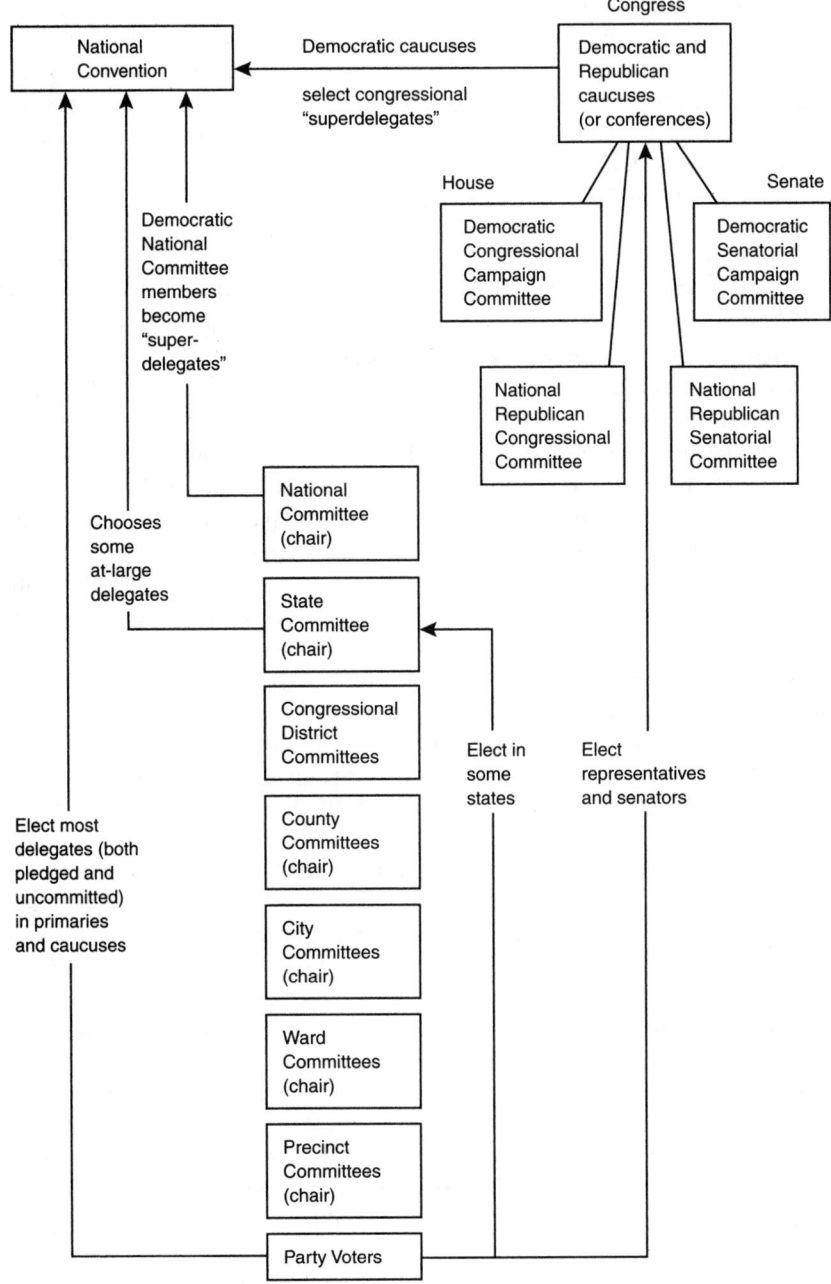

represented by three members: the state party chair, a national committeeman, and a national committeewoman.

To know what the national committee is, it is necessary to look at what it does.[47] One of its principal responsibilities is to make arrangements for the national convention every four years. In this capacity it chooses the site, prepares a temporary roster of delegates, and selects speakers and temporary officers who will manage the convention in its opening phase. The committee is especially active during presidential campaigns—coordinating campaign efforts, publicizing the party and its candidates, and raising money.

The national party committee has evolved into a fund-raising machine. Until loopholes in the campaign finance laws (covered in greater detail in chapter 4) were closed following the 2002 election cycle, the national parties were able to raise unlimited sums of money to engage in "party building" activities. As the national parties found innovative ways to spend these funds to support individual federal candidates, well-heeled donors found the parties to be attractive places to contribute large sums of money. These "soft money" donations made the national party committees into clearinghouses for campaign money, which the parties deployed in competitive federal contests to support individual party candidates or—more often—to attack opposition party candidates. In the 2001–2002 election cycle, the last that permitted the raising and distributing of soft money, Republican national party committees raised $250 million in soft money, and Democratic national party committees raised $246 million.[48] Changes in the campaign finance system stemmed the tide of soft money, but the parties have become more adept at raising hard money—money regulated by federal election laws. In the 2007–2008 election cycle, the Republican Party raised a total of $920.3 million, an increase of 3.5 percent over the previous presidential election cycle despite the party's flagging popularity. The Democrats raised even more: $960.7 million in that same election cycle, a 32 percent increase over 2003–2004.[49]

The influence of presidents on their parties' national committees is substantial. "I don't think the Republican National Committee can ever really be independent," a committee staff member said. "[The committee has] a responsibility to the leader. Policy is always made at the White House, not here."[50] The same is true for the DNC. "The president likes a party that serves as a supportive tool for the president," observed a state party chair during the Carter administration. "An independent organization is looked upon as a nuisance."[51] Nevertheless, tension between the national committee and the White House exists. Sometimes it stems from a perception that the administration is too demanding—in particular, that it expects the national committee to center its efforts on the president's reelection, even at the expense of other offices. A former DNC chair, then-Colorado governor Roy Romer, complained in 1996 that the national party had not paid sufficient attention to the election of its congressional and gubernatorial candidates. "You've got to have a very close working relationship with the president and vice president because they help you raise the money," he remarked. "But don't think that the DNC ought simply to be the campaign finance arm of the executive branch."[52]

For decades, the RNC was more effective than the DNC in raising campaign funds and in providing services for its party's candidates. That gap has largely disappeared. During the 2007–2008 election cycle, the Republican Party's three national-level committees (national, senatorial, and congressional) raised $640.3 million, and the three Democratic committees raised $599.1 million.[53] Although the RNC beat the DNC to the punch in making a variety of technical services available to party candidates at both the national and state level—including fund-raising assistance, consultant advice, candidate training, public opinion surveys, and computer analyses of voting behavior—the parties find themselves on almost equal footing today.[54]

The National Chair

The head of the national party is the national chair. Although chairs are officially selected by the members of the national committee, in practice they are chosen by the party's presidential candidate shortly after the national convention has adjourned. Very few leaders in either party have held the position for an extended period. The chair of the party winning the presidency sometimes receives a major appointment in the new administration, and the chair of the losing party is replaced by a new leader selected by the national committee. Factional conflicts may come to the surface when the committee must find a replacement, because the leading candidates usually will be identified with certain wings of the party.

The central problem with which the national chair must come to terms in presidential election years is the direction and coordination of the national campaign. Initially, the Republican national organization far outstripped its Democratic rival in adapting to the candidate-centered campaign environment. One major reason is that national chairs such as Ray C. Bliss (1965–1969) and Bill Brock (1977–1981) concentrated their efforts on organizational reform, seeking in particular to strengthen state and local Republican organizations by providing them with all kinds of "electioneering" assistance.[55] A successful fund-raising program, based on more than 2 million small contributors, made these efforts possible.[56] An absence of adequate financial resources was particularly burdensome for the Democratic Party's national chair for many years. Kenneth M. Curtis, who resigned in 1978 after only one year in office, described what his job was like:

> Have you ever tried to meet the payroll every two weeks of a bankrupt organization and deal with 363 bosses [national committee members] and 50 state chairs? . . . I tried it for a year and simply decided I'd like to do something else with my life. It's not the sort of job that you lay down in the street and bleed to keep.[57]

A succession of energetic national chairs brought the Democratic Party up to speed. Under Charles Manatt (1981–1985), Paul Kirk (1985–1989), and Ron Brown (1989–1992), the party expanded its contributor base; became more competitive in raising funds; strengthened itself organizationally; and increased its support of candidates, state party organizations, and party-building activities. The DNC continued to make strides in these areas under Howard Dean (2005–2009), who implemented the so-called "50-state strategy" designed to expand the party's electoral reach beyond swing states and those where the party was already strong. As a result, the national Democratic Party is better poised organizationally to challenge its Republican counterpart in election campaigns than it has been before. Still, in 2007–2008, the RNC retained its historical fund-raising advantage over the DNC, out-raising it by $420.6 million to $260.1 million. The DNC's smaller haul—it raised nearly $40 million less than it did in 2004—may partly reflect Obama's decision to refuse public funding in the general election, which allowed him to raise private funds in the postconvention period.[58] Obama's extraordinary fund-raising—$153 million in September alone and more than $700 million overall—may well have siphoned off contributions that would have ordinarily gone to the DNC.

Congressional and Senatorial Campaign Committees

The other principal units of the national party organization are the congressional and senatorial campaign committees, one committee for each party in each house. These committees, composed of members of Congress, are independent of the national committees and are an outgrowth of the need of members of Congress to have organizations concerned exclusively with their political welfare. As such, they raise campaign funds for members, help to develop campaign strategies, conduct research, and otherwise provide assistance to members running for reelection.[59] A certain degree of informal cooperation occurs between the party committees of Congress and the national committees, but for the most part they go their separate ways: the former focused on securing reelection of incumbent legislators and on improving the party's prospects for winning or retaining control of Congress, the latter preoccupied with the presidential race.

Over the years, Republican campaign committees have tended to be the most active and best financed, but that changed fundamentally in 2008. In 2004 the National Republican Congressional Committee raised twice as much money for Republican congressional candidates as the Democratic Congressional Campaign Committee did for its candidates. But in 2008, the DCCC out-raised the NRCC, $176.2 million to $118.3 million. On the Senate side, the Democratic Senatorial Campaign Committee widened its advantage over its Republican counterpart. In 2004 the DSCC brought in $88.6 million to the NRSC's $79.0 million.[60] In 2008 Senate Democrats enjoyed an advantage of nearly $70 million ($162.8 to $94.4). This difference surely proved to be vital to the significant gains made by Democratic congressional candidates in 2008. Indeed, by November 3, the DCCC had made $1 million or more in (hard money) independent expenditures in thirty-eight close House races, and it spent more than $2 million in ten House contests. The NRCC spent $1 million in only four House races.[61] The shift also suggests how important viability is to campaign contributors. Early in 2008 it was already clear that the Democrats would keep their majorities in both houses of Congress. The only question was how large the majorities would be.

State Committees

Midway between the national party apparatus and local party organizations are the state party committees, often called state central committees. So great are the differences between these committees from state to state—in membership selection, size, and function—that it is difficult to generalize about them. In some states the membership is made up of county chairs; more commonly, state committee members are chosen in primaries or by local party conventions. Their numbers range from fewer than a hundred members to several hundred. In some states the state central committee is a genuinely powerful party unit and is customarily charged with drafting the party platform, slating statewide candidates, and waging an intensive fund-raising campaign. In other states the committee's impact on state politics is scarcely perceptible. In a fashion similar to that found at the national level, the party's gubernatorial candidate ordinarily selects the state chair. And like the national chair, the state leader is usually a principal adviser to the governor on party affairs, particularly on matters involving the distribution of patronage.[62] As with the national committees, many state parties have greatly increased their organizational capacities.[63]

Many state legislatures now have campaign committees that serve functions similar to the congressional campaign committees. Members of the legislature run these committees, and they are concerned almost exclusively with electing fellow partisans to their legislative chamber. Such committees are more likely to be found in states with professionalized legislatures, and state legislative leaders often raise the bulk of the committees' campaign funds.[64]

Local Party Organization

Below the state party committee is the county committee, ordinarily a very large organization composed of all the precinct officials within the county. At the head of this committee is the county chair, who is usually elected by the members of the county committee. Often an important figure in local party organizations, the county chair is active in campaign planning, recruitment and slating of party candidates, supervision of campaign financing, and allocation of patronage to the party faithful. In many counties, leaders' power is enhanced by their active recruitment of candidates for precinct committee members—the very people who in turn elect them to office. Some states have congressional district party organizations, developed around the office of the U.S. representative.

Where these committees exist, they function essentially as the member's personal organization, set off from the rest of the party and preoccupied with the member's reelection. Although local party officials, such as the county chair, may be instrumental in controlling the original congressional nomination, their influence on the representative's policy orientations is virtually nil. Indeed, one of the dominant characteristics of congressional district organization is its autonomy.

Some members of Congress operate what are essentially their own informal local machines, wielding substantial influence over local politics and even over nominations to local, state, and federal offices.[65] Further down the line are the city and ward committees, which vary in size and importance throughout the country. Their activities, like those of other committees, are centered on campaigns and elections.

The cornerstone of American party organization is the precinct committee, organized within the tens of thousands of election or voting districts of the nation. In metropolitan areas a precinct is likely to number one thousand or two thousand voters; in rural areas, perhaps only a dozen. The complexity of party organization at the precinct level is mainly a function of precinct size. The precinct committee member is chosen in one of two ways: by the voters in a primary election or by the vote of party members attending a precinct caucus.

In the lore of American politics, elections are won or lost at the precinct level. A strong precinct organization, the argument runs, is essential to party victory, and the key to a strong organization is a precinct leader bent on carrying the precinct. In attempting to advance their party's fortunes, the committee members engage in four main activities: tasks associated with the campaign, party organizational work such as recruitment and organization of workers, promulgation of political information, and identification and recruitment of candidates for local office. For most jurisdictions, it appears, the most important activities are those related to the campaign, such as persuading people to register, contacting voters, raising money, campaigning for votes, and transporting voters to the polls.

Undoubtedly, differences exist in the role perceptions of party officials. A study of precinct leaders in Massachusetts and North Carolina, for example, found that about 60 percent saw their principal task as that of mobilizing voters.[66] In Connecticut and Michigan the leading activities of precinct officials were fundraising, canvassing, and distributing literature.[67] And in Pittsburgh, Pennsylvania, about two-thirds of the committee members described their most important task as electoral—but here they tended to be indifferent to organizational goals and more supportive of particular candidates than of the party slate as a whole.[68] Another study showed that the organizational vitality of local parties (as measured by the presence of officials, allocation of time to party business, regular meetings, the existence of a budget, and participation in various kinds of campaign activities) is highest in the East and the Midwest and lowest in the South.[69] As with the national and state committees, many local committees have gradually adapted to the contemporary campaign environment. Even some old-style party machines have made the transformation to modern, service-oriented organizations.[70]

Does the strength of local party organizations make a difference in electoral politics? A study by John P. Frendreis, James L. Gibson, and Laura L. Vertz provides a two-part answer. First, the presence of well-organized and active local party organizations does not have a significant direct effect on what voters think and how they vote. Those effects appear to be the domain of candidate organizations.

Second, and of overlooked importance, in jurisdictions where a party organization is active, the party is likely to be involved in recruitment and therefore able to field a full slate of candidates. Party building, in other words, comes one step at a time. The structural strength of the party, this study suggests, provides a base for the eventual development of competitive party politics.[71]

The Changing Parties: "Old Style" and "New Style" Politics

In the late nineteenth and early twentieth centuries the best examples of strong party organization could be found in the large cities of the Northeast and Midwest—New York City, Boston, Philadelphia, Jersey City, Kansas City, and Chicago. Well-organized and strongly disciplined, the urban machine was virtually invincible. Precinct and ward officials maintained steady contacts with their party constituencies—finding jobs for people out of work; helping those in trouble with the law; aiding others in securing government benefits such as welfare payments; assisting neighborhoods to secure government services; helping immigrants cope with a new society; and helping merchants and tradespeople to obtain contracts, licenses, and the like. The party organization was at the center of community life, an effective mediator between the people and their government. Party officials were "brokers," exchanging information, access, and influence for loyalty and support at the polls.

The picture is very different today. Many factors have contributed to the parties' loss of function: the growth of civil service systems and the corresponding decline in patronage, the relative decline in the value of patronage jobs, the arrival of the welfare state with its various benefits for low-income groups, the steady assimilation of immigrants, the growing disillusionment among better-educated voters over many of the unsavory features of machine politics, and the coming of age of the mass media with its potential for contacts between candidates and their publics. Where the parties have suffered a loss of function, it is reasonable to assume that they have also suffered a loss of vitality. The result has been a decline in their ability to deliver the vote on election day.

"Controlling" votes, except perhaps in a few big city wards, is a lost art. Today, the most important players are the media, and what counts in a campaign is a candidate's image. As Peter Hart, a well-known pollster, observed, "A campaign is not played out anymore so much for people or voters; it's played out for the media."[72] Assisted by their advisers, candidates plan steadily for ways to establish good relationships with print and broadcast media, in hopes of generating favorable news stories or acquiring a few seconds of exposure on television. An "old style" party leader of the 1930s or 1940s would be left incredulous at the scope of today's campaign activities that fall outside the purview of the party organization.

Television is central to major campaigns because "retail" politics has given way to "wholesale" politics.[73] Candidates no longer rely as much on precinct organization, and they have less time to march in parades or visit an array of plants, businesses, and farms. Another city or state (or airport) is on the day's agenda. As opportunities for personal visits with voters, including party, civic, labor, and business leaders, have diminished, emphasis has shifted to the wholesale politics of short television commercials and Web videos. The mediating function of local leaders, reflected in their assessments of candidates and their interpretations of issues for rank-and-file voters, has atrophied in the face of electronic mass media. This trend seems likely to continue as technological developments—everything from blogs to social networking sites to YouTube—allow a greater number of voices to compete for influence in the electoral process.[74]

In short, *candidate-centered* campaigns have by and large replaced party-centered campaigns. Candidates now have their own campaign organizations that make decisions on campaign strategies, issues, worker recruitment, voter mobilization, and the raising and spending of funds. To assist them, candidates often hire campaign management firms, public relations specialists, and political consultants. These professionals conduct public opinion surveys; prepare films and advertising; raise money; buy media time; write speeches; provide computer analyses of voting behavior; and develop strategies, issues, and images. This is not to say that parties have no role in managing candidate campaigns, setting campaign agendas, and financing campaign communications; they do, and party officials occasionally still even have the clout to exercise considerable influence over candidate campaigns.[75] But party efforts are largely intended to augment campaigns organized by individual candidates and designed for a candidate-centered environment.

Candidate-centered campaigns revolve around candidate-centered fundraising. Typically, House candidates obtain about half of their funds and Senate candidates receive almost three-fifths of theirs from individual contributors. Political action committees (PACs) rank next in importance. House incumbents in 2008 received 45 percent of their campaign funds from PACs; Senate incumbents received 27 percent. In addition to these regulated donations, interest groups can make hard money independent expenditures from their federal PACs, and they can employ a variety of tax-exempt groups to make soft money expenditures. The latter are commonly referred to as 501(c) and 527 committees, designated as such because of the section of the Internal Revenue Code under which they are organized. Under the 1971 Federal Election Campaign Act and its amendments, limits are placed on the amount of money an individual or PAC can give to a federal candidate. But no limit exists on the amount of money that supporters of federal candidates can spend to aid their campaigns as long as the funds are raised under federal limits and spent *independently*—that is, without contact with the candidates or their campaign organizations. Soft money expenditures by interest groups, which are made with funds raised outside of federal limits, lie largely beyond the scope of federal regulators.[76]

As a result, groups of all kinds spend heavily, especially in media advertising, to support or oppose candidates. In the 2008 general election, hard money independent expenditures by PACs exceeded $135.2 million, more than double the amount spent in 2004 and 250 percent more than in 2006. About 75 percent was allocated to the presidential race.[77] Soft money expenditures by interest groups totaled roughly $400 million in 2008.[78] The intense involvement of groups in campaigns has changed the nation's political ambiance and its political structures, serving to promote the independence of candidates and officeholders from party control while making them more reliant on interest groups and, presumably, more sensitive to their claims.

For years, many observers have felt that these changes signaled the end of parties. David Broder's 1972 book, *The Party's Over,* captured the conventional wisdom.[79] Reports of the death of party, however, turned out to be greatly exaggerated. Parties have redefined themselves in ways that have increased their relevance. Instead of relying on the physical labor of party workers to turn out votes, parties now rely on capital, using their money and other resources to compete in a candidate-centered world. The introduction of soft money in the mid-1990s made parties relevant again. In the 1991–1992 election cycle, the major parties raised a "mere" $86 million for "party-building activities." In 2007–2008, even without the benefit of unlimited soft money contributions, the parties raised nearly $2 billion combined. Moreover, because the most recent revisions to the campaign finance laws increased the limits on hard money contributions to the parties and indexed them for inflation, these receipts stand to continue to grow in the future.

Along with stronger national party organizations, party responsibility in Congress is more pronounced, with a sizable increase in the percentage of party-line votes over the last two decades. In fact, party voting is more pronounced in Congress today than it has been since the late nineteenth century.[80] Scholarly concerns about party weakness have been replaced by concerns about party polarization. Third party fixture Ralph Nader may see the major parties as interchangeable and ineffectual, but Republicans and Democrats today stake out strikingly clear positions on issues across the political spectrum, from abortion to the environment to Social Security to tax policy. As a result, ordinary citizens are more likely to think about politics in terms of the major parties. The party is far from over. It is simply being driven by a different beat.

NOTES

1. James Madison, Federalist No. 10, in Alexander Hamilton, James Madison, and John Jay, *The Federalist Papers*, ed. Clinton Rossiter (New York: New American Library, 1961). Consider the development and components of a party model based on the idea that the only standard useful in evaluating the vitality of American parties is the ability of a party to win office. Using this standard, Joseph Schlesinger argues that the major parties are healthier now than they were in the past. See "On the Theory of Party Organization," *Journal of Politics* 46 (May 1984): 369–400.

2. E. E. Schattschneider, *Party Government* (New York: Holt, Rinehart and Winston, 1942), 1.

3. Ibid., 37.

4. Leon Epstein, *Political Parties in Western Democracies* (New York: Praeger, 1967), 9.

5. Edmund Burke, *Works*, vol. I (London: G. Bell and Sons, 1897), 375.

6. Anthony Downs, *An Economic Theory of Democracy* (New York: Harper, 1957).

7. V. O. Key Jr., *Politics, Parties, and Pressure Groups* (New York: Crowell, 1964), 200–201.

8. Schattschneider, *Party Government*, 1.

9. Agreement among students of political parties on the nature of party functions, their relative significance, and the consequences of functional performance for the political system is far from complete. Frank J. Sorauf points out that among the functions attributed to American parties are the following: to simplify political issues and alternatives, produce automatic majorities, recruit political leadership and personnel, organize minorities and opposition, moderate and compromise political conflict, organize the machinery of government, promote political consensus and legitimacy, and bridge the separation of powers. The principal difficulty with such a list, according to Sorauf, is that "it involves making functional statements about party activity without necessarily relating them to functional requisites or needs of the system." He suggests that emphasis should be given to the *activities* performed by parties to avoid the confusion arising from the lack of clarity about the meaning of function, the absence of consensus on functional categories, and the problem of measuring the performance of functions. See his instructive essay, "Political Parties and Political Analysis," in *The American Party Systems: Stages of Political Development*, ed. William Nisbet Chambers and Walter Dean Burnham (New York: Oxford, 1967), 33–53.

10. In about four-fifths of the states, judges are chosen in some form of partisan or nonpartisan election. In the remaining states they come to office through appointment. A few states employ the so-called Missouri Plan of judge selection, under which the governor makes judicial appointments from a list of names supplied by a nonpartisan judicial commission composed of judges, lawyers, and laypeople. Under this plan, designed to take judges out of politics, each judge, after a trial period, runs for reelection without opposition; voters may vote either to retain or to remove the judge from office. If a majority of voters casts affirmative ballots, the judge is continued in office for a full term; if the vote is negative, the judge loses office and the governor makes another appointment in the same manner. But even under this plan, governors may give preference to aspirants of their own party. Irrespective of the system used to choose judges, party leaders and party interest will nearly always be involved.

11. Michael Teitelbaum, "Heated Maryland Primary Rematch Gets Personal," *CQ Politics*, February 8, 2008. See www.cqpolitics.com.

12. For insight into the power of informal party networks in nomination processes, see Marty Cohen, David Karol, Hans Noel, and John Zaller, *The Party Decides: Presidential Nominations Before and After Reform* (Chicago: University of Chicago Press, 2008). See also Seth Masket, *No Middle Ground: How Informal Party Organizations Control Nominations and Polarize Legislatures* (Ann Arbor: University of Michigan Press, 2009).

13. L. Sandy Maisel, "American Political Parties: Still Central to a Functioning Democracy?" in *American Political Parties: Decline or Resurgence?* ed. Jeffrey E. Cohen, Richard Fleisher, and Paul Kantor (Washington, D.C.: CQ Press, 2001). Also see Cornelius P. Cotter, James L. Gibson, John F. Bibby, and Robert J. Huckshorn, *Party Organization in American Politics* (New York: Praeger, 1984); and James L. Gibson, Cornelius P. Cotter, John F. Bibby, and Robert J. Huckshorn, "Whither the Local Parties? A Cross-Sectional and Longitudinal Analysis of the Strength of Party Organizations," *American Journal of Political Science* 29 (February 1985): 139–160.

14. For a similar set of findings, see Thomas A. Kazee and Mary C. Thornberry, "Where's the Party? Congressional Candidate Recruitment and American Party Organizations," *Western Political Quarterly* 43 (March 1990): 61–80. For a discussion of the role of the national parties in recruiting candidates for Congress, see Paul S. Herrnson, *Party Campaigning in the 1980s* (Cambridge, Mass.: Harvard University Press, 1988), 48–56.

15. Theodore J. Lowi, "Party, Policy, and Constitution in America," in *The American Party Systems*, 263.

16. See a discussion of the party role in "the aggregation of interests" in Gerald M. Pomper, "The Contributions of Political Parties to American Democracy," in *Party Renewal in America: Theory and Practice*, ed. Gerald M. Pomper (New York: Praeger Special Studies, 1980), 5–7. Race may be an exception to the claim that parties are willing to make an effort to satisfy any group's demands. Paul Frymer argues that African Americans are electorally "captured" by the Democratic Party because Republicans (fearing the loss of the largely white GOP base) make no attempt to appeal to black voters. This allows Democrats to pay less attention to African American interests they would if the African American vote was up for grabs. Paul Frymer, *Race and Party Competition in the United States* (Princeton, N.J.: Princeton University Press, 1999).

17. Bart Jansen and Kathleen Hunter, "Sen. Specter Switches to Democratic Party," *CQ Weekly*, May 4, 2009, 1038. The Club for Growth continues to target Republicans it views as insufficiently conservative on fiscal issues. In 2008 GOP House member Wayne T. Gilchrest of Maryland lost in the primary to Andy Harris, a challenger bankrolled by the Club for Growth. Harris lost in the general election.

18. Few facts about the political participation of Americans are of greater significance than those that reveal its social class bias. A disproportionate number of the people highly active in politics are drawn from the upper reaches of the social order, those who hold higher-status occupations, are more affluent, and better educated. Only about 10 percent of the participants highly active in politics come from lower socioeconomic levels. See Sidney Verba and Norman H. Nie, *Participation in America: Political Democracy and Social Equality* (New York: Harper and Row, 1972), especially chapter 20. Sidney Verba, Kay Schlozman, and Henry Brady, *Voice and Equality* (Cambridge, Mass.: Harvard University Press, 1996). The result is that lower-income constituencies tend to be less well represented than upper-income constituencies. Larry Bartels, *Unequal Democracy: The Political Economy of the New Gilded Age* (Princeton, N.J.: Princeton University Press, 2008).

19. Harvey Fergusson, *People and Power* (New York: Morrow, 1947), 101–102.

20. This proposition is debatable. For the opposite position—one that stresses the capacity of parties to shape themselves—see Austin Ranney, *Curing the Mischiefs of Faction: Party Reform in America* (Berkeley: University of California Press, 1975), especially chapter 1.

21. In addition to using terms such as "candidate," "legislator," "member," and "representative" to apply to men and women in politics, we occasionally refer to them in the masculine gender—"he," "him," "his." This is simply a matter of style. These pronouns are employed generically.

22. For a study of ideological polarization in state party systems, see Robert D. Brown and Gerald C. Wright, "Elections and State Party Polarization," *American Politics Quarterly* 20 (October 1992): 411–426. Some states, such as Utah and California, are highly polarized (liberal Democrats versus conservative Republicans), whereas in other states, such as Louisiana and Arizona, there is little difference in the ideology of the party coalitions (both are conservative). In states in which the parties are ideologically polarized, there is less split-ticket voting, fewer party defections, less vote swing, and less volatility in election results.

23. David R. Mayhew, *Placing Parties in American Politics* (Princeton, N.J.: Princeton University Press, 1986).

24. Andrew M. Appleton and Daniel S. Ward, *State Party Profiles: A Fifty-State Guide to Development, Organizations, and Resources* (Washington, D.C.: CQ Press, 1997).

25. Mayhew, *Placing Parties in American Politics*, particularly chapters 2 and 7.

26. Single-member districts clearly play a significant role in protecting the American major parties from the incursions of minor parties. For an enlightening essay on how proportional representation might affect the two-party system in American states, see Douglas J. Amy, "Proportional Representation and the Future of the American Party System," *American Review of Politics* 16 (Fall-Winter 1995): 371–383.

27. For studies of the effects of divisive primaries on party unity and election outcomes, see Donald B. Johnson and James R. Gibson, "The Divisive Primary Revisited: Party Activists in Iowa," *American Political Science Review* 68 (March 1974): 67–77; Patrick J. Kenney and Tom W. Rice, "The Relationship between Divisive Primaries and General Election Outcomes," *American Journal of Political Science* 31 (February 1987): 31–44; and Paul S. Herrnson and James G. Gimpel, "District Conditions and Primary Divisiveness in Congressional Elections," *Political Research Quarterly* 48 (March 1995): 117–150.

28. Stephen Ansolabehere, Mark Hansen, Shigeo Hirano, and James M. Snyder Jr., "The Incumbency Advantage in U.S. Primary Elections," *Electoral Studies* 26 (September 2007): 660–668.

29. Although Howard Dean, the former governor of Vermont, was the Democratic presidential front-runner in the preprimary period in 2003–2004, he was certainly not the party's choice. Many believe that party regulars recruited Gen. Wesley Clark into the race to defeat Dean. When Dean's campaign began to sputter in early 2004 with his disappointing showings in Iowa and New Hampshire, party regulars breathed a sigh of relief with the emergence of John Kerry as front-runner.

30. Cohen et al., *The Party Decides.*

31. John Aldrich, *Why Parties* (Chicago: University of Chicago Press, 1996).

32. See Barry Burden, "The Polarizing Effect of Congressional Primaries," in *Congressional Primaries and the Politics of Representation,* ed. Peter Galderisi, Marni Ezra, and Michael Lyons (Lanham, Md.: Rowman and Littlefield, 2001).

33. Federal Election Commission, press release, November 2004.

34. Lucian W. Pye and Sidney Verba, eds., *Political Culture and Political Development* (Princeton, N.J.: Princeton University Press, 1965), 513.

35. Jack Dennis, "Support for the Party System by the Mass Public," *American Political Science Review* 60 (September 1966): 600–615. Also see Thomas M. Konda and Lee Sigelman, "Public Evaluations of the American Parties, 1952–1984," *Journal of Politics* 49 (August 1987): 814–829.

36. Survey by *Newsweek,* conducted by Princeton Survey Research Associates International, June 20–21, 2007.

37. See *The American Enterprise* (January/February 1993): 107–108.

38. NBC News/*Wall Street Journal* poll, conducted by Hart and Newhouse Research Companies, October 4–5, 2008.

39. A system of "responsible parties" would be characterized by centralized, unified, and disciplined parties committed to the execution of programs and promises offered at elections and held accountable by the voters for their performance. For an analysis of this model, see chapter 7.

40. Survey by Gallup Organization, September 8–11, 2008.

41. This question was not asked in the 2008 NES. A question asking which party would better handle the economy was asked, and a plurality of respondents chose the Democrats.

42. Larry M. Bartels, "Partisanship and Voting Behavior, 1952–1996," *American Journal of Political Science* 44 (January 2000): 35–50.

43. David W. Rohde, *Parties and Leaders in the Post-Reform House* (Chicago: University of Chicago Press, 1991).

44. Marc J. Hetherington, "Resurgent Mass Partisanship: The Role of Elite Polarization," *American Political Science Review* 95 (September 2001): 619–631. Similar treatments of party resurgence in the electorate include David G. Lawrence, "On the Resurgence of Party Identification in the 1990s," and Richard Fleisher and Jon R. Bond, "Evidence of Increasing Polarization Among Ordinary Citizens," in *American Political Parties;* and Geoffrey C. Layman and Thomas M. Carsey, "Party Polarization and 'Conflict Extension' in the American Electorate," *American Journal of Political Science* 46 (October 2002): 786–802.

45. See Jeffrey Stonecash, *Class and Party in American Politics* (Boulder, Colo.: Westview, 2000), for a discussion of the increase in class-based voting in the 1990s.

46. Data are taken from the 2000 and 2004 exit polls.

47. Two studies that trace the growing importance of the national party are Charles H. Longley, "National Party Renewal," and John F. Bibby, "Party Renewal in the National Republican Party," in *Party Renewal in America,* 69–86, 102–115.

48. Federal Election Commission, press release, May 2003.

49. Data from opensecrets.org, based on information released by the Federal Election Commission, May 1, 2009.

50. *Congressional Quarterly Weekly Report,* February 16, 1974, 352.

51. *Congressional Quarterly Weekly Report,* January 14, 1978, 61.

52. *New York Times,* March 27, 1997.

53. Federal Election Commission, press release, May 12, 2005.

54. Paul S. Herrnson, "The National Parties at Century's End," in *The Parties Respond: Changes in Parties and Campaigns,* 3rd ed., ed. L. Sandy Maisel (Boulder, Colo.: Westview Press, 1998).

55. See Cornelius P. Cotter and Bernard C. Hennessy, *Politics without Power: The National Party Committees* (New York: Atherton Press, 1964), 67–80. The authors see the roles of the national chair as "image-maker, hell-raiser, fund-raiser, campaign manager, and administrator."

56. F. Christopher Arterton, "Political Money and Party Strength," in *The Future of American Political Parties,* ed. Fleishman, 105.

57. *Congressional Quarterly Weekly Report,* January 14, 1978, 58.

58. Obama is the first presidential candidate to decline public funding in the general election since the law went into effect in 1976.

59. The job of chair of a congressional campaign committee is a major political plum. The chair concentrates on fund-raising, "signs the checks" for the party's candidates, and inevitably gains the gratitude of winners.

60. Federal Election Commission, press release, May 2005.

61. Campaign Finance Institute, "A First Look at Money in the House and Senate Elections," press release, November 6, 2008.

62. For an examination of the strength of party organizations at the state level, see John F. Bibby, Cornelius P. Cotter, James L. Gibson, and Robert J. Huckshorn, "Trends in Party Organizational Strength, 1960–1980," *International Political Science Review* 4 (January 1983): 21–27.

63. John Aldrich, "Southern Parties in State and Nation," *Journal of Politics* 62 (August 2000).

64. Anthony Gierzynski, *Legislative Party Campaign Committees in the American States* (Lexington: University of Kentucky Press, 1992); Daniel M. Shea, *Transforming Democracy: Legislative Campaign Committees and Political Parties* (Albany: SUNY Press, 1995). Cindy Simon Rosenthal, "New Party or Campaign Bank Account? Explaining the Rise of State Legislative Campaign Committees," *Legislative Studies Quarterly* XX (May 1995): 249–268.

65. Seth Masket, *No Middle Ground.*

66. Lewis Bowman and G. R. Boynton, "Activities and Role Definitions of Grassroots Party Officials," *Journal of Politics* 28 (February 1966): 121–143.

67. Barbara C. Burrell, "Local Political Party Committees, Task Performance and Organizational Vitality," *Western Political Quarterly* 39 (March 1986): 48–66.

68. Michael Margolis and Raymond E. Owen, "From Organization to Personalism: A Note on the Transmogrification of the Local Political Party," *Polity* 18 (Winter 1985): 313–328.

69. See Maisel, "American Political Parties"; and Gibson et al. "Whither the Local Parties?" 139–160.

70. William C. Binning, Melanie J. Blumberg, and John C. Green, "Change Comes to Youngstown: Local Political Parties as Instruments of Power," in *The State of the Parties: The Changing Role of Contemporary American Parties,* 3rd ed., ed. John G. Green and Daniel M. Shea (Lanham, Md.: Rowman and Littlefield, 1999).

71. John P. Frendreis, James L. Gibson, and Laura L. Vertz, "The Electoral Relevance of Local Party Organizations," *American Political Science Review* 84 (March 1990): 225–235. Indicators of the structural strength of a party organization include the presence of a constitution and bylaws, a complete set of officers, an active chair, bimonthly meetings, a year-round office, staff, and a budget.

72. Quoted in Albert R. Hunt, "The Media and Presidential Campaigns," in *Elections American Style,* ed. A. James Reichley (Washington, D.C.: Brookings Institution, 1987), 53.

73. See column by R. W. Apple Jr. in *New York Times,* February 11, 1988.

74. Michael Cornfeld, "Game Changers: New Technology and the 2008 Presidential Election," in *The Year of Obama: How Barack Obama Won the White House,* ed. Larry J. Sabato (New York: Longman, 2009).

75. Gary Jacobson notes that after spending more than $2.4 million dollars on behalf of Colorado Republican House candidate Bob Beauprez in 2002, the NRCC demanded an oversight role in his campaign. Gary C. Jacobson, *The Politics of Congressional Elections,* 7th ed. (New York: Pearson-Longman), 78–79. See also David C. W. Parker, *The Power of Money in Congressional Campaigns, 1880–2006* (Norman: University of Oklahoma Press, 2008).

76. Campaign Finance Institute, press release, "Outside Soft Money Groups Approaching $400 million in Targeted Spending in 2008 Election," October 31, 2008.

77. Federal Election Commission, press release, "Growth in PAC Activity Slows," April 24, 2009.

78. Campaign Finance Institute, press release, "Outside Soft Money Groups Approaching $400 million in Targeted Spending in 2008 Election," October 31, 2008.

79. David S. Broder, *The Party's Over: The Failure of Politics in America* (New York: Harper and Row, 1972).

80. Hahrie Han and David W. Brady, "An Extended Historical View of Congressional Party Polarization" (paper presented at the Congress and History Conference, Stanford University, June 11–12, 2004).

2 AMERICAN PARTIES: CHARACTERISTICS AND COMPETITION

THE MAJOR PARTIES ARE FIRM LANDMARKS on the American political scene. In existence for more than 175 years, the parties have made important contributions to the development and maintenance of a democratic political culture and to democratic institutions and practices. In essence, the parties form the principal institution for popular control of government, and this achievement is remarkable given the limitations under which they function. This chapter examines the chief characteristics and the competitiveness of the American party system.

Characteristics of Parties

Viewed at a distance, the party organizations may appear to be neatly ordered and hierarchical—committees are piled one atop the other from the precinct to the national level, conveying the impression that power flows from the top to the bottom. In reality, the American party is not nearly so hierarchical. State and local organizations have substantial independence in most party matters, and at one time they dictated policy to the national parties. The national parties' emergence as successful fund-raisers and their ability to transfer funds to state parties have given the national organizations substantially more power. Even so, the practices that state and local parties follow, the candidates they recruit or help to recruit, the campaign money they raise, the auxiliary groups they form and re-form, the innovations they introduce, the organized interests to which they respond, the campaign strategies and issues they create, and, most important, the policy orientations of the candidates who run under their labels—all bear the distinctive imprints of local and state political cultures, leaders, traditions, and interests.[1] Rather than being top-down organizations, parties traditionally have reflected the bottom-up differences between members. As a result, American parties, which value winning elections over everything else, have had strong incentives to at least be perceived as moderate and inclusive in an attempt to knit together as large a coalition as possible, especially at the national level. As party coalitions have become more distinct, and congressional elections less competitive, however, parties have become markedly more ideological in nature.

Dispersed Power

One important characteristic of American political parties is decentralization. Because of the legal and constitutional design of the American political system, parties must find their place within a federal system where powers and responsibilities lie with fifty states as well as with the national government. The basic responsibility for the electoral system in which the parties compete is given to the states, not to the nation. Not surprisingly, party organizations have been molded by the electoral laws under which they contest for power. State and local power centers have naturally developed around the thousands of governmental units and elective offices in the states and localities. Typical officeholders—with their distinctive constituencies (frequently safe districts), their own coteries of supporters, and their own sources of campaign money—have a remarkable amount of freedom in defining their relationships to their party. Their well-being and the party organization's are not identical, and officeholders continuously evaluate party claims and objectives in light of their own career aspirations. When the party's claims and the officeholder's aspirations diverge, the party usually loses out. A federal system, with numerous elective offices, opens up an extraordinary range of political choices to subnational parties and, especially, to individual candidates.

Candidates in subnational elections are much better able to adopt and reflect the ideological profile of the state or locality than candidates in national elections. Although the national Republican Party and almost all of its candidates for president and Congress are now quite conservative, Republican gubernatorial candidates still often do well in liberal states. A Republican presidential candidate could not hope to win in California, Connecticut, Hawaii, Rhode Island, or Vermont under nearly any circumstances these days, but all have elected liberal Republican governors since 2006. The same is true for Democratic governors in conservative states. No Democratic presidential candidate has won in Kansas, Oklahoma, or Wyoming since 1964, yet since 2006 all three have elected conservative Democratic governors.

For all of its significance for the party system and the distinctiveness of American politics, however, federalism is but one of several explanations for the fragmentation of party power. Another constitutional concept—separation of powers—also contributes to this condition. A frequent by-product of the separation of powers is a truncated party majority: one party controls one or both houses of the legislature, and the other controls the executive office. Since the

1960s this arrangement has often been the case at the federal level, but divided party control also is quite common at the state level. At worst, the result is a dreary succession of narrow partisan clashes between the branches; at best, an occasional clarification of differences between the parties may occur. At no time, however, does a truncated majority help in the development and maintenance of party responsibility for a program of public policy.

A third factor in the fragmentation of party power is the method used to make nominations. As noted earlier, nominations for national office are sorted out and settled at the local level, ordinarily without interference from national party functionaries. One of the principal supports of local control over nominations is the direct primary. Its use virtually guarantees that candidates for national office will be tailored to the measure of local specifications. To the extent that American localities differ from one another in economic interests, culture, and political attitudes, the national parties will be ideologically heterogeneous and show differing degrees of cohesion from issue to issue.[2]

As politics has become more nationalized over the last generation, however, the heterogeneity that stems from local control has become less problematic. As an example of homogeneity, Stephen Ansolabehere, James Snyder, and Charles Stewart find that Republican candidates for Congress today are always more conservative than Democratic candidates. In addition, present-day candidates are less responsive to the ideological preferences of people in their districts than in generations past, following their own preferences instead.[3] Although Robert Erikson and Gerald Wright demonstrate that ideological extremity decreases candidates' vote share to some degree,[4] the ideologically extreme still have little to worry about because their districts are so safe for one party or the other. Those who draw congressional district lines create districts that are either solidly conservative or solidly liberal. As a result, policy-driven candidates can be more extreme than their reelection constituencies without fear of being defeated by the other party.

Fourth, the distribution of power within the parties is affected by patterns of campaign finance. Few, if any, campaign resources are more important than money. Although parties are now raising and spending more money on behalf of candidates than ever before, the vast majority of political donations in any given year still go directly to the campaign organizations of individual candidates instead of to the party organizations. Moreover, parties typically spend money in only the most competitive contests—of which there are relatively few, especially in most American legislatures. Parties still maintain some influence over their candidates' fund-raising fortunes. Indeed, as James Gimpel, Frances Lee, and Shanna Pearson-Merkowitz show, at least some of the money from individuals and interest groups is steered toward the candidates by the parties, which serve as intermediaries in the political money market.[5] The aggressive GOP congressional party leaders who emerged in the 1990s took such steering to new levels, warning interest groups against contributing to Democrats.[6] Nevertheless, most if not all serious candidates (especially incumbents) have their own network of donors and fund-raisers, placing them in a relatively strong position vis-à-vis the party organization and allowing them to maintain their independence.[7] Whether candidates can remain independent from the deep-pocketed individuals and interest groups that pour money into their campaigns is another question.

Fifth, a pervasive spirit of localism dominates American politics and adds to the decentralization of political power. Local interests find expression in national politics in countless ways. Even the presidential nominating process may become critical for the settlement of local and state political struggles. Prominent political leaders who align themselves with the candidate who eventually wins the presidential nomination, particularly if their support comes early in the race, can improve their political profile by gaining access to the nominee and the increased visibility that comes with it. If their party wins the presidency, they may even be offered appointments in the new administration. In January 2008 Kathleen Sebelius, the Democratic governor of Kansas, endorsed Barack Obama's presidential candidacy even though Hillary Clinton was the obvious front-runner. As a result, Sebelius found herself on the short list of potential Obama vice-presidential candidates. Joe Biden was the eventual VP choice, but Obama tapped Sebelius to lead the Department of Health and Human Services, an important cabinet position given the Obama administration's plans for health care reform. Another early Obama endorser, Gov. Janet Napolitano of Arizona, was named Obama's secretary of the Homeland Security Department, another politically important post.

Congress has always shown a remarkable hospitality to the idea that government power should be decentralized. A great deal of the major legislation passed in recent decades has been designed to make state and local governments participants in the development and implementation of public policies— arrangements from which locally based political organizations profit. A basic explanation for Congress's defense of state and local governments lies in the backgrounds of the members themselves. Many served in state or local offices prior to their election to Congress; they are steeped in local lore, think in local terms, meet frequently with local representatives, and work for local advantage. Their steady attention to the local dimensions of national policy helps safeguard their own careers and promote the interests of the politicians "back home" who look to Washington for assistance in solving community problems. The late Speaker of the House, Thomas P. "Tip" O'Neill Jr. (D-Mass.), had it right when he said, "All politics is local."[8]

Finally, the fragmentation of party power owes much to the growing importance of outsiders in the political process. Chief among them are the media, campaign management firms, and interest groups. Today, virtually all candidates for important offices hire expert consultants to organize their campaigns, shape their strategies, and mold their images. They strain for media coverage that presents them in a favorable light—an ever more complex undertaking with the emergence of political comedy shows such as *The Colbert Report* and *The Daily Show*. What counts, candidates know, is how the voters perceive them.

As for interest groups, their role in campaigns, particularly in financing, has grown in importance. In 2008 federal PACs contributed about $413 million to the campaigns of candidates for Congress—$41 million more than in 2004 and roughly nine times as much as they gave in 1978.[9] Additionally, the 501(c) and 527 organizations associated with interest groups—many of which also give from PACs—spent roughly $400 million in soft money in the 2008 elections.[10] And in all likelihood, their influence on officeholders has increased.[11] Indeed, many critics of the campaign finance system blame it for the string of corporate scandals that came to light in 2002, including those involving Enron, WorldCom, Global Crossing, and Tyco. All were major political contributors who sought and received from Congress lax federal regulation of their industries' business and accounting practices.

The Power of Officeholders

Writing in the 1960s, James M. Burns sketched the organizational strength of state parties:

> At no level, except in a handful of industrial states, do state parties have the attri-butes of organization. They lack extensive dues-paying memberships; hence, they number many captains and sergeants but few foot soldiers. They do a poor job of raising money for themselves as organizations, or even for their candidates. They lack strong and imaginative leadership of their own. They cannot control their most vital function—the nomination of their candidates. Except in a few states, such as Ohio, Connecticut, and Michigan, our parties are essentially collections of small cliques and they are often shunted aside by the politicians who understand political power. Most of the state parties are at best mere jousting grounds for embattled politicians.[12]

Is the situation different today? It is, in many respects. Later research has shown that the parties are stronger organizationally than they were in the 1960s. Most state parties now maintain permanent headquarters with professional staffs in the state capital. State party budgets have grown in size, and systematic fund-raising by leaders and staff has become a more important function. Party organi-zations are better equipped to provide candidates with services, including research assistance and campaign money, largely because of massive cash transfers from the national parties. They are also more effective in recruiting candidates for public office in many jurisdictions. Scholarly treatments of state parties consis-tently suggest that the Republican state parties are stronger than their Demo-cratic counterparts, although Democrats now appear to match Republicans in candidate recruitment, county party assistance, and voter identification.[13] John Aldrich notes that Republican state parties are particularly strong in the South where, until thirty years ago, the Republican Party barely existed.[14]

State parties have become stronger largely because of the greater ability of national parties to fund them. The Federal Election Campaign Act (FECA) helps national parties in this regard. Although the national parties are limited in the amount of money they can give candidates (see chapter 4), parties can transfer unlimited sums of hard money for "party building" activities at the state level. In the 2007–2008 election cycle, the Democratic National Committee (DNC) transferred $66 million to its state parties. The largest amounts went to Florida ($5.5 million), Pennsylvania ($3.1 million), and Ohio ($2.5 million)—states with closely contested races in the presidential campaign.[15] The Republican National Committee (RNC) transferred $24.2 million over the same period to its state parties. The same three states received the bulk of the RNC's money, with $7.3 million going to Florida.[16] With this kind of money at their disposal, parties can be effective in the states.

Important everywhere, however, are the candidates and officeholders. They dominate the campaign and election process. Aided by hired consultants and assorted handlers, they develop strategies and issues, raise funds, recruit workers, interact with interest groups, assemble coalitions, cultivate the media, make news, and mobilize voters. The party organization may facilitate campaigns by providing useful services to the candidates, but that is usually the extent of its involvement. Moreover, the parties tend to aid candidates in only the most competitive races. As congressional races, in particular, have become significantly less competitive, the parties involve themselves in relatively few contests, although they spend more where their participation is likely to matter. For the most part, candidates shape their own campaigns and win largely on their own efforts and on their own terms. The perspective of Barbara G. Salmore and Stephen A. Salmore is instructive:

> Technology is the development most responsible for ending party primacy in campaigns. . . . What made the advent of television and the computer unique was that they provided candidates everywhere with an effective alternative means of getting information about themselves to the voters. Newspapers, magazines, and radio paled in comparison with what television offered—a powerful combination of visual and aural messages. Candidates could enter voters' homes and give party organizations competition they had never had before. . . . Once candidates learned that they could independently compete with party organizations and that they had the direct primary as the vehicle to do it, why should they give up their independence and control of their messages to the party organizations?[17]

Coalitional in Nature

The American political party is much less a collection of individuals than it is a collection of social interests and groups. In the words of Maurice Duverger, "A party is not a community but a collection of communities, a union of small groups dispersed throughout the country."[18] Functioning within a vastly heterogeneous society, the major parties have naturally assumed a coalitional form. Groups of all kinds—social, economic, religious, and ethnic—are organized to press demands on the political order. In the course of defending or advancing their interests, they contribute substantial energy to the political process—by generating innovations, posing alternative policies, recruiting and endorsing candidates, conducting campaigns, and so on. No party seriously contesting for office could ignore the constellation of groups in American political life.

Table 2-1 Loyal Groups in the Party Coalitions

	Presidential Election Year				
Groups	1992	1996	2000	2004	2008
Percentage points more Democratic than the nation as a whole					
African Americans	40	35	42	40	42
Jews	37	29	31	26	25
Hispanics	18	23	15	5	14
Unmarried women	10	13	15	14	17
Union households	12	10	11	13	6
Percentage points more Republican than the nation as a whole					
White fundamentalist or evangelical Christians	23	24	32	27	28
Southern whites	11	15	19	19	32
High income	10	10	6	7	3
Whites	2	5	6	7	9

Source: Developed from data in Voter News Service national exit polls from 1992 to 2000 and Edison/ Mitofsky exit polls in 2004 and 2008.

Note: High income in 2008 is defined as $100,000 and over. Of the total vote in 2008, African Americans made up 13 percent; Hispanics, 9 percent; Jews, 2 percent; unmarried women, 21 percent; and union households, 21 percent. Whites cast 74 percent of the total vote.

Traditionally, each party has had relatively distinct followings in the electorate, a characteristic illustrated in Table 2-1. The urban working classes, union families, racial minorities (especially African Americans), Jews, and persons at the lower end of the income scale have been mainstays of the Democratic Party since the 1930s. At one time, southerners, Catholics, and those at the low end of the education scale also were Democrats. The Republican coalition has had a disproportionate number of supporters from big business, industry, farmers, small-town and rural dwellers, whites, Protestants, upper-income (although not as strongly in 2008), and "old stock" Americans. More recently, evangelical Christians have also supported the GOP in disproportionate numbers. These group inclinations make coalition politics a major feature of successful election campaigns.

Today, these coalitions are in flux. Nowhere is this more evident than in the South, where Republicans have made major gains and in many ways dominate the region on the federal level. Changes in public opinion and voting behavior tend to be glacial to the extent that they occur at all, so the change in southern politics over the past sixty years has been nothing short of breathtaking. In 1948 Republican presidential candidate Thomas Dewey failed even to appear on the ballot in several southern states, but George W. Bush carried every state in the former Confederacy in both 2000 and 2004. Even in defeat, John McCain won all but two states (Virginia and North Carolina) in this region. Among southern white voters, McCain ran a remarkable 32 percentage points ahead of his national showing. In ten straight elections from 1972 to 2008, southern white voters cast a plurality of their votes for the Republican presidential candidate. Only Jimmy Carter of Georgia, with the aid of many southern blacks, ran a stronger campaign in the region than he did nationally. In addition, Republicans went from a mere 6 percent of the House seats in the South in 1953 to more than 55 percent after the 2008 election.[19] The change in the Senate has been even more dramatic. In 1953 there were no Republican senators from the southern states. In 2009 Republicans held fifteen of the twenty-two seats, even after losing the 2006 and 2008 election cycles.

Race was the root cause of the beginning of this southern realignment. Until the 1960s the Democratic Party was the main political vehicle for the continuation of racial segregation and the beneficiary of nearly unanimous support from white voters in the South. Under Democrats John F. Kennedy and Lyndon B. Johnson, however, the party embraced racial integration and voting rights for African Americans, which won the Democrats the support of nearly all black voters. Uncomfortable with this change in policy, many southern whites bolted to Barry Goldwater's presidential campaign in 1964; the Republican candidate promised to leave decisions on racial issues to the states. Indeed, other than his home state of Arizona, the only states Goldwater won were the five Deep South states. Today, southern Democrats are disproportionately African American and hail from urban centers, while the suburban and rural parts of the South, which make up most of the region, lean strongly Republican.

Andrew Gelman demonstrates that today the dividing line in southern white voting behavior is more class based than race based.[20] Well-off voters in wealthy northeastern states like Connecticut, New Jersey, and New York are about equally likely to vote either Republican or Democratic, but middle- and high-income voters in the South are more likely to cast their ballots for Republicans than Democrats in national elections. Apparently, the GOP's lower-tax, smaller government philosophy is attractive to high-income voters in this region, while the low-income voters tend to vote Democratic. The South's growing prosperity over the last thirty years has produced a larger percentage of Republican voters.

High-income voters outside the South, however, have become a significantly less reliable Republican constituency over time. Gelman argues that two explanations are at the root of this change. First, upper-income voters are disproportionately liberal on "culture war" issues such as abortion and gay rights. Although Thomas Frank, in his provocative book *What's the Matter with Kansas*, argues that Republicans have used these issues to attract the support of socially conservative low-income voters, Gelman demonstrates that the culture war is really being fought by middle- to upper-income voters. Low-income voters, by and large, do not feel the luxury to vote on noneconomic grounds. Second, high-income voters earn their money doing a range of different things. Traditional managers, administrators, and property and business owners always were and continue to be strongly Republican, but those who are termed "professionals"—doctors, lawyers, software engineers, and the like—who used to identify as Republicans have now become Democrats. As high-income professionals have become a larger chunk of America's service-based economy, their voting behavior has become more evenly divided. This trend explains why the states with the highest median incomes (Connecticut, Maryland, Massachusetts, and New Jersey) vote Democratic for president.

The voting behavior of certain religious groups also has changed over time, to the detriment of Democrats. With one of their own, John Kennedy, at the top of the Democratic ticket in 1960, Catholics voted 28 percentage points more Democratic than the electorate as a whole (78 percent to 50 percent). Protestants, in contrast, voted 12 percentage points more Republican than the national average (62 percent to 50 percent). Even in 1964, with Lyndon Johnson replacing Kennedy as the Democrats' standard-bearer, Catholics voted strongly Democratic (76 percent as contrasted with Johnson's national average of 61 percent). Since then, however, Catholic support for Democratic presidential candidates has declined. In fact, non-Hispanic Catholics cast a majority of their ballots (52 percent) for Bush in 2000 and 2004 and for John McCain in 2008.[21]

There are two main reasons for this change. First, Catholics are no longer as economically distinct as they were generations ago. As new immigrants for much of the early twentieth century, Catholics tended to be disproportionately poor, making the pro–welfare state Democratic Party a more attractive option for them. Second, the politicization of abortion and gay rights may dispose some Catholics to vote Republican, as the GOP and the Catholic Church are strongly antiabortion and oppose the gay rights agenda. In more general terms, the Republicans' recent emphasis on "family values" issues may also hold a particular attraction for certain Catholic voters as well as for Protestant fundamentalists. As evidence, the degree of religious devotion now divides Democrats from Republicans, with those who go to church less often supporting Democrats, and those who go to church more often supporting Republicans. Not all Catholics have been drifting toward the Republican Party at the same rate. Most of this change has been among those who attend Mass regularly.

Other demographic changes have favored the Democrats. According to the 2000 Census, the fastest growing racial and ethnic groups in the United States are Latinos and Asians; and Latinos have overtaken African Americans as the largest minority population in America. Traditionally, Latinos have been strong Democratic supporters, often voting for Democratic presidential candidates by a two-to-one margin. This pattern was again evident in 2008 with Obama winning the Latino vote, 68 percent to 31 percent. Moreover, the clustering of Latinos in certain states has the potential to strengthen the group's political punch. Substantial Latino populations in Colorado, Florida, Nevada, and New Mexico were important in moving these states from the Republican column in presidential voting in 2004 to the Democratic column in 2008.[22] And, even though Latinos still make up less than 5 percent of the population of North Carolina, the rate of increase there was the fastest in the country from the 1990s to the 2000s, making their vote consequential in a state decided by about 20,000 votes.

Still it is important not to overstate the impact of Latino voters on the future of Democratic successes. A high percentage of Latinos living in the United States have not yet progressed through the naturalization process, which means they are not citizens and cannot vote. In addition, Latinos tend to turn out to vote at lower rates than those from other racial and ethnic groups. In presidential elections, Latino voter turnout is typically less than 30 percent, whereas turnout is typically more than 60 percent among whites and more than 50 percent among African Americans. Moreover, Republican efforts to attract Latinos have been at times successful. President Bush increased his support among Latinos by nine percentage points between 2000 and 2004 by advertising on Spanish-language radio, speaking Spanish on the stump, and appealing to Latinos' conservative position on social issues such as abortion.[23]

In a more general sense, it is significant that the parties are increasingly divided by race. As recently as 1992 those who identify themselves as white divided their votes equally between the major parties (the difference was a statistically insignificant two percentage points). In 2008 whites were nine percentage points more Republican than the electorate as a whole, although white voters under age thirty favored Obama over McCain by ten points. The Democrats are becoming a party of racial minorities. In 2008 nonwhites made up 27 percent of the electorate, and every nonwhite racial classification provided overwhelming support to Obama: 95 percent among African Americans, 67 percent among Latinos, 62 percent among Asian Americans, and 64 percent among those who chose "other" racial classifications. As the United States becomes a more diverse and racially tolerant nation, the Democrats' electoral advantage with minority groups becomes more consequential.

American parties are fragile because they are coalitions. Demands by one coalition partner might be at odds with the interests of others. Social conservatives in the Republican Party tend to oppose immigration reform that would provide illegal immigrants with a path to citizenship, but economic conservatives in the party favor such reform efforts. Social liberals in the Democratic Party support gay marriage and gay adoption, but working-class whites and racial minorities oppose these rights. At times, these coalitions seem to be held together by nothing more than generality, personality, and promise. Perhaps what is surprising, all things considered, is that they hold together as well as they do.

Theoretically Moderate and Inclusive, but Less So in Practice

Because their main role is to knit together coalitions of groups that may have conflicting goals, American parties have an incentive to be moderate and inclusive. As a result, they have been mostly "catchall" parties in which all but the most extreme and intractable elements in society can find a place and, in the process, stake a claim to a piece of the action. All groups are invited to support the party, and in some measure all do. Even though only about 10 percent of African Americans vote Republican, the GOP has appealed to black voters by highlighting its support for school vouchers and its opposition to gay rights, which are popular positions in this community. In addition, Michael Steele was elected chair of the Republican National Committee in 2009, the first African American to hold that post. Almost everything about a major party at election time represents a triumph for those who press for accommodation in American politics. Platforms and candidate speeches, offering something to virtually everyone, provide the hard evidence that parties attempt to be inclusive rather than exclusive in their appeals and to draw in a wide rather than a narrow band of voters. "No matter how devoted a party leadership may be to its bedrock elements," V. O. Key Jr. wrote, "it attempts to picture itself as a gifted synthesizer of concord among the elements of society. A party must act as if it were all the people rather than some of them; it must fiercely deny that it speaks for a single interest." [24] Even the ideologically polarized parties of the contemporary era each *claim* to represent all Americans. Key's observation is exemplified by the preamble to the 2008 Republican Party platform: "We stand united today because we are the one party that speaks to all Americans—conservatives, moderates, libertarians, independents, and even liberals." [25]

The inclusivity of the major American parties means that they occupy virtually all of the political space in the political system. Minor parties, then, are forced to search for distinctiveness. Some fashion narrow appeals, others press unusual or hopeless causes, and still others maneuver only at the ideological fringes, seeking to address extreme left-wing or right-wing audiences. Their dilemma is that only a relative handful of voters are at each ideological pole and only a few will be attracted to a narrow or single-issue appeal. The result is that most minor parties struggle to secure candidates, financing, media attention, and credibility. The major parties' inclusiveness, not to mention their institutional control, causes minor parties to struggle just to stay in business.

The Founders established an intricate system of divided powers, checks and balances, and auxiliary precautions to reduce the government's vulnerability to factions. The "Madisonian system"—separation of powers, staggered terms of office, bicameralism, federalism, life appointments for federal judges, and fixed terms of office for the president and members of Congress, among other things— makes it difficult for any group (faction or party) to gain firm control of the political system. Today's parties qualify as James Madison's factions, but with an unexpected twist: they are in no way a factional threat. Their historical inclusivity and relative moderation represent at least as great an obstacle to factional domination of government as do formal constitutional arrangements. Because the major parties include all kinds of interests, they are not free to favor a single interest or a small cluster of interests to the exclusion of others.

Even though the parties have pursued a more ideological course recently, they still make efforts to reach out to the political middle. Democrat Bill Clinton championed and signed into law the 1996 Welfare Reform Act, perhaps the most significant rollback of the American welfare state in U.S. history. Clinton also pushed hard for the North American Free Trade Agreement (NAFTA), a measure that garnered more support from congressional Republicans than Democrats. On the other hand, Republican George W. Bush campaigned for and signed into law a prescription drug benefit for older Americans under the Medicare program, which represented the largest expansion of the welfare state since the 1960s. And in the first months of the Obama administration, the government continued to direct huge infusions of cash into troubled banks, not something liberal Democrats tend to embrace.

Standing party policies are an expression of earlier settlements among divergent interests. Virtually every new policy can be contested by interested party elements. Every affected interest expects a hearing, and bargaining occurs as a matter of course, usually leading to accommodations that can at least be tolerated by most participants. The broad consequences are that policymaking is a slow process and that policy changes are introduced incrementally. The parties' moderation ordinarily means that no one wins or loses completely—a consequence of which is that the public often has difficulty deciding which party to single out for credit and which to blame. (See Figure 2-1.)

Ideologically Heterogeneous in Theory, but Less So in Practice

To win elections and gain power is the unabashedly practical aim of the major parties. Given that the United States is such a large and diverse country, parties need to build coalitions such that the policy goals of the groups and candidates in a given party are subordinated to their capacity to contribute to electoral victory. The natural outcome of a campaign strategy designed to attract a wide variety of groups is that the party's ideology is not brought into as sharp a focus as it might be.

One way to consider how the ideological heterogeneity of the nation's representatives challenges the parties is to examine the Americans for Democratic Action (ADA) ratings of members of the U.S. Senate. The ADA, well known for its identification with liberal causes, rates legislators based on how often they vote in accordance with its liberal principles. Those who support laws to close corporate tax loopholes, protect the environment, and raise the minimum wage, for example, receive high scores from the ADA; those who do not, receive low scores. Figure 2-2 displays a summary of ADA scores prior to the 2006 election. The average Democratic senator supported the ADA position 89 percent of the time; the average Republican senator, a mere 9 percent of the time. The party differences are not difficult to detect.

Nevertheless, important cleavages *within* the parties are quite apparent. Two of the most distinctive are regional: the Northeast (defined here as the eleven states running from Maine to Maryland) is known for its liberalism, and the South (defined here as the eleven states of the former Confederacy) for its conservatism. Many Republican senators have ADA scores of either 5 or 0, but northeastern Republicans score an average of 34, significantly more liberal than most members of their party. One of those northeastern Republicans was Rick Santorum of Pennsylvania, who was defeated in 2006 largely because the voters saw him as too conservative for the state. If we eliminate him from the calculation,

Figure 2-1 Moderate Parties and Policymaking

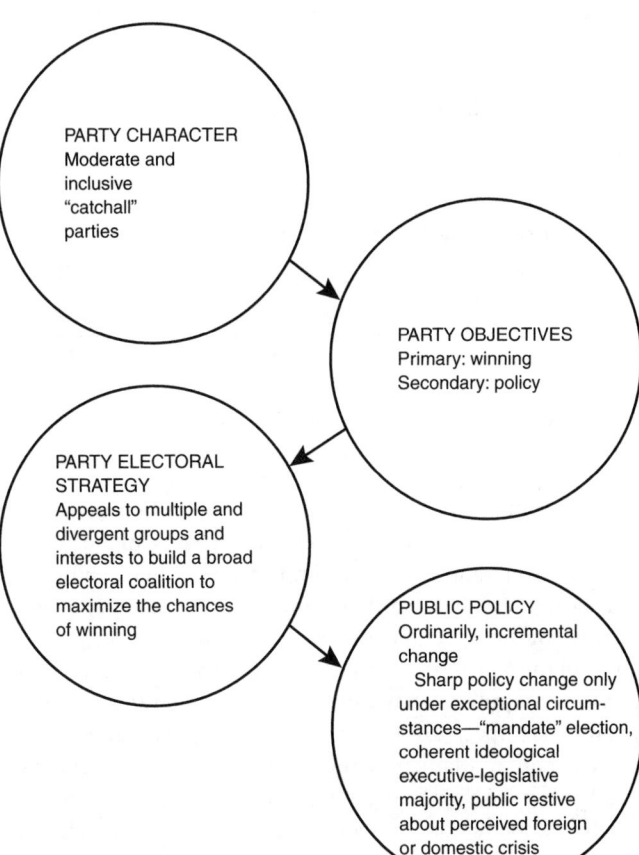

PARTY CHARACTER
Moderate and
inclusive
"catchall"
parties

PARTY OBJECTIVES
Primary: winning
Secondary: policy

PARTY ELECTORAL
STRATEGY
Appeals to multiple and
divergent groups and
interests to build a broad
electoral coalition to
maximize the chances
of winning

PUBLIC POLICY
Ordinarily, incremental
change
   Sharp policy change only
under exceptional circum-
stances—"mandate" election,
coherent ideological
executive-legislative
majority, public restive
about perceived foreign
or domestic crisis

the average northeastern Republican voted with the ADA's position 40 percent of the time. Not surprisingly, northeastern Democrats were particularly liberal, chalking up an average ADA score of 95.

The picture in the South is the reverse. Southern Democratic senators had an average ADA score of 72, compared to the party average of 89. And southern Republicans were more conservative than the caucus as a whole. The average ADA score for these members was 4, which means that the average southern Republican senator voted with the ADA's position less than once out of twenty votes.

Intraparty divisions have become less confounding over the last two decades. Conservative southern Democrats and liberal northeastern Republicans are dying breeds. In Congress, ideological heterogeneity is becoming a smaller problem for party leaders as conservatives have come to dominate the Republican Party, and

Figure 2-2 Democratic and Republican Support of Americans for Democratic Action (ADA) Positions, by Region, 109th Congress, Second Session

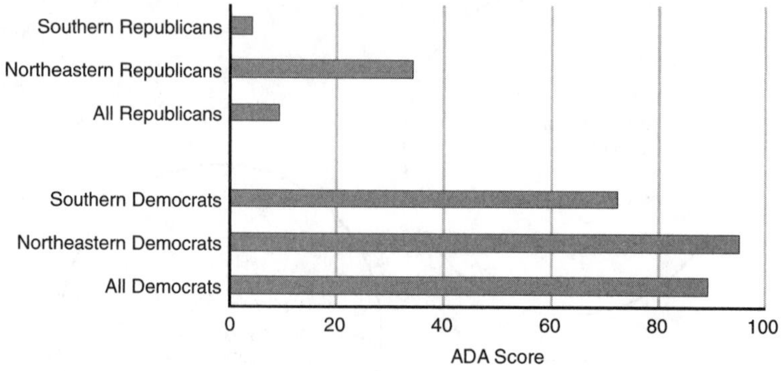

ADA Score

Source: www.adaction.org.

liberals the Democratic Party. In 1986 the Democrats held twelve of the twenty-two Senate seats in the southern states. Such a large bloc of mostly conservative Democrats had a moderating influence on the party. Their seniority, moreover, boosted their power well beyond their numbers. After the 2008 election, however, only seven southern Democrats remained in the Senate.

An analysis of the Northeast turns up a similar pattern. Eleven of the twenty-two senators were Republicans in 1986, but only three remained after the 2009 party switch of Arlen Specter of Pennsylvania.[26] Two of them, Susan Collins and Olympia Snowe, both of Maine, are the most moderate members of the caucus. The third, Judd Gregg of New Hampshire, is retiring at the conclusion of his term in 2011. Moreover, the reason for Specter's switch from Republican to Democrat is instructive. His moderate voting record over his more than twenty years in the Senate had attracted a challenge for the nomination in the 2010 Republican primary from Patrick Toomey, a conservative former member of the House, who had narrowly lost to Specter in the 2004 Republican primary. Specter believed his moderate voting record might be a liability in the Republican primary and that his reelection prospects would improve if he changed parties and faced Toomey in the general election. In the 2006 Pennsylvania Senate race, Santorum was stomped by Democrat Robert Casey by 18 points, making Specter's political calculation a bit easier.[27] Similar results have occurred in the U.S. House. The 2008 defeat of moderate Republican Chris Shays, who had represented Connecticut's increasingly Democratic Fourth District since 1987, left the GOP without a single U.S. House seat in New England for the first time since the party's founding in 1854.[28]

The disappearance of the ideological middle in Congress means that the parties' positions on major issues are more transparent today than they have been for generations. Democratic members of Congress and Democratic congressional candidates are more likely to support social welfare legislation and an expanded role for the federal government than are Republican officeholders and candidates. Programs to advance minority rights, make federal funds available for environmental protection, improve the lot of low-income individuals and families, support family planning programs (including abortion counseling at federally funded clinics), provide for government-sponsored health care, curtail different forms of defense spending, regulate business, and promote the interests of labor typically produce substantial disagreement between the parties, with almost all Democrats aligned on the liberal side and almost all Republicans aligned on the conservative side. And, even though some high-profile party members occasionally march to the beat of a different drummer, most are usually in step with their parties.

An Interest Group

Certain kinds of issues or policy questions that come before legislatures present a party with an opportunity to advance its interests as an organization—in much the same fashion as political interest groups attempt to secure or block legislation that would improve or impair their fortunes. As E. E. Schattschneider wrote many years ago, within each party is a "public" and a "private" personality.[29] The public dimension of the party is on display when larger questions of public policy are brought before the legislature.

The major political parties' public appearance, in the judgment of many critics, often leaves much to be desired. The fundamental flaw is that a party nominally in control of government, but weakened by division, cannot be held responsible by the public for its decisions. The problem is not that party unity collapses on all issues but that it collapses with sufficient frequency to make it a less than dependable agent for carrying out commitments made to the electorate.

This critique may be less applicable today than it was twenty or thirty years ago. To begin with, the greater homogeneity of each party's constituency has made it easier for members to support their party. Compared to thirty years ago, there is simply less difference between what a member's party favors and what his or her constituents favor. But leadership also matters. From 1995 to 2006 GOP majority party leaders in the House aggressively minimized defections from the party line. Since taking back the House in 2006, House Democratic leaders have been similarly successful in enforcing party loyalty on the party's main policy priorities. Senate rules make it considerably more difficult for party leaders to hold party members in line, a subject covered in chapter 5. But, as Kathryn Pearson shows, party loyalty rates have increased substantially even in the Senate since 1987, and leadership tactics seem to be at least partly responsible.[30]

Despite the renewed partisanship in Congress, cross-party coalitions still occur on some of the weightiest issues. In early 2005, Senate Democrats threatened to filibuster several of President Bush's nominees to federal courts whom they deemed too conservative. Because it takes sixty votes to end a filibuster, and the

Republicans had only fifty-five senators, they would have needed the support of a handful of Democrats to approve these nominees. In response to the filibuster threat, Republican Party leaders threatened to invoke the so-called "nuclear option," a parliamentary ruling that would make the filibuster of judicial nominations illegal. Upholding such a ruling would require only a simple majority or fifty-one votes. Uncomfortable with the potential for fundamental change to Senate rules, a bipartisan group of moderate senators banded together to form the Gang of Fourteen. The group's seven Democrats agreed not to filibuster the president's judicial nominees except in "extraordinary circumstance" in return for a promise from the seven Republicans not to vote in favor of the nuclear option if Democrats did decide to filibuster a truly unacceptable nominee. This coalition dealt a sharp blow to the leadership of Majority Leader Bill Frist (R-Tenn.) and to President Bush.

Indeed, it is relatively easy to find examples of major policy passed or defeated by incumbents crossing party lines. Edward Kennedy (D-Mass.) led a majority of Senate Democrats in supporting Bush's No Child Left Behind education bill in 2001, and eleven Senate Democrats and nine Senate Republicans defected from their party's position on Bush's Medicare Prescription Act of 2003. In September 2008 a bipartisan force of House Democrats and Republicans joined to defeat Bush's emergency financial bailout bill—a measure with enormously important stakes for the nation's economy. A few days later, an alternative measure was passed in the House by a similar bipartisan vote. (Underscoring the looseness of the American party system, Republican candidate Melissa Hart, running in Pennsylvania's Fourth Congressional District for the seat she had lost two years earlier, said she would attack Democratic incumbent Jason Altmire *whichever* way he voted on the bailout measure.[31]) Finally, in 2009, three GOP senators—Collins, Snowe, and Specter (before he switched parties)—provided crucial votes in the Senate for President Obama's American Recovery and Reinvestment Act.

In sharp contrast to the public persona is the private personality of a party. Although it would be an exaggeration to argue that a party is engaged in steady introspection, it is surely true, as Schattschneider has observed, that "the party knows its private mind better than it knows its public mind."[32] It has a sharp sense of where the best opportunities lie for partisan advantage and of the perils and pitfalls that can threaten or damage party interests. Numerous occasions arise for transmitting benefits to the party organization and its members. Staff positions in the offices of elected officials provide rewards for a party's loyal activists.[33] At the national level, "senatorial courtesy" guarantees that senators will have the dominant voice in the selection of candidates to fill various positions, such as district court judges and U.S. marshals. This custom calls on the president, before nominating a person for a position in a state, to consult with the senators of that state (if they belong to the same party as the president) to learn their preference for the position. If someone objectionable to the senators of that state is nominated, the prospects are strong that the full Senate will reject the nominee, irrespective of the nominee's qualifications. On questions of this sort—those that touch the careers and political fortunes of members—party unity is high and predictable.

Legislators have never won reputations for queuing up behind proposals that might limit maneuvering in the interest of their careers or their party's welfare. With only a few exceptions, they have opposed plans to extend the merit system, to take judges out of politics, and to empower independent boards or commissions to assume responsibility for reapportionment and redistricting. The private side to such public questions is that to extend the merit system is to cut back party patronage; to remove judges from the election process is to cut off a career avenue for legislators with their sights on the court; and to give a nonlegislative commission control over redistricting is to run the risk of a major rearrangement of legislative districts and a resultant loss of offices.

Legislators and the parties they represent take seriously their role as guardians of the welfare of the organization and the personal interests of its members. As a collectivity, the American party is most resourceful and cohesive when it is monitoring party business—and party business is about as likely to intrude on the great public questions as it is on those of narrow or parochial concern. Opportunities to advance the party cause—through debate, legislation, or investigations—are limited only by a failure of imagination.

Party Competition

Vigorous two-party competition in all political jurisdictions is clearly unattainable. Even when elections are competitive, as in the 2000 and 2004 presidential contests, they may not be competitive everywhere. The American party system is in some places and at some times strongly two-party, and dominantly one-party in others. Competition between the parties is a condition not to be taken for granted, despite the popular tendency to bestow the two-party label on American politics.

Presidential Elections

Contests for the presidency provide the best single example of authentic two-party competition. The 2000 presidential contest illustrates how close elections sometimes can be; out of the more than 101 million votes cast, only about 500,000 separated the major party candidates. Although Bush's win by three percentage points in the popular vote in 2004 may seem like a landslide in comparison, the Electoral College result was still close by historical standards. The 2000 and 2004 elections featured the two closest Electoral College outcomes since 1916. Indeed, with but three exceptions in all *two-party* presidential contests since 1940, the losing presidential candidate has received at least 45 percent of the popular vote.[34] Even though Obama comfortably defeated McCain in 2008 by seven percentage points, McCain still received a healthy 46 percent. In addition to 2000 and 2004, several other elections of the past several decades have been particularly close: in 1960 John Kennedy received 49.7 percent of the popular vote to Richard Nixon's

Table 2-2 The Shrinking Battlefield: Competition in Five Presidential Elections

	1960	1976	2000	2004	2008
National vote margin	0.2%	2.1%	0.5%	2.8%	7.2%
Average state margin	8.0%	8.9%	13.8%	14.8%	16.25%
Number of states that were:					
Blowouts (GT 20%)	6	6	14	17	16
One-sided (10–19.99%)	10	13	14	13	19
Competitive (5–9.99%)	16	11	10	10	9
Battlegrounds (0–4.99%)	18	20	12	10	6
Electoral votes of:					
Blowout states	56	34	124	121	181
Battleground states	244	299	139	106	84

Source: *Congressional Quarterly's Guide to U.S. Elections,* 4th ed. (Washington, D.C.: CQ Press, 2003). For 2004 and 2008 elections: www.uselectionatlas.org.

49.5 percent, and in 1968 Nixon obtained 43.4 percent to Hubert H. Humphrey's 42.7 percent (with George C. Wallace receiving 13.5 percent). In another extremely close race in 1976, Jimmy Carter received 50.1 percent of the vote to Gerald R. Ford's 48.0 percent.

That present-day presidential elections tend to be close does not necessarily mean that they are competitive in all states. State presidential outcomes have exhibited great continuity. In the five presidential elections from 1992 to 2008, thirty-one states cast their electoral votes for the same party all five years. Put another way, more than 60 percent of states have voted for the same party in five straight elections. There was almost no difference in the Electoral College map between 2000 and 2004, with only three states switching (Iowa and New Mexico from Democratic to Republican, and New Hampshire from Republican to Democratic). Although Obama's more sizable victory in 2008 moved nine states (Colorado, Florida, Indiana, Iowa, Nevada, New Mexico, North Carolina, Ohio, and Virginia) from the Republican to the Democratic column, the electoral map still shows more continuity than change. Candidates routinely find certain states so uncompetitive that they do not even bother to campaign in them, even the large, electorally important states. Many political strategists criticized George W. Bush for visiting California in 2000 several times in the campaign's final weeks because he had little chance of winning it. Obama spent no time to speak of in Texas during the 2008 general election campaign, although it is second only to California in the electoral vote count.

Viewed at the state level, presidential elections actually have become *less* competitive over time. Table 2-2 traces the voting behavior of states in four nationally competitive elections—1960, 1976, 2000, and 2004—and the 2008 contest, which was less competitive. Between 1960 and 2004, the average margin of victory by state nearly doubled from eight percentage points to about fifteen. The number of blowouts—states decided by more than twenty percentage points— nearly tripled, from only six in 1960 to seventeen in 2004. The 1976 and 2004 elections produced almost identical popular vote margins (Carter won by

Figure 2-3   2008 Electoral College Map

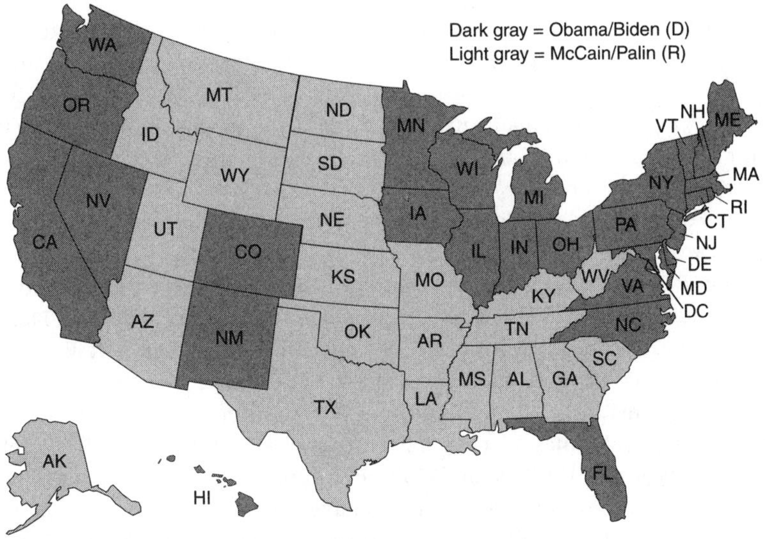

Dark gray = Obama/Biden (D)
Light gray = McCain/Palin (R)

Source: Mark Newman, "Maps of the 2008 US presidential election results," www.personal.umich
.edu/~mejn/election/2008/.

2.1 points, Bush by 2.8), yet there were half as many battleground states (those
decided by five percentage points or less) in 2004 compared with 1976. Because
several of the twenty battleground states in 1976 were large, 299 electoral votes
were up for grabs. In contrast, only 106 electoral votes were similarly up for grabs
in the ten battleground states in 2004. In 2008, with the Democratic candidate
winning a comfortable but not a landslide victory, state-level competition was
even weaker. The number of blowout states held steady, but the electoral votes
in these most uncompetitive environments increased from 121 to 181 between
2004 and 2008. The number of one-sided states (those decided by between ten
and twenty points) increased by six. At the other end of the continuum, the
number of states decided by five points or less dropped from ten to six, and in
2008 they represented only 84 electoral votes.

Both parties derive state support from clearly defined regions. The 2008 electoral map (see Figure 2-3) is a snapshot of the major parties' strength in presidential elections. Democrats dominated the Northeast, upper Midwest, and Pacific
coast. Indeed, of the Middle Atlantic and New England states, which run from
Pennsylvania and New Jersey to Maine, only New Hampshire was decided by less
than 10 percentage points. The Pacific coast is even less competitive, with Obama's
closest victory in that region coming in Oregon by 16.8 percentage points. Obama
swept the entire upper Midwest, from Ohio to Minnesota and Iowa, although the
vote in some of these states was close. Indiana and Ohio, two states that voted
twice for George W. Bush, went to Obama by less than five percentage points.

Republicans, on the other hand, dominated the South and the states running from the Mississippi River to the Rocky Mountains, although not to the extent that they have in the recent past. In 2004 Bush did not lose a single state in the South, and the sweep of his victory ran without interruption from the southern coast of the Atlantic to the desert Southwest and Rocky Mountains. In 2008, however, the Democrats made inroads in these areas, as Obama won two coastal southern states (Virginia and North Carolina) and three states in the West (Nevada, Colorado, and New Mexico).

When elections are close nationally, the states that are decided by the smallest margins are known as "swing states." A state-by-state analysis of the 2000 and 2004 presidential elections suggests that thirteen swing states are most central to understanding who wins and who loses presidential elections: Colorado, Florida, Iowa, Maine, Michigan, Minnesota, Nevada, New Hampshire, New Mexico, Ohio, Oregon, Pennsylvania, and Wisconsin. Each was decided by less than ten percentage points in 2000 and 2004. Because the Democratic candidate won Maine, Michigan, Minnesota, Oregon, Pennsylvania, and Wisconsin in both elections and still lost in the Electoral College, future Democratic candidates must continue to win these six swing states to have even a chance at victory. Three (New Hampshire, Iowa, and New Mexico) voted Republican in one election and Democratic in the other. A Democrat winning all nine would win the election by the narrowest of margins. The remaining four (Colorado, Florida, Nevada, and Ohio) voted Republican in both 2000 and 2004, usually by reasonably healthy margins. Obama, however, won all four of them in 2008, suggesting the Republicans' advantage is not insurmountable. Moreover, he also demonstrated that states that seem like safe bets might not be so safe in a year when one party has a strong advantage, as the Democrats did in 2008. The Republicans were saddled with a mounting economic crisis, an unpopular war, and an incumbent president with low approval ratings. Although Virginia had not voted for a Democratic presidential candidate since 1964, it voted for Obama by a comfortable six percentage points. North Carolina and Indiana, two other Republican presidential stalwarts, also went to Obama, but by a single point or less.

The heterogeneity of these toss-up states, not to mention each party's desire to extend its strength into the other's home turf, suggests the need to present an ideologically moderate front in presidential elections. The candidates cannot risk appearing too conservative without alienating voters in states like Minnesota, Pennsylvania, and Wisconsin, or too liberal without alienating voters in states like Colorado, Florida, and Ohio. In 2008 McCain decided to run a "play-to-the-base" campaign to shore up support among conservatives, who at times have expressed distrust in him because of his sometimes moderate voting record. Although it is impossible to know how the outcome would have differed, it would have been interesting to see the outcome if he had run on his voting record. The reality is that presidential candidates have to perform a balancing act to win general elections.

Figure 2-4 1976 Electoral College Map

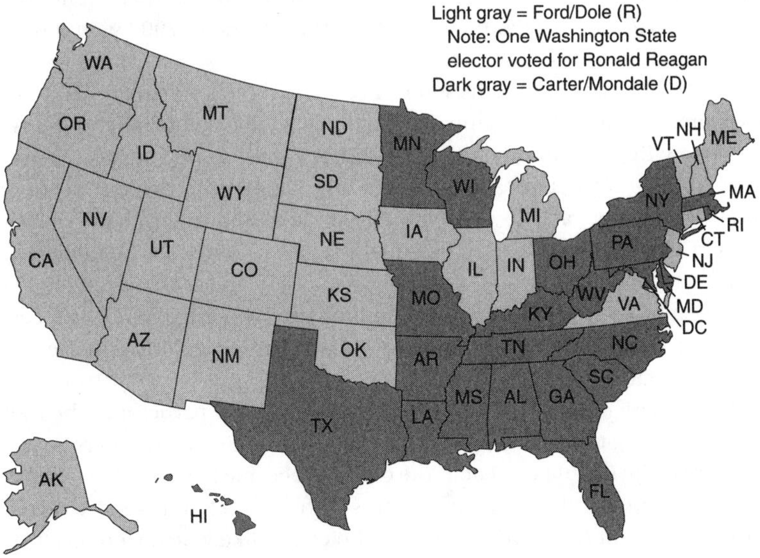

Light gray = Ford/Dole (R)
Note: One Washington State
elector voted for Ronald Reagan
Dark gray = Carter/Mondale (D)

Source: Presidential Elections, 1789–2000 (Washington, D.C.: CQ Press, 2002), 221.

It is also worth noting that the electoral map has undergone a stunning trans-formation since 1976. (See Figure 2-4.) In 1976, with Georgia governor Jimmy Carter topping the ticket, the Democrats dominated the South, winning every state in the region except Virginia. The Democrats also did well in the East, but not in New England, where Connecticut, Maine, New Hampshire, and Vermont all voted for Gerald Ford. In addition, the upper Midwest was not the Democratic stronghold that it is today, with both Illinois and Michigan voting Republican. Perhaps most notably, the Republicans won every state west of Minnesota except Hawaii and Texas.

Of all the changes in regional voting behavior, that of the South is starkest. From shortly after the Civil War to the mid-twentieth century, the Democratic Party maintained a virtual monopoly in the South. The cohesion stemmed from the experience of secession and collective bitterness over the loss of the war, from the durable economic interests of an agricultural society, and most important, from a widespread desire to maintain segregation and white supremacy by excluding African Americans from the political system. Except for Carter's near sweep in 1976, Republicans have come to dominate the region. In 1980 Ronald Reagan received 53.6 percent of the southern major party vote, and in 1984 his percentage jumped to 62.6. In 1988 George H. W. Bush substantially exceeded his national showing by winning 58.8 percent of the southern vote. In 1992 and

1996, even with Clinton, a former governor of Arkansas at the top of the Democratic ticket, Republicans carried more than half of the southern states in each election. In 2000 and 2004, they swept the region, and in 2008 won nine of the eleven southern states.

At the other end of the scale, some once-Republican strongholds have become either more competitive or now fall regularly in the Democratic camp. At one time solidly Republican, Maine and Vermont almost always support Democrats today. In 2000 New Hampshire was the only Republican holdout north of the Mason-Dixon Line, and it went to Kerry in 2004 and to Obama by nearly ten points in 2008. Most notably, California, a state that voted for Republican presidential candidates in every election between 1968 and 1988, is largely beyond their reach today, with Obama winning the state by nearly twenty-five percentage points. In addition, Oregon and Washington now regularly vote Democratic by wide margins.

The decrease in ideological heterogeneity within the parties is at the root of a trend toward regional party strongholds. As conservative southerners have come to dominate the Republican Party, the GOP has become less attractive to northern and western moderates and to immigrants in the desert Southwest. An economic conservative from New York who is prochoice will likely be uncomfortable with the highly conservative southern Republicans who strongly influence the party. Similarly, as the Democrats appeal to their increasingly homogenous liberal constituency, moderates from the South and the Great Plains states may find little in common with the national Democratic Party.

Congressional Elections

Presidential elections are usually rather close, but U.S. House elections are not. Many congressional districts have a long history of one-party or incumbent domination. The diversion of House and Senate elections from the mainstream of competitive politics is obvious (see Table 2-3). In the typical election during the 1990s, about 20 percent to 25 percent of House elections were marginal—that is, elections in which the winning candidate received less than 55 percent of the vote. Since then, these elections have become decidedly less competitive. In 2000 only about 13 percent were marginal, the same percentage as in 2008.

Table 2-3   Marginal, Safe, and Uncontested Seats in Congressional Elections: 2000, 2004, and 2008 (by percentage of total seats)

	House			Senate		
	2000	2004	2008	2000	2004	2008
Marginal	13.2	7.4	13.6	32.4	23.5	28.6
Safe	82.7	87.1	79.5	67.6	76.5	68.6
Uncontested	4.1	5.5	6.9	0	0	2.9

Sources: Congressional Quarterly Weekly Report, November 11, 2000, 2694–2703; New York Times, November 4, 2004, P12–13; for 2008 election: http://elections.nytimes.com/2008/index.html.

Table 2-4 The Incumbency Advantage in Congressional Elections: 1978–2008

Year		Defeated in Primary	Total Number of Incumbents			Percentage of Incumbents Running in General Election Elected
			Running in General Election	Elected in General Election	Defeated in General Election	
1978	House	5	377	358	19	94.96
	Senate	3	22	15	7	68.18
1980	House	6	392	361	31	92.09
	Senate	4	25	16	9	64.00
1982	House	4	383	354	29	92.42
	Senate	0	30	28	2	93.33
1984	House	3	408	392	16	96.07
	Senate	0	29	26	3	89.65
1986	House	2	391	385	6	98.46
	Senate	0	28	21	7	75.00
1988	House	1	408	402	6	98.53
	Senate	0	27	23	4	85.18
1990	House	1	406	391	15	96.31
	Senate	0	32	31	1	96.88
1992	House	19	351	327	24	93.16
	Senate	1	27	23	4	85.18
1994	House	4	382	345	37	90.31
	Senate	0	26	24	2	92.31
1996	House	2	381	360	21	94.49
	Senate	1	19	18	1	94.74
1998	House	1	401	395	6	98.50
	Senate	0	29	26	3	89.66
2000	House	3	400	394	6	98.50
	Senate	0	29	23	6	79.31
2002	House	8	390	383	7	98.20
	Senate	1	25	23	2	92.00
2004	House	2	401	394	7	98.39
	Senate	0	26	25	1	96.00
2006	House	2	404	384	20	95.05
	Senate	1[a]	29	23	6	79.31
2008	House	4	397	380	17	95.72
	Senate	0	30	25	5	83.33

Sources: Various issues of *Congressional Quarterly Weekly Report* and *CQ Weekly.*

[a] Sen. Joseph Lieberman (D-Conn.) was defeated in the Democratic primary but won reelection as an Independent.

Incumbency is the major factor in limiting turnover of congressional seats. Both parties thrive on safe-district politics, and in most elections fewer than a dozen House seats switch party hands. As would be expected, party control is most likely to shift when a seat is open—when no incumbent is running.

As Table 2-4 shows, the incumbency advantage is enormous in the House. In the typical election, well over 90 percent of incumbents on the ballot are returned to Washington. With few exceptions, these percentages reach the high nineties, particularly in the last years of a redistricting cycle.[35] Even in "bad" years for incumbents, such as 2006 and 2008, 94 percent and 95 percent of incumbents running for reelection, respectively, were returned to Washington, although some by closer than usual margins. The 2006 and 2008 elections were extremely difficult for the GOP, but 90 percent of Republican House incumbents retained their seats. The blunt truth is that the House is an arena for two-party politics not because its members are produced by competitive environments but because both parties have managed to develop and protect large blocs of noncompetitive seats. Incumbency is a major factor in each party's success in reducing competition.[36] So is the electoral map. In 2008 only 83 of the 435 House districts yielded split results—a House and presidential candidate of different parties winning the district. The number of split districts in 2008 was the second lowest since 1952, trailing only the 59 split districts in 2004.

Because House members are not often threatened electorally, they typically do not need to appeal to the political center like presidential candidates do. Although they often overestimate their vulnerability,[37] their recent behavior suggests that they understand their freedom. A conservative like Rep. Jeff Flake (R-Ariz.) can be as conservative as he wants without much fear of losing his seat in his like-minded district. A liberal like Maxine Waters (D-Calif.) has little need to appeal to the middle in her liberal Democratic district. This lack of competition has helped to make the party's positions on policy issues more distinct.

Unlike the House, elections for Senate seats evince strong party competition. In 2008 fully ten of the thirty-five victors won with less than 55 percent of the vote (see Table 2-3). In addition, five of the thirty incumbents who ran for reelection were defeated, for an 83 percent incumbency reelection rate, much lower than in the House (see Table 2-4). In a strongly Democratic year in which all Democratic incumbents were reelected, Republican Senate incumbents proved particularly vulnerable; only fifteen of the twenty Republican incumbents kept their seats. After the 2008 election eleven states had one Republican and one Democratic senator. Of the thirty-nine states with two members of the same party, five (Arkansas, Maine, Montana, North Dakota, and West Virginia) voted for the presidential candidate of the party opposite their senators. If either party can win a Senate election or a presidential race, it suggests reasonably strong party competition. Even in states with two senators of the same party, and that voted for that party's presidential candidate in 2008, a Senate victory is not automatic. Mitch McConnell (R-Ky.), the Senate minority leader, won his race with only 53 percent of the vote.

Even though Senate races are often close, party has become a fairly reliable predictor of the winners. Party fortunes in Senate elections now tend to follow the direction of a state's presidential voting. Compared with the eleven split-party delegations after the 2008 elections, twenty-four states featured one senator of each party after the 1976 election when partisanship was weak. Of the twenty-six states with two senators of the same party, ten voted for the presidential candidate of the opposite party of their senators in the 1976 election, compared with five in 2008. Put differently, fully thirty-four states in 2008 had two senators of the same party and voted for that party's candidate in the presidential election. In 1976 only sixteen, or less than half the number in 2008, did. Of the five GOP incumbents who were defeated in 2008, three—Norm Coleman (Minn.), John Sununu (N.H.), and Gordon Smith (Ore.)—represented states that now typically vote for Democratic presidential candidates and where the other senator is a Democrat.

Congressional elections also produce interesting regional variations. Table 2-5 shows the party shares in each region in 1953, 1981, and 2007. Several findings are noteworthy. In 1953 Republicans in the South held no seats in the Senate and only 6 percent of the 106 House seats. In 2007 they held 59 percent of the seats in the House and 77 percent of the Senate seats. Of further consequence, population shifts favoring the South have increased the number of House seats in this region to 131. People are essentially sorting themselves by their political affiliation even when they relocate. A liberal moving from the North to the South is more likely to choose an urban area, which is more progressive and very likely already represented by a Democrat. Conversely, southern conservatives are moving into suburban areas, which are traditionally more conservative and probably already represented by Republicans. Migration patterns, oddly enough, are serving to make districts less competitive.

Outside of the South and border states, the trends favor the Democrats. In 1953 the Republicans held 75 percent of Senate seats and 65 percent of House seats in the East. By 2007 Democrats dominated the eastern states, holding about three quarters of the seats in each house. The number of House seats in the East over this period has, however, declined from 116 in 1953 to 84 in 2007, making Democratic gains in this region less impressive than Republican gains in the South. The same is true in the Midwest. In the 1950s Republicans held three quarters of the House seats and 86 percent of the Senate seats in the region. In 2007 the House delegation was almost a 50–50 split, and the Democrats dominated the Senate delegation by 64 percent to 36 percent. A Republican stronghold in the 1950s, western states—driven by partisan changes in California, Oregon, and Washington—now elect a majority of Democrats to the House.

State-Level Competition

As one study of state and local politics notes, "Party competition in the states is stronger today than at any time in recent history."[38] One indication of competition is the number of divided state governments. Table 2-6 shows that governors in a majority of states regularly face at least one house of the legislature controlled by the other party. After the 2008 election, twenty-two states had divided governments, which suggests not only that both parties are viable players in these states but also that the public may well prefer not to consolidate power in one party.[39]

Figure 2-5 more systematically examines party competition in the states. The degree of interparty competition was calculated for each state by blending four

Table 2-5 Party Shares of Regional Delegations in Congress: 1953, 1981, and 2007

Region	1953			1981			2007		
	Democrats (%)	Republicans (%)	(N)	Democrats (%)	Republicans (%)	(N)	Democrats (%)	Republicans (%)	(N)
House									
East	35	65	(116)	56	44	(105)	74	26	(84)
Midwest	23	76	(118)[a]	47	53	(111)	49	51	(91)
West	33	67	(57)	51	49	(76)	58	42	(98)
South	94	6	(106)	64	36	(108)	41	59	(131)
Border	68	32	(58)	69	31	(35)	48	52	(31)
Total	49	51	(435)	56	44	(435)	54	46	(435)
Senate									
East	25	75	(20)	50	50	(20)	75	25	(20)[b]
Midwest	14	86	(22)	41	59	(22)	64	36	(22)
West	45	55	(22)	35	65	(26)	46	54	(26)
South	100	0	(22)	55	45	(22)	23	77	(22)
Border	70	30	(10)	70	30	(10)	50	50	(10)
Total	49	51	(96)	47	53	(100)	51	49	(100)

Source: Paul R. Abramson, John H. Aldrich, and David Rohde, *Change and Continuity in the 2004 and 2006 Elections* (Washington, D.C.: CQ Press, 2007).

Note: Numbers in parentheses are the totals on which percentages are based.

[a] Includes one Independent.

[b] Includes two Independents.

Table 2-6 Incidence of Party Division Following the 2000, 2004, and 2008 Elections

Relation between Governor and Legislature	Following 2000 Election		Following 2004 Election		Following 2008 Election	
	Number	Percentage	Number	Percentage	Number	Percentage
Governor opposed[a]	22	63	20	40	22	63
Governor unopposed	27	37	30	60	27	37

Sources: Various issues of *Congressional Quarterly Weekly Report, CQ Weekly,* and *National Conference of State Legislatures* publications.

[a] At least one house controlled by a majority of the other party.

separate state scores: the average percentage of the popular vote received by Democratic gubernatorial candidates; the average percentage of Democratic seats in the state senate; the average percentage of Democratic seats in the state house of representatives; and the percentage of all terms for governor, state senate, and state house in which the Democrats were in control. Taken together, these percentages constitute an "index of competitiveness" for each state. In about 40 percent of the states, party competition for state offices lacks an authentic ring. Over the period of this study—2000 to 2005—eight states were classified as modified one-party Democratic and eleven states as modified one-party Republican. Thirty-one states met the test of two-party competition.[40] No state was strictly one-party, although many states were in the past, particularly in the once solidly Democratic South.

The results of this analysis contain some surprises. In contrast to the national level, the Democratic Party remains competitive for state offices in the Deep South. Of the eleven southern states, seven feature authentic two-party competition, and two (Alabama and Louisiana) lean Democratic at the state level. Even though most northeastern states vote for Democratic presidential candidates, virtually all of them are competitive at the state level. Republicans have enjoyed majorities in both legislative houses in Pennsylvania for most of the last twenty years, although Democrats captured the House in 2006. Other regions are more consistent with their national profiles. As the competitiveness of federal elections foreshadowed, the Republican Party dominates many of the states between the Mississippi River and the Rocky Mountains, such as Idaho, Utah, and Wyoming. Two-party states are found throughout the country and include Colorado, Iowa, and New Jersey. All this suggests that party competition must be explored along several dimensions.

It is noteworthy that Republicans have made tremendous gains at the state level, especially in the South. Contrast Figure 2-6, which replicates the previous analysis using election returns from 1989–1994, with Figure 2-5. In a decade, eleven states moved categories toward the Republicans, with five of these changes occurring in the South (Arkansas, Georgia, and Mississippi from modified Democratic to two-party, and Florida and Texas from two-party to modified one-party

Figure 2-5   The Fifty States Classified According to Degree of Interparty Competition: 2000–2005

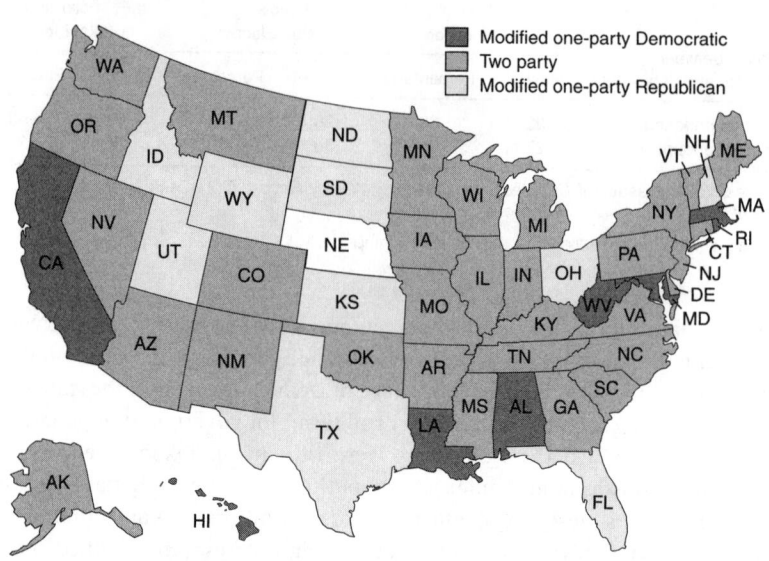

Source: Compiled by authors based on the classification of John F. Bibby and Thomas M. Holbrook, "Parties in State Politics," in *Politics in the American States: A Comparative Analysis*, ed. Virginia Gray and Herbert Jacob (Washington, D.C.: CQ Press, 1996). The classification scheme was originally developed by Austin Ranney.

Republican). There is little reason to doubt that Alabama and South Carolina will almost certainly become Republican strongholds in the future. Republicans have also made gains in Kentucky and Oklahoma. In contrast, the Democrats have made state-level gains in only two states, Arizona and California.

That party strength differs between the state and federal levels points both to the power of the parties and to their ideological weakness. Weak at one level, strong at another, is a common party pattern. Oklahoma and Wyoming elected Democratic governors in 2002 and 2004, respectively, even though no Democratic presidential candidate had won or even come close to winning either state since 1964. In 2008 West Virginia's Democratic governor, Joe Manchin, won reelection with 70 percent of the vote, but Obama tallied only 43 percent of the state's popular vote for president. The same was true in Montana, where Democratic governor Brian Schweitzer ran eighteen points ahead of Obama's showing. Following the 2008 elections, Alabama, Arkansas, and Mississippi had Democratic majorities in both houses of their state legislatures, but all three went for McCain.[41] But it is also important to note that state-level Democrats who win in the South today are ideologically more like national Republicans than national Democrats. For the most part, state political figures bear a stronger ideological resemblance to their state or region than to their national party.

Figure 2-6   The Fifty States Classified According to Degree of Interparty Competition: 1989–1994

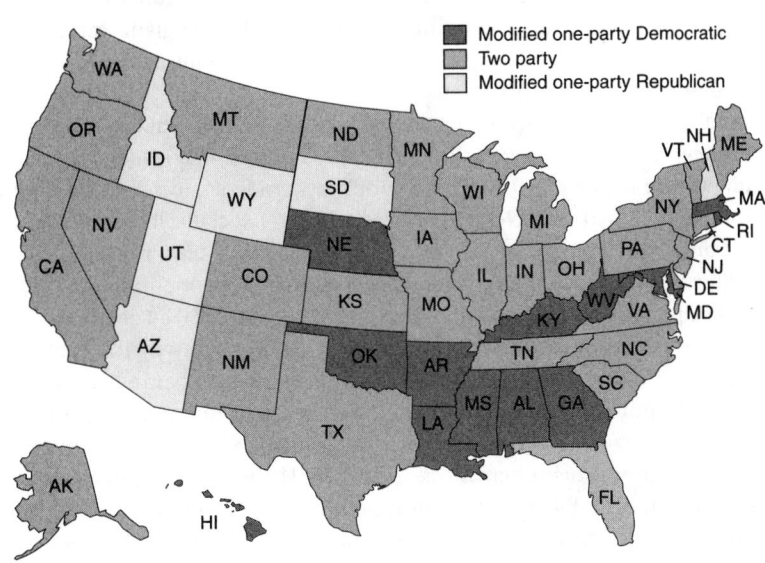

Source: Based on the classification of John F. Bibby and Thomas M. Holbrook, "Parties in State Politics," in *Politics in the American States: A Comparative Analysis,* ed. Virginia Gray and Herbert Jacob (Washington, D.C.: CQ Press, 1996), 105. The classification scheme was originally developed by Austin Ranney.

Party Competition and Issue Positions

Critics of the two major parties, such as George Wallace in the 1960s and Ralph Nader today, have argued that "there's not a dime's worth of difference between them." Although true to some extent when Wallace contended for the presidency, the observation is simply not true today. The strategies of the presidential candidates, however, can make it appear that way.

In a political system with only two political parties, Anthony Downs argues, each party has a strong incentive to appeal to the center to minimize the differences that exist between the parties and the median voter.[42] With only two candidates in the contest, one party needs to get only one more vote than the other to win the election. In an ideologically heterogeneous jurisdiction, the median voter, by definition, settles in the political center. In presidential campaigns, both parties make distinct and continuing appeals to moderates as they seek to form a winning coalition. It made sound strategic sense for George W. Bush to characterize himself as a "compassionate conservative" so as to declare his conservatism to his party's faithful and his moderation to the centrist voters who would ultimately determine the election outcome. Obama embraced "the politics of hope," an appeal that is apparently divorced completely from ideology. Who is opposed to hope?

Most congressional candidates, however, do not have to move toward the center or to camouflage their ideological colors. Republicans from the Deep South can espouse their conservatism, and liberals from New England can advertise their liberalism, with neither group much concerned about its electoral future. They know what counts in their districts.

The disconnect between the presidential and congressional levels affects not only policymaking but also political fortunes. Congressional leaders can pull the president from the center toward the periphery, or ideological pole. In 1992 Bill Clinton campaigned as a New Democrat who was socially liberal and fiscally conservative, but during the first two years of his administration he followed the more liberal Democratic congressional leadership in implementing the most liberal public policy course of any president since the mid-1960s. For this and other reasons, he paid a price. Dissatisfied voters in 1994 took away the Democrats' congressional majority for the first time in forty years. Obama faces a similar challenge. Republicans could make gains in the 2010 midterm elections if his administration is not perceived as sufficiently centrist, a very real possibility given how liberal many of his congressional allies are. The point is that every administration party faces a balancing act in representing its multiple interests and in shaping public policy; how well any one succeeds determines whether or not a party can keep its coalition intact.

The Persistent Two-Party (Not Multiparty) System in America

Political competition in the United States generally comes down to competition between the two major parties. American politics has been receptive to a two-party rather than a multiple-party system, as in many European democracies, because of the election system, public law, and party behavior.

The election system is a major support for the two-party system. Most important, the single-member district, first-past-the-post election system offers no rewards for coming in second or third. Minor parties would benefit from a proportional representation system, as used in much of Europe, because it would reward a relatively good showing with an opportunity to gain influence in the government. Because third parties cannot hope to win elections outright in the United States, they have less incentive to challenge the major parties.

Given that members of the two major parties write the election laws, it is not surprising that the laws treat minor parties badly. Only the most well-organized and well-financed third parties can even hope to gain a place on the ballot. The major parties almost always receive places on the ballot automatically, but minor parties have to go through an arduous petition process, gathering enough signatures to secure a line on the ballot. The petition rules vary by state, with some states requiring few signatures and others a great many. Moreover, state rules differ as to when the signatures can be gathered and who is eligible to sign a petition. The crux of the problem for a minor party presidential effort is that it has to coordinate signature campaigns in numerous states, taking into account a cornu-copia of different rules.[43] This effort requires a well-schooled, well-funded, and disciplined organization in fifty states—requirements that are foreign to most minor parties. Independent candidate John Anderson in 1980 spent more than half of the money he raised in an attempt to get his name on all fifty state ballots.[44]

Campaign finance laws do not treat third parties well either. The Federal Election Campaign Act of 1974 provides block grants to the major party presidential candidates to run their general election campaigns, should they decide to accept it, after they receive their party's nomination. This money is paid out in the late summer *before* the general election. The law treats third parties differ-ently. Unless a minor party has received more than 5 percent of the vote in a previous presidential election—which is, historically speaking, an unlikely occurrence[45]—its candidate receives federal money *after* the election, and only if he receives 5 percent of the popular vote. This money is helpful for retiring a campaign debt but not for competing on equal footing with the major parties. (See chapter 4 for a more detailed account of the system.)

In addition to the rules, the diversity and flexibility that characterize the two major parties contribute to the preservation of the two-party system. The policy orientations of the parties are rarely so firmly fixed as to preclude a shift in emphasis or direction to attract emerging interests within the electorate. More-over, each party is made up of officeholders with different views. Almost any political group, as a result, can discover some officials who share its values and predilections and who are willing to represent its point of view. Primary elections, moreover, allow candidates with diverse perspectives to compete *within* a party, decreasing the need for additional parties. The adaptability of the parties and the officeholders not only permits them to siphon off support that otherwise might contribute to the development of third parties but also creates a great deal of slack in the political system. Groups pressing for change know that there is always some chance that they can win acceptance for their positions within the existing party framework.

In addition, strange as it may seem, the dominance of one party may enhance the two-party system. Each party has a number of areas (states or districts) that vote consistently and heavily for its candidates, irrespective of the intensity of forces that play on voters there and elsewhere. Therefore, even when one of the major parties has a particularly bad election year, it is never threatened with extinction. Republicans may clean up in outstate and downstate Illinois, but Chicago will remain safely Democratic. Most of the rural, less-populous counties of Pennsylvania will vote Republican 'til the cows come home, but Philadelphia, Pittsburgh, and other urban, industrial areas will vote to elect Democratic candi-dates. Year in and year out, for most offices, Maryland and Rhode Island turn to the Democrats, while Kansas and Utah faithfully vote Republican. One-party areas remove some of the mystery that surrounds American elections. Each major party owes something to them, counts on them, and is not often disappointed.

Table 2-7   Third-Party and Independent Presidential Candidates Receiving 5 Percent or More of Popular Vote

Candidate (party)	Year	Percentage of Popular Vote	Electoral Votes
Theodore Roosevelt (Progressive)	1912	27.4	88
Millard Fillmore (Whig-American)	1856	21.5	8
Ross Perot (Independent)	1992	18.9	0
John C. Breckinridge (Southern Democrat)	1860	18.1	72
Robert M. LaFollette (Progressive)	1924	16.6	13
George C. Wallace (American Independent)	1968	13.5	46
John Bell (Constitutional Union)	1860	12.6	39
Martin Van Buren (Free Soil)	1848	10.1	0
James B. Weaver (Populist)	1892	8.5	22
Ross Perot (Reform)	1996	8.4	0
William Wirt (Anti-Masonic)	1832	7.8	7
John B. Anderson (Independent)	1980	6.6	0
Eugene V. Debs (Socialist)	1912	6.0	0

Source: Congressional Quarterly Weekly Report, October 18, 1980, 3147 (as adapted and updated).

A final, central explanation for the durability of the two-party system in America is found in a tradition of dualism.[46] Early political conflict occurred between those who favored adoption of the Constitution and those who opposed it. Subsequently, dualism was reflected in struggles between Federalists and Anti-federalists and, later still, between Democrats and Whigs. Since the Civil War, the main party battle has been fought between Democrats and Republicans. In sum, the main elements of conflict within the American political system have ordinarily found expression in competition between two dominant groups of politicians and their followings.

Although the deck is stacked against them, minor parties have been around as long as the major parties. The Jacksonian Era, which ran roughly from 1828 through 1860, was the first period of true party competition in the United States, and it was also the period when third parties had the most success. (See Table 2-7.) Indeed, internal divisions within the Whig Party, at the time the alternative to the Democrats, led to its being replaced by the Republican Party as the second major party in the late 1850s. This is the only time that such a change has occurred. There are, however, identifiable periods when minor parties do better than others.

Steven Rosenstone, Roy Behr, and Edward Lazarus identify a number of factors that help determine the success of challengers to the major parties.[47] Chief among them is fielding an experienced, well-financed candidate. National reputation is critical. Theodore Roosevelt, a former president who ran as a Bull Moose in 1912, was by far the most successful; George Wallace of Alabama did quite well in 1968, especially in the South, because of his national reputation as an opponent of racial integration. Given the major parties' near monopoly on power, however, few well-known politicians are willing to risk their careers by becoming the candidate of a third party. John Anderson, a Republican presidential candidate in 1980, formed his own party after losing the nomination to Ronald Reagan. Although he was a relatively successful third party candidate, winning 6.6 percent of the popular vote, Anderson was never again a significant force in Republican politics. In fact, his third party maneuvering doomed his political career.

Access to money is critically important to all parties. Because established interest groups are inclined to give their money to candidates they believe can win, they favor those of the major parties. Therefore, it helps to be independently wealthy to launch a third party candidacy, which is why Ross Perot did so well in 1992. He spent nearly $100 million of his own fortune, roughly the same amount of money as did Clinton and George H. W. Bush. It is not surprising that he won nearly 20 percent of the popular vote, a percentage that likely would have been much higher had he not dropped out of the race for several months in the summer. Even so, Perot's showing was the best third party vote since Roosevelt's Bull Moose candidacy in 1912.

Third parties also do better when people hold the major parties in particularly low esteem, as in 1992. The nation was mired in recession, Congress had been wracked by the House banking scandal, and Washington was beset by gridlock. Perot became a more viable option. The importance of partisanship also bears on the chances of third parties; no third party candidate received as much as 5 percent of the vote between 1928 and 1968, a period when party ties in the electorate were strong. With parties again more salient to voters in the early twenty-first century, it is easy to understand why Ralph Nader received only about 3 percent of the vote in 2000 and less than 1 percent in 2004 and 2008.[48]

In sum, two major parties have dominated American politics for nearly two hundred years. Because of the election system and election laws adopted by representatives of the major parties, this situation is likely to persist. Conditions affect the success of third parties: when they can field good candidates, when partisanship is weak, and when political dissatisfaction is high, their candidates do relatively well. Yet, they do not win; most, in fact, do not stay on the political stage very long.

Minor parties nevertheless can be important. In isolated cases, they can affect election outcomes. In 2000 Nader attacked corporate power and entrenched special interests, a line of argument that was much more attractive to liberals than to conservatives or moderates. Had Nader not been in the race, those who supported him would have voted disproportionately for Gore. Even though Nader received only about 3 percent of the national vote, he snatched more than enough votes to cost Gore the election. Just an additional handful of votes for Gore in either Florida or New Hampshire would have elected him president. Roosevelt's Bull Moose candidacy almost certainly cost Republican William Howard Taft the 1912 election. With Republicans splitting their votes between Taft and Roosevelt, Woodrow Wilson led the Democrats to victory.[49]

Third parties also can place issues on the political agenda that the major parties might otherwise ignore. In 1992 Perot made the growing federal budget deficit a central feature of his campaign. The deficit had ballooned during the 1980s under Reagan and George H. W. Bush, Republican presidents who confronted consistent Democratic majorities in the House. As a result, neither Republicans nor Democrats were disposed to talk much about this issue—which, in turn, meant the public was not inclined to care much about it. By concentrating on the deficit, Perot's campaign moved public concern about the issue to the top of the political agenda, which almost certainly provided the impetus for the balanced budgets achieved in the late 1990s. Both parties wanted to attract the nearly 20 percent of voters who registered their dissatisfaction by voting for Perot. Absent Perot's candidacy, such swift attention to this problem probably would not have occurred.

The Party Condition

The party in the United States is the center of the political process, but its grip on political power is far from secure. To be sure, the people recruited for party and public offices, the issues they bring before the electorate, the campaigns in which they participate, and the government they help to organize and direct—all are influenced by party. But no party is able to control all the routes to political power. In some jurisdictions, nonpartisan election systems have been developed to try to remove parties from politics, and to a degree they have succeeded. Moreover, so thoroughly are some states and localities dominated by one party that party itself has come to have little relevance for the kinds of people recruited for office or for the voters in need of cues for casting their votes. Devices such as the direct primary have also cut into the power of the formal party organization, serving in particular to discourage national party agencies from attempting to influence nominations, including those for national office, and to open up the nominating process to all kinds of candidates and informal coalitions of activists and groups.[50] In addition, divided party control of government has become a chronic problem of both state and national governments. Typically, one party winds up controlling the executive branch and the other one or both houses of the legislative branch. Determining which party is accountable for policy outcomes is not always easy.[51]

On the whole, the nation's political culture is a hostile environment for parties. From the perspective of party leaders, the Constitution is a vast wasteland, scarcely capable of supporting vigorous parties. Federalism, separation of powers, checks and balances, and staggered elections have all proved inimical to the organization of strong parties. The party itself is an uneasy coalition of individuals and groups fused together for limited purposes. Within government, power is about as likely to be lodged in nooks and crannies as it is in central party agencies. Conflict within the parties is sometimes as intense as it is between the parties. Even in this era of strong polarized parties, it is not difficult to find incumbents defecting from their party's position on major policy initiatives. Parties compete vigorously in some states and scarcely at all in others. As for individual party members, they have a great many rights but virtually no responsibilities for the well-being of the parties. Public skepticism concerning the parties is pervasive.

Still, party competition has rarely been more vigorous in the nation's history. Fewer than 1 million votes separated the 2000 presidential candidates, the closest election since the late nineteenth century. Although the 2006 and 2008 election cycles have provided the Democrats substantial majorities in both the House and Senate, partisan control of Congress has generally been close lately, at least by historical standards. Indeed, the 2000 elections produced a U.S. Senate with a fifty-fifty partisan split. At the state level, formerly one-party areas such as the South now exhibit real two-party competition. And increases in party competition may well be good for American democracy. Charles Barrilleaux shows that when party majorities receive stiff competition from the other major party, the result is public policy more in keeping with the preferences of the electorate.[52] In other words, a competitive party system is likely to give the people what they want in terms of public policy.

Although most Americans may not think highly of parties, they still structure our political world. Compared with European democracies, American parties will never be particularly strong, but they have strengthened over the last two decades, and there is little to suggest a return to the weak-party 1970s any time soon.

NOTES

1. *The People, the Press, and Politics, 1990* (Washington, D.C.: Times Mirror Center for the People and the Press, 1990), 2, 32.

2. Stephen Ansolabehere, Shigeo Hirano, and James M. Snyder Jr., "What Did the Direct Primary Do to Party Loyalty in Congress?" in *Party, Process, and Political Change In Congress, Vol. 2: Further New Perspectives on the History of Congress*, ed. David W. Brady and Mathew D. McCubbins (Stanford, Calif.: Stanford University Press, 2007).

3. Stephen Ansolabehere, James M. Snyder Jr., and Charles Stewart III, "Candidate Positioning in U.S. House Elections," *American Journal of Political Science* 45 (January 2001): 136–159.

4. Robert S. Erikson and Gerald C. Wright, "Voters, Candidates, and Issues in Congressional Elections," in *Congress Reconsidered*, 9th ed., ed. Lawrence C. Dodd and Bruce I. Oppenheimer (Washington, D.C.: CQ Press, 2009).

5. James Gimpel, Frances E. Lee, and Shanna Pearson-Merkowitz, "The Check Is in the Mail: Indirect Funding Flows in Congressional Elections," *American Journal of Political Science* 52 (2008): 373–394.

6. Jacob S. Hacker and Paul Pierson, *Off Center: The Republican Revolution and the Erosion of American Democracy* (New Haven, Conn.: Yale University Press, 2005).

7. Peter Francia, John C. Green, Paul S. Herrnson, Lynda Powell, and Clyde Wilcox, *The Financiers of Congressional Elections* (New York: Columbia University Press, 2003).

8. Thomas P. O'Neill with William Novak, *Man of the House: The Life and Political Memoirs of Speaker Tip O'Neill* (New York: Random House, 1987), 26.

9. Federal Election Commission, press release, April 13, 2005.

10. Campaign Finance Institute, press release, "Outside Soft Money Groups Approaching $400 Million in Targeted Spending in the 2008 Election" October 31, 2008.

11. See the interesting evidence of the influence of moneyed interests on congressional decision making marshaled by Richard L. Hall and Frank M. Wayman, "Buying Time: Moneyed Interests and the Mobilization of Bias in Congressional Committees," *American Political Science Review* 84 (September 1990): 797–820.

12. James M. Burns, *The Deadlock of Democracy: Four Party Politics in America* (Englewood Cliffs, N.J.: Prentice Hall, 1963), 236–237. For an instructive study of state party organizations and leaders, see Robert J. Huckshorn, *Party Leadership in the States* (Amherst: University of Massachusetts Press, 1976).

13. See John Aldrich, "Southern Parties in State and Nation," *Journal of Politics* 62 (August 2000); Cornelius P. Cotter, James L. Gibson, John F. Bibby, and Robert J. Huckshorn, *Party Organizations in American Politics* (New York: Praeger, 1984).

14. Aldrich, "Southern Parties in State and Nation."

15. Federal Election Commission, press release, March 2, 2005; corrected March 14, 2005.

16. Ibid.

17. Barbara G. Salmore and Stephen A. Salmore, *Candidates, Parties, and Campaigns: Electoral Politics in America*, 2nd ed. (Washington, D.C.: CQ Press, 1989), 255–256.

18. Maurice Duverger, *Political Parties* (New York: Wiley, 1965), 17.

19. Paul R. Abramson, John H. Aldrich, and David W. Rohde, *Change and Continuity in the 2004 Elections* (Washington, D.C.: CQ Press, 2006).

20. Andrew Gelman, *Red State, Blue State, Rich State, Poor State: Why Americans Vote the Way They Do* (Princeton, N.J.: Princeton University Press, 2008).

21. Ibid., 98.

22. John B. Judis and Ruy Teixeira, *The Emerging Democratic Majority* (New York: Scribner, 2002).

23. Edison-Mitofsky exit poll, 2004.

24. V. O. Key Jr., *Politics, Parties, and Pressure Groups* (New York: Crowell, 1964), 221.

25. Republican platform, www.gop.com/2008Platform/Preamble.htm.

26. According to Larry Sabato of the Center for Politics at the University of Virginia, the two most vulnerable Republican incumbents in 2006 were both northeasterners—Rick Santorum of Pennsylvania and Lincoln Chafee of Rhode Island.

27. The Pennsylvania GOP has lost some 200,000 party registrants since Specter narrowly defeated Toomey in 2004. If these departures were mostly moderate voters, Specter would face an even more difficult primary race as a Republican.

28. Tim Storey and Edward Smith, "Election 2008: History Making," *State Legislatures,* December 2008, 16.

29. E. E. Schattschneider, *Party Government* (New York: Holt, Rinehart, and Winston, 1942), 133–137.

30. Kathryn Pearson, "Party Loyalty and Discipline in the U.S. Senate"; and Erin Bradbury, Ryan A. Davidson, and C. Lawrence Evans, "The Senate Whip System: An Exploration," in *Why Not Parties? Party Effects in the U.S. Senate,* ed. Nathan W. Monroe, Jason Roberts, and David W. Rohde (Chicago: University of Chicago Press, 2008).

31. David M. Herszenhorn, "Word Reaches Congress: As the Market Goes, So Goes the Electorate," *New York Times,* October 2, 2008, www.nytimes.com. Altmire voted against the bailout legislation twice and won reelection.

32. Schattschneider, *Party Government.*

33. Seth Masket, *No Middle Ground: How Informal Party Organizations Control Nominations and Polarize Legislatures* (Ann Arbor: University of Michigan Press, 2009).

34. The exceptions occurred in 1964 (Barry Goldwater received 39 percent of the vote), 1972 (George McGovern, 38 percent), and 1984 (Walter F. Mondale, 41 percent).

35. Marc J. Hetherington, Bruce A. Larson, and Suzanne Globetti, "The Redistricting Cycle and Strategic Candidate Decisions in U.S. House Races," *Journal of Politics* 65 (November 2003): 1221–35.

36. The literature on legislative-constituency relations, which includes examination of the incumbency factor in elections, is impressive. A sampling from it includes: David R. Mayhew, "Congressional Elections: The Case of the Vanishing Marginals," *Polity* 6 (Spring 1974): 295–317; Gary C. Jacobson, "The Effects of Campaign Spending in Congressional Elections," *American Political Science Review* 72 (June 1978): 469–491; Jon R. Bond, Gary Covington, and Richard Fleisher, "Explaining Challenger Quality in Congressional Elections," *Journal of Politics* 47 (May 1985): 510–529; Donald A. Gross and James C. Garrand, "The Vanishing Marginals, 1824–1980," *Journal of Politics* 46 (February 1984): 224–237; John C. McAdams and John R. Johannes, "Constituency Attentiveness in the House: 1977–1982," *Journal of Politics* 47 (November 1985): 1108–39; Melissa P. Collie, "Incumbency, Electoral Safety, and Turnover in the House of Representatives, 1952–1976," *American Political Science Review* 75 (March 1981): 119–131; and John R. Alford and John R. Hibbing, "Increased Incumbency Advantage in the House," *Journal of Politics* 43 (November 1981): 1042–61.

37. See Fenno, *Home Style: House Members in Their Districts*, especially chapter 1; and Gary Jacobson, *The Politics of Congressional Elections*, 7th ed. (New York: Longman, 2009), especially chapter 3.

38. Thomas R. Dye, *Politics in States and Communities*, 10th ed. (Upper Saddle River, N.J.: Prentice Hall, 2000).

39. See Morris P. Fiorina, *Divided Government*, 2nd ed. (Boston: Allyn Bacon, 1996). For a different view, see Barry C. Burden and David C. Kimball, "A New Approach to the Study of Ticket Splitting," *American Political Science Review* 59 (September 1998): 533–544.

40. Nebraska cannot be included in the analysis because it does not have two legislative bodies. See John F. Bibby and Thomas M. Holbrook, "Parties in State Politics," in *Politics in the American States: A Comparative Analysis*, ed. Virginia Gray and Herbert Jacob (Washington, D.C.: CQ Press, 1996), 103–109.

41. See Dye, *Politics in States and Communities*, for a more general treatment of party competition in states as opposed to federal elections.

42. Anthony Downs, *An Economic Theory of Democracy* (New York: Harper, 1957).

43. For an analysis of ballot access laws, see Bruce W. Robeck and James A. Dyer, "Ballot Access Requirements in Congressional Elections," *American Politics Quarterly* 10 (January 1982): 31–45. Also see Richard Winger, "How Ballot Access Laws Affect the U.S. Party System," *American Review of Politics* 16 (Winter 1995): 321–350.

44. Steven J. Rosenstone, Roy L. Behr, and Edward H. Lazarus, *Third Parties in America*, 2nd ed. (Princeton, N.J.: Princeton University Press, 1996).

45. Since the advent of public funding in presidential elections, only one minor party candidate—Ross Perot—qualified for public funding (in 1996) proportional to his showing in the previous (1992) election.

46. For analysis of the dualism theme, see Key, *Politics, Parties, and Pressure Groups*, 207–208.

47. Rosenstone, Behr, and Lazarus, *Third Parties in America*.

48. A similar line of argument is true for increasing trust in government throughout the 1990s. See Marc J. Hetherington, "The Effect of Political Trust on the Presidential Vote, 1968–1996," *American Political Science Review* 93 (June 1999), 311–326. For an opposing point of view, see Morris P. Fiorina, "Parties and Partisanship: A 40-Year Retrospective," *Political Behavior* 24 (June 2002): 93–115.

49. Although many commentators have suggested that Ross Perot may have cost George H. W. Bush the 1992 election, political scientists have turned up little evidence to support this assertion. See R. Michael Alvarez and Jonathan Nagler, "Economics, Issues and the Perot Candidacy: Voter Choice in the 1992 Presidential Election," *American Journal of Political Science* 39 (August 1995): 714–744; and Dean Lacy and Barry C. Burden, "The Vote-Stealing and Turnout Effects of Ross Perot in the 1992 U.S. Presidential Election," *American Journal of Political Science* 43 (January 1999): 233–255.

50. Masket, *No Middle Ground*.

51. The extent to which divided control matters for policymaking is an open question. David Mayhew has found that unified and divided national governments produce very similar amounts of important legislation, but Sarah Binder has found that unified national governments tend to be more successful in advancing the nation's policy agenda. David Mayhew, *Divided We Govern: Party Control, Lawmaking, and Investigations, 1946–2002*, 2nd ed. (New Haven, Conn.: Yale University Press, 2005); Sarah Binder, *Stalemate: Causes and Consequences of Legislative Gridlock* (Washington, D.C.: Brookings, 2003).

52. Charles Barrilleaux, "Party Strength, Party Change and Policy Making in the American States," *Party Politics* 6, no. 1 (2000): 61–73. Thomas Brunell provides an alternative perspective, arguing that intense electoral competition minimizes voter satisfaction with representation because it maximizes the number of voters whose preferred candidate loses. Thomas Brunell, *Redistricting and Representation: Why Competitive Elections Are Bad for America* (New York: Routledge, 2008).

3 POLITICAL PARTIES AND THE ELECTORAL PROCESS: NOMINATIONS

IT IS PROBABLE THAT NO NATION has ever experimented as fully or as fitfully with mechanisms for making nominations as has the United States. The principal sponsor of this experimentation is the federal system itself. Under it, responsibility for the development of election law lies with the states. Their ingenuity, given free rein, has often been remarkable, and they have tried out a wide variety of caucuses, conventions, and primaries—the three principal methods of making nominations. The devices that lasted owe their survival not so much to widespread agreement on their merits but to the inability of opponents to settle on alternative arrangements and to the general indifference of the public at large to major institutional change.

Party Nominating Methods: A Brief History

Caucus

The oldest device for making nominations in the United States is the caucus. In use prior to the adoption of the Constitution, the caucus was an informal meeting of political leaders held to decide questions concerning candidates, strategies, and policies. The essence of the caucus idea, when applied to nominations, was that by sifting, sorting, and weeding out candidates before the election, leaders can assemble substantial support behind a single candidate and decrease the possibility that the votes of like-minded citizens will be split among several candidates. Historically, the legislative caucus was the most important form of this nominating procedure; until 1824, it was used successfully to nominate candidates for state and national offices, including the presidency. The major drawback

71

to the legislative caucus was that membership was limited to the party members in the legislature, which exposed the caucus to the charge that it was unrepresentative and undemocratic. A modest reform in the legislative caucus occurred when provisions were made for seating delegates from districts held by the opposition party. Nevertheless, when the (Jeffersonian) Republican caucus failed to nominate Andrew Jackson for the presidency in 1824, it came under severe criticism from many quarters and shortly thereafter was abandoned as a method for selecting presidential nominees.

Today, another form of the caucus survives in the presidential nominating process: the caucus-convention system for choosing delegates to the parties' national nominating conventions, which we discuss below. Modern caucuses, such as Iowa's, are typically open to all registered party voters. They should not be confused with the elite legislative caucuses used to nominate candidates in the early republic.

Party Conventions

Advocates of reform to the nominating process turned to the party convention, already in use in some localities, as a substitute for the legislative caucus. The great merit of the convention system, they argued, was that it could provide for representation, on a geographical basis, of all elements within the party. The secrecy of the caucus was displaced in favor of a more public arena, with nominations made by conventions composed of delegates drawn from various levels of the party organizations. As the convention method gained in prominence, so did the party organizations, and state and local party leaders came to play dominant roles in the selection of candidates.

The convention system, used for the nomination of presidential candidates since the 1830s, ultimately failed to live up to its early promise. Critics found that it suffered from essentially the same disabling properties as the caucus. In their view, it was sheer pretense to contend that the conventions were representative of the parties as a whole; instead, party bosses ran them without regard either for the views of the delegates or for the rules of fair play. A great many charges were aired involving corruption in voting practices and procedures, and many of them were true. Stricter regulation of conventions by the legislatures failed to assuage the public's doubts. The direct primary came into favor as reformers saw its potential for dismantling the structure of "boss and machine" influence and for introducing popular control over nominations.

Direct Primary

Popular control of the political process has always been an important issue to reformers. The direct primary, with its emphasis on voters instead of on party organization, was hard to resist. Once Wisconsin adopted it for nomination of candidates for state elective offices in 1903, its use spread steadily throughout the country. In 1975 Indiana became the last state to adopt it for nominating statewide candidates.

Part of the attractiveness of the primary is its apparent simplicity. From one perspective, it is a device for transferring control of nominations from the party leadership to rank-and-file voters; from another, it shifts this control from the party organization to the state. The primary rests on state law: it is an official election held at public expense on a date set by the legislature and is supervised by public officials. It has often been interpreted as an attempt to institutionalize intraparty democracy.

It is not surprising that the direct primary has had a better reception in reformist circles than anywhere else. For the party organization, however, it poses problems, not opportunities. If the party organization becomes involved in a contested primary for a major office, it probably will have to raise large sums of money for the eventual candidate's campaign. If it remains neutral, it may wind up with a candidate who is either hostile to the organization or unsympathetic to its programs and policies. Even if the party supports the candidate, there is no guarantee that he will win. In fact, a good many political careers have been launched in primaries in which the unendorsed candidate has convinced the voters that a vote for him is a vote to crush the "machine." Finally, the primary often works at cross-purposes with the basic party objective of harmonizing its diverse elements by creating a balanced ticket for the general election. Voters are much less likely to nominate a representative slate of candidates, one that recognizes all major groups within the party, than is the party leadership. Moreover, if the primary battle turns bitter, the winner may enter the general election campaign with a sharply divided party behind him.[1]

Even so, as Alan Ware shows, many party regulars cooperated in enacting state primaries far more than conventional wisdom holds. It would have been difficult, Ware points out, for progressive reformers to enact primaries if strong state parties had opposed them, and strong-party states were just as likely as weak-party states to adopt primaries. Many party regulars simply did not see primaries as inimical to their interests. Indeed, strong state parties believed they could continue to exercise control over nominations through the primary system.[2]

Types of Primaries

To choose candidates for state offices, parties at one time could choose from five basic types of primaries: closed, open, blanket, nonpartisan, and runoff. In 2005 the U.S. Supreme Court invalidated the blanket primary. Since then, the three states that used this type, Alaska, California, and Washington, have had to choose among the other options. Presidential primaries are distinct in many ways and are analyzed in a separate section on the presidential nomination process later in the chapter.

Closed Primary

Twenty-eight states use a closed primary of one sort or another to make nominations, meaning that only those registered with a party may participate in that party's primary. In fifteen of these states, registration with the party in whose primary a voter wants to participate is required, although voters may change their party affiliation before primary election day. Sometimes the amount of time allowed for such a change is quite generous, as in Connecticut, where voters have up until the day before the primary; in other states, including New York and Kentucky, the deadline to declare an affiliation is much earlier—eleven months before the primary election to be exact. The mean time is roughly two months before the primary. In thirteen other closed primary states, independents can vote in a party primary or voters can register with a party on election day. So states such as Iowa, which allows people to declare an affiliation at the polls, are palpably open. Some closed primary states prohibit voters from switching parties once the candidates have filed their declarations of candidacy; other, less restrictive, states allow "voter floating" by permitting changes in party registration after candidates have declared themselves.

Other differences in closed primary systems stem from the 1986 U.S. Supreme Court ruling in *Tashjian v. Republican Party of Connecticut.* The case arose from the efforts of Connecticut's GOP to attract independents by permitting them to vote in its primary elections. Unable to change the state's closed primary law in the legislature, the party successfully challenged it in court. The Supreme Court ruled, 5–4, that states may not require political parties to hold closed primaries that permit only voters previously enrolled in a party to vote. This ruling leaves the choice of primary system to the parties instead of to state legislatures. A state party may choose to open its primary to unaffiliated (or independent) voters, or it may choose to bar their participation. Within a year of the Court's decision, seven other states enacted legislation under which a party could permit unaffiliated voters to vote in its primary. The trend is clearly toward openness. In 2004 more than half of the Democratic *presidential* primaries and caucuses were open to registered independents, as were more than two-thirds of Republican contests. The *Tashjian* decision does not outlaw closed primaries, however, and presumably many state parties will continue to permit only registered party members to vote in their primaries.[3]

Open Primary

From the point of view of the party organization, the open primary is less desirable than the closed primary. Fifteen states (not counting those that use runoff or nonpartisan primaries) have some form of open primary—defined as one in which voters can be registered with any party or as independents and still participate in the party primary of their choice. Provisions for open primaries differ from state to state. In nine states the voter is given the ballots of all parties, with instructions to vote for the candidates of only one party and to discard the other ballots.[4] In six other states, voters can cast ballots in any primary, but they have to publicly declare their choice of a party ballot at the polling place. In either case, nothing can prevent Democrats from voting to nominate Republican candidates or Republicans from voting to nominate Democratic candidates. One study has shown that in Wisconsin roughly 8–11 percent of all voters in presidential primaries are partisan crossovers. And a surprising one-third of each party's primary participants are self-styled independents. As Karen Kaufmann, James Gimpel, and Adam Hoffman demonstrate, one benefit of open primaries is that they attract an electorate far more representative of the general electorate than do closed primaries.[5]

Yet party leaders in open primary states suffer from a special anxiety: the possibility that voters of the competing party will raid their primary, hoping to nominate a weak candidate who would be easy to defeat in the general election. Moreover, a study by Lynn Vavreck suggests that many candidates in open primary states produce campaign advertisements that make no mention of party but instead highlight issues that tend to be of interest to partisans of the other party, which may undermine the role of the party faithful.[6] Although a study of Arkansas voters by Gary D. Wekkin finds that most crossover voters are not mischievous,[7] it seems clear that voters may be motivated to vote in the other party's primary when there is an exciting contest between candidates. Indeed, one of the central arguments asserted by the state of Connecticut in *Tashjian* was the party's need to protect itself from raiding by members of the other party.

In the 2008 battle for the Democratic presidential nomination such concerns were well founded. Talk radio host Rush Limbaugh launched what he called "Operation Chaos" in March to encourage fellow conservatives to vote for presidential hopeful Hillary Clinton in the Democratic primaries. It is not that Limbaugh was an admirer of Clinton; rather, he hoped to "bloody up" Barack Obama after he had won a string of primary and caucus victories over Clinton, so he would not cruise unscathed to his party's nomination. Limbaugh believed that a long and protracted Democratic primary battle would aid John McCain, who had all but secured the Republican nomination. Although it is difficult to assess with certainty the impact of Operation Chaos, this much is certain: the number of party crossover voters in Democratic primaries in competitive states like Ohio and Texas—where Limbaugh focused much of his attention—was much higher than usual, and these voters overwhelmingly favored Clinton. Even if encouraging the supporters of one party to vote in the other party's primary seems like dirty politics, it is not against the law. In Ohio crossovers are asked to sign a form that states they support the principles of the party in whose primary they vote. But voter intent is almost impossible to establish in a legal sense, and voting clearly enjoys First Amendment protection.[8]

In a close race, the presence of outsiders can make a difference in the outcome, as McCain—a reform-minded, moderate Republican—demonstrated in the 2008 presidential primaries. Exit polls showed that Republican identifiers favored other candidates over McCain in all four states holding caucuses or primaries in January, the important first month of the season. But Independents and Democrats liked McCain more in those four states, carrying him to the early victories that made his nomination all but inevitable. Obama owed much of his early competitiveness to independent voters. Of the sixteen primaries held on Super Tuesday, exit polls showed that Democratic self-identifiers favored Clinton in all but four states, but Obama carried seven of these states and was competitive in six more. Without the disproportionate support of Independent self-identifiers, Obama might have found himself all but eliminated from contention at the beginning of February rather than using his better than expected showing as a springboard for the nomination.[9]

A federal court ruling suggests that jurists are now taking concerns about raiding other parties' primaries more seriously, if only for minor parties. In August 2002 a federal judge struck down the 1998 law proposed by the Arizona state legislature and approved by voters that implemented an open primary system. In the suit brought by the Arizona Libertarian Party, the judge ruled that the fact that non-Libertarians, who greatly outnumber Libertarians in Arizona, might determine the Libertarian Party's nominee violated party members' right of free association. In December 2003 the Ninth Circuit Court of Appeals upheld the lower court ruling, but tailored the finding narrowly to affect only the Libertarian Party's concerns rather than those of the major parties.[10]

Blanket Primary

The states of Alaska, California, and Washington traditionally used a "blanket" or "jungle" primary system. No other primary is as open, nor does any other type offer voters a greater range of choice. Under its provisions the voter is given a ballot that lists all candidates of all parties under each office. A candidate needs no approval from a party to affiliate with the party on the ballot. Voters may vote for a Democrat for one office and a Republican for another, or they may vote for a third party candidate. They cannot, however, vote for more than one candidate per office. Independents are allowed to participate. For a given office, the top vote-getting candidate for a party becomes the party's general election nominee. The blanket primary is an invitation to ticket-splitting. This system, consistent with the emergence and consolidation of candidate-centered politics, is anathema to anyone who believes parties stand for something and that they should be held accountable for the performance of government.

Providing some good news for parties, the federal courts have cast a disapproving eye on blanket primaries. In *California Democratic Party v. Jones* (2000) the Supreme Court ruled the California jungle primary, adopted in 1996, unconstitutional. Writing for the majority, Justice Antonin Scalia argued that blanket primaries violated a party's right to limit its internal selection process to its own membership. Providing the precedent for the Arizona open primary cases, the Court ruled that "the burden [California's voting system] places on [the political parties'] rights of political association is both severe and unnecessary."[11] In 2003 an appeals court ruled the blanket primary system in Washington unconstitutional, saying it too violates the parties' rights of free association.[12] As a result of these rulings, Alaska, California, and Washington have chosen different nominating arrangements—closed, modified closed, and a hybrid blanket-runoff primary, respectively. We discuss Washington's hybrid blanket system in greater detail below.

Nonpartisan Primary

In a number of states, judges, school board members, and other local government officials are selected in nonpartisan primaries. State legislators in Nebraska are also selected on this basis. The scheme is simple: the two candidates who receive the greatest number of votes are nominated; in turn, they oppose each other in the general election. No party labels appear on the ballot in either election. The nonpartisan primary is defended on the grounds that partisanship should not be permitted to intrude on the selection of certain officials, such as judges. By eliminating the party label, runs the assumption, the issues and divisiveness that dominate national and state party politics can be kept out of local elections and offices. Although nonpartisan primaries muffle the sounds of party, they do not eliminate them. It is not uncommon for the party organizations to slip quietly into the political process and to recruit and support candidates in these primaries; in such cases, about all that is missing is the party label on the ballot.

Runoff Primary

The runoff, or second primary, is a by-product of a one-party political environment. As used in many southern states, this primary provides that if no candidate obtains a majority of the votes cast for an office, a runoff is held between the two leading candidates. The runoff primary is an attempt to come to terms with a chronic problem of a one-party system—essentially all competition is jammed into the primary of the dominant party.

With numerous candidates seeking nomination for the same office, the vote is likely to be sharply split, with no candidate receiving a majority. A runoff between the top two candidates in the first primary provides a guarantee, if only statistical, that one candidate will emerge as the choice of a majority of voters. This was no small consideration in those southern states in which the Democratic primary was traditionally the real election and where factionalism within the party was so intense that no candidate stood much of a chance of consolidating his party position without two primaries—the first to weed out the losers and the second to endow the winner with the legitimacy a majority can offer.

Louisiana boasts the most interesting runoff primary; it combines the runoff with a nonpartisan primary.[13] Under this system, all candidates for an office are grouped together in a primary election, which is actually held on election day in November. A candidate who receives a majority of the primary vote is elected, which eliminates the need for a general election. If no candidate obtains a majority of the votes cast, the top two, irrespective of party affiliation, face each other in a runoff general election in early December. Although the Supreme Court has ruled unconstitutional some variants of blanket primaries, it has stated explicitly that runoff primaries are, in fact, constitutional, and that blanket primary states ought to consider Louisiana's approach.[14]

In fact, following the 2003 appeals court decision striking down Washington's blanket primary, the state put in place a system similar to Louisiana's. Instead of the top vote-getting candidate for each party becoming the party's nominee for a given office—as in Washington's former blanket primary—the new system advances to the general election the two top vote-getting candidates *regardless of their party affiliation.* Therefore, as in Louisiana, two candidates with the same party affiliation can potentially face each other in the general election. Although the change from Washington's former blanket primary may seem subtle, it was the focus of the Supreme Court, which upheld Washington's new system in *Washington State Grange v. Washington State Republican Party* (2008). The Court's reasoning was that the new system does not actually select the *parties'* nominees; rather, it winnows down the field of general election candidates. Washington's parties, the Court additionally noted, remained free to nominate their candidates outside of the primary because the same law that enacted the new primary also repealed the state's prior regulations on party nominations.[15] The new Washington State system differs from Louisiana's in that Washington holds its primary *prior* to the national election day and requires a general election contest regardless of whether a primary candidate receives a majority in the primary election. A similar primary system proposal was defeated in Oregon in 2008, and another will be on the California ballot in 2010.

Runoff primaries do have a number of negative effects: incumbents enjoy a pronounced advantage; voter turnout often drops substantially from the first primary to the second; a growing number of candidates face the voters with no party affiliation; campaigns tend to cost significantly more; and, perhaps most important, institutionalized multifactionalism develops, marked by intensified campaigning at the primary stage with numerous candidates competing for the same office. Party obviously counts for less in these settings. Even the ballot has been modified, changing from party column to office block as a means of inhibiting straight party voting.[16] A wholesale move to this type of primary would certainly be bad news for parties.

An Assessment of the Direct Primary

The great virtue of the direct primary, from the perspective of its early Progressive Era sponsors, was its democratic component, its promise for changing the accent and scope of popular participation in the political system. Its immediate effect, they hoped, would be to diminish the influence of political organization on political life. What is the evidence that the primary has accomplished its mission? What impact has it had on political party organization?

On the positive side, an important outcome of having the primary system is that party leaders have been sensitized to the interests and feelings of the most active rank-and-file members. Fewer nominations are cut and dried, and even though candidates who secure the organization's endorsement win more frequently than they lose, their prospects often are uncertain. The possibility of a revolt against the organization, carried out in the primary, forces party leaders to take into account the elements that make up the party and to pay attention to the claims of potential candidates. There is always a chance—in some jurisdictions, a strong possibility—that an aspirant overlooked by the leadership will decide to challenge the party's choice in the primary. The primary therefore fosters caution among party leaders. A hands-off policy—one in which the party makes no endorsement—is sometimes its only response. If the party has no candidate, it cannot lose; party leaders can stay in business by avoiding the embarrassment that comes from primary defeats. In some jurisdictions, party intervention in the primary is never even considered, so accustomed is the electorate to party-free contests. For the public at large, the main contribution of the primary is that it opens up the political process.[17]

For the most part, the direct primary has had a decidedly negative impact on party leaders. Malcolm E. Jewell and Sarah A. Morehouse show that when the percentage of contested primaries increased moderately into the mid-1990s, the proportion of party-endorsed candidates winning contested races dropped precipitously, at least in gubernatorial elections. From 1960 to 1978, 79 percent of endorsed candidates for governor in contested primaries won the party nomination, but only 53 percent did so from 1980 to 1994.[18] Endorsements are most effective when the party organizations provide their favored candidates with organizational assistance, financing, and personnel—resources not all state and local parties have in large supply.[19]

Although the primary has not immobilized party organizations completely, it has caused a number of problems for them. The party leaders' lack of enthusiasm for primaries is not hard to understand given that, among other things, the primary:

1. greatly increases party campaign costs (if the party backs a candidate in a contested primary);
2. diminishes the capacity of the organization to reward its supporters through nominations;
3. makes it difficult for the party to influence nominees who establish their own power bases in the primary electorate;
4. creates opportunities for people hostile to party leadership and party policies to capture nominations;
5. permits anyone to wear the party label and opens the possibility that the party will have to repudiate a candidate who has been thrust upon it; and
6. increases intraparty strife and factionalism.[20]

Despite all of this, the primary still has not fulfilled the expectations of its sponsors. Most notably, primaries have not made politics significantly more competitive. A total of four Senate incumbents have been defeated in primaries since 1980, and, over the same period, only once (in 1992) did more than ten House incumbents lose. Most incumbents face token opposition for the nomination, if they face any at all. Yet politicians always worry, often irrationally, about reelection; even though House members normally win with 70 percent of the vote, many never think their districts are safe enough.

The surprising number of nominations won by default has several causes. First, uncontested primaries may be evidence of party strength—that is, potential candidates stop short of entering the primary because their prospects appear slim for defeating the organization's choice. Second, the deserted primary simply may demonstrate the pragmatism of politicians: they do not struggle to win nominations that are unlikely to lead anywhere. As V. O. Key Jr. and others have shown, primaries are most likely to be contested when the chances are strong that the winner will be elected to office in the general election, and are least likely to be contested when the nomination appears to have little value.[21] Therefore, the tendency is for electoral battles to occur in competitive districts or in the primary of the dominant party. Third, the presence of an incumbent reduces competition for a nomination. In fact, over the last twenty years, less than 2 percent of incumbent members of Congress have actually lost their party's nomination. Overall, the prospects for a primary contest are greatest in districts where the party has a chance to win in November and where no incumbent is in the race.

Experience with the primary has also shown that it is one thing to shape an institution so as to encourage popular participation and quite another to realize such participation. No fact about primaries is more familiar than that large numbers of voters assiduously ignore them. A majority of voters almost always stays away from the polls on primary day, even when major statewide races are to be settled. Consider the following evidence from 2008. Twenty-one states held their primaries for state offices such as governor or U.S. senator on a day different from their presidential primary. In those states, turnout was a mere 14 percent, a record low. In the states that held their primaries for governor or senator concurrently with the presidential primary, turnout was 26.5 percent—the highest rate of turnout since 1972.[22] Although the latter figure is much higher, it is still true that barely a quarter of eligible voters participated in these primary elections despite the stimulus of the most competitive presidential nomination contest in decades.

Presidential Selection

The presidential nominating process is unusually complicated. Those citizens who understand it know that it is an awkward mix of conventions, primaries, and caucuses regulated both by public law and party rules and that the parties differ in the methods they use to select their nominees.

The National Convention

The American national convention is surely one of the most remarkable institutions in the world for making nominations. In use since the early to mid-1800s, it is the official agency for the selection of each party's candidates for president and vice president and for the ratification of each party's platform. At the same time, it is a party's supreme policymaking authority, empowered to make the rules that govern party affairs.

The national convention historically has served another function of prime importance to the parties. It has been a meeting ground for the party itself, one in which leaders could tap into rank-and-file sentiments and in which the divergent interests that make up each party could, at least in some fashion, be accommodated. In its classic role, the national convention presents an opportunity for the national party—the fifty state parties assembled—to come to terms with itself, permitting leading politicians to strike the necessary balances and to settle, at least temporarily, the continuing questions of leadership and policy. Under the pressure of other changes in the presidential nominating process, however, the party role in conventions has been diminished.

Until the 1970s national convention decisions could best be explained by examining the central role of national, state, and local party leaders, and the behavior of state delegations. These were the "power points" in the classic model of convention politics, aptly described by the authors of *Explorations in Convention Decision Making:*

> Historically, state delegations have been thought to be the key units for bargaining in conventions; operating under the unit rule, they bargain with each other and with candidate organizations. The rank-and-file delegates are manipulated by hierarchical leaders holding important positions in national, state, and local party organizations. In order to enhance their bargaining position, these leaders often try to stay uncommitted to any candidate until the moment that their endorsement is crucial to victory for the ultimate nominee. After the presidential balloting is over, the vice-presidential nomination is awarded to a person whose selection will mollify those elements of the party who did not support the presidential choice. At the end of the convention, all groups rally around the ticket and the party receives a boost in starting the fall campaign.[23]

The classic model of convention decision making bears only modest resemblance to the patterns of influence at play in the most recent party conventions. In broad terms, decentralization of power is now the chief characteristic of the struggle for the presidential nomination. State delegations have given way to candidate blocs in importance, and party leaders have been displaced by the leaders of candidate organizations. Party leaders have few resources with which to bargain in those state delegations split among candidates, and any influence they wield is largely a product of their affiliation with one of the candidate organizations.

The decline of party presence in national conventions results from a confluence of forces: the delegate selection rules that opened up the parties to amateur activists and contributed to the spread of presidential primaries, the capacity of candidates to dominate campaign fund-raising by using government subsidies or by raising substantial funds from private donors, and the general weakness of state and local party organizations.[24] What matters to the candidate is winning the immediate primary or placing well enough, as judged by the mass media, to attract new funds and build momentum for the next contest. In the modern scheme of campaigning, expert consultants, an active personal organization spread out across the state, and the mass media are more important to the candidates than party structures and party leaders.

Selection of Delegates

National convention delegates are chosen by two methods: presidential primaries and caucus-conventions. Each state chooses its own system, and it is not unusual for a state to switch from one method to another between elections in response to criticisms from the press, the public, and politicians unhappy about the latest outcomes.

Loosely managed by the parties, the caucus-convention system provides for the election of delegates by rank-and-file members (mixed with candidate enthusiasts) from one level of the party to the next—ordinarily from precinct caucuses to county conventions to the state convention, and from there to the national convention. The first-tier caucuses (mass meetings at the precinct level) are crucial because they establish the delegate strength of each candidate in the subsequent conventions, including the national convention. Candidates and their organizations must turn out their supporters for these initial party meetings; a loss at this stage cannot be reversed.

At one time, the chief criticism of the caucus-convention system was that it was essentially closed, dominated by a few self-selected party leaders, key public officials, "fat cats" (major financial contributors), and lesser party officials as delegates. The democratizing reforms of the 1970s opened up the caucuses to participation by average party members and short-term activists willing to spend an afternoon or evening discussing and voting. Today, competing candidate organizations and their enthusiasts dominate the delegate-selection caucuses, and prominent party officials may or may not be found in their ranks. Preoccupied with the struggle for delegates, the media pay scant attention to the caucus as a party event. Popular participation is low in caucus states. In 2008, 239,000 voters took part in the Iowa Democratic caucuses, whereas 288,000 voted in the Democratic primary in New Hampshire, a state with about half the population of Iowa.[25] Although the participant count was close in 2008—an especially exciting presidential election—New Hampshire's first-in-the-nation primary usually produces twice as many participants as Iowa's first-in-the-nation caucus. Other than Iowa, turnout in caucus states is particularly low.[26]

In addition, the caucus-convention system poses major problems for party leaders.[27] In most caucus states party regulars have been reduced to bystanders as candidate organizations, bolstered by amateur enthusiasts, vie with one another for votes and delegates. Intraparty conflict also appears to occur more frequently in caucus states than in primary states. Finally, party leaders have become sensitive to the charge that caucus results may not be representative of general voter sentiment. For these reasons, particularly the latter, states that change their nominating systems in the future are more likely to switch to primaries than to caucuses.[28]

Used by the most populous states, presidential primaries are easier for the public to understand. A large majority of each state's delegates is chosen on primary day by the direct vote of the people; the remaining delegates are chosen through party processes following the primary. Like the direct primary used to nominate national, state, and local officials, the presidential primary was designed to wrest control of nominations from the bosses (the party professionals) and place it in the hands of the people by permitting them to choose the delegates to the nominating conventions in a public election. Just into the twentieth century, Florida became the first state to adopt a presidential primary law. In little more than a decade, about half of the states had adopted some version of it. Following the Progressive Era, its use dropped, with only fourteen states and the District of Columbia holding presidential primaries in 1968. In the 1970s and 1980s, however, the popularity of presidential primaries once again exploded, and by 2000, one or both parties held presidential primaries in forty-one states. In 2008 Democrats chose 86 percent of their delegates in primaries; Republicans, 80 percent.[29]

The broad objective of presidential primaries, as opposed to caucuses, is to encourage popular participation in the selection of presidents, but, historically, many voters have not attached much importance to the nominating process, even when the presidency is at stake (see Table 3-1).[30] In 2004 about 24 million voters participated in choosing the nominees, as contrasted with 121 million who voted in the general election. The 2008 nomination process, however, produced an enormous increase in voter participation. Driven mostly by the fierce primary fight that went the distance on the Democratic side, turnout reached its highest levels ever. More than 57 million people participated—36.7 million on the Democratic side and 20.6 million on the Republican side. Despite the increase, the overall turnout rate in the nomination phase for the highest office in the country was only about 30 percent of the eligible electorate.[31]

Table 3-1 Presidential Primary Turnout: 1968–2008

Year	Number of States Holding Primaries	Democratic Vote	Republican Vote	Total Major Party Vote
1968	14 and D.C.	7,535,069	4,473,551	12,008,620
1972	20 and D.C.	15,993,965	6,188,281	22,182,246
1976	26 and D.C.	16,052,652	10,374,125	26,426,777
1980	35 and D.C.	18,747,825	12,690,451	31,438,276
1984	29 and D.C.	18,009,192	6,575,651	24,584,843
1988	36 and D.C.	22,961,936	12,165,115	35,127,051
1992	38 and D.C.	20,239,385	12,696,547	32,395,932
1996	41 and D.C.	10,947,364	13,991,649	24,939,013
2000	41 and D.C.	14,665,119	20,717,198	35,382,317
2004	37 and D.C.	15,975,066	7,940,331	23,915,397
2008	41 and D.C.	36,731,478	20,613,383	57,348,121

Sources: Rhodes Cook, *Race for the Presidency: Winning the 2008 Nomination* (Washington, D.C.: CQ Press, 2008), as updated; and Center for the Study of the American Electorate, 2008 "The Primary Turnout Story," www1.media.american.edu/electionexperts/2008%20Primary%20Turnout_Final.pdf.

Delegate selection systems vary from state to state and from party to party. On the Democratic side, national party rules mandate that voters in primaries used for delegate selection must declare themselves as Democrats when they cast ballots (that is, only Democrats or registered Independents who declare themselves as Democrats on primary day), with the exception of a few states like Wisconsin that have open primary traditions. Twelve states use caucuses instead of primaries. Some use both primaries and caucuses; typically, in this arrangement, the caucus selects the delegates to reflect the primary results. For Republicans, the most common method for selecting delegates is the open primary; it is used in more than half of the states, including populous Illinois, Ohio, and Texas. Just under a quarter of the states, including Florida, California, New York, and Pennsylvania, use closed primaries. About one-fifth of the states use caucuses; in 2008 most of these were closed caucuses. Like the Democrats, Republican caucus states tend to be rural, with smaller populations, and in the Midwest (Iowa and Minnesota) or West (Alaska, Nevada, North Dakota, and Wyoming). Thirteen states used a caucus system in 2008 to select Republican delegates.

Whether a state used a primary or a caucus affected the 2008 election outcomes profoundly, particularly on the Democratic side. Of the fourteen states that employed a caucus, Obama won thirteen, often by wide margins. The only exception was the Nevada caucus early in the nomination process, which Clinton won narrowly. The targeting of caucus states was perhaps the Obama campaign's most important tactical move. Most Democratic caucus states have small populations, and many of them tend to vote in general elections for Republicans. As a result, Clinton ignored them. But, because Clinton failed to organize in these states, Obama was able to win these caucuses by huge margins, racking up a disproportionate number of delegates from caucus states, which offset Clinton's strength in the larger primary states.[32]

Rules of Delegate Selection

Prior to the 1970s, the manner in which national convention delegates were selected was left to the states. Today, the Democratic Party in particular tightly regulates the methods of delegate selection. The rules make it clear that not much is left to chance or to the discretion of individual state parties.

An amalgam of recommendations by five party study commissions stretching from 1969 to 1985, the rules were designed to serve several major objectives:

1. to stimulate the participation of rank-and-file Democratic voters in the presidential nominating process;
2. to increase the representation of certain demographic groups (particularly women, African Americans, and young people) in the convention through the use of guidelines on delegate selection;
3. to eliminate procedures held to be undemocratic (such as the unit rule, under which a majority of a state delegation could cast the state's total vote for a single candidate);

4. to enhance the local character of delegate elections (by requiring 75 percent of the delegates in each state to be elected at the congressional district level or lower); and

5. to provide through proportional representation that elected delegates fairly reflect the presidential candidate preferences of Democratic voters in primary states and Democratic participants in caucus-convention states. (The proportional representation rule was relaxed in the 1980s but is mandatory today.)

For many members of the first commission, the McGovern-Fraser Commission, the underlying objectives were to diminish the power of party professionals in the convention and to increase that of party members and activists at the local level. They succeeded to an extraordinary degree. A new type of participant, to whom candidates and issues were central, came to dominate the Democratic convention. Party leaders and public officials, thoroughly overshadowed in the 1972 and 1976 conventions, gradually have been readmitted since then. Following a recommendation of the Winograd Commission, in 1980 the Democratic National Committee (DNC) adopted a provision to expand each state delegation by 10 percent to include prominent party and elected officials. Since then, the number of these officials, who gain their seats automatically (that is, without facing the voters), has grown. "Superdelegates," as they are called, made up nearly 20 percent of the 2004 and 2008 Democratic conventions. Composed of Democratic members of Congress, Democratic governors, members of the DNC, and various prominent state party officials, the superdelegations are potentially influential in steering the nomination process, but only if the race is very close.

Superdelegates were introduced to the delegate-selection process to provide peer review of candidates by professional politicians and, at the same time, to diminish the influence of amateur activists and interest groups. They were to be the new power brokers of the convention. But it has not worked out that way. Because candidates campaign for the superdelegates' votes just as they campaign for popular support, most superdelegates arrive at the convention not as free agents but as delegates fully committed to individual candidates. Like other politicians in search of influence, superdelegates want to endorse the ultimate winner and often do so as early as possible, when endorsements count the most.

The story of 2008 was slightly more complicated in that superdelegates were, in fact, positioned to affect the outcome of the nomination process for the first time since 1984. The early endorsements went disproportionately to Hillary Clinton, who was the unquestioned front-runner before the primary and caucus season began. But a smaller than usual percentage of superdelegates had made formal endorsements early in the process, which gave them flexibility to back the stronger candidate at the end of the process. As Obama moved ahead of Clinton in the pledged delegate count—the delegates chosen by primaries and caucuses—the superdelegates began to support him. In other words, when an insurgency candidate was on the verge of toppling the party leaders' initial choice—exactly the scenario that superdelegates were created to stop—superdelegates still endorsed the opinion of Democratic primary and caucus voters.[33] The same situation occurred in 1984 when Walter Mondale led Gary Hart in pledged delegates, but, like Obama, did not have quite enough pledged delegates to secure the nomination. In both cases, the superdelegates chose the candidate who was ahead rather than chart an independent course.

The way delegates are allocated to candidates has been a persistent problem for the Democrats. Tinkering and temporizing, the party has vacillated between winner-take-all and proportional representation since the 1970s. In 1988 the national Democratic rules permitted state parties to choose from among three plans. First, states could select the *proportional representation* method, under which any Democratic candidate who reached the 15 percent threshold of the primary or caucus vote was entitled to a proportionate share of the delegates; candidates who failed to reach the threshold did not qualify for any delegates. Second, states could adopt what amounts to a *winner-take-all* system. In this direct-election form, voters cast ballots for individual delegates who either were pledged to candidates or uncommitted. The candidate who came in first in a district could win all or most of the delegates instead of sharing them with the trailing candidates. Third, states could choose a *winner-take-more* plan. Here, the winning candidate in each district was given a bonus delegate before the rest were divided proportionally. For the last five conventions, Democratic Party rules required all states to allocate their publicly elected delegates on a proportionate basis, giving each candidate who reached the 15 percent threshold the appropriate share of delegates.

Proportional representation has several side effects, not all of them positive. A party's first objective must be to minimize divisiveness, and contested primaries cause divisiveness. Enmities and resentment among party elites and voters generated in the nominating process can have a significant influence on their behavior in general elections. An analysis of Democratic presidential primaries, caucuses, and general election outcomes over a sixty-year period by James I. Lengle, Diane Owen, and Molly W. Sonner found that divisiveness at the nominating stage hurt the party's prospects for winning the general election. From 1932 to 1992 Democratic presidential candidates lost more than three-fourths of the states that experienced divisive primaries but only half of those with nondivisive primaries or those with caucuses.[34]

The Democrats' reliance on proportional representation in delegate selection certainly does not help in this regard. Although proportional representation enables the front-runner to secure delegates even in states won by another candidate, it still takes a long time for him or her to assemble a majority of delegates. In contrast, winner-take-all systems allow front-runners to land knockout blows at any point and end ugly intraparty struggles. As Priscilla L. Southwell notes, proportional representation can be advantageous for some lesser-known, outsider candidates because their second- and third-place finishes in the early caucuses and primaries will entitle them to delegates and perhaps keep their candidacies alive.[35] In the end, proportional representation leads to longer nomination struggles, more contested primaries, and more negative feelings within the party in the general election campaign. The 2008 nomination fight was long and protracted on the Democratic side, although it did not ultimately cost Obama, the eventual nominee, the general election. Still, the general themes of the scholarly literature on divisive primaries hold. Reliance on proportional representation made the process longer and more expensive than it would have been with a winner-take-all system.

As Larry Sabato neatly demonstrates, Obama's electoral strategy during the primaries and caucuses was central to his victory because it accounted for the realities of a proportional representation delegate selection system. Facing twenty-two elections on Super Tuesday, the candidates had to make strategic decisions about where to focus attention. Clinton targeted the large, delegate-rich states that Democrats typically win in the general election—California, New Jersey, and New York—to convince the rank and file and superdelegates that she could defeat the Republican nominee in the fall. Indeed, she won all the large states on Super Tuesday, except Obama's native Illinois. But she did not win by overwhelming margins, which led to an almost even split of delegates. Obama tried to stay competitive in the big states and also target small states like Idaho, North Dakota, and Utah. As a result, Obama won five caucuses by more than two-to-one margins in states that the Clinton campaign ignored, all but canceling out Clinton's slight advantage in the big states. Contrasting Idaho and New Jersey provides a particularly useful example. In Idaho, Obama collected fifteen of the eighteen delegates awarded by the state, a twelve-delegate advantage. Clinton won the much bigger state of New Jersey, but just by ten points, which netted her only eleven more delegates than Obama. In other words, even though only about 20,000 people in Idaho participated in the Democratic caucuses, Obama's landslide victory there offset Clinton's delegate advantage in New Jersey where more than 1 million people voted.

It is also noteworthy that a winner-take-all system, which rewards victories, particularly in big states, likely would have made Clinton the 2008 Democratic nominee. Sabato calculated that Clinton won states with a total of 1,835 delegates, while the states Obama won totaled only 1,574 delegates. Although this result would not have given Clinton enough pledged delegates to win the nomination, the superdelegates likely would have broken disproportionately to her as the pledged delegate leader, propelling her to the nomination. Instead, because of the proportional representation system, Obama led by 117 delegates after the primaries and caucuses were over, winning him the support of the superdelegates and the nomination. There are few better examples in American politics demonstrating that the rules matter. The Obama campaign's attentiveness to the rules provided the underdog with a chance to overtake the front-runner. The Clinton campaign's inattentiveness to these same rules cost her a clear path to the nomination. Indeed, Clinton's primary strategist, Mark Penn, apparently believed (erroneously) that Democratic delegates were awarded on a winner-take-all basis.[36]

The Republican Party in the 1970s and 1980s was considerably less active than the Democratic Party in restructuring its delegate selection rules, but it did make a few changes. Its current rules require open meetings for delegate selection, ban automatic (ex officio) delegates, and provide for the election, not the selection, of congressional district and at-large delegates (unless otherwise provided by state law). State Republican parties are urged to develop plans for increasing the participation of women, young people, minorities, and other groups in the presidential nominating process, but they are not required to do so. The push to nationalize party rules, pronounced among Democratic reformers for the last several decades, finds only limited support among Republicans, who continue to stress the federal character of their party. The basic authority to reshape delegate selection rules remains with state parties.[37]

The delegate selection practices of Republicans differ in several major respects from those of Democrats. First, Republicans have not adopted proportionality in delegate allocation, but continue with some version of winner-take-all. In 2008 most Republican primaries used either statewide winner-take-all or a hybrid statewide-district winner-take-all. A few Republican state parties use winner-take-all but provide for proportional representation if no candidate receives a majority of the vote. Second, the GOP has no provision for the automatic selection of party or public officials, or superdelegates, in Democratic nomenclature. Third, the party has no requirement that state delegations be evenly divided between men and women, a rule imposed on state Democratic parties beginning in 1980. (Women delegates made up only 32 percent of the total number of Republican delegates in 2008.)[38] Fourth, each state Republican Party is free to schedule its primary or caucus as it sees fit. On the Democratic side, the primary-caucus calendar is tightly regulated by national party rules. Party differences in delegate selection reflect basic party differences in philosophy and organization that can be summed up in the appellations "federal" Republicans and "national" Democrats.

Evaluating Presidential Primary and Caucus-Convention Systems

Sometimes it seems as if the only persons satisfied with the presidential nominating process are the winners—the nominees and their supporters—and everyone else can find reasons to be unhappy or frustrated.

To initiated and uninitiated voters alike, the primaries and caucuses are a mass of paradoxes. Unpredictability reigns, victory in a single state can be the key to the nomination, and victories in the early primaries and caucuses are usually crucial. Consider these outcomes. In the judgment of many observers, on the day that John F. Kennedy defeated Hubert H. Humphrey in the West Virginia primary in 1960—a Catholic winning in an overwhelmingly Protestant state—he sewed up the nomination. Al Gore and George W. Bush clinched their parties' nominations within two months of the start of the 2000 primary and caucus season. The Democratic nomination followed a similar pattern in 2004. Although Howard

Dean had party support before any voters spoke, John Kerry used his victories in Iowa and New Hampshire to take home the nomination by the second week in March.

The timing of state victories makes a difference. The first-in-the-nation contests in Iowa and New Hampshire give these states disproportionate influence. George McGovern in 1972 and Jimmy Carter in 1976, both long shots to win the nomination, owed their success to their strong showings in these states. In 2008 these early contests had their usual outsized effect on the nomination contests. By winning Iowa handily, Obama legitimized his candidacy and gained strong momentum. Many commentators suggested that a win by Obama in New Hampshire might destroy Clinton's candidacy, but she posted a come-from-behind win there, setting the stage for the most competitive nomination season since voters became an integral part of the process in 1972.

If a candidate fails to win one of these two early contests, it is almost impossible to recover. In the months leading up to 2008, former Massachusetts governor Mitt Romney and former New York City mayor Rudy Giuliani led the competitors in the polls, but they quickly faded because of defeats in Iowa and New Hampshire. Romney finished second to Mike Huckabee in Iowa and to John McCain in New Hampshire. Romney outspent all his rivals in these states and was running from a state bordering New Hampshire, but his showings were not deemed good enough by political watchers, and he dropped out of the race. Giuliani tried to bypass these first two contests in favor of states later in the nomination process, such as Florida. By the time Florida came around, however, McCain and to a lesser extent Huckabee had seized the momentum, and, after a string of poor showings in the states where he thought he would do well, Giuliani was eliminated from contention. His experience suggests that it is not advisable for a candidate to bypass all of the early contests.

The most important result of an early victory or unanticipated good showing is the free media coverage it produces. Even though the race between Carter and Morris Udall was very close in New Hampshire in 1976 (Carter received 28 percent of the vote to Udall's 23 percent), the press hailed Carter as the clear-cut winner. As a result, he received 2,600 lines of the coverage in *Time* and *Newsweek* in the week following New Hampshire to Udall's 96 lines, a proportion mirrored on both television news and in major newspapers.[39] For anyone except their residents, it is simply mind-boggling to learn that Iowa and New Hampshire, which comprise about 3 percent of the nation's population, receive nearly 30 percent of the media coverage given the entire campaign for the presidential nomination.[40] Many find this focus problematic because neither state has a major metropolitan area, a large urban (unionized) workforce, or a sizable minority population—characteristics of special importance for Democrats. In short, the voters in these states are patently not a cross section of the nation as a whole.[41]

Regional variation in candidate strength also can be decisive. The South is gaining population and exerting more influence over the choice of party nominees. Southern primaries and caucuses were crucial for George H. W. Bush in

1988, Bill Clinton in 1992, Robert Dole in 1996, George W. Bush in 2000, and Barack Obama in 2008. It is hardly surprising, then, that between 1988—when most southern states started to hold their primaries on Super Tuesday—and 2008, more than half of the major party nominees have had some kind of connection to the South. Although Obama is not a southerner, his appeal among African Americans was critical in this region. He won big in South Carolina, the first contest after his loss in New Hampshire. On Super Tuesday, he won huge victories in Georgia and Alabama, and a week later he won decisively in Mississippi. In all these states, African Americans made up half or more of the primary electorate in 2008. Sequence and region obviously affect the choice of nominees.

Front-Loading and Its Effects

The opening weeks of the nominating process are absolutely critical. In an effort to be meaningful, states continue to shift their primaries and caucuses forward to the early part of the season. In the argot of analysts and political junkies, they are "front-loading." Since 1992 California has moved its presidential primary date from June to the fourth Tuesday in March (1996) to the first Tuesday in March (2000, 2004) to the first Tuesday in February (2008), ostensibly to increase its influence in the process. With other populous states following suit, February and March are now the pivotal months in securing the presidential nomination. That February has become such an important month is a new development. The percentage of Republican delegates chosen in February nearly quadrupled between 2000 and 2008 from 15 percent to 57 percent. The Democratic Party traditionally barred states other than New Hampshire from scheduling presidential primaries in February, but relaxed this rule in 2004. In 2008 the trend toward front-loading continued, with fully 60 percent of delegates chosen before March 1. More than 40 percent of the delegates for both parties were chosen on Super Tuesday (February 5), which featured races in twenty-four states, including several with large populations.

Front-loading has several critical effects. Potential candidates must begin raising money, building campaign organizations, and securing endorsements at least a year or more before the primary season officially begins. This period is often referred to as the *invisible primary*—an interval in which no official contests occur but candidacies are made or broken. For all intents and purposes George W. Bush had secured his party's nomination even before 2000. His campaign had raised more than $36 million by July 1999, much more than any of his competitors. As a result, he was able to lock up important endorsements from many governors, members of Congress, and other party leaders.

Money separates the serious candidate from the dilettante or the rank outsider. There is never enough of it, and the law does not make it easy to get. Under the 2002 Bipartisan Campaign Reform Act (BCRA), no individual can contribute more than $2,000 indexed for inflation ($2,300 in 2008) to any campaign. Moreover, candidates can qualify for matching federal funds only after they have raised $100,000 in small sums ($250 or less, $5,000 per state) in each of twenty states. After a candidate qualifies, the federal government will match up to $250 of an individual donor's total contributions to the candidate's campaign. Political action committees may contribute up to $5,000 to a candidate, but their gifts are not eligible for matching public money. Candidates are therefore compelled to develop a large network of small contributors, spread around the country—making fund-raising a chore for all candidates and a major obstacle for some. Plans and activities to raise money must be launched long in advance of the election year. It is easy to mark the opening of a new campaign; it begins with the creation of fund-raising committees and the scramble for money.

The fund-raising contest for the 2008 primary elections highlighted the growing importance of the Internet for attracting money from small donors, which marked a fundamental change in financing campaigns. This is especially evident in the comparison of Clinton's and Obama's fund-raising. Although Clinton narrowly outraised Obama in 2007, she used the more traditional approach of targeting big donors with the means to give the maximum donation at fund-raising events. Obama successfully targeted many thousands of individuals willing to make small donations primarily over the Internet. These small donors, many of whom were targeted via the enormous e-mail address list assembled by the campaign, helped Obama keep the fund-raising battle close during the invisible primary season and, perhaps more important, allowed him to raise historic sums of money after his victory in the Iowa caucuses. In fact, he raised $28 million through online donations alone in January 2008, and 90 percent of these contributions were under $200.[42] Access to this wide base of small donors allowed Obama to overcome Clinton's well-established fund-raising network and focus more time on campaign events rather than traditional fund-raisers. This experience suggests that future candidates who do not prioritize online fund-raising do so at great peril. Obama also raised substantial sums from traditional large donors, and such donors will remain essential to presidential campaign finance.[43]

Next, candidates must get out of the blocks quickly. Slow starters usually find themselves out of the race in a matter of weeks. Bill Clinton had the 1992 Democratic nomination nailed down before half of the states, including many big ones, had even voted. In contrast, late starts by Republican Fred Thompson in 2008 (and to a lesser extent Giuliani) doomed their campaigns. For most candidates who do poorly in early contests, financial coffers run dry, fund-raising becomes impossibly difficult, and plans to exit the race quickly take shape. Although the Democrats took their nomination fight almost all the way to the convention in 2008, McCain had vanquished his rivals that year by March 4, a much more typical outcome with a front-loaded calendar. Without doubt, front-loading gives an advantage to well-known candidates with campaign organizations in place, to those with large amounts of money on hand, and to those with significant national followings.[44]

In addition, front-loading makes it difficult for dark-horse candidates to translate momentum, built on stronger than expected showings in states like Iowa and New Hampshire, into strong showings elsewhere. After Jimmy Carter won his

Table 3-2   Number and Timing of Presidential Primaries and Caucuses: 1976–2008

Month	1976	1980	1984	1988	1992	1996	2000	2004	2008
January	0	0	0	0	0	0	0	1	4
February	1	1	1	2	2	5	6	11	21
March	5	9	8	20	15	24	20	14	5
April	2	4	3	3	5	1	2	1	1
May	13	13	11	7	10	8	9	7	6
June	6	9	7	5	7	4	5	3	2
Total	27	36	30	37	39	42	42	37	39

Source: Rhodes Cook, *Race for the Presidency: Winning the 2008 Nomination* (Washington, D.C.: CQ Press, 2008).

surprise victory in New Hampshire in late February 1976, he had to prepare for only seven primaries in the next two months. Most primaries were then held in May. Mike Huckabee enjoyed no such luxury in 2008. A little-known former governor of Arkansas, Huckabee was considered a long-shot candidate through 2007, raising less than $5 million in the first nine months of the year leading up to the election and receiving only single-digit support in national public opinion polls. His campaign was rewarded for its laser-like focus on the Iowa caucus with a surprising victory, making him an overnight contender for the nomination. But he lacked the time to build on his win. The next week, he had to face the voters of New Hampshire where he had only just begun to campaign, and he finished third behind the well-organized McCain and Romney. (See Table 3-2.) Huckabee's lack of organization hurt him again later in January when he finished a close second to McCain in South Carolina, a state that many thought he could win because of its high concentration of evangelical social conservatives. Although Huckabee won a small handful of Super Tuesday states, McCain dominated the day. With an extra month, perhaps even an extra week, to organize in South Carolina, Huckabee might have won, which would have made him a stronger contender on Super Tuesday.

The inability to field new campaign organizations after an early victory slows a candidate's momentum. Another obstacle used to be the need to raise money quickly, but the Internet has helped candidates overcome that. Huckabee did not do well in national polls in 2007, but he began to make inroads in polls in Iowa, which allowed him to raise more than twice as much money in the two months preceding the caucus there than he had raised in the rest of 2007.[45] Much of the fund-raising occurred online, aided by the marketing videos featuring his celebrity endorser, Chuck Norris. This fund-raising surge allowed Huckabee to quickly gain the financial resources necessary to compete, but it did not provide time to build an effective organization.

Nevertheless, evidence suggests it is not impossible for an underdog candidate to emerge. In 2004 Howard Dean went from being a relatively unknown former governor of a very small state to leading in the polls even before the primaries and caucuses got started. In the year leading up to the nomination fight, Dean used the Internet to build a fund-raising and volunteer-organizing juggernaut. In fact, in the third quarter of 2003, Dean raised more than $15 million; no one else in the field raised even $5 million. He was by far the best-funded Democratic presidential aspirant, and in late 2003 his campaign looked sufficiently strong that former vice president Al Gore endorsed his candidacy. Although Dean's fortunes ultimately nose-dived for a number of reasons, one of his notable missteps was to spend a significant chunk of money in states with later contests. This strategy was risky for a candidate who had only recently emerged on the scene. In addition, Dean seemed to wilt under the hot lights of increased scrutiny from the national press in the early weeks of 2004. After poor showings in Iowa and New Hampshire, he was no longer a factor.

In 2008 Obama became the first underdog candidate to secure a major party nomination since Carter did it in 1976, proving that front-loading does not preclude such an outcome. His campaign possessed some of the best characteristics of Dean's and Huckabee's. Like Dean and, in fact, using some of his campaign operatives from 2004, Obama raised significant money early. Even though Clinton was the obvious front-runner, Obama still raised a remarkable $103.8 million in the year leading up to the election.[46] And, like Huckabee, he was able to use his victory in Iowa as a springboard to even more successful fund-raising. In fact, Obama raised a remarkable $36 million in January alone, compared with only $13.5 million for Clinton.[47] Unlike Huckabee, Obama had raised early money, which had been invested wisely in later primary and caucus states. When Super Tuesday arrived, Obama was competitive in nearly all of the more than twenty contests. And, unlike Dean, Obama used his early money to win early victories, due largely to his remarkable campaign skills. These victories kept the money coming in, whereas Dean's had quickly dried up in 2004.

No matter who runs for president in the future, a protracted struggle for the nomination is still more likely to be the exception than the rule. Front-loading has led to a more compact process and to a strengthened opportunity for a quick knockout. In 2008 more than 70 percent of Republican and Democratic delegates had been decided by the end of February (see Table 3-3), which indicates that early money and standing organizations are more important than ever. Once the campaign begins in this tighter schedule of events, scant time is available to raise money, solicit endorsements, shape issues, or put an organization in place. For serious contenders, the nominating campaign must begin two or more years in advance of the presidential year. No one can wait around for lightning to strike.

Up through the 2000 election cycle, the Democratic Party sought to diminish the significance of the early phase of the presidential nominating process by adopting rules to restrict the nominating season (the caucus-primary "window"). According to David Redlawsk, Daniel Bowen, and Caroline Tolbert, these efforts actually *increased* the significance of the first few contests.[48] In the 1990s the Democrats mandated that all their primaries had to occur between March and June, except for Iowa and New Hampshire. This step provided the impetus for

Table 3-3   Percentage of Delegates Allocated: 2008

Month	Republican		Democratic	
	Percentage of Delegates Allocated	Cumulative Percentage Allocated to Date	Percentage of Delegates Allocated	Cumulative Percentage Allocated to Date
January	14%	14%	13%	13%
Feb. 5 (Super Tuesday)	41	55	47	60
Rest of February	16	71	13	73
March	12	83	12	85
April	3	86	4	89
May	11	97	9	98
June	3	100	2	100
Total	100		100	

Source: Rhodes Cook, *Race for the Presidency: Winning the 2008 Nomination* (Washington, D.C.: CQ Press, 2008), viii–ix, as updated.

Super Tuesday, as many states scrambled to move their primaries to the start of the window to increase their importance. In 2001 the Democrats adopted a plan to widen the window to include February. In response, no fewer than eighteen states moved their nominating contests to February in 2004.

The Republican Party has also become sensitive to the scheduling of nominating events. In an effort to combat front-loading and to stretch out the nominating process, the 1996 Republican convention approved changes in party rules that gave states a bonus in delegates if they moved their caucus or primary to a later date in 2000; any state that voted after May 15 would receive 10 percent more delegates, but those that voted in the last half of April or the first half of May received only a 7.5 percent increase. The convention also restricted the nominating season by barring delegate-selection events in January.[49] In the end, however, there was no rush to move primaries back in the calendar; only sixteen states held their contests in April, May, or June in 2000, only three more than in 1996. Ultimately, the appeal of extra delegates was weaker than the appeal of holding the vote before the contest was effectively decided. As a result, the Republicans have stopped offering such incentives.

After seeing the results of the 2004 nomination process, the Democratic Party's Commission on Presidential Nomination Timing and Scheduling offered recommendations that would further front-load the system, with the specific intent of reducing the influence of Iowa and New Hampshire.[50] In the end, the party moved the contests in Iowa and New Hampshire from two weeks apart to about a week apart and inserted the Nevada caucuses between them. They then allowed South Carolina to hold its primary the week after New Hampshire, but the week before Super Tuesday. The Democratic National Committee clearly meant business when they finalized this calendar: when Florida and Michigan scheduled their contests for January, which was not within the DNC-approved window of time, the DNC stripped these states of their delegates and refused to acknowledge their primaries.

In sum, the electoral results in the early caucus-convention and primary system are peculiar to the presidential nominating process. And overemphasis of the results by the media is the norm. Often speaking with greater finality than the voters themselves, the media create winners and losers, front-runners and also-rans, candidates who should "bail out," and candidates who have earned "another shot." Voters learn who did better than expected and who did worse; they even start to evaluate the candidates on these terms rather than on policy.[51] Winning or placing well is translated into a major political resource, with the psychological impact greater than the number of delegates won. The rewards for capturing the media's attention are heightened visibility, an expanded and more attentive journalistic corps, television news time, interest group cynosure, endorsements, campaign funds, and a leg up on the next contest.[52] The truth is that in the nominating process the media have become the new parties.[53]

Primaries and the End of Party Boss Influence

The system of caucus-conventions and presidential primaries is a crazy quilt of activity. Candidates fly from one end of the country to the other and back again, emphasizing certain states, de-emphasizing others, and doing their best to impose their interpretations on the most recent results. Candidates are never wholly confident about how or where they should spend their time or money, and voters are not quite sure of what is going on. Yet there is more to the system than its awkwardness, complexity, and unpredictability.

Popular participation in the presidential nominating process generally was not of much consequence prior to the reforms of the 1970s. Candidates, following their instincts and the advice of assorted national and state politicians, chose to enter primaries, to avoid them, or to participate in certain ones and skip others. As recently as 1968, only fourteen states even held primaries, and Humphrey captured the Democratic nomination that year without running in any of them. In states using the caucus-convention system, the chief method of nomination, one or a few leaders typically controlled the selection of delegates and therefore the outcome. To win the nomination, candidates spent much of their time cultivating influential state party leaders. Only a few candidates at any time, moreover, were thought to be "available" for the office; that is, they possessed attributes that would prompt party leaders throughout the country and the media to take them seriously. Presidential nominees were chosen in a relatively closed system from among a very select group.

That world and the rules and practices that controlled it have disappeared. Today, the system is remarkably open, and the impact of party leaders and organizations is more diffuse. No single leader can "deliver" a state. Candidates rarely write off a primary or caucus, although they often downplay the significance of certain contests. And, most important, rank-and-file voters are central to the presidential nominating process. Whether the new system produces better presidential candidates (or better presidents) than those previously chosen in smoke-filled rooms is another matter.

Marty Cohen and his colleagues argue that the waning of party influence in presidential nominations is overstated. Parties just look different now than prior to the McGovern-Fraser reforms. A constellation of political insiders and policy demanders who work together for a candidate, the new party elite includes an amalgam of organized interests, party leaders, fund-raisers, pollsters, media consultants, and even citizen activists. When this web of political insiders unites around a candidate, it can be a potent political force, targeting money and endorsements toward the preferred candidate in the invisible primary and beyond. In 2000 George W. Bush, instead of McCain, received the early support of an important network of GOP insiders. McCain failed to get the endorsement of even one Republican governor. The party's primary voters took their cues from insiders, handing Bush the nomination. Similar dynamics characterized Al Gore's early defeat of Democratic rival Bill Bradley in 2000. Although the coalition of insiders usually unites around a candidate, sometimes they do not. In 2008 the Democrats left it to the voters to decide between Obama and Clinton, who were backed by separate camps of Democratic insiders.[54]

Presidential primaries, because they tap into voters' preferences in a more direct fashion than caucuses and involve a much larger sector of the electorate, present a particularly good opportunity for testing candidates, policies, and issues in a variety of states.[55] When Carter, an outsider, won a large majority of the 1976 Democratic primaries, it revealed the intensity of voters' resentment toward the "Washington establishment." Voter attitudes toward conservatism were brought to light in 1980 when Ronald Reagan easily won the first primary in New Hampshire and then twenty-seven of the next thirty-one primaries he entered. In 1992 Clinton demonstrated his personal resiliency and the appeal of his centrist message in an often-bruising beginning to the primary season; he won more primaries—thirty-two—than any previous Democratic candidate. In 2008 many of the attacks absorbed by Obama in the primaries returned in the general election. By then, however, they carried less punch because the primary and caucus season had already exposed people to the information.

What has been the overall impact of the preconvention struggle on the choice of nominees? The primary and convention-caucus process has become decisive, all but eliminating the significance of the national conventions in the selection of presidential nominees. Since the adoption of the McGovern-Fraser reforms, one of the few convention uncertainties to be settled is which state will cast the votes (of already committed delegates) that will push the winning candidate over the top. Everyone has known the winner for months.

The Convention Delegates

The emphasis on popular participation in the delegate-selection process, coupled with affirmative action requirements to promote the representation of disadvantaged groups, has sharply changed the composition of the Democratic National Convention. Prior to the 1970s, Democratic delegates were preponderantly male, middle-aged, and white. They were usually party regulars—officials of the party, important contributors, and reliable rank-and-file members. Public officeholders were prominent in all state delegations. The selection process was dominated by state and local party leaders.

The reforms have produced a new breed of delegate. As a result of the guidelines adopted by the McGovern-Fraser Commission, the representation of women, African Americans, and the young in the national convention has increased quickly. For example, the proportion of women delegates grew from 13 percent in 1968 to 40 percent in 1972, and that of African Americans from 5.5 percent to 15 percent. Under current rules, each state Democratic Party is required to develop outreach programs to raise the number of delegates from groups significantly underrepresented in the past, such as individuals sixty-five and over, the physically disabled, or those with low or moderate incomes. Another affirmative action rule specifies that in the selection of at-large delegates, preference should be given to African, Hispanic, Native, and Asian/Pacific Americans, and to women. All state delegation-selection plans must provide for equal numbers of men and women. These mandated changes have had a profound impact on the composition of state delegations.

The chief losers in the reforms of the 1970s were Democratic Party professionals and public officeholders, as they were replaced in state after state by delegates animated by particular issues or candidates ("amateurs," in broad terms). The addition of superdelegates has restored some power to party regulars. It is now typical to see more than half of the delegates holding some sort of party post or elected office, suggesting that professional politicians have come back after being sidelined by various party reform commissions. Whether their presence has the potential to alter the outcomes remains to be seen, as the conventions merely anoint the nominees chosen by primary voters and caucus participants. Even when nominations have been close, as in 1984 and 2008, superdelegates chose to back the candidate who was ahead in the pledged delegate count. It seems clear that superdelegates do not want to be seen as overturning the will of the primary electorate.

Changes in the composition of delegates to the Republican National Convention have come more gradually. Even so, a larger proportion of women, African Americans, and young people are being elected as delegates than ever before. Amateur activists are also more numerous in Republican conventions, but not on the scale found on the Democratic side. Party leaders, long-time party members, and public officials continue to play their parts.

Amateur or professional, convention delegates reflect neither a cross section of the population nor of the party membership. Two particular characteristics differentiate delegates from the wider public and rank-and-file party members: high income and substantial education. In 2008 more than 80 percent of Republican and Democratic delegates were college graduates, compared with about one-third of the population as a whole. Better than 65 percent of delegates in each party reported incomes in excess of $75,000 annually, compared with less than a third of all Americans.[56]

The racial and gender differences in the parties are reflected in their delegates for the 2008 nominating conventions. African Americans made up 23 percent of the Democratic delegates and 2 percent of the Republican delegates. The percentage of Hispanic Democratic delegates was 11 percent, compared with 5 percent among Republican delegates. Women made up 50 percent of the Democratic delegates, and 32 percent of the Republican delegates. It is noteworthy that the Republican delegates were significantly more likely to be white and male in 2008 than in 2004, reversing a trend toward more racial and gender balance on the Republican side over the last few elections.

Liberals are regularly overrepresented in the Democratic convention, and conservatives in the Republican convention. In 2008, 19 percent of the Democratic delegates described themselves as "very liberal," in contrast to 15 percent for the Democratic membership as a whole. Sixty-three percent of rank-and-file Republicans identified themselves as "very conservative" or "somewhat conservative," but 72 percent of the Republican delegates described themselves in that fashion. Fully 40 percent of all Republican delegates, in fact, identified themselves as very conservative—a proportion 10 percentage points higher than found among Republican voters. Less than 1 percent of Republican delegates identified themselves as liberals, as contrasted with 5 percent for GOP voters. Even more striking, only 3 percent of the Democratic delegates described themselves as somewhat or very conservative, in contrast to 16 percent for rank-and-file party members.[57] Ideologically, these two-party elites are quite different. What is more, ideological distinctiveness is more characteristic of delegates than of average party voters.

The Politics of the Convention

Three practical aims dominate the proceedings of a national party convention: to nominate presidential and vice-presidential candidates, to draft the party platform, and to lay the groundwork for party unity in the campaign. The way the party addresses itself to the tasks of nominating the candidates and drafting the platform is likely to determine how well it achieves its third objective: to heal party rifts and forge a cohesive party. To put together a presidential ticket and a platform that satisfies the principal elements of the party is difficult. The task of reconciling divergent interests within the party occupies the convention from its earliest moments until the final gavel—at least in most conventions. By and large, convention leaders have been successful in shaping the compromises necessary to keep the national parties, such as they are, from flying apart.

The Convention Committees

The initial business of a convention is handled mainly by four committees. The *committee on credentials* is given the responsibility for determining the permanent roll (official membership) of the convention. Its specific function is to ascertain the members' legal right to seats in the convention. In the absence of challenges to the right of certain delegates to be seated, or of contests between two delegations from the same state trying to be seated, the review is handled routinely and with dispatch. Most state delegations are seated without difficulty. When disputes arise, the committee holds hearings and takes testimony; its recommendations for seating delegates are then reported to the convention, which ordinarily (but not invariably) sustains them. The *committee on permanent organization* is charged with selecting the permanent officers of the convention, including the chair, the clerks, and the sergeant at arms. The *committee on rules* devises the rules under which the convention will operate and establishes the order of business. Decisions made by the committees can be critical. Meeting in May 2008, the DNC's committee on rules and bylaws was forced to reconsider what to do with the delegates from Florida and Michigan, who were initially not counted because the states had held their primaries outside of the time period approved by the DNC. Having Michigan and Florida's delegates counted in full was the only scenario under which Hillary Clinton would have a chance to win the Democratic nomination.[58] Ultimately, the committee opted to give each state half of its delegate vote.

The most important convention committee is the *committee on resolutions* which is in charge of drafting the party platform. The actual work of this committee begins many weeks before the convention, so that a draft of the document is ready when the convention opens and the formal committee hearings begin. When a president seeks reelection, the platform is likely to be prepared under his direction and accepted by the committees (and later by the floor) without major changes.

Conventions are major public relations opportunities for the parties. In 2000 the Republicans, concerned about their reputation as antiminority and antigay, made an effort to highlight their diversity. Although fewer than 5 percent of their delegates were actually black, a number of noteworthy African Americans— from Colin Powell, who spoke favorably about affirmative action, to the Rock, a professional wrestler—addressed the convention. Arizona representative Jim Kolbe, who is gay, spoke as well. (The Texas delegation threatened to boycott Kolbe's speech, but instead the members waged a silent protest by removing their cowboy hats and mouthing prayers.) The 2004 Republican convention, which renominated George W. Bush, was remarkable for its timing. It occurred in early September, much later than national party conventions ordinarily take place. The reason? To take advantage of the third anniversary of the September 11 terrorist attacks, an especially potent symbol given that the convention was held in New York City. As many people saw Bush's performance in the aftermath of 9/11 as his finest hour, framing the convention in these terms greatly benefited the Republican ticket.

The 2004 Democratic convention was less successful. John Kerry worked hard to promote his heroic Vietnam War service in an effort to blunt Republican attacks that suggested liberal Democrats were not sufficiently tough to combat terrorism. In the weeks that followed, however, Kerry's campaign was badly damaged by unsubstantiated charges that he had exaggerated his wartime heroism. Barack Obama, who would be elected senator from Illinois later in the year, made a stirring keynote address in which he argued that Democrats cared about values and religion just like Republicans, yet Kerry did even worse among regular churchgoers in the election than Al Gore had four years before.

In 2008 party unity was particularly important for the Democrats. The party believed it had a great opportunity to win the presidency, as Bush had become so unpopular with the public. Still, the Democrats had to put the acrimonious nomination struggle between Obama and Clinton behind them. Preconvention polls suggested that a substantial minority of Clinton's primary and caucus supporters would not vote for Obama in the general election. Clinton, however, made a remarkable speech at the convention, arguing that her strong showing in the primaries was "not about me" and urging her supporters to back Obama because she agreed with him on the issues most important to Democrats. Her pleas were successful, as an overwhelming majority of Clinton supporters fell in line behind Obama.

The 2008 Republican convention had its share of drama as well. The base of the Republican Party had long distrusted McCain because of his independent voting record on issues important to the party's base. Such concerns were of central import in the days leading up to the convention, as speculation centered on whether McCain would choose Joe Lieberman, a long-time Democratic senator who had recently become an independent, as his running mate. Ultimately, McCain picked Sarah Palin, the popular governor of Alaska and a darling of the social conservative movement. Although most eventually came to see Palin as a liability on the ticket, her electrifying performance at the convention energized Republicans and drew McCain and Palin into a statistical tie with Obama and Joe Biden in the week after the Republican convention. McCain did, in fact, shore up his support with conservative evangelical Christians in 2008, winning roughly the same percentage of votes from this group in 2008 as Bush did in 2004.

Selecting the Presidential Ticket

Some party leaders believe the best convention is the one that opens with significant uncertainties and imponderables—a good, but not surefire, prescription for generating public interest in the convention, the party, and its nominees.[59] Both parties' 2008 conventions featured such uncertainties, which led to unprecedented public attention to them. According to the Nielsen ratings, the Republican affair was the most watched of all time, and McCain's acceptance speech attracted nearly 39 million viewers. Obama's acceptance speech drew only about a half million fewer. Such uncertainties, however, are far from the norm. They are usually limited to the choice of vice-presidential candidates, as the names at the top of the ticket are almost sure to be known months before.

Although the 2008 contests were a departure from the norm, experience tells us that the front-runner going into the election year nearly always wins the nomination. The first two post–McGovern-Fraser elections produced Democratic surprises, with the nominations of McGovern in 1972 and Carter in 1976, but the only real surprise in the last seven elections was Obama. Some early front-runners may wobble for several weeks, as Bob Dole did in 1996 and McCain did in 2008, but their superiority in organizing and fund-raising generally leads to their nomination. Open conventions have all but disappeared. In fact, first-ballot nominations have occurred at both conventions every year from 1956 through 2008.[60]

The final major item of convention business is the selection of the party's vice-presidential nominee. Here the task of the party is to come up with the right political formula—the candidate who can add the most to the ticket and detract the least. Most often the presidential nominee makes the choice after rounds of consultation with various party and candidate organization leaders. Although a great deal of suspense is usually created over the vice-presidential nomination, convention ratification comes easily once the presidential nominee has decided and cleared the selection with party leaders.

Unless the presidential nominee is inclined to take a major risk to serve the interest of his own faction or ideology, he has traditionally selected a candidate who can help balance the ticket and unify the party.[61] Carter's choice of Walter Mondale fits neatly into this category (a southern moderate and a midwestern liberal), as do several other pairs, including Kerry's choice of John Edwards (a northeastern liberal and a southern moderate), and McCain's choice of Palin (a western moderate and a western conservative). As Kerry's and McCain's experience suggests, however, such regional or ideological balancing does not ensure success. Other vice-presidential choices do not follow this pattern. Mondale's selection of Geraldine A. Ferraro in 1984 broke with major party tradition in more ways than one: Representative Ferraro was the first woman to be nominated for the vice presidency, the first Italian American to be nominated for national office, and the first nominee to be anointed prior to the opening of the convention. Similarly, George H. W. Bush's surprising selection of a young, telegenic U.S. senator, Dan Quayle of Indiana, in 1988, reflected his desire to merge conservative and generational appeals. And in 2000 Gore chose Lieberman, a fellow moderate, although Lieberman was perceived as somewhat more conservative than Gore on so-called "morality" issues. The selection of Lieberman, the first Jewish vice-presidential nominee, energized Democrats, providing the ticket with a double-digit bounce in the polls the week following the convention.

Arguably, regional and ideological balancing have become less important in recent years. Seeking to give the Democratic Party a moderate and youthful image in 1992, Clinton chose Gore, a senator from Tennessee, as his running mate, creating the party's first all-southern ticket since 1852.[62] The strategy proved successful: stressing change, the "new Democrats" carried five southern states and received strong support from younger (and older) voters throughout the country. In 2000 George W. Bush from Texas won the White House after choosing a fellow westerner, Dick Cheney of Wyoming, who had been living in Texas for nearly a decade. Both Bush and Cheney brought strong conservative credentials to the race. Obama's choice of Biden brought together two relatively liberal senators. Although Biden hailed from Delaware and Obama from Illinois, it did not appear that region was important in the selection process. Rather, Biden was seen as one of the party's leading members on national security, an area of weakness for Obama.

Furthermore, recent experience suggests certain pitfalls in choosing a running mate who is not in ideological agreement with the top of the ticket. For almost everyone, including the pundits, Dole's choice of Jack Kemp as his running mate in 1996 was surprising, not only because of their strained personal relationship but also because of their incompatibility on certain issues. In the press, Dole's choice of Kemp was framed as cynical—he hoped to get a lift in the polls, to reenergize his campaign, to unify his party, and to make his economic plan (to cut taxes while also balancing the budget) the centerpiece of his campaign. Similarly, McCain and Palin seemed to be working at cross-purposes at times toward the end of the 2008 election season. Palin was at her strongest when trumpeting socially conservative views and questioning Obama's commitment to "American values," but McCain seemed uncomfortable with this line of attack as the campaign wound down.

The main point is that the presidential candidate has a great deal of leeway in choosing the vice-presidential nominee. Naturally, the need to reward or placate a certain party element reduces the list of possible choices. Except for the most doctrinaire presidential candidate, the prime consideration is to choose a running mate who strengthens the ticket in terms of the party's strategy for winning the election.

The Media, the Nominating Process, and the Parties

It would be hard to exaggerate the importance of the print and electronic media in shaping the presidential nominating process. Not surprisingly, media influence is as controversial as it is pivotal. Critics charge that the media are preoccupied with the competitive, or "horse race," aspects of the presidential campaign and give too little attention to the candidates' records and issue positions. Horse race stories are easy for journalists to write, for television reporters to portray, and for the public to understand. These stories have a standard format: where the candidates have been and where they are going; how their strategies have emerged; how crowds and organized groups are responding to them; how politicians evaluate them and their campaigns; how they have dealt with events and mistakes; who has endorsed them; and, most important, who is winning and who is losing. What the campaign is all about—the issues and policy questions—is ordinarily lost in these accounts.

Numerous studies have shown that more than half of all stories on presidential campaigns have a horse race theme.[63] During the 2008 election season, 71 percent of coverage focused on winning and losing, while only 13 percent was devoted to substantive issues.[64]

Another feature of media coverage of nominating campaigns singled out by critics is the practice of focusing on front-runners at the expense of providing information on other candidates' campaigns. The early public opinion polls provide the initial impetus to prepare press and television stories on the front-runners. Thin on evidence, these stories nevertheless generate additional coverage of the leaders, even before the first caucus or primary is held. In natural progression, the candidates who win or place well in the Iowa precinct caucuses, the New Hampshire primary, or both become media darlings and gain even more coverage. The "spin" put on the election by candidates, handlers, and the media is what really counts. A narrow win can sometimes be translated into a striking victory in the next day's news or treated as a virtual loss, because the winner's vote failed to meet expectations set by the media.[65] Ed Muskie "lost" the 1972 Democratic primary in New Hampshire to McGovern despite receiving 46 percent of the vote to McGovern's 37 percent. *Washington Post* reporter David Broder had declared that Muskie could "win" only if he garnered more than 50 percent of the vote, an interpretation adopted by the rest of the news media. Muskie's candidacy soon collapsed.

The media are particularly influential in the early phase of the presidential nominating process. Television and press journalists sort out the candidates (ranking them as "the hopeless, the plausible, and the likely, with substantial differences between the three in the amount and quality of coverage"),[66] establish performance expectations, boost some campaigns while writing off others, and launch the bandwagons. Their evaluations create winners and losers. Candidates who capture the media's attention are rewarded out of proportion to the significance of the contests and perhaps to their shares of the vote. Early winners and surprise candidates gain momentum in this system of "lotteries driven by media expectations and candidate name recognition."[67]

The media also play a critical role in publicizing the factional appeals of candidates in primaries and caucuses, as the candidates forsake coalition building and instead seek to mobilize narrow ideological, religious, ethnic, or sectional followings. The more crowded the field, the greater the probability that an active, passionate, well-organized faction can keep the candidate in contention from one Tuesday to the next in the crucial early weeks of the season. Through extensive coverage of the campaign, the media help the candidates to attract, instruct, and mobilize their distinctive factional followings.[68]

Campaign schedules, speeches, and statements all revolve around the media. Candidates fly from one airport tarmac or television market to the next in their quest for press attention and free media time on local television stations. Nothing may be more important. Brief stops are the order of the day. It is not uncommon in the days leading up to Super Tuesday—when most of the action is concentrated—for some candidates to visit five or six states (or, more accurately, assorted airports in these states) in a single day, not to see crowds of voters but to secure a few seconds of exposure on the local evening news—and, with luck, a snippet on the network news.

The influence of the media on the presidential nominating process is obviously pervasive. But two broad effects stand out. The first is that the media have undercut the position of party elites. Free media time and paid advertising are a much more effective means for influencing mass electorates than working through party leaders and party organizations. The media also provide an excellent opportunity for candidates, tutored by media consultants, to raise campaign money by gaining public attention. Impressive televised speeches sometimes produce a flood of campaign contributions. The media are now used to "deliver" votes and money in a way that state and local politicians did a generation ago. What is more, political consultants and handlers are at least as important as any party professional in shaping campaign decisions.

Second, the media have, to a large extent, transformed the national party convention. They did so by becoming the vehicle by which candidates and candidate organizations distanced themselves from the party organization. Today's conventions are run by candidates and their organizations; the influence that party and elected officials wield is a function of their affiliation with candidate organizations. Typically, the nominee is known long in advance of the convention. In virtually every phase, then, the party convention is a media event. Activities are scheduled at times that will produce maximum television audiences. Deals are struck to avoid controversy. Politics is sanitized. Celebrities are properly honored. Speeches are kept brief. Trivial events and "news" are magnified by television reporters scurrying around for interviews. Orchestration and entertainment pervade the convention agenda as leaders strive to showcase their candidates, enhance the party's image, and hold an audience notorious for its short attention span. Elaborate efforts are made to avoid boring the viewers.

National party conventions have turned into spectacles, or made-for-TV shows, because they no longer actually choose the candidate; because they are trying to stay in business in a mass-oriented political system; because they are driven by the entertainment imperative; because party leaders prefer choreography to controversy; and because the media control the interpretation, and thus shape the politics, of the preconvention season. Not a great deal—maybe nothing—is left for the convention to decide.

NOTES

1. Does a hard-fought, divisive primary hurt the party's chances in the general election? Although the question is not settled, the preponderance of evidence suggests that conflictual (or competitive) primaries do have an adverse impact on the parties' chances for victory in the general election. Support for this interpretation appears in Patrick J. Kenney and Tom W. Rice, "The Effect of Primary Divisiveness in Gubernatorial and Senatorial Elections," *Journal of Politics* 46 (August 1984): 904–915; and Robert A. Bernstein, "Divisive Primaries Do Hurt: U.S. Senate Races, 1956–1972," *American Political Science Review* 71 (June 1977): 540–545. But for a study that finds the relationship weak, see Richard Born, "The Influence of House Primary Divisiveness on General Election Margins, 1962–76," *Journal of Politics* 43 (August 1981): 640–661. Preoccupation with the effects of divisive primaries may, however, lead researchers to ignore the positive, *mobilizing* effects of participation in nominating campaigns. See the study by Walter J. Stone, Lonnie Rae Atkeson, and Ronald B. Rapoport, "Turning On or Turning Off? Mobilization and Demobilization Effects of Participation

in Presidential Nominating Campaigns," *American Journal of Political Science* 36 (August 1992): 665–691.

2. Alan Ware, *The American Direct Primary: Party Institutionalization and Transformation in North America* (New York: Cambridge University Press, 2002).

3. *Tashjian v. Republican Party of Connecticut,* 479 U.S. 208 (1986). See a comprehensive analysis of the *Tashjian* decision by Leon D. Epstein, "Will American Political Parties Be Privatized?" *Journal of Law and Politics* 5 (Winter 1989): 239–274.

4. The states with the purest form of open primary are Hawaii, Idaho, Michigan, Minnesota, North Dakota, Utah, Vermont, and Wisconsin. See a comprehensive classification scheme for state primary systems in Malcolm E. Jewell and David M. Olson, *Political Parties and Elections in American States* (Chicago: Dorsey Press, 1988), 89–94.

5. Karen Kaufmann, James Gimpel, and Adam Hoffman, "A Promise Fulfilled? Open Primaries and Representation," *Journal of Politics* 65 (2003): 457–476.

6. Lynn Vavreck, "The Reasoning Voter Meets the Strategic Candidate: Signals and Specificity in Campaign Advertising, 1998," *American Politics Research* 29 (September 2001): 507–529.

7. Gary D. Wekkin, "Why Crossover Voters Are Not 'Mischievous Voters': The Segmented Partisanship Hypothesis," *American Politics Quarterly* 19 (April 1991): 229–257.

8. See "Limbaugh Safe from Voter-Fraud Charges," *Columbus Dispatch,* March 28, 2008.

9. See "Clinton and McCain Win in California, Obama Stays Close as G.O.P. Rivals Lag," *New York Times,* February 5, 2008.

10. See "Federal Judge Strikes Down Arizona's Open Primary," *Congress Daily,* August 6, 2002, 12. See also "Appeals Court Rules Part of Open Primary Violates Party Rights," Associated Press, December 9, 2003.

11. See *California Democratic Party v. Jones,* 530 U.S. 567 (2000). Also see "Court Strikes Down California Primary Placing All Parties on a Single Ballot," *New York Times,* June 27, 2000.

12. *Democratic Party of Washington State v. Reed,* 343 F. 3d (2003).

13. For a complete treatment of the effects of two-stage primary elections, see James Adams and Samuel Merrill, "Candidate and Party Strategies in Two-Stage Elections Beginning with a Primary," *American Journal of Political Science* 52 (April 2008): 344–359.

14. See "Court Strikes Down California Primary."

15. *Washington State Grange v. Washington State Republican Party,* 552 U.S. ____ (2008), at 10.

16. The observations made in this paragraph are based mainly on an analysis by Charles D. Hadley, "The Impact of the Louisiana Open Elections System Reform," *State Government* 58, no. 4 (1986): 152–157. For a general analysis of factionalism, see Earl Black, "A Theory of Southern Factionalism," *Journal of Politics* 45 (August 1983): 594–614.

17. For an unorthodox argument that the intraparty competition afforded by primaries encourages the parties to be responsive to voters, see John G. Geer and Mark E. Shere, "Party Competition and the Prisoner's Dilemma: An Argument for the Direct Primary," *Journal of Politics* 54 (August 1992): 741–761.

18. See Malcolm E. Jewell and Sarah A. Morehouse, "What Are Party Endorsements Worth? A Study of Preprimary Gubernatorial Endorsements," *American Politics Quarterly* 24 (July 1996): 338–362.

19. Jewell and Olson, *Political Parties and Elections,* 94–104. Also see a study of the various factors that influence the value of a political party's preprimary endorsement to the candidate who received it.

20. These themes appear in Frank J. Sorauf, *Party Politics in America* (Boston: Little, Brown, 1980), 220–224.

21. Thomas Mann and Norman Ornstein, *Vital Statistics on Congress* (Washington, D.C.: American Enterprise Institute, 2001).

22. See American University's Center for the Study of the American Electorate, "The Primary Turnout Story," October 1, 2008.

23. Denis G. Sullivan, Jeffrey L. Pressman, and F. Christopher Arterton, *Explorations in Convention Decision Making* (San Francisco: Freeman, 1976), 17.

24. Ibid., 20–21.

25. These data were taken from the Federal Election Commission's Web site, www.fec.gov.

26. See the caucus turnout figures at http://elections.gmu.edu/Turnout_2008P.html.

27. Ideologically extreme candidates tend to run better in caucus states than in primary states. See Barbara Norrander, "Nomination Choices: Caucus and Primary Outcomes, 1976–88," *American Journal of Political Science* 37 (May 1993): 343–364.

28. Changing from one system to another has unanticipated consequences. Richard W. Boyd has shown that frequent elections depress turnout. States that switch from caucus-convention systems to direct primaries will have a lower general election turnout. See his article, "The Effects of Primaries and Statewide Races on Voter Turnout," *Journal of Politics* 51 (August 1989): 730–739.

29. Stephen J. Wayne, *The Road to the White House 2000* (Boston: Bedford/St. Martins, 2001), 340–343; and Rhodes Cook, *Race for the Presidency: Winning the 2004 Nomination* (Washington, D.C.: CQ Press, 2004).

30. Turnout in presidential primaries tends to be highest in the states with high levels of education, facilitative legal provisions on voting, and competitive two-party elections. High turnout is not associated with high levels of campaign spending. See Patrick J. Kenney and Tom W. Rice, "Voter Turnout in Presidential Primaries: A Cross-Sectional Examination," *Political Behavior* 7, no. 1 (1985): 101–112.

31. American University's Center for the Study of the American Electorate, "The Primary Turnout Story."

32. For discussion of Obama's strategic approach, see Justin Sizemore, "How Obama Did It," *Center for Politics*, June 5, 2008.

33. Clinton maintained a lead in superdelegate support until early May when Obama's superdelegate count began to surge. See "On Day of Last Primary, Obama's Superdelegate Surge," *New York Times*, June 3, 2008.

34. James I. Lengle, Diane Owen, and Molly W. Sonner, "Divisive Nominating Mechanisms and Democratic Party Electoral Prospects," *Journal of Politics* 57 (May 1995): 370–383.

35. Priscilla L. Southwell, "Rules as 'Unseen Participants': The Democratic Presidential Nominating Process," *American Politics Quarterly* 20 (January 1992): 64.

36. Barry C. Burden, "The Nominations: Rules, Strategies, and Uncertainty," in *The Elections of 2008*, ed. Michael Nelson (Washington, D.C.: CQ Press, 2009), 36; and James Ceaser, Andrew E. Busch, and John J. Pitney, *Epic Journey: The 2008 Elections and American Politics* (Lanham, Md.: Rowman and Littlefield, 2009), 117.

37. William J. Crotty, *Political Reform and the American Experiment* (New York: Crowell, 1977), 255–260.

38. *New York Times*, September 1, 2008.

39. Thomas Patterson, *Out of Order* (New York: Knopf, 1993).

40. See William C. Adams, "As New Hampshire Goes . . . ," in *Media and Momentum: The New Hampshire Primary and Nomination Politics*, ed. Gary R. Orren and Nelson W. Polsby (Chatham, N.J.: Chatham House, 1987), 42–49.

41. Are the voters who take part in presidential primaries ideologically unrepresentative? To some extent, it depends on the type of primary. Kaufmann et al. show that ideologically, open primary voters resemble general election voters more than do closed primaries voters. Kaufmann et al., "A Promise Fulfilled? Open Primaries and Representation."

42. See "Small Online Contributions Add Up to Huge Fund-Raising Edge for Obama," *New York Times*, February 20, 2008.

43. Campaign Finance Institute, press release, "Reality Check: Obama Received About the Same Percentage from Small Donors in 2008 as Bush in 2004," November 24, 2008, www.cfinst.org/pr/prRelease.aspx?ReleaseID=216.

44. For a study of how state party leaders seek to enhance media coverage of their state's primary or caucus, see David S. Castle, "Media Coverage of Presidential Primaries," *American Politics Quarterly* 19 (January 1991): 33–42.

45. See "Clinton, Obama Top $100 Million for 2007," *Wall Street Journal*, January 1, 2008.

46. Ibid.

47. See "Small Online Contributions Add Up."

48. David Redlawsk, Daniel Bowen, and Caroline Tolbert, "Comparing Caucus and Registered Voter Support for the 2008 Presidential Candidates in Iowa," *PS: Political Science & Politics* 41 (January 2008):129–138.

49. *Congressional Quarterly Weekly Report*, August 17, 1996, 2299.

50. See Dan Balz, "Democratic Unit Votes to Add Early '08 Contests," *Washington Post*, December 11, 2005, A11; and Adam Nagourney "Democratic Panel Calls for More Early Contests in '08," *New York Times*, December 11, 2005, A51.

51. Larry M. Bartels, *Presidential Primaries* (Princeton, N.J.: Princeton University Press, 1988).

52. For evidence that heavy candidate spending influences the outcome of the presidential nominating process, see Audrey A. Haynes, Paul-Henri Gurian, and Stephen M. Nichols, "The Role of Candidate Spending in Presidential Nomination Campaigns," *Journal of Politics* 59 (February 1997): 213–225.

53. No one articulates this thesis better than Patterson in *Out of Order*.

54. Marty Cohen, David Karol, Hans Noel, and John Zaller, *The Party Decides: Presidential Nominations Before and After Reform* (Chicago: University of Chicago Press, 2008).

55. But see a study of the 1980 presidential primaries that finds that voters made little use of candidates' issue positions in deciding how to vote. The most frequent correlates of vote choice are the qualities of the candidates. Barbara Norrander, "Correlates of Vote Choice in the 1980 Presidential Primaries," *Journal of Politics* 48 (February 1986): 156–166.

56. *New York Times*, September 1, 2008.

57. *New York Times*, August 25, 2008, and September 1, 2008.

58. Barry C. Burden, "The Nominations: Rules, Strategies, and Uncertainty," in *The Elections of 2008*.

59. One of the most important functions of the convention is the "rally function"—bringing the party together and creating enthusiasm for the ticket. A manifestation of its effect is that candidates usually realize a "bump" of five to seven percentage points in public opinion surveys. See James E. Campbell, Lynna L. Cherry, and Kenneth A. Wink, "The Convention Bump," *American Politics Quarterly* 20 (July 1992): 287–307.

60. An exception to this rule occurred in 1956 when Adlai Stevenson, the Democratic presidential nominee, created a stir by declining to express a preference for his vice-presidential running mate. Left to its own devices, the convention quickly settled

on a choice between Sens. Estes Kefauver and John F. Kennedy. Kefauver, who had been an active candidate for the presidency, won a narrow victory. Kennedy came off even better; he launched his candidacy for the presidential nomination in 1960.

61. The preference of party professionals for a balanced ticket grows out of their instinct for the conservation of the party and their understanding of the electorate. In the view of party professionals, the ticket should have broad appeal, not an ideological or sectional focus. The factors that ordinarily come under review in the consideration of balance are geography, political philosophy, religion, and factional recognition.

62. Does balancing a ticket geographically make a difference? The answer is that it makes some positive difference if the candidate is from a small state, but "it is the presidential candidates who dominate the nation's politics." See Robert L. Dudley and Ronald B. Rapoport, "Vice Presidential Candidates and the Home State Advantage: Playing Second Banana at Home and on the Road," *American Journal of Political Science* 33 (May 1989): 537–540.

63. Doris A. Graber, *Mass Media and American Politics*, 4th ed. (Washington, D.C.: CQ Press, 1993), 273–275. The tendency to treat elections as horse races did not begin with television, but horse race coverage increased dramatically in the television era. Although coverage of policy issues has declined somewhat in recent years, Lee Sigelman and David Bullock report, it is still greater than it was during the newspaper era. See their article, "Candidates, Issues, Horse Races, and Hoopla: Presidential Campaign Coverage, 1888–1988," *American Politics Quarterly* 19 (January 1991): 5–32.

64. Tom Rosenstiel and Bill Kovach, "Lessons of the Election," www.stateofthe newsmedia.org/2009/printable_special_chapter.htm.

65. See Christine F. Ridout, "The Role of Media Coverage of Iowa and New Hampshire in the 1988 Democratic Nomination," *American Politics Quarterly* 19 (January 1991): 48–53.

66. William G. Mayer, "The New Hampshire Primary: A Historical Overview," in *Media and Momentum*, ed. Orren and Polsby, 16.

67. Henry E. Brady and Richard Johnston, "What's the Primary Message: Horse Race or Issue Journalism?" in *Media and Momentum*, ed. Orren and Polsby, 128.

68. Nelson W. Polsby, *Consequences of Party Reform* (New York: Oxford University Press, 1983), 67.

4 CAMPAIGNS AND CAMPAIGN FINANCE

POLITICAL CAMPAIGNS ARE DIFFICULT TO DESCRIBE for one very good reason: they come in an extraordinary variety of shapes and sizes. Whether there is such a thing as a typical campaign is open to serious debate. Campaigns differ depending on the office sought (executive, legislative, or judicial), the level of government (national, state, or local), the legal and political environments (partisan or non-partisan election, competitive or noncompetitive constituency), and the initial advantages or disadvantages of the candidates (incumbent or nonincumbent, well known or little known), among other things.

Standards by which to measure and evaluate the effectiveness of campaigns are not easy to develop because of the many variables that intrude on campaign decisions and on voter choice. Does the winning party owe its victory to a superior campaign or would it have won anyway? Data needed to answer this question are elusive. What is evident is that strategies appropriate to one campaign may be less appropriate or even inappropriate to another. Tactics that work at one time or in one place may not work under other circumstances. Organizational arrangements that satisfy one party may not satisfy the other. Campaigns are loaded with imponderables that neither the party organizations nor the candidates can control. In most cases it is not immediately clear when a miscalculation has been made, how serious it may be, or how best to repair the damage.

Despite the variability and uncertainty that characterize political campaigns, a few general requirements are imposed on all candidates and parties. Candidates making a serious bid for votes must acquire certain resources and meet certain problems. Whatever their perspective of the campaign, candidates will have to deal with matters of organization, strategy, and finances.

Campaign Organization

Very likely the single most important fact to know about campaign organization is that the regular party organizations are ill equipped to organize and conduct campaigns by themselves. Of necessity, they look to outsiders for assistance in all kinds of party work and for the development and staffing of auxiliary campaign organizations. A multiplicity of organizational units is created in every major election for the promotion of particular candidacies.[1] Some in business will organize to support the Republican nominee, and others will organize to support the Democratic nominee. And the same is true for educators, lawyers, physicians, advertising executives, and even political independents, to mention but a few. Seth Masket has noted the influence of what he labels "informal party organizations," consisting of influential officeholders, interest groups, political activists, and brokers (fund-raisers, lobbyists, and campaign consultants).[2] At times these groups may work in harmony with the regular party organizations (perhaps to the point of being wholly dominated by them), and at other times they function as virtually independent units, seemingly oblivious to the requirements for communication or for coordination of their activities with those of other party or auxiliary units.

The regular party organizations share influence with an array of powerful interest groups that employ a variety of committees to shape political campaigns. Many groups contribute and spend money on behalf of candidates through political action committees (PACs). Among the best known PACs are the American Medical Association Political Action Committee, the Realtors Political Action Committee, the Sierra Club Political Action Committee, the National Rifle Association Political Victory Fund, and the AFL-CIO Committee on Political Education. In 2008 PACs contributed $386 million to candidates for Congress, a little more than 31 percent of total campaign receipts. In addition, interest groups use an array of "soft money" committees to spend substantial sums in federal elections. Known as 527 and 501(c) committees because of their tax code status, these groups—especially 501(c) committees—are regulated largely by the IRS, not the Federal Election Commission (FEC). As a result, their receipts and expenditures are difficult to track. Some soft money committees are sponsored by well-known interest groups that also sponsor a PAC. The Service Employees International Union, a labor union with a sizable federal PAC, spent more than $25 million in soft money from its 527 committee in the 2008 elections. Other soft money committees have close ties to major industries. An example is America's Agenda: Healthcare for Kids, a 501(c)4 committee that spent more than $13 million a month before the 2008 election and is supported largely by the pharmaceutical industry. Still other soft money outfits, such as Freedom's Watch, which supports Republicans, and America Votes, which backs Democrats, are closely aligned with their respective parties. Regulating this growing group activity is a challenge for the FEC.[3]

At the top of the heterogeneous cluster of party and auxiliary campaign committees are the campaign organizations created by the individual candidates. Virtually all candidates for important, competitive offices develop personal campaign organizations to counsel them on strategy and issues, assist with travel arrangements and speeches, raise money, defend their interests in party circles, and try to coordinate their activities with those of other candidates and campaign units. The size of a candidate's personal organization is likely to vary according to the significance of the office and the competitiveness of the constituency. A member from a safe congressional district, who is used to easy elections, has less need for an elaborate campaign organization than does a candidate from a competitive district.

In some campaigns the regular party organization is reduced to the status of just another spectator. Rather than rely on the party organizations to direct their campaigns, these candidates employ professional management firms.[4] Most facets of American politics today come under the influence of public relations specialists and advertising firms. Possessing resources that the party organizations cannot match, they raise funds, recruit campaign workers, develop issues, gain endorsements, write speeches, arrange campaign schedules, direct the candidate's television appearances, and prepare campaign literature, films, and advertising. Indeed, they often create the overall campaign strategy and dominate day-to-day decision making.

Given all of this, it should not be surprising that few aspects of American politics have changed more dramatically than the way candidates contend for office. Barbara G. Salmore and Stephen A. Salmore wrote:

> The role of the party boss has been taken over by the political consultant; that of the volunteer party worker by the paid telephone bank caller. Most voters learn about candidates not at political rallies but from television advertising and computer-generated direct mail; candidates generally gather information about voters not from the ward leader but from the pollster. The money to fuel campaigns comes less from the party organizations and "fat cats" and more from direct mail solicitation of individuals and special-interest political action committees. In short, candidates have become individual entrepreneurs, largely set free from party control or discipline.[5]

This is not to say that parties have no influence in campaigns. Indeed, the parties' ability to spend heavily in close contests can help tip the balance in such races. But in *most* contests, party efforts supplement those of the candidate and are designed to help candidates succeed in a candidate-centered environment.

Campaign Strategy

The paramount goal of all major party campaigns is to form a coalition of sufficient size to bring victory to the candidate or party. Ordinarily, the early days of the campaign are devoted to developing and testing a broad campaign strategy designed to produce that winning coalition. In the most general sense, strategy should be seen as "an overall plan for acquiring and using the resources needed for a campaign." In developing this broad strategy, candidates, their advisers, and party leaders must take into consideration a number of factors, including:

1. the principal themes to be developed during the campaign;
2. the issues to be emphasized and exploited;

3. the candidate's personal qualities to be emphasized;[6]
4. the specific groups and geographical areas to which appeals will be directed;
5. the acquisition of financial support and endorsements;
6. the timing of campaign activities;
7. the relationship of the candidate to the party organization and to factions within it; and
8. the uses to be made of the communications media, particularly television.[7]

To the casual observer, there appear to be no limits to the number of major and minor strategies open to a resourceful candidate. In reality, important constraints shape and define the candidate's options. Campaign strategy is affected by the political, social, and economic environments; the competitiveness of the district; the nature of the electorate; the quality and representativeness of the party ticket; the unity of the party; the presence of an incumbent; the election timetable (a presidential or off-year election); and the predispositions and commitments of political interest groups. Although it is difficult to weigh its significance, the temper of the times also affects the candidate's overall plan of action. Whatever the impact of these constraints, most are beyond the control of the candidate; they are simply conditions to which the candidate must adjust and adapt. The candidate's overall strategy must be consonant with the given restrictions of the campaign environment.[8]

Do Campaigns Matter?

Some evidence suggests that the campaign environment matters so much that it all but renders the campaign itself meaningless. The earliest studies of political behavior showed that very few people actually changed their vote intention from the beginning of the campaign to the end. Almost without exception, those who said in September that they planned to vote for Dwight D. Eisenhower or Adlai Stevenson actually voted for Eisenhower or Stevenson in November.[9] Indeed, a number of economists and political scientists have devised relatively simple ways to predict election outcomes based on the country's economic performance. Political scientists Michael Lewis-Beck and Tom Rice have predicted the winner of thirteen of the past sixteen presidential contests—and ten of eleven before 1992—using data collected months before the campaigns ever began.[10]

Nevertheless, campaigns are far from meaningless. In the same way that well-known consumer brands like Coca-Cola and McDonald's advertise vigorously, well-known political candidates take their campaigns seriously. If they fail to engage the public, they are likely to lose market share to their competitors. In that sense, it is important to realize that campaigns are designed to do much more than change people's voting intentions. Instead, the most important goal of a political campaign is to *get core supporters out to vote*. A campaign needs to reinforce the existing predispositions of regular voters. A great many elections are won or lost depending on the turnout of the party faithful; so a campaign must take great pains to fire up its base by whatever means it can. One reason negative advertising is used so often in close races is that it increases turnout, especially among supporters of the candidate running the negative advertisement.[11] The choice of issues to highlight can also be important in firing up the party faithful. In 2004 conservative groups placed initiatives to ban gay marriage on the ballots of thirteen states in an effort to increase turnout among conservative voters. Some believe that this move in Ohio may have been decisive in providing George W. Bush with his margin of victory. In 2006 liberal activists placed a stem cell initiative on the Missouri ballot that may have energized enough left-of-center voters to tip the Senate election that year to Democrat Claire McCaskill over incumbent Republican Jim Talent.

Unlike campaigns waged a few decades ago, when attracting moderate voters was the goal, recent elections have emphasized activating core supporters. In 2004 the Bush campaign's pollsters decided months before the election that most Americans had already made up their minds and few undecided voters remained to be won. The campaign believed that the key to winning the election was to be more effective than their opponents at turning out their committed supporters. As a result, they adopted a "play-to-the-base" strategy, in which Bush highlighted issues of particular import to staunch conservatives, and the Bush win convinced some political professionals that such a strategy is the most effective. Playing to the base can, however, carry certain costs. In 2008 John McCain also ran a campaign designed to fire up his conservative base. It worked with conservatives but alienated moderate voters, who voted overwhelmingly for Barack Obama (60 percent to 39 percent).

Second, candidates must *activate latent support.* Successful campaigns often turn on the ability of candidates to activate potential voters among the groups that ordinarily support their party.[12] For the Democratic candidate, this means that special efforts must be directed toward African Americans, Hispanics, Jews, blue-collar workers, union members, urban residents, women, and members of low-income households. For the Republican candidate, this rule dictates a similar effort to motivate Protestants (especially evangelical Christians), whites, suburban or rural residents, and business and managerial elements. Efforts may also be made to motivate powerful single-issue groups, such as those in the pro-choice and pro-life movements. It is important to minimize defections to third party candidates. Indeed, had Al Gore received even a tiny portion of the more than ninety thousand votes cast for Ralph Nader in Florida, he would have been elected president in 2000.

The third general strategy produces the weakest results, but it aims to *change the opposition.*[13] The massive party defections seen in the 1964, 1972, and 1984 elections occur less often today because voters discern important differences between the parties. Although many partisans cast ballots for third party candidate Ross Perot in 1992 and 1996, few voted for the other major party nominee.[14] In terms of major party voters, the winning party can generally count on the support of about 90 percent of its identifiers; the losing party generally gets the vote of around 85 percent of its partisans. In 2008, 89 percent of Democrats voted for Obama, and 90 percent of Republicans voted for McCain.[15]

Sunshine Hillygus and Todd Shields persuasively show that the most effective way for campaigns to change the opposition is to highlight certain issues. Because not all Democrats agree with their party on every issue, and the same is true of Republicans, effective campaigns identify the issues on which a substantial number of their opponents' partisans disagree with their party and draw attention to those issues. Many working-class Democrats are conservative on social issues such as gun rights and abortion, so Republican campaigns can target these voters with mailings or phone calls emphasizing the Democratic candidate's stand in favor of gun control or abortion rights. Similarly, many upper-income Republicans do not share their party's position on stem cell research and immigration, which provides Democratic campaigns with opportunities to target these cross-pressured voters. The key to a successful campaign is making the issues on which partisans disagree with their party more important to them than the issues on which they do agree with their party.[16]

Fourth, campaigns also attempt to mobilize new voters. Realizing how hard it is to get a Republican to vote for a Democratic candidate or vice versa, campaigns may find it useful to try to change the potential universe of voters. Obama's campaign team worked to bring nontraditional voters into the process by suggesting that he was a different kind of politician. His efforts with people under age thirty, ordinarily the least participatory group in American public life, were remarkably successful. Exit polls showed that fully 11 percent of voters in 2008 were voting for the first time and that they favored Obama over McCain by 69 percent to 30 percent. Such a strategy is fraught with danger, however. Regular nonparticipants are among the most difficult people for campaigns to reach, and if a campaign fails to energize them, it has wasted precious campaign resources. But, if these efforts are successful, the payoff can be significant. Eric Plutzer demonstrates that voting is a tough habit to break.[17] Moreover, once people vote for candidates of one party in one election, they tend to do so in future elections. Taken together, Obama's success mobilizing first time voters in 2008 could be a boon to the Democratic Party for years to come.

Once campaigns attract the attention of voters, day-to-day events, whether large or small, tend to be meaningful. Examining presidential campaigns in particular, Daron R. Shaw demonstrates that a number of campaign occurrences, such as party conventions, debates, campaign appearances, and gaffes, significantly affect a candidate's standing in the polls.[18] If a candidate does well in a debate or makes an embarrassing mistake on the campaign trail, his support in the polls will increase or decrease to some degree. Indeed, at least one political observer boldly declared that Gore's excessive sighing during his first debate with Bush in 2000 cost him the election.[19] A presidential candidate's visit to a state increases his poll-standing there. Although events affect subsequent, immediate *poll results* more than they do *election outcomes*, Shaw confirms that they have some effect on the outcome. That said, these short-term forces do not necessarily determine who wins and who loses. In 2004, most observers agreed that John Kerry won all three of his debates with George W. Bush, but he still lost the election. It is likely, however, that Bush would have won more comfortably had Kerry not done so well in the debates.

No one is really certain what does or does not work from campaign to campaign. Myths and facts are mixed in about equal proportion in the lore of campaign strategy. Indeed, it is scarcely ever apparent in advance which strategies are likely to be most productive and which least productive or even counterproductive. A common mistake of postmortems is to assert that a certain event or stand or mannerism of a candidate caused him to win or lose. Often no one knows whether the election result was because of this factor or despite it. A spectacular event—whether a dramatic proposal, an attack, or something in the news outside the campaign—is like a revolving door. It wins some votes and loses others.

Indeed, campaign decisions may be shaped as much by chance and the ability of the candidate to seize on events as by the careful formulation of a broad and coherent plan of attack. During the 1960 presidential campaign John F. Kennedy decided to telephone Coretta Scott King to express his concern over the welfare of her husband, the Reverend Dr. Martin Luther King Jr., who had been jailed in Atlanta following a sit-in at a department store. There is no evidence that Kennedy's decision—perhaps as critical as any of the campaign—was based on a comprehensive assessment of alternatives or possible consequences. Instead, according to Theodore H. White, the decision "was impulsive, direct, and immediate. . . . The entire episode received only casual notice from the generality of American citizens in the heat of the last three weeks of the Presidential campaign. But in the [African American] community the Kennedy intervention rang like a carillon."[20]

In contrast to such dramatic moments at the presidential level, congressional campaigns and election outcomes carry few surprises. Candidates generally win where they are expected to win and lose where they are expected to lose. Incumbent House members who lose in their bids to retain office are almost as rare as some entries on the endangered species list. Because states are ordinarily more heterogeneous than House districts, senators have more reason to worry over what the voters will deal them, but they too campaign from a position of strength. Congressional campaigns go as expected for three major reasons.

First, incumbents enjoy overwhelming advantages: a public record to which they can point, resources that permit them to assist constituents with their problems, the franking privilege (permission to mail without paying postage), generous travel allowances, and a staff and offices. Voters also are more familiar with incumbents than with their challengers.

Second, members of Congress campaign year-round. Their staffs handle constituent problems, and members return home almost every weekend. Everyone in the member's entourage knows that reelections are won in nonelection years.

Third, incumbents have a much easier time raising money than challengers typically do. In 2008 the average House incumbent raised and spent more than four times as much money as did the average House challenger.[21] That greater campaign resources translate into easy victories for incumbents provides further evidence that campaigns do, in fact, matter. When campaign resources are more evenly balanced, as in presidential elections, victory is uncertain. When one side has a pronounced advantage, it almost always triumphs.

Issues and Campaigns

Donald Stokes distinguishes between two types of campaign issues: *position* and *valence*.[22] Position issues are those on which the parties have taken differing stances on policy questions, such as government spending on programs that benefit the poor or support for affirmative action. These concerns may be significant, but modern election campaigns are dominated by valence issues. According to John J. Dilulio Jr., these are:

> issues on which the voters distinguish parties and candidates not by their real or perceived differences on position issues but by the degree to which they are linked in the voters' minds with conditions, symbols, or goals that are almost universally approved of or disapproved of by the electorate, such as economic prosperity, public corruption, and resolute leadership.[23]

The development of specific stands on positional issues is of somewhat limited importance in designing campaign strategy. Because most Americans do not follow politics closely, if at all, voters frequently are unable to identify the positions of the candidates, particularly in congressional elections.[24] Also, although some voters are sensitive to the specific issues generated in a campaign, many others are preoccupied with a candidate's image, personality, and style. Candidates are often judged less by what they say than by how they say it, less by their achievements than by their personalities. Voters' perceptions of a candidate's character are highly important, especially in presidential contests. Scandals in government typically have a major impact on the strategies of subsequent campaigns, serving to heighten the significance of a candidate's alleged personal virtues—particularly those of honesty and sincerity—and to diminish the significance of positional issues. "I don't think issues mean a great deal about whether you win or lose," observes a U.S. senator. "I think issues give you a chance to [demonstrate] your honesty and candor."[25] Along the same lines, a Democratic media consultant contends, "I don't think inflation is an issue. Who's for it? . . . The real issue is which of the two candidates would best be able to deal with [it]."[26]

According to exit polls conducted in 2008 as analyzed by Gerald Pomper, voters favoring Obama or McCain cited sharply different reasons for their choices. Obama supporters stressed concerns about the economy, health care, energy, and Iraq, and McCain voters focused on terrorism. The issue that was important to a higher percentage of Americans by far was not a position issue, but the economy. By and large, Americans do not care much about the means followed to improve the economy; they are more interested in the outcome. Although Obama held the advantage on the issues, the split between the candidates was more even on voters' evaluations of the candidates' personal traits. Voters who preferred McCain emphasized his experience and believed that he shared their values. Those drawn to Obama singled out his ability to bring about change and their perception that he cares about people (see Table 4-1).[27]

To the extent that issues matter, they are driven less by the specifics of the plans of competing candidates and more by people's general views about the parties' ability to solve different types of problems. Voter preference for the Republican

Table 4-1   Sources of the Presidential Vote: 2008

	Percentage Mentioning	Percentage Voting for		Contribution to Vote of	
		Obama	McCain	Obama	McCain
Issue					
Energy	4%	52%	48%	2%	2%
Iraq	6	60	40	4	3
Economy	39	55	45	21	17
Terrorism	6	13	87	1	5
Health Care	6	74	26	4	5
Totals	61			32	32
Traits					
Shares my values	13	33	67	4	8
Can bring change	14	91	9	13	1
Experience	8	7	93	1	8
Cares about people	5	75	25	4	1
Totals	40			22	18

Source: Gerald Pomper, "The Presidential Election," in *The Elections of 2008*, ed. Michael Nelson (Washington, D.C.: CQ Press, 2009), 146.

candidate on national defense, foreign affairs, and morality, and for the Democratic candidate on social welfare issues and the environment has been consistent since the 1970s. John Petrocik refers to this constancy as *issue ownership*.[28] Bill Clinton's support for the Family and Medical Leave Act of 1993 and George W. Bush's stance on Iraq illustrate both presidents' constancy. In this interpretation, elections are decided by which candidate is best able to bring his party's issues to the top of the campaign agenda.

Table 4-2 provides snapshots, taken in January 2004 and July 2008, of the issues that each party "owns" in the public mind. A random cross section of Americans was asked, "When it comes to dealing with [insert issue], which party do you think would do a better job—the Democratic Party, the Republican Party, both about the same, or neither?" The Democrats owned most domestic issues: on Social Security, health care, prescription drugs for senior citizens, and the environment, the Democrats held an advantage of at least twenty percentage points. Americans preferred the Republican Party on foreign policy and security issues: on most of these issues, such as national defense, homeland security, and terrorism, the public gave the Republicans an edge of twenty percentage points or more. The public also favored Republicans by a wide margin on "moral values." If Republicans can focus elections on national defense and strength abroad, they tend to do well—as was evidenced by their strong showing in the 2002 midterm elections when homeland security dominated the campaign agenda. If Democrats can make elections turn on domestic programs, as Obama did in 2008 with health care and the environment, they tend to do well.

Although parties usually own issues over long stretches of time, it is worth noting that performance can affect public perceptions. Iraq is a perfect example. In a January 2004 poll, the Republicans held a 48 percent to 23 percent

Table 4-2   Issues "Owned" and "Leased" by the Major Parties: 2004 and 2008

Issue	Favor Democrats	Favor Republicans	Difference
2004			
Democratic Issues			
Prescription drugs for seniors	42%	20%	22%
Health care	48	22	26
Environment	51	18	33
Education	35	29	6
Federal deficit	37	26	11
Energy policy	37	25	12
Social security	45	25	20
Republican Issues			
Foreign policy	29	43	−14
National defense	16	53	−37
Homeland security	18	47	−29
Iraq	23	48	−25
Terrorism	23	46	−23
Moral values	23	45	−22
Leased Issues			
Economy	36	36	0
Taxes	35	37	−2
2008			
Democratic Issues			
Health care	49%	18%	31%
Energy policy	42	22	20
Homeownership issues	36	17	19
Republican Issues			
Iraq	37	39	−2
Terrorism	29	40	−11
Moral values	24	35	−11
Immigration	27	27	0
Leased Issues			
Economy	41	25	16
Taxes	37	36	1

Source: NBC News/*Wall Street Journal* Poll, January 10–12, 2004, and July 11–18, 2008.

advantage over the Democrats on this issue, not surprising given the public's general preference for Republicans on foreign affairs. Moreover, the war effort had proceeded relatively smoothly to that point. As violence escalated in Iraq with a spike in bombings and American casualties, public support for the Iraq war deteriorated, as did the Republicans' advantage on the issue. An NBC News/*Wall Street Journal* poll taken in July 2008 showed that 39 percent of those questioned favored the Republicans on Iraq and 37 favored the Democrats.

Not all issues are owned by one party or the other. Issues such as the economy and taxation are what Petrocik refers to as "leased." Either party can gain an advantage in these areas if it manages them well or if its opponent manages them poorly. The period between 2004 and 2008 demonstrates that when the public perceives a party has governed poorly, as was the case with the electorate and the

Republicans during this period, leased issues can become an advantage for the other party, and even owned issues can become less safe than they once were. The same NBC News/*Wall Street Journal* poll revealed that in mid-2008 voters favored the Democrats over the Republicans on the economy by sixteen percentage points, although preferences on taxes, another leased issue, remained a statistical dead heat. The Republicans had a 23-point advantage on terrorism and a 22-point advantage on moral values in 2004, but those advantages had narrowed to 11 points for both in 2008. These data illustrate how difficult it was for McCain to run a successful presidential election in such an anti-Republican environment.

Campaign Money

Of all the requirements for successful campaigns, none may be more important than money. Political money does not lend itself to easy analysis, nor is it simple to trace how it is raised and how it is spent. In a federal and fragmented system, campaign money is collected and spent by many competing political actors and institutions. In addition, the effects of money on elections, political behavior, and public policy are not fully understood. One point about which there is substantial agreement, however, is that campaign spending has grown dramatically in recent years.

The spiraling costs of running for office result from a number of factors. One is inflation: the steady increase in the general price level affects everything, including the cost of campaigns. The growth in population and the enlargement of the electorate also make campaigning more expensive. The utilization of modern techniques, such as direct mail and computerized voter databases, added to the costs of campaigns in the 1970s and 1980s. More recently, however, the Internet has given parties, interest groups, and candidates a relatively inexpensive way to deliver their messages and contact supporters.[29] The substitution of presidential primaries for caucus-convention systems also appears to have increased campaign expenditures. Candidates spend considerable sums hiring political consultants to direct their campaigns. And the availability of private money in large quantities, particularly from large individual donors and the political action committees of interest groups, encourages candidates to add to their campaign treasuries.[30] Congressional incumbents believe (and probably rightly so) that the best way to discourage challengers is to amass a large campaign fund well in advance of the next election.[31] It is therefore common for members of Congress to raise substantial sums of campaign money, even when they have no serious competition. Moreover, congressional party leaders encourage incumbents to share their campaign funds with party committees and fellow party candidates in need of financial assistance (a development we discuss in more detail below).[32] This trend has ratcheted up the pressure on incumbents to raise even more money because now they need enough for themselves and their party.

Spending campaign money intelligently is problematic to say the least. Candidates spend as heavily as they do because neither they nor their advisers know which expenditures are likely to produce the greatest return in votes. Lacking systematic information, they jump at every opportunity to contact and persuade voters—and every opportunity costs money. As one political consultant reportedly said, "Half of all the money spent on political campaigns is wasted; the problem is we don't know which half."

Broadcast advertising in particular has driven up campaign costs. Television, critics contend, is the real culprit. Lynn Vavreck found that 62 percent of the $343 million dollars spent on the 2000 presidential campaign was for paid television advertising.[33] David Broder has estimated that U.S. Senate candidates allocate 70 percent to 80 percent of their funds to paid television, turning them, as one senator put it, into "bag men for the TV operators."[34] Paul S. Herrnson, however, suggests that the numbers often cited by critics are greatly inflated. He notes that about 22 percent of House campaign budgets and 30 percent of Senate campaign budgets, on average, are spent on television ads, but he focuses on all races in any given year.[35] These percentages are significantly higher in very competitive races and significantly lower in noncompetitive races.

One point is indisputable: campaign costs have increased dramatically. In 1952 expenditures for the nomination and election of public officials at all levels of government came to about $140 million. By 1968 this figure had climbed to $300 million. In 1984 candidates and parties spent approximately $1.8 billion. The numbers went up from there: $3.2 billion in 1992, just short of $4 billion in 2000, and slightly more than $4 billion in 2004.[36] By 2008 congressional and presidential candidates alone spent $3.4 billion, with the national parties spending an additional $1.1 billion.[37] On the congressional level, House and Senate candidates collectively spent about $195 million in 1978. By 1992 congressional campaign spending had jumped to $678 million, and in 2000 it cleared the $1 billion mark. By 2008, spending in congressional elections had reached $1.35 billion, making it the most expensive congressional election ever.[38] Put another way, over a twenty-year period spending on congressional elections experienced a five-fold increase.

Some observers argue that it is useful to examine these numbers relative to money spent on advertising by private firms. Anthony Gierzynski notes that Apple Computer spent $100 million on one week's worth of advertising for its iMac computer.[39] Frank J. Sorauf claims that Sears had an advertising budget of $1.4 billion in 1990.[40] And, in a different twist, Bradley Smith observes that Americans spend two times as much on potato chips every year as candidates spend on political campaigns.[41]

Figure 4-1 presents data on House and Senate spending by winning candidates from 1981 to 2008. Over this twenty-two-year period, expenditures by successful House candidates more than tripled, and expenditures by winning Senate candidates jumped by three-and-a-half times.

Spending is particularly heavy in the most competitive races, especially when a challenger takes aim at an incumbent. In the House elections of 2008, winning

Figure 4-1   Total Spending by Winning Congressional Candidates: 1981–2008

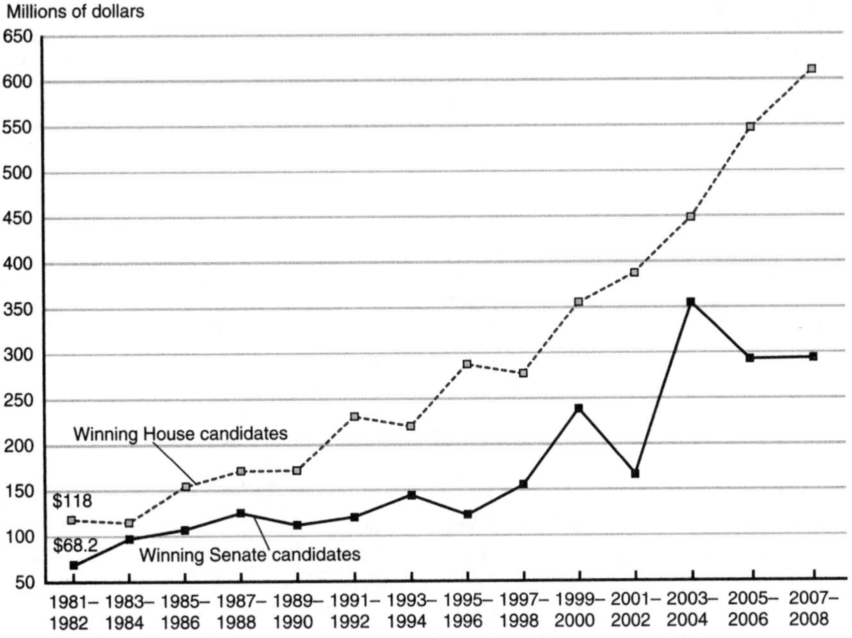

Millions of dollars

Sources: For 1981–1982 through 2003–2004: Federal Election Commission, press release, June 9, 2005; for 2005–2006 and 2007–2008: authors' analysis of Federal Election Commission data.

Note: Spending is for all campaigns, including primaries, runoffs, and general elections. An election cycle is for two years, the election year and the year preceding.

Democratic challengers had median expenditures of more than $2.1 million in defeating Republican incumbents, whose median expenditures were almost $2.3 million. The median expenditures for successful Republican challengers were $1.6 million, as contrasted with $2.4 million for losing Democratic incumbents (see Table 4-3). In the past, open-seat contests also tended to be more competitive in terms of spending. But redistricting has produced districts that are safe for one or the other party, not just for the particular incumbents running in them. In 2008 the median expenditure of a House open-seat winner was more than twice as much ($1.9 million) as the median expenditure of the opponent ($900,000). Even when an incumbent retires, the other party does not necessarily view it as an opportunity to pick up the seat.

Several broad conclusions can be drawn concerning spending in House campaigns. First, the most expensive races involve incumbents who think or know they are in trouble with the voters. Incumbents who garnered 55 percent of the vote or less in 2008 spent an average of nearly $2.3 million, compared to $1.2 million spent by incumbents who won with more than 55 percent of the vote. Even safe House incumbents spent an average of $1.32 million in 2008.[42] Second, with few exceptions, incumbents outspent their challengers, many of

Table 4-3   Spending to Defeat Incumbents and to Win Open Seats and
Close Races, U.S. House Elections: 2008

No. of Districts	Median Expenditures			Median Expenditures
	Winning Challengers and Losing Incumbents			
5	Winning Republican challengers	$1,597,768	Losing Democratic incumbents	$2,385,202
14	Winning Democratic challengers	$2,116,562	Losing Republican incumbents	$2,269,425
	Open Seats			
17	Winning Republicans	$1,352,282	Losing Democrats	$855,329
19	Winning Democrats	$1,994,533	Losing Republicans	$1,234,163
	Close Races[a]			
21	Winning Republican incumbents	$1,728,339	Losing Democratic challengers	$1,189,406
9	Winning Democratic incumbents	$2,218,166	Losing Republican challengers	$1,416,883

Source: Calculated from Federal Election Commission data.

[a] Winners received less than 55 percent of the vote.

whom are severely underfinanced; indeed, as a group, House incumbents ended the 2008 election cycle with almost as much *left over* in their campaign war chests ($184 million) as challengers *raised* ($218 million) during the entire cycle. Third, challengers who win or make a good showing generally are well financed. Fourth, spending in campaigns for open seats is usually heavy, particularly in competitive districts. Fifth, the costs of some House campaigns border on the scandalous. In New York's Twentieth Congressional District in 2008, Sandy Treadwell, the Republican candidate spent $7 million unsuccessfully attempting to defeat the one-term Democratic incumbent, Kirsten Gillibrand, who spent $4.5 million. Put another way, the two candidates combined spent roughly $40 on each voter who showed up to vote in the contest. Less than three months later, Gov. David Patterson appointed Gillibrand to fill the U.S. Senate seat vacated by Hillary Rodham Clinton, who had been appointed secretary of state. Gillibrand's departure set the stage for a special election in April 2009 in which the two candidates combined to spend yet another $3.5 million in the district. (Democrat Scott Murphy won in a close race.)

Expenditures in U.S. Senate contests depend on which states have seats in contention. Senate contests in competitive states with high-priced media markets can be extraordinarily expensive. Two Senate races in 2000 broke records for the most expensive campaigns ever. In New Jersey, billionaire investment banker Jon Corzine, a Democrat, won a Senate seat by spending more than $60 million of his own money to defeat Republican Bob Franks, who spent about a tenth as much. In New York, Hillary Clinton, the Democratic candidate, spent $30 million to defeat her Republican opponent, Rep. Rick Lazio, who spent $40.6 million.

The 2008 Senate contests were characteristically expensive, and vulnerable Senate incumbents typically spent more than safe incumbents. While victorious Senate incumbents spent an average of $8.1 million, losing Senate incumbents spent an average of $12 million.[43] Money also mattered for challengers. The average amount spent by winning Senate challengers was $8.8 million, while losing Senate challengers spent an average of only $1.6 million.[44] As with successful House challengers, victorious Senate challengers, although typically unable to outspend their incumbent opponents, were able to raise sufficient funds to mount effective campaigns. Senate challengers in 2008 were also typically supplemented by sizable national party expenditures, which we discuss later in the chapter.

In the five open-seat Senate contests of 2008, money was associated with victory; winning candidates raised an average of $7.4 million, and losing candidates an average of $3.4 million. The open-seat Senate contest in Virginia saw particularly lopsided fund-raising, with early favorite Democrat Mark Warner raking in nearly $13 million to GOP candidate Jim Gilmore's $2.6 million. The most expensive U.S. Senate contest in 2008 was in Minnesota, where GOP incumbent Norm Coleman and Democratic challenger Al Franken spent a combined $42 million. Plainly, congressional campaign politics is not a poor person's game, at least not for candidates who want to be taken seriously.

The Regulation of Campaign Finance

The public has long been restive over the role of money in American politics. Dissatisfaction focuses on two main complaints. The first is simply that campaign costs have risen to such an extent that candidates with limited resources are seriously disadvantaged in the electoral process. The idea persists that some talented people never seek public office because they lack financial support or are unwilling to solicit funds from others because of the risk of incurring political indebtedness and compromising their independence. Moreover, the high cost of elections may mean that the public hears only one side of the campaign—that of the candidate with access to large sums of money.

The second complaint is that the donors who contribute lavishly to parties and candidates may be able to buy influence and gain preferments in return for the money they channel into campaigns. Ironically, post-Watergate federal and state disclosure reforms, which have made campaign finance systems considerably more transparent than they were in the past, have likely increased public suspicions of influence-peddling by revealing the sources and sums in play. Whether influence is being bought and sold may not be as important as the fact that the public believes that it is. In some measure, public suspicion about campaign financing contributes to public suspicion of government.

To deal with a variety of maladies associated with the financing of federal political campaigns, Congress has passed a number of regulatory measures, starting as early as 1910 with the Tillman Act, which banned corporate contributions to federal candidates. The Federal Corrupt Practices Act of 1925 included contribution and expenditure limits and disclosure rules, but provided little means for effective enforcement. The 1939 Hatch Act banned federal employees from partisan political activities in federal elections, and the 1940 Hatch Act extended the prohibition to state and local employees whose jobs were funded by federal dollars. (The 1940 act also included contribution limits for individual donors, but they were easily circumvented.) The Smith-Connally Act of 1943 temporarily banned labor union contributions to federal candidates, and the Taft-Hartley Act of 1946 made the ban permanent. Labor unions responded to these prohibitions by setting up financing committees separate from their (dues-funded) treasuries that instead raised political money through voluntary contributions made by their members. These committees were the first PACs.[45]

The contemporary campaign finance regime began in 1971, when Congress passed the Federal Election Campaign Act of 1971 (FECA). Adopted prior to the Watergate incident, it anticipated public financing of federal election campaigns by providing that taxpayers could earmark $1 on their personal income tax returns for use in the 1976 presidential election. This provision represented the first effort at public funding of political campaigns. Of at least equal importance, the act provided for rigorous disclosure requirements concerning campaign contributions, expenditures, and debts. Finally, it carried a provision to stimulate private contributions to political campaigns by allowing taxpayers to deduct small campaign contributions from their tax obligations. In retrospect, the extraordinary dimensions of the 1972 presidential election scandal would not have been uncovered without the disclosure requirements for political contributions and expenditures contained in the law.

Largely in response to the Watergate scandal, Congress passed comprehensive amendments to the Federal Election Campaign Act in 1974.[46] Designed to curtail the influence and abuse of money in campaign politics, these amendments placed tight restrictions on contributions, expenditures, disclosure, and reporting. Most important, the 1974 amendments provided for at least partial public financing of presidential primaries, elections, and nominating conventions. In 1979 Congress passed another amendment that allowed political parties to spend an unlimited sum of hard dollars on certain grassroots activities—a provision designed to enhance the parties' role in campaigns.[47] The main features of the nation's campaign finance law, including changes adopted in the Bipartisan Campaign Reform Act of 2002, are included in Box 4-1.

The constitutionality of the 1974 provisions relating to the presidential electoral process was promptly tested in the courts. In *Buckley v. Valeo* (1976) the Supreme Court held that the act's limitations on spending (either by a candidate or by individuals or groups spending independently on behalf of a candidate)

Box 4-1   Major Provisions for the Regulation of Campaign Financing
in Federal Elections

Contribution Limits
- An individual may contribute up to $2,000 indexed for inflation ($2,300 in 2008) to any candidate or candidate committee per election. (Primary, runoff, and general elections are considered separate elections.)
- An individual may contribute up to $25,000 per calendar year indexed for inflation ($28,500 in 2008) to a national party committee and up to $5,000 per calendar year to any other political committee. An individual's total biennial federal contributions cannot exceed $95,000 indexed for inflation ($108,200 in 2008).
- A multicandidate committee (one with more than fifty contributors that makes contributions to five or more federal candidates) may contribute no more than $5,000 to any candidate or candidate committee per election, no more than $15,000 to the national committee of a political party, and no more than $5,000 to any other political committee per calendar year.
- The national committee and the congressional campaign committee may each contribute up to $5,000 to each House candidate, per election; the national committee, together with the senatorial campaign committee, may contribute up to a combined total of $35,000 to each Senate candidate for the entire campaign period (including a primary election).
- Political action committees formed by businesses, trade associations, or unions are limited to contributions of no more than $5,000 to any candidate in any election. No limits apply to their aggregate contributions.
- Banks, corporations, and labor unions are prohibited from making contributions from their treasuries to federal election campaigns. Government contractors and foreign nationals are similarly restricted. Contributions may not be supplied by one person but made in the name of another person. Contributions in cash are limited to $100.

Expenditure Limits
- Candidates are limited to an expenditure of $10 million each indexed for inflation in all presidential primaries (the 2008 limit was $42.5 million), provided they accept public funding.
- Major party presidential candidates who accept public funding may spend no more than $20 million indexed for inflation in the general election (a total of $84.1 million each in 2008).
- Presidential and vice-presidential candidates who accept public funding may spend no more than $50,000 of personal funds in their campaigns.
- Each national party may spend up to two cents per voter in coordination with its presidential candidate ($19.1 million in 2008); $20,000 indexed for inflation *or* two cents per voter indexed for inflation (whichever is greater) in coordination with its U.S. Senate candidates; and $10,000 indexed per inflation in coordination with its U.S. House candidates ($42,100 in 2008; $84,100 for states with one House district).
- As a result of the Supreme Court's decision in *Buckley v. Valeo* (1976), there are no limits on how much House and Senate candidates may collect and spend in their campaigns (or on how much they may spend of their own or their family's money).
- Also in keeping with *Buckley v. Valeo,* there are no limits on the amount that individuals and groups may spend on behalf of any presidential or congressional candidate so long as the expenditures are independent—that is, not arranged or controlled by the candidate.
- As a result of the Court's decision in *Colorado Republican Federal Campaign Committee v. FEC* (1996), political parties may now make unlimited *independent* expenditures on behalf of or against federal candidates as long as these expenditures are financed with hard money and not coordinated with the candidates or their campaigns. "Independent" expenditures, in other words, are entitled to First Amendment protection and are not to be treated as indirect campaign contributions subject to regulations.

Public Financing
- Major party candidates for the presidency qualify for full funding ($20 million indexed for inflation) prior to the campaign, the money to be drawn from the federal income tax dollar checkoff. In 2008 the Democratic and Republican nominees were each eligible to receive

(*continued*)

Box 4-1 *(continued)*

$84.1 million in campaign funds if they chose to participate in the public funding program. Candidates may decline to participate in the public funding program and finance their campaigns through private contributions. Candidates who accept public funding may not accept private contributions.

- Minor party and independent candidates qualify for lesser sums, provided their candidates received at least 5 percent of the vote in the previous presidential election. New parties or parties that received less than 5 percent of the vote four years earlier qualify for public financing after the election, provided they drew 5 percent of the vote.
- Matching public funds up to $5 million plus COLA (cost-of-living adjustment) are available for presidential primary candidates, provided that they first raise $100,000 in private funds ($5,000 in contributions of no more than $250 in each of twenty states). Once that threshold is reached, the candidate receives matching funds up to $250 per contribution.
- Presidential candidates who receive less than 10 percent of the vote in two consecutive presidential primaries become ineligible for additional campaign subsidies. Subsidies are renewed if the candidate receives 20 percent in a subsequent primary.
- Optional public funding of presidential nominating conventions is available for the major parties, with lesser amounts for minor parties.

Disclosure and Reporting
- Each federal candidate is required to establish a single, principal campaign committee to report on all contributions and expenditures on behalf of the candidate.
- Frequent reports on contributions and expenditures are to be filed with the Federal Election Commission.

Enforcement
- Administration of the law is the responsibility of a six-member, bipartisan Federal Election Commission. The commission is empowered to make rules and regulations, to receive campaign reports, to render advisory opinions, to conduct audits and investigations, to subpoena witnesses and information, and to seek civil injunctions through court action.

Source: Federal Election Commission.

---

were unconstitutional because they interfered with the right of free speech under the First Amendment.[48] Political money, the Court ruled, is political speech. The Court upheld the limitations on contributions to campaigns, the disclosure requirements, and the public funding provisions for presidential primaries and elections. In 1996 the Court extended its protection of hard money independent expenditures to political parties, ruling that parties have a First Amendment right to spend without limit on their candidates as long as the spending is done independently of the candidates.[49] In a 2000 decision, the Court reaffirmed the constitutionality of reasonable contribution limits.[50]

No provision is made for the public financing of campaigns for Congress, and that has increased the pressure on candidates to raise vast sums of money from individuals and organized interests. Many members of Congress have become weary of the struggle. To raise the $25,832,567 he spent in his 2006 campaign, former senator Rick Santorum of Pennsylvania would have needed to bring in $11,800 per day, every day, for his entire six-year term. Obviously, the time spent in fund-raising takes significant time away from members' ability to legislate.

As Sen. Robert C. Byrd (D-W.Va.) observed:

> The present system does not even allow the incumbents with new ideas to get them into place. We are too busy out there engaging in the money chase. We cannot be here in the committees, we cannot be here on the floor doing our work. . . . We are kept so busy out there knocking on doors all over the country, seeking money, asking for money, begging for money, getting on our hands and knees for money, we do not have time to give thought to new ideas and to be putting them into creative legislation.[51]

In addition, the pressure to raise large sums of campaign money drives parties and candidates to cut corners and to engage in questionable (if not illegal) practices.[52] Following the 1996 election, it was discovered that the White House had been rewarding and beguiling Democratic Party contributors by letting them spend a night in the Lincoln Bedroom, that numerous White House coffees had been held for prospective big donors, and that Vice President Al Gore had placed fund-raising telephone calls from the White House, a possible violation of a law that prohibits soliciting funds on federal property. Evidence of illegal foreign donations to the Democratic Party from Indonesia and China also surfaced. Topping it off, the Democratic National Committee (DNC) had to return a number of suspicious or illegal donations because their true source could not be established. Special access, money-hustling, favor-seeking, and buying influence were the central themes in story after story involving the White House's unusual efforts to raise money to compete with the Republican Party's highly successful money chase. Moreover, these charges continued to dog Gore during his run for president in 2000.

In late 2005, however, a fund-raising scandal that centered on Republican super-lobbyist Jack Abramoff helped to end the party's dominance in Washington. Abramoff funneled tens of millions of dollars in fees that he collected from representing Native American groups into the coffers of friendly campaign organizations, often doing so illegally. In addition, he gave members of Congress gifts that exceeded congressional rules, including golf vacations, expensive dinners, and skybox seats at sporting events. In return, Abramoff clients apparently received preferential treatment in public policy outcomes. Abramoff was sent to federal prison for his actions, and his dealings directly or indirectly led to federal corruption charges against several prominent members of Congress, including House Majority Leader Tom Delay (R-Texas).

Soft Money

Discontent over the parties' fund-raising practices derives not only from concern over sleazy behavior but also from the perception that campaign finance laws are riddled with loopholes. Consider the matter of contribution limits. One of the major purposes of the FECA was to place sharp restrictions on the amount of money that could be given to federal campaigns by individuals and organizations, but donors found ways around these restrictions. Prior to 2002 wealthy individuals, corporations, and unions could give political parties "soft money" donations, which were not subject to the "hard" limitations of the FECA. Parties could then spend the money on a variety of party building activities, as long as the activities did not expressly advocate the election or defeat of specific federal candidates.

The soft money loophole emerged from several FEC rulings during the 1970s that allowed state and national political parties to use soft money to finance the nonfederal portion of generic party activities and expenses.[53] The national parties took advantage of these rulings to use soft money to pay for the nonfederal share of many activities that benefited the entire party ticket. By 1996, however, the DNC had begun to exploit the loophole by using soft money to finance so-called "issue advocacy advertisements." Clearly designed to bolster President Clinton's reelection, the ads looked no different from a typical candidate ad to the average viewer. But because they stopped short of using the "magic words"—such as "vote for" or "vote against"—identified by the Supreme Court to distinguish between election and issue communications, the ads were legally considered issue advocacy rather than election advocacy, allowing them to be financed with soft, rather than hard, money. The Republican Party soon followed suit in using soft money to finance issue ads. It became abundantly clear that the Court's "magic words" test was not particularly meaningful in distinguishing issue advocacy from outright electioneering. Indeed, a study by Craig Holman and Luke McLoughlin of the 2000 elections shows that a mere 10 percent of advertisements produced by congressional candidates advocating their own election actually asked for a vote.[54]

The amount of soft money raised and spent by parties exploded with the 1996 election. In the 1992 election cycle, the parties combined brought in less than $100 million in soft money. In the 2000 election cycle, they raised nearly $500 million (see Figure 4-2). Ordinarily, fund-raising increases in presidential years and declines in off-year elections, but the parties actually raised more soft money in the 2002 election cycle than they did in 2000. For 2002 the Democrats collected $246 million in soft money, and the Republicans $250 million—overall, more than twice that raised in 1995–1996. As Ellen Miller of the Center for Responsive Politics observes, "The parties find it a lot easier to raise $100,000 in soft money with one call to a corporation than to try to collect $1,000 donations from individuals."[55]

Soft money represented a huge financial boon to the parties. Yet parties did not necessarily use this money to create a significantly more party-centered electoral environment. Instead, they chose to use it to further candidate-centered elections. According to the Brennan Center for Justice, only 8.3 percent of soft money in 2000 was spent on party building, get-out-the-vote campaigns, and voter education efforts. In contrast, 38 percent was spent on issue advocacy ads, and even these were not party centered. Fully 99.8 percent mentioned a specific candidate's name; only 8 percent identified a political party.[56] Moreover, the parties focused their efforts strategically on a small number of competitive races to get the biggest bang for their buck. In 2000 the parties aired their issue ads in only forty-eight House races, concentrating one-third of their overall spending in six

Figure 4-2   Soft Money Party Receipts Reported to the FEC through Twenty Days after the General Election: 1992–2002

Millions of dollars

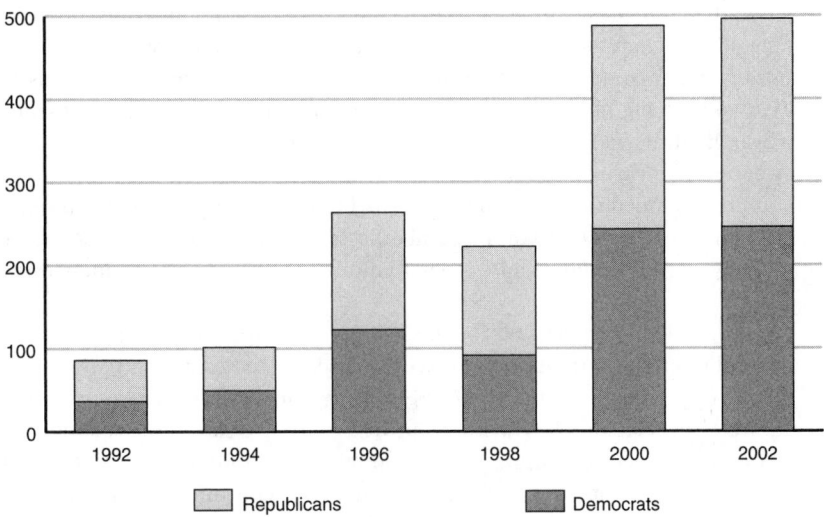

Source: Press release, Federal Election Commission, December 18, 2002.

of them.[57] The parties have resigned themselves to the reality of the candidate-centered campaign.

The parties were not the only organizations to deploy soft money-financed issue advocacy ads; interest groups got into the game as well. In the 1996 election a large portion of the AFL-CIO's $35 million soft money budget was spent on issue advocacy ads designed to defeat GOP House incumbents. Republican-oriented interest groups soon followed suit. As David Magleby, J. Quin Monson, and their team of researchers show, by 2002 it was not uncommon in competitive contests for soft money spending by parties and interest groups to exceed spending by the candidates themselves.[58]

In sum, no fund-raising practice provided a more direct assault on the mission of the FECA than soft money. The 1974 legislation had sought to limit the influence of wealthy interests by limiting individuals to $1,000 contributions per candidate per election, or $5,000 for a PAC. The emergence of soft money reopened the door to big, potentially corrupting, influences. A soft money contribution of $1 million or $2 million, or even several hundred thousand, to a party captures the attention of the beneficiary in a way quite distinct from the impression made by a $5,000 PAC gift. PACs are influential when viewed collectively, but one enormous soft money donation could surely be problematic. After 1996 reformers sought to eliminate the soft money loophole. In 2002 they succeeded, but only partially, with the passage of the Bipartisan Campaign Reform Act of 2002.

Reforming Campaign Finance Reform

The Bipartisan Campaign Finance Reform Act (BCRA), also known as the McCain-Feingold act, was signed into law in March 2002 by President George W. Bush. In the 2000 presidential campaign, Bush, like most Republicans, opposed any significant changes to the campaign finance system, under which Republicans consistently outperform Democrats. Following the corporate scandals in 2001 involving big political contributors such as Enron and Global Crossing, however, Bush bowed to public pressure and signed the reform bill.

Among the measure's numerous provisions, four stand out. First, and most important, it banned the national parties (including the congressional and senatorial campaign committees) and federal officeholders from raising and spending soft money. Parties are now limited to hard money contributions from individuals and PACs.

Second, to help compensate for the lost revenue from the soft money ban, some hard money contribution limits were raised and indexed for inflation. One of the major problems with the 1974 FECA amendments was that contribution limits were set relatively low, with no provision for increases. BCRA sought to mitigate this problem by raising the individual contribution limit to $2,000 per candidate, per election. As the amount would rise with inflation, in 2008 the individual contribution limit was $2,300. The limit on individual contributions to national parties was increased from $20,000 to $25,000, and indexed for inflation; the 2008 limit was $28,500. The reform also raised the total amount that individuals could contribute to federal candidates, parties, and PACs during a two-year election cycle from $50,000 to $95,000, with these sums to grow at the pace of inflation. The limit for 2008 was $108,200.[59]

Third, the law attempted to prevent corporations, labor unions, and nonprofit groups from running soft money–financed issue advocacy ads by prohibiting the expenditure of soft money on what BCRA termed "electioneering communications." Such communications were defined by Congress as "any broadcast, cable, or satellite communication that (1) refers to a clearly identified candidate for federal office, (2) is transmitted within 30 days of a primary or 60 days of a general election for the office that a candidate is seeking, and (3) is targeted to the relevant electorate."[60] These ads had been criticized in particular for distorting the records of candidates so close to election day that candidates lacked adequate time to respond to them. By creating a new category of political advertisement called "electioneering communications," BCRA essentially broadened the Supreme Court's "magic words" test of express advocacy.

Fourth, through the so-called "millionaires' amendment," BCRA set contribution limits three to six times higher for candidates facing opponents who exceed a threshold amount of self-financing.[61] Incumbents, it appears, became concerned about the possibility of a challenge from a multimillionaire candidate such as Corzine. The ways the reform legislation altered the flow of money are depicted in Figure 4-3.

Figure 4-3 How the BCRA Alters the Money Flow

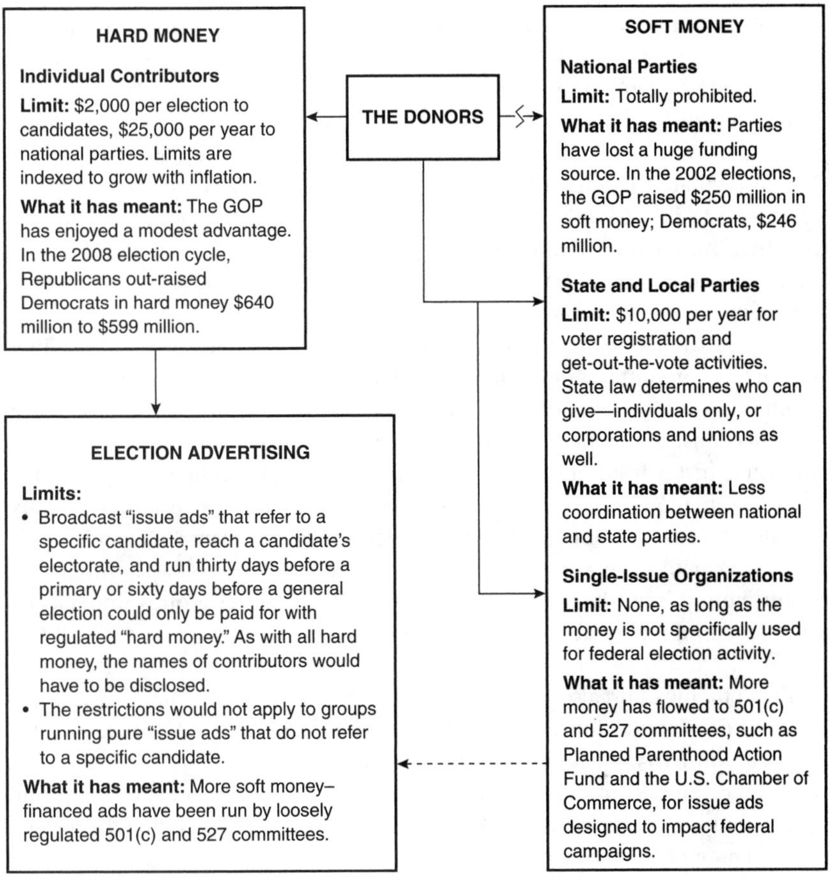

HARD MONEY		SOFT MONEY

HARD MONEY

Individual Contributors

Limit: $2,000 per election to candidates, $25,000 per year to national parties. Limits are indexed to grow with inflation.

What it has meant: The GOP has enjoyed a modest advantage. In the 2008 election cycle, Republicans out-raised Democrats in hard money $640 million to $599 million.

THE DONORS

SOFT MONEY

National Parties

Limit: Totally prohibited.

What it has meant: Parties have lost a huge funding source. In the 2002 elections, the GOP raised $250 million in soft money; Democrats, $246 million.

State and Local Parties

Limit: $10,000 per year for voter registration and get-out-the-vote activities. State law determines who can give—individuals only, or corporations and unions as well.

What it has meant: Less coordination between national and state parties.

ELECTION ADVERTISING

Limits:

- Broadcast "issue ads" that refer to a specific candidate, reach a candidate's electorate, and run thirty days before a primary or sixty days before a general election could only be paid for with regulated "hard money." As with all hard money, the names of contributors would have to be disclosed.
- The restrictions would not apply to groups running pure "issue ads" that do not refer to a specific candidate.

What it has meant: More soft money–financed ads have been run by loosely regulated 501(c) and 527 committees.

Single-Issue Organizations

Limit: None, as long as the money is not specifically used for federal election activity.

What it has meant: More money has flowed to 501(c) and 527 committees, such as Planned Parenthood Action Fund and the U.S. Chamber of Commerce, for issue ads designed to impact federal campaigns.

Source: Adapted by authors from *Congressional Quarterly Weekly Report*, March 23, 2002, 800.

Since its passage, BCRA has been weakened by the federal courts, the FEC, and by groups that quickly learned how to escape the law's regulatory reach. The FEC initially helped limit BCRA's reach by declining to extend the law to 527 groups.[62] As a result, 527 groups were free to use soft money on issue advocacy ads, just as the national parties had done prior to BCRA. They needed only to steer clear of coordination with a candidate and express advocacy.[63]

Freed from most restrictions, the 527 committees flourished, spending $426 million in the 2004 elections. The liberal 527s vastly outnumbered and outspent conservative groups. Billionaire businessman George Soros bankrolled America Coming Together, the most heavily financed 527 group in the 2004 election; it raised and spent in excess of $75 million. A conservative 527, Swift Boat Veterans for Truth, spent less than a third of this amount, but its advertisements, which accused John Kerry of exaggerating his war record, are often cited as critical in explaining his inability to gain traction following the Democratic National Convention. Despite BCRA's efforts to keep soft money out of the system, 527 groups have brought it back in.

The line between issue advocacy, which these organizations are purportedly designed for, and candidate advocacy can be blurry. Moreover, it is nearly impossible to regulate the amount of coordination between 527s and campaigns. In 2004 Joe Sandler, a Washington-based attorney, worked for both the DNC *and* the MoveOn.org Voter Fund, a heavily funded liberal 527 group, and the Swift Boat Veterans for Truth had several staff members in common with the Bush campaign.

To close the loophole, the FEC tightened its regulations on 527s and fined several 527 committees for failing to register as political committees.[64] The FEC's actions account for some of the decrease in expenditures by 527 groups in the 2008 elections. But money spent by 527s did not just disappear from the electoral landscape; instead, soft money migrated to 501(c) organizations, which are less regulated than 527 groups and are not even required to disclose their donors. Spending by 501(c) groups in 2008 rose roughly threefold from 2006, and Republicans appear to have a sizable advantage with these groups.[65] The migration of soft money from the national parties to 527s to 501(c) groups underscores a fundamental reality about campaign money: like running water, it will find an outlet.

The Supreme Court also has weakened BCRA's attempts to regulate soft money–financed communications. The initial legal challenge to BCRA focused on the law's ban on party soft money and its restrictions on financing electioneering communications. In an expedited decision rendered in December 2003, the Court upheld both parts of the act in a 5–4 decision.[66] Most observers thought the soft money ban would survive judicial scrutiny, but that the electioneering communication regulations would not. In 2007, however, the Court ruled that political communications can be regulated only if they are "susceptible of no reasonable interpretation other than as an appeal to vote for or against a specific candidate."[67] The ads at the center of the controversy, run by a 501(c)(4) group called Wisconsin Right to Life (WRTL), encouraged viewers to urge Sen. Russ Feingold, who was up for reelection in 2004, to oppose the filibustering of President Bush's federal court nominees. In its decision, the Court did not completely overturn BCRA's financing restrictions on electioneering communications. It did, however, rule that the financing restrictions were unconstitutional *as applied* to WRTL's particular ads. As such, the Court opened the door for even more unregulated interest group money in elections.[68]

In 2008 the Supreme Court further weakened BCRA by striking down the millionaires' amendment. As is often true in campaign finance cases, First Amendment concerns were front and center for the Court. In his majority opinion, Justice Samuel Alito wrote, "While BCRA does not impose a cap on a candidate's expenditure of personal funds, it imposes an unprecedented penalty on any candidate who robustly exercises that First Amendment right, requiring him to choose between the right to engage in unfettered political speech and subjection to discriminatory fundraising limitations." [69]

Although parts of the 2002 BCRA have been weakened, its prohibition on national party soft money remains intact. Moreover, the national parties have adapted to the post-BCRA regulatory environment by substantially increasing their hard money receipts. We discuss this in greater detail later in the chapter.

Sources of Campaign Financing

Presidential Contests

Most of the cost of American elections is borne by private individuals and groups. Only in presidential elections is public financing (funding from the government) available. Under amendments to the FECA, candidates for the presidential nomination can qualify for matching public funds. Once the nominations have been settled, the candidates can choose to receive full federal funding in the general election campaign.

The public funding option has, however, become less attractive for presidential candidates. Public funding for the primaries began to fall out of favor in 2000, when GOP candidate George W. Bush opted not to take it. In 2004 Bush again decided to reject public funding in the primary, as did Democratic candidates Howard Dean and John Kerry. In 2008, all of the top-tier candidates except John Edwards rejected the public funding option in the primaries. The reason is that nearly all serious presidential candidates can now raise far more than the spending limit—$42.5 million in 2008—that accompanies the acceptance of public funds. In 2008 Barack Obama and Hillary Clinton raised $414 million and $224 million, respectively, in the Democratic primaries, and John McCain and Mitt Romney raised $221 million and $110 million, respectively, in the Republican primaries. Candidates who accept public funds in the primaries are also saddled with burdensome state-by-state limits. Clearly, the matching funds system in presidential primaries has lost its effectiveness.

More worrisome for public funding advocates is that Obama opted not to take the $84 million public funding grant for the *general* election, making him the first major party candidate to reject public funding in the general election since the program went into effect in 1976. Confident that he could raise—and therefore spend—more than the $84 million, Obama raised $153 million in September alone. In all, he raised a staggering $741.6 million dollars—more than any single candidate in the history of U.S. elections. Much of Obama's fund-raising success came from 3 million online donors who gave small amounts (an average of $80).[70] But Obama also relied on large donors. In fact, roughly 47 percent of his receipts came from donors who gave $1,000 or more. For GOP nominee McCain, however, this figure was 60 percent.[71]

The national party committees have the capacity to be important players in presidential general election contests. In 2008 the DNC spent roughly $260 million, and the RNC spent approximately $428 million.[72] National party money is spent on a variety of campaign items—everything from polling to television advertisements to wide-ranging voter mobilization efforts.[73]

Federal law also allows the national committees to make *coordinated expenditures* on behalf of their presidential candidates. Permitted only in the general election, these are party expenditures made in conjunction with a party's presidential campaign. Indexed for inflation and computed on the basis of the country's voting age population, the coordinated expenditure limit for the 2008 presidential election was $19.1 million. In 2008 the RNC made $18.9 million in coordinated expenditures on behalf of McCain, and the DNC spent $6.4 million in coordination with the Obama campaign.[74]

Although BCRA prohibits the national parties from running soft money–financed issue advocacy ads, they are permitted by federal law to make unlimited *independent expenditures* on behalf of their presidential candidates. Independent expenditures are hard dollars spent by the parties on express advocacy, but not spent in coordination with their candidates' campaigns. They can either advocate the election of the party's candidate or the defeat of the opposing party candidate. Following BCRA, the FEC wrote new rules to ensure that national party independent expenditures were genuinely independent of the presidential campaigns.[75] In 2008 the RNC spent more than $53 million on independent expenditures opposing Obama, but the DNC spent only $1.1 million against McCain. The small sum of DNC independent expenditures likely reflects the fact that much of the Obama ad campaign was run out of the Obama organization itself.

Finally, the national parties can also influence presidential contests by transferring funds to state parties. In 2008 the DNC transferred $77.7 million to its state parties, and the RNC transferred $45.6 million to GOP state committees. Naturally, much of the money transferred by the national committees to state party committees is targeted to battleground states. But consistent with BCRA, all national party transfers to state parties must now be hard dollars, and the overall sums of transfers have declined in the post-BCRA period.[76]

Although PACs play almost no role in funding presidential races, scores of 527s and 501(c) groups spent money trying to influence the 2008 presidential contests. The American Issues Project, a 501(c)4 group, spent roughly $3 million on ads detailing Obama's relationship with William Ayers, a former member of the radical Weather Underground group. Other groups, such as America Votes, a Democratic-oriented 527 committee, undertook substantial voter mobilization efforts.[77] This sort of group activity has been difficult to regulate, and it may well be a permanent fixture on the American electoral landscape.

Congressional Contests

Congressional elections are obviously different from presidential contests, and the financing of House and Senate campaigns reflects that. By looking at the sources and sums of funds in the 2008 congressional campaigns, we can learn a great deal about the forces at work in congressional campaign finance.

Raising campaign money is a relentless pursuit for members of Congress and their aides. House and Senate rules permit each office to have at least one staff member assigned to receive campaign contributions. Many members hire professional fund-raisers to advise them on the techniques for soliciting money (to ask for the "right" amount—not too much, not too little) and to travel across the country with them to court contributors. The hunt for money has prompted members to seek funds from sources outside their home states, and, although the two parties' voting bases differ regionally, incumbents of both parties tend to raise campaign money from the same (mostly affluent) regions of the country.[78] In addition, fund-raising events at Washington watering holes occur night after night, attracting lobbyists and assorted contributors who know that gifts are acknowledged with the promise of access. Members solicit and accept out-of-state political money, first, because it is readily available, and second, because it is easier than asking their own constituents and perhaps offending them.[79]

Several aspects of the money hustle of the 2008 election (covering the two-year election cycle of primary, runoff, and general elections) stand out. First, the contributions of individuals represent the major source of campaign money for congressional candidates. In 2008 individual contributions made up 54 percent of the funds received by House candidates and 67 percent of those raised by Senate candidates.

Second, PACs continue to be a major source of money for congressional candidates. In the 2007–2008 election cycle, PACs contributed $386.9 million to congressional campaigns ($225.3 million to Democrats and $161.6 million to Republicans). PAC contributions amounted to 36 percent of receipts for all House races and 21 percent for all Senate races. Incumbents in particular depend on PAC money. In the House, Democratic incumbents received 48 percent of their receipts from PACs, and Republican incumbents received 41 percent. Although they are less dependent on interest groups, Senate incumbents nevertheless raised 27 percent of their funds from PACs.[80]

Third, congressional campaign fund-raising is an incumbent-dominated system. Challengers do not fare nearly as well in the PAC sweepstakes. (See Table 4-4.) Overall, 82 percent of all PAC funds in 2008 (both parties, both chambers) went to incumbents, and a combined 18 percent went to challengers and candidates for open seats.[81] The average House incumbent received $646,672 from PACs, whereas the average House general election challenger received roughly $113,414. Especially in the House, where the majority party has a tight hold on the legislative process, majority party members typically enjoy significant fund-raising advantages with PACs. This was certainly true in 2008: House Democratic incumbents raised an average of $690,604 from PACs, and House GOP incumbents collected an average of $587,492. Five House incumbents—four Democrats and one Republican—raked in more than $2 million in PAC dollars in 2008.

Table 4-4   Sources of Funding for Congressional Candidates: 2008

	Individual Contributions	PAC/Nonparty Contributions	Candidate Contributions	Loans	Direct Party Contributions
House					
Dem. incumbents	50%	49%	*	*	*
Dem. challengers	69	18	2	11	*
Dem. open seats	57	26	11	5	*
Rep. incumbents	55	43	*	1	*
Rep. challengers	68	10	12	9	1
Rep. open seats	57	19	*	23	1
Senate					
Dem. incumbents	67	32	2	*	*
Dem. challengers	79	9	*	11	*
Dem. open seats	81	18	*	1	*
Rep. incumbents	67	28	1	4	*
Rep. challengers	75	7	1	17	1
Rep. open seats	72	25	*	3	*

Source: Federal Election Commission data.

Notes: PAC/nonparty committee contributions include contributions from all PACs and other nonparty committees (such as candidates' principal campaign committees). Party contributions include only direct party contributions, not coordinated or independent expenditures made by political parties. Figures do not include funds transferred by candidates to their principal campaign committee from other authorized committees.

* Less than 1 percent.

The overall growth of PAC contributions has been substantial. (See Table 4-5.) PACs contributed nearly seven times as much money to House and Senate candidates in 2008 as they did in 1980. The numbers are instructive: a total of $55.2 million was contributed in the 1980 election cycle and $386.9 million in the 2008 election cycle.

Political action committees target their gifts carefully, taking into consideration factors such as incumbency, party, and legislative position. Labor PACs tend to be strongly allied with Democrats, and in 2008, 93 percent of the $60.8 million that labor PACs contributed to congressional candidates went to Democrats. Corporate PACs tend to be more pragmatic than ideological: they favor members of the majority party.[82] In 2008, 52 percent of the $103.16 million given by corporate PACs to House incumbents went to Democrats, a dramatic shift from 2004, when Republicans held majority control of the House. In that year, 67 percent of corporate PAC dollars contributed to House incumbents went to Republicans.[83] Committee chairs and party leaders tend to be major beneficiaries of interest group largesse.[84] Committee membership is also taken into consideration. Members of the tax and commerce committees invariably receive more PAC money than members of the judiciary or foreign policy committees. The pattern of contributions is illustrated by these observations:

> The main goal is to support our friends who have been with us most of the time.
> —*an official of the United Auto Workers*

Table 4-5 Contributions of Political Action Committees to Congressional Campaigns in Presidential Election Years: 1980–2008 (in millions of dollars)

	1980	1984	1988	1992	1996	2000	2004	2008
PAC Dollars								
Total	$55.2	$105.4	$147.9	$180.5	$201.4	$243.2	$289.0	$386.9
House cands.	37.9	75.7	102.3	128.6	155.8	192.8	225.3	308.1
Senate cands.	17.3	29.7	45.6	51.9	45.6	50.4	63.7	78.8
As pct. of receipts for								
House cands.	26%	34%	37%	33%	31%	32%	32%	36%
Senate cands.	17	17	23	20	16	14	13	21

Sources: Data from Federal Election Commission, press releases, May 16, 1985; February 24, 1989; April 9, 1989; March 4, 1993; April 14, 1997; May 15, 2001; June 8, 2005; April 24, 2009.

> The prevailing attitude is that PAC money should be used to facilitate access to incumbents.
> —*the director of governmental and political participation for the Chamber of Commerce of the United States*

> We're inclined to support incumbents because we tend to go with those who support our industry. We are not out looking to find challengers. Our aim is not to change the tone of Congress.
> —*a spokesperson for the Lockheed Good Government Program*

> We're looking especially for members who serve on key committees, and people who help us on the floor.
> —*a spokesperson for the Automobile and Truck Dealers Election Action Committee*[85]

In addition to making direct contributions to candidates, PACs are permitted to make unlimited independent expenditures for or against congressional candidates, but they are prohibited from consulting candidates concerning these expenditures. In 2008 such independent expenditures by PACs totaled $35.9 million, with $23.9 million spent on behalf of candidates and $12 million spent against them.[86] Under the FECA, direct PAC contributions to any candidate in a federal election are limited to $5,000. Independent spending is a way to circumvent this restriction. Interest groups also use soft money–financed 527 and 501(c) groups to spend in congressional campaigns, a development we discuss later in the chapter.

So popular are PACs that many members of Congress have created their own political action committees—informally known as "leadership PACs"—to raise and disburse campaign funds. The thrust of some leadership PACs is simply to help reelect partisan or ideological allies or to help the party win a majority.[87] But for at least some leadership PACs, the dominant purpose appears to be self-promotion. The most active congressional PACs are those created by members who hold, or aspire to hold, powerful party and committee leadership positions in the House, such as Speaker, floor leader, whip, or the chair of an important committee. These PACs distribute campaign funds to candidates as a way of building good will and creating support for the sponsoring member's goals. The contributions also send a signal to the PAC sponsor's congressional colleagues that he is willing and able to help the party and its candidates with campaign funds—a requirement for congressional leaders in the contemporary era. Indeed, with the demise of the seniority system for choosing party leaders and top committee chairs, leadership PACs have become more important for those hoping to rise to leadership positions.[88] Since the 1990s the number of leadership PACs sponsored by House and Senate incumbents has grown from a handful to well over two hundred. Even for presidential hopefuls, having one's own PAC is invaluable in meeting the expenses of political travel necessary to capture public attention or to campaign for other congressional candidates.[89]

The availability of PAC money makes life easier for incumbents. They and their aides understand the PAC network and know how to curry favor with specific PACs (or at least how to avoid their enmity), how to solicit funds from them, and how to respond to their initiatives. Members are largely comfortable in this world of organization money, even though they resent the amount of time required to raise funds and worry over possible obligations to their benefactors. Access to PAC money is not, however, the most important advantage of incumbents. Their main advantages are simply the opportunities and resources attached to holding congressional office, the most important of which is a large staff. "The Hill office," writes David R. Mayhew, "is a vitally important political unit, part campaign management firm and part political machine."[90] The office is a political unit financed by the U.S. Treasury Department, and the contributions to incumbents are substantial. Michael Malbin estimates that House incumbents enjoy perquisites of office that support constituent contact worth at least $1 million over the period of a two-year term ($400,000 for constituent service staff; $400,000 for district office expenses, travel, phones, computers, and the like; and $250,000 for unsolicited mailings to constituents).[91] Indeed, it might be argued that the United States *has* publicly funded congressional campaigns—but only for incumbents. The heavy support of political action committees is simply icing on the cake—double rich.

As in presidential contests, interest groups spend money in congressional campaigns through 527 and 501(c) committees. The Washington-based Campaign Finance Institute (CFI) has done the difficult work of monitoring the activities of these groups. According to the CFI, some of the committees that spent heavily in the 2008 elections, such as the U.S. Chamber of Commerce's 501(c), also have sizable federal PACs that contribute to congressional candidates. Other committees are bankrolled by major trade groups. Still others, such as the American Future Fund—a 501(c)4 committee—appear to be smaller operations run by political operatives. These groups, especially the 501(c)s, are only loosely regulated, and they are a growing force in congressional campaigns.[92]

The parties, however, have regained importance in congressional campaigns, mostly through the four congressional campaign committees, also known as the

"Hill committees": the Democratic Congressional Campaign Committee (DCCC), the National Republican Congressional Committee (NRCC), Democratic Senatorial Campaign Committee (DSCC), and the National Republican Senatorial Committee (NRSC). The two national committees, the DNC and the RNC, concern themselves mostly with presidential elections and statewide contests, but sometimes help House and Senate candidates.

Federal law severely constrains the direct financial assistance parties can provide to congressional candidates. The national parties and congressional campaign committees may each give $5,000 per candidate per election to House candidates. Senate candidates may receive up to $17,500 in combined direct contributions from the national committee and the senatorial campaign committee in a calendar year. State and local party committees can make limited direct contributions to congressional campaigns. These are small sums in campaigns that routinely cost millions.

As in presidential contests, the parties can also make coordinated expenditures on behalf of their congressional candidates, and these expenditures can be decidedly more generous than direct party contributions. For House candidates in 2008, coordinated expenditure limits were $42,100 (except in states with only one member, where the limit was $84,100).[93] For Senate candidates, coordinated expenditure limits are based on state voting-age population, and they can be sizable for the most populous states; for California in 2008 the limit was $2.3 million.

In congressional elections, the parties enjoy the most regulatory freedom in making independent expenditures. The parties have the right to make such expenditures without limit, as long as the expenditures are financed with hard money and made independently of the benefited candidate.[94] Such expenditures can either advocate the election of the party's candidates or the defeat of opposing party candidates.

In 2008 the congressional campaign committees spent relatively little on direct contributions and coordinated expenditures, opting instead to deploy substantial resources on independent expenditures. Indeed, the direct contributions made by all four Hill Committees in 2008 amounted to only $4.8 million, while the committees' coordinated expenditures added up to a slightly larger $10.3 million. But these committees made $296.5 million in independent expenditures in the 2008 congressional elections.[95] Prohibited from raising soft money to finance issue advocacy ads, the congressional campaign committees have turned to hard money independent expenditures as their weapon of choice.

Independent expenditures made by the Hill committees can very likely influence the outcome of close races. In fact, in several competitive contests in 2008, party independent expenditures exceeded candidate expenditures. In the 2008 U.S. Senate race in Oregon, the DSCC spent more than $12 million opposing the Republican incumbent, Gordon Smith—nearly double the sum Jeff Merkley, the Democratic candidate (and winner), spent. The DCCC pumped $2.4 million in independent expenditures into the House contest in New Hampshire's First Congressional District. This amount was $800,000 more than the $1.6 million spent in the race by first-term Democratic incumbent Carol Shea-Porter.[96] Most of the independent expenditures made by the Hill committees advocated the defeat of the opposing party candidate rather than the election of the party's own candidate, and this trend is likely to increase the negativity in House and Senate campaigns.

Clearly, the Hill committees were not on equal financial footing in 2008. On the House side, the DCCC's sizable fund-raising advantage over the NRCC translated into significant differences in the two committees' ability to spend in their candidates' campaigns. The DCCC spent $1 million or more in forty House races, but the NRCC was able to spend that much in only nine House contests.[97] On the Senate side, both party campaign committees poured the bulk of their independent spending into just five competitive contests: Minnesota, Mississippi, New Hampshire, North Carolina, and Oregon. But the DSCC outspent the NRSC in all five races, and it did so by a 2-1 margin in North Carolina and Oregon. Democrats won all but the Mississippi race. The RNC helped the Republican Hill committees by making coordinated expenditures in some close House and Senate contests.

Hill committee expenditures are also supplemented by campaign contributions from congressional incumbents, who give from their principal reelection accounts and leadership PACs to help the party's candidates.[98] In the 2008 election cycle, Charles Rangel (D-N.Y.), chair of the House Ways and Means Committee, contributed $899,000 to Democratic congressional candidates from his leadership PAC and another $399,900 from his principal reelection account. On the House Republican side, Eric Cantor (R-Va.) gave more than $1 million to candidates from his leadership PAC and $54,000 from his principal campaign committee.[99] (For his efforts, Cantor was elected House Republican whip by his House GOP colleagues for the 111th Congress.) For candidates in tight races, these "party-connected" contributions can be a substantial boost. In 2008 embattled GOP House incumbent Steve Chabot (R-Ohio), who lost his bid for reelection, received $325,118 from the leadership PACs and reelection accounts of his Republican colleagues. Since passage of BCRA, congressional incumbents have become a vital part of the parties' fund-raising machinery, as the leaders lean on even junior members to share their campaign wealth with the party campaign committee and its needy candidates.[100]

Finally, the congressional campaign committees also indirectly assist their candidates by transferring funds to state parties. In 2008 the DSCC transferred $22.1 million to Democratic state parties, and the DCCC gave $16.2 million. These funds were almost certainly intended to help Democratic congressional candidates in close races. The Republican Hill committees transferred far fewer dollars to state parties in 2008, reflecting the GOP's more precarious financial situation.

Ultimately, party support for congressional candidates can be quite substantial and affect the outcomes of close contests. The party campaign committees, however, share the electoral arena with powerful interest groups that contribute large sums from PACs directly to candidates (mostly incumbents) and that make significant soft money expenditures through 527 and 501(c) groups. If the behavior of officeholders is influenced by campaign money, as Herbert E. Alexander observes, the parties surely have only a partial claim for preference.[101] That said, the parties' claims are far stronger today than they were twenty years ago.

Evaluating the Campaign Finance System

Although campaign finance reform has been effective in some ways, it has failed to meet the expectations of reformers in a number of the most important areas. One of the main goals of the FECA was to limit the cost of campaigns. In this regard, it has failed miserably. The Supreme Court's ruling in *Buckley v. Valeo* (1976) that restrictions on the personal and total expenditures of candidates for Congress were unconstitutional led to an explosion of spending. Winning candidates for the Senate in 1976 spent a total of $20 million; in 2008 they spent $279 million, more than fourteen times as much. Winning candidates for the House in 1976 spent a total of $38 million; in 2008 they spent roughly $637 million, nearly 17 times as much.[102]

The FECA has also failed in its effort to curtail the influence of organized interests. Indeed, much of the spending increase is the direct result of greater activity of PACs and various soft money committees run by interest groups. The impact of interest groups is especially pronounced at the congressional level. In 1974 PACs made campaign contributions of about $12.5 million to congressional candidates. In 2008 their contributions totaled $386.9 million—more than thirty times as much. Currently there are nearly four thousand PACs, almost seven times as many as there were in 1974. Additionally, the 501(c) and 527 committees organized by interest groups funneled an estimated $400 million into campaigns in 2008. These committees pose a particular problem for the campaign finance system because they are so difficult to regulate. Moreover, as the Court continues to define express advocacy narrowly, these committees have significant latitude to run soft money–financed issue ads, precisely the kind of activity BCRA sought to eliminate.[103]

Under Chief Justice John Roberts, the Court may well continue to loosen campaign finance regulations. At the time of this writing, the Court had just heard oral arguments in *Citizens United v. Federal Election Commission,* in which it revisited the constitutionality of government-imposed restrictions on corporate independent expenditures. At issue is a highly critical ninety-minute documentary about Hillary Clinton produced by a conservative nonprofit 501c(4) corporation, Citizens United, during the 2008 primary season and paid for with funds raised outside of federal restrictions. Claiming that the documentary was the "functional equivalent" of election advocacy, the FEC argued that Citizens United's use of unregulated corporate funds to finance the film violated BCRA's ban on such funds to pay for election advocacy.[104] In theory, the Court could resolve this case with a narrow ruling in favor of Citizens United by striking down the provision in BCRA subjecting nonprofit corporations to the same restrictions as for-profit corporations or by arguing that the group's film is not the type of political communication BCRA was intended to regulate.[105] Some observers believe a conservative majority on the Court may use the case as a vehicle for setting aside established precedent and overturning *all* government prohibitions on corporate independent expenditures—those made by nonprofit ideological corporations and business corporations alike.[106]

The FECA also sought to stimulate the involvement of ordinary citizens in the financing of campaigns. At first, that goal appeared to be a success: in 1976, 16 percent of Americans reported having made a contribution to help a campaign, twice the percentage recorded just ten years earlier.[107] In addition, 29 percent of all taxpayers took advantage of the federal income tax checkoff option in 1980. By 1992, however, this percentage had dropped to less than 20 percent, where it has remained. Mirroring the decline in the income tax checkoff, only 9.6 percent of Americans reported that they contributed money to help a campaign in 2004, about half the percentage reported in 1976.[108] Obama's campaign may well have boosted these numbers in 2008, but his campaign can clearly be considered exceptional.

The direct influence of wealthy contributors on electoral politics has probably declined, although not as much as reformers had hoped. To be sure, direct contributions to federal candidates, now capped at $2,300 per candidate, per election, are effectively limited. But in other ways, federal regulations are hardly constraining. One may give a total of $108,500 of hard money per election cycle, a sum few ordinary Americans can afford. Of these funds, $28,500 may go to the national parties. Well-connected individuals can also "bundle" contributions, a practice that involves raising contributions for a candidate from a large number of individual donors and then delivering the contributions to the candidate en masse. Wealthy individuals can also spend an unlimited amount of money to help elect a candidate if the money is spent independently of the candidate's campaign. The proliferation of 527 and 501(c) groups has only furthered this kind of activity. Indeed, many of the 501(c) committees operating in the 2008 elections were reportedly funded by extremely wealthy individuals.[109] To be sure, BCRA's soft money ban has prevented wealthy individuals from making six- and seven-figure contributions to the national parties. But many of these donors have simply found outlets for their political cash in the growing number of 527 and 501(c) committees. It is therefore a myth that strict limitations control contributions to federal campaigns. People and groups have always found ways to inject money into the political system, and undoubtedly they always will.

The matching fund system for funding presidential primaries was also intended to increase the influence of small contributors. As provided by the FECA, matching federal funds become available for presidential primary and caucus candidates who have raised $100,000 in small sums—by obtaining $5,000 in contributions of $250 or less in each of twenty states. Once a candidate has reached the $100,000 threshold, the government matches the first $250 of any individual contribution. This encourages candidates to raise money in smaller chunks, something that ordinary people might be able to afford. To receive federal matching funds, however, presidential candidates must agree to certain spending limits and grapple with state spending ceilings, which are determined by population. In 2008 candidates could spend $841,000 in a small state like New Hampshire and $18.3 million in California, the largest state.[110]

To avoid these limitations, presidential candidates may refuse federal funding and raise their funds exclusively from private or personal sources. In 2000 George W. Bush demonstrated that such an approach could be successful, and John Kerry and Howard Dean followed suit in 2004, opting out of federal funding in the primaries because they could raise significantly more money through private means. In 2008, nearly every serious presidential candidate turned down public financing in the primaries, and the top-tier candidates in each party raised staggering sums of private money. Obama argued that his large number of small individual donors constituted a new model of public funding, but he also raised a significant sum of campaign money from large donors.[111] Just how large a departure from the 1970s fund-raising regime this represents cannot be overstated. In the 1976 presidential primaries, nearly 50 percent of funds spent by candidates came from the federal government. In 2008, the figure was 2 percent.

In at least one area, the FECA has not been a complete failure. Opportunities to misuse money in federal elections have been constrained to some extent. The risks of detection are greater as a result of timely and comprehensive disclosure provisions, requirements for centralized accounting of contributions and expenditures, curbs on cash contributions, and the existence of a full-time agency—the FEC—to administer the law and to investigate alleged infractions. Every major presidential and congressional campaign employs accountants and lawyers to analyze and monitor its financial activities. Moreover, the FEC has begun to clamp down on 527 groups. But substantial problems remain. The 501(c) groups remain largely free of disclosure requirements, making these groups unaccountable to the public. Moreover, knowing that legal action by the chronically understaffed and underfunded FEC will not be taken until well after the election doubtlessly tempts some candidates and groups to play fast and loose with the rules on campaign finance.

In terms of the parties, the FECA has aided them in some respects and weakened them in others. Among the provisions of the law that benefit the parties are:

1. individual contributors can give more money to the national parties ($28,500) than they can to candidates ($2,300);
2. each national party can spend money on behalf of its presidential and congressional candidates (coordinated expenditures);

3. each national party can spend unlimited sums of hard money on express advocacy, as long as the money is spent independently of its presidential and congressional candidates (independent expenditures);
4. both national and state party committees can make direct contributions to House and Senate candidates; and
5. public funds are available to defray the costs of presidential nominating conventions.

Other provisions of the law, however, do not serve the party interest. The public funds made available in the nominating and election phases go directly to the candidates instead of to the parties. In this, the law is plainly candidate-centered. By contrast, many European democracies, and even a few U.S. states, allocate public funds to political parties.[112] Moreover, with the passage of BCRA in 2002, the national parties can no longer raise soft money, forcing them to spend more time and money raising hard dollars in smaller increments.

Despite the restrictions on the parties in raising and spending funds, the parties are reclaiming their role in campaigns. As Anthony Corrado points out, in 2004—the first election after BCRA took effect—the DNC and the RNC raised more hard dollars than they had raised in hard *and* soft dollars in 2000.[113] And party fund-raising continues to keep pace. The three Democratic national committees (national, senatorial, and congressional) raised $599.1 million in 2008 (up from $586.2 million in 2004), while the corresponding GOP committees raised $640.3 million in 2008 (down from $657.1 million in 2004). The parties have offset the loss of soft money in several ways: by pushing for larger contributions from regular donors, by using the Internet to expand their small donor base, and, as Diana Dwyre and her colleagues note, by the efforts of congressional party leaders, especially in the House, to persuade well-heeled incumbents to share their campaign funds with the congressional campaign committees.[114] In 2008 Democratic House incumbents transferred $38.9 million to the DCCC—22 percent of the DCCC's total receipts in 2008; and, although GOP incumbents faced a more difficult electoral environment, they still managed to give $22.8 million to the NRCC.[115]

In the 2008 elections, both national committees and their presidential candidates also increased their fund-raising capacity through the use of joint fund-raising committees. Such committees benefit the parties and their presidential candidates by allowing them to raise money concurrently from the same donors. Donors to joint fund-raising committees simply combine the contribution limits that would apply if they gave to each committee separately.[116]

Some observers mistakenly predicted that BCRA's soft money ban would harm the Democratic Party more than the Republican Party.[117] Compared with the 1970s and 1980s, when the RNC often outraised the DNC by five to one, the gap has narrowed considerably, although Republicans still maintain a substantial advantage. As Table 4-6 demonstrates, the Democrats were originally able to narrow the Republican advantage through the use of soft money. In 2000 soft money

Table 4-6 National Party Fund-Raising, Hard and Soft Money: 1998–2008 (in millions of dollars)

	Presidential Year			Off Year		
	2000	2004	2008	1998	2002	2006
Democrats						
Hard money	$212.9	$586.2	$599.1	$153.4	$162.3	$392.1
Soft money	257.0	—	—	91.5	246.2	—
Total	469.7	586.2	599.1	244.9	408.5	392.1
Republicans						
Hard money	$361.6	$657.1	$640.3	$273.6	$352.9	508.1
Soft money	258.1	—	—	131.0	250.0	—
Total	619.7	657.1	640.3	404.6	602.9	508.1
GOP advantage	$150	$70.9	$41.2	$159.7	$194.4	$116.0

Source: Federal Election Commission, press release, March 2, 2005, as corrected March 14, 2005. Federal Election Commission, press release, May 28, 2009. The national parties include the national committees, the congressional campaign committees, and the senatorial campaign committees.

made up 47 percent of the Democrats' total receipts but only 35 percent of the Republicans'.[118] In 2004, when soft money was banned for the first time, the Democrats further cut the Republicans' advantage to $101 million dollars, the smallest difference between the parties ever. The DNC ($404.3 million) actually outraised the RNC ($392.4) in 2004, but the RNC regained its financial edge in 2008. On the Hill, the DCCC and DSCC, enjoying a favorable political climate and the fund-raising leverage afforded by majority party control, had sizable financial advantages over their GOP counterparts in 2008.

Neither the adoption of the FECA and its amendments nor BCRA has solved all the problems of financing American elections. Inequities, confusion, and uncertainties persist, especially since the appearance of 527 and 501(c) groups on the political landscape. Have campaigns become too costly? Some close observers argue that they are underfinanced.[119] Should congressional as well as presidential campaigns be publicly financed? Thus far, Congress has said no. In theory, the public supports the concept, but Americans have expressed no desire to pay for public funding. Indeed, even the presidential public financing system now appears hopelessly out of date. And what of interest groups, now spending with a vengeance and undoubtedly gaining improved access to policymakers and securing questionable preferments? How much regulation of soft money expenditures by interest groups will the Supreme Court permit? Is it realistic to think of passing new campaign finance legislation that makes elections more competitive by diminishing the advantages of incumbents over their challengers?

As it stands, the massive advantages of office for incumbents leave challengers with no more than an outside chance of winning, particularly in House elections. Law and practice have combined to build a comprehensive incumbent protection system. Can campaign finance legislation be designed to strengthen the parties, and should this be a public policy goal? These are some of the questions that will inform future debate on campaign finance and its reform. Answers do not come easily. The consequences of change, moreover, are difficult to anticipate. Protecting the status quo may be the best safeguard against the unanticipated outcomes that invariably accompany change.[120]

The manner in which political campaigns are financed has long been a source of controversy. Devising acceptable public policy on the subject has proven to be difficult. But the objectives of regulation have been clear: to increase public confidence in the political process by curbing the abusive uses of political money, to enhance the opportunities for citizens to participate in politics by running for public office or contributing to political campaigns, to facilitate healthy levels of electoral competition, and to reduce the vulnerability of candidates and public officials to the importunings and pressures of major benefactors. The campaign finance law has contributed only marginally to the achievement of these objectives. A solid majority of the public still thinks that the government is run for a small number of big interests rather than for the nation as a whole, and large contributors continue to dominate the fund-raising system. Overall, the reform laws have created some new problems, accentuated certain old ones, conferred advantages on incumbent politicians and disadvantages on challengers, and, arguably, done more to weaken the parties than to strengthen them.

NOTES

1. For an analysis of these party networks, see John F. Bibby, "National-State Integration, Allied Groups, and Issue Activists," in *The State of the Parties: The Changing Role of Contemporary Parties*, 3rd ed., ed. John C. Green and Daniel Shea (Lanham, Md.: Rowman and Littlefield, 1999).

2. Seth Masket, *No Middle Ground: How Informal Party Organizations Control Nominations and Polarize Legislatures* (Ann Arbor: University of Michigan Press, 2009).

3. Campaign Finance Institute, press release, "Soft Money Political Spending by 501(c) Nonprofits Tripled in the 2008 Election," February 25, 2009. Also see Center for Responsive Politics at www.opensecrets.org/527s/index.php.

4. See Paul S. Herrnson, *Congressional Elections: Campaigning at Home and in Washington*, 5th ed. (Washington, D.C.: CQ Press, 2008); and Dennis W. Johnson, *No Place for Amateurs: How Political Consultants Are Shaping Democracy* (New York: Routledge, 2001).

5. Barbara G. Salmore and Stephen A. Salmore, *Candidates, Parties, and Campaigns* (Washington, D.C.: CQ Press, 1989), 215–216.

6. A study of women's and men's campaigns for the U.S. House of Representatives shows that they have more similarities than differences. The most important difference is that women are more likely than men to stress social issues, such as children, poverty, and education. See Kirsten la Cour Dabelko and Paul S. Herrnson, "Women's and Men's Campaigns for the U.S. House of Representatives," *Political Research Quarterly* 50 (March 1997): 121–135. For a complete treatment of gender differences in campaigns, see Kim Fridkin Kahn, *The Political Consequences of Being a Woman: How Stereotypes Influence the Conduct and Consequences of Political Campaigns* (New York: Columbia University Press, 1996).

7. Daniel Shea, *Campaign Craft: The Strategies, Tactics, and Art of Political Campaign Management* (Westport, Conn.: Praeger, 1996).

8. Ibid.; Salmore and Salmore, *Candidates, Parties, and Campaigns*. For an interesting argument that negative campaigning is not necessarily bad campaigning, see William G. Mayer, "In Defense of Negative Campaigning," *Political Science Quarterly* 111 (Fall 1996): 437–455.

9. Just how minimal the effect of campaigns is depends on the study. Paul Lazarsfeld, Bernard Berelson, and Hazel Gaudet, *The People's Choice* (New York: Columbia University Press, 1944), find it to be between five and eight percentage points. Steven E. Finkel, "Reexamining the 'Minimal Effects' Model in Recent Presidential Campaigns," *Journal of Politics* 55 (March 1993): 1–21, finds a similar effect in a more contemporary study. Larry M. Bartels, "Electioneering in the United States," in *Electioneering: A Comparative Study of Continuity and Change,* ed. David Butler and Austin Ranney (New York: Oxford University Press, 1992), finds the effect of political campaigns to be only about two percentage points.

10. See Michael Lewis-Beck and Tom Rice, *Forecasting Elections* (Washington, D.C.: CQ Press, 1992); and Steven J. Rosenstone, *Forecasting Presidential Elections* (New Haven, Conn.: Yale University Press, 1983).

11. Stephen Ansolabehere and Shanto Iyengar, *Going Negative* (New York: Free Press, 1995). See also John G. Geer, *In Defense of Negativity: Attack Ads in Presidential Campaigns* (Chicago: University of Chicago Press, 2006).

12. Bartels, "Electioneering in the United States."

13. Lewis A. Froman Jr., "A Realistic Approach to Campaign Strategies and Tactics," in *The Electoral Process,* ed. M. Kent Jennings and L. Harmon Zeigler (Englewood Cliffs, N.J.: Prentice Hall, 1966), 7–8.

14. See Marc J. Hetherington, "The Effect of Political Trust on the Presidential Vote," *American Political Science Review* 93 (June 1999): 311–326.

15. Edison-Mitofsky exit poll, 2008.

16. D. Sunshine Hillygus and Todd Shields, *The Persuadable Voter* (Princeton, N.J.: Princeton University Press, 2008).

17. Eric Plutzer, "Becoming a Habitual Voter: Inertia, Resources, and Growth in Young Adulthood," *American Political Science Review* 96 (March 2002): 41–56.

18. Daron R. Shaw, "A Study of Presidential Campaign Event Effects from 1952–1992," *Journal of Politics* 61 (May 1999): 387–422. Also see Daron R. Shaw, "The Effect of TV Ads and Candidate Appearances on Statewide Presidential Votes, 1988–96," *American Political Science Review* 93 (June 1999): 345–362; Thomas Holbrook, *Do Campaigns Matter?* (Thousand Oaks, Calif.: Sage Publications, 1996); and John G. Geer, "The Effects of the Presidential Debates on the Electorate's Preferences for Candidates," *American Politics Quarterly* 16 (May 1988): 486–501.

19. Charles Cook of the Cook Political Report is the political analyst in question. It is worth noting that Gore had a several-point lead in the polls in the days leading up to this debate but trailed from then until election day.

20. From Theodore H. White, *The Making of the President, 1960* (New York: Atheneum, 1961). For an analysis of the major models of campaign decision making, see Karl A. Lamb and Paul A. Smith, *Campaign Decision-Making: The Presidential Election of 1964* (Belmont, Calif.: Wadsworth, 1968).

21. Federal Election Commission, press release, June 9, 2005.

22. Donald E. Stokes, "Spatial Models of Party Competition," *American Political Science Review* 57 (June 1963): 368–377.

23. John J. Dilulio Jr., "Valence Voters, Valence Victors," in *The Elections of 1996,* ed. Michael Nelson (Washington, D.C.: CQ Press, 1997), 172.

24. Salmore and Salmore, *Candidates, Parties, and Campaigns,* 113.

25. "Campaign Consultants: Pushing Sincerity in 1974," *Congressional Quarterly Weekly Report,* May 4, 1974, 1105.

26. Salmore and Salmore, *Candidates, Parties, and Campaigns,* 113.

27. Voter News Service exit poll.

28. John R. Petrocik, "Issue Ownership in Presidential Elections, with a 1980 Case Study," *American Journal of Political Science* 40 (August 1986): 825–850.

29. Michael Cornfeld, "Game Changers: New Technology and the 2008 Presidential Election," in *The Year of Obama: How Barack Obama Won the White House,* ed. Larry J. Sabato (New York: Pearson-Longman, 2009).

30. See an article by Frank J. Sorauf that examines the organizational lives of PACs, the role of donors to PACs, and PAC accountability: "Who's in Charge? Accountability in Political Action Committees," *Political Science Quarterly* 99 (Winter 1984–1985): 591–614. Also see the studies of PAC goals, organization, and decision making by Theodore J. Eismeier and Philip H. Pollock III, "An Organizational Analysis of Political Action Committees," *Political Behavior* 7, no. 2 (1985): 192–216; and "Strategy and Choice in Congressional Elections: The Role of Political Action Committees," *American Journal of Political Science* 30 (February 1986): 197–213. The authors distinguish three PAC roles: *accommodationist* (seek access in Congress through gifts to incumbents); *partisan* (basically financial auxiliaries of the major parties); and *adversary* (seek to defeat members whom they regard as hostile to their interests).

31. The scholarly verdict is mixed on the extent to which war chests can discourage competition. See Janet Box-Steffensmeier, "A Dynamic Analysis of the Role of War Chests in Campaign Strategy," *American Journal of Political Science* 40 (1996): 352–371; and Jay Goodliffe, "War Chests as Precautionary Savings," *Political Behavior* 26 (2004): 289–315.

32. Eric Heberlig and Bruce A. Larson, "Redistributing Campaign Funds by U.S. House Members: The Spiraling Costs of the Permanent Campaign," *Legislative Studies Quarterly* XXX (November 2005): 597–624; Marian Currinder, *Money in the House: Campaign Funds and Congressional Party Politics* (Boulder, Colo.: Westview Press, 2009); Damon Cann, *Sharing the Wealth: Member Contributions and the Exchange Theory of Party Influence in the U.S. House* (Albany, N.Y.: SUNY Press, 2008); Paul S. Herrnson, "Money and Motives: Spending in House Elections," in Lawrence C. Dodd and Bruce I. Oppenheimer, eds., *Congress Reconsidered,* 6th ed. (Washington, D.C.: CQ Press, 1997).

33. Lynn Vavreck, "More than Minimal Effects: Explaining the Differences between Clarifying and Insurgent Presidential Campaigns in Strategy and Effect," Ph.D. diss., University of Rochester, 2001.

34. *Washington Post,* June 15, 1987.

35. Herrnson, *Congressional Elections,* 81–82. Herbert E. Alexander also held that television costs in overall political spending are not as great as critics contend. He observed that only about one-half of the candidates for the U.S. House of Representatives ever purchase television time.

36. See Herbert E. Alexander, *Financing the 1980 Election* (Washington, D.C.: CQ Press, 1983); William J. Crotty and Gary C. Jacobson, *American Parties in Decline* (Boston: Little, Brown, 1980), 816–823; and Frank J. Sorauf, *Money in American Elections* (Glenview, Ill.: Scott Foresman/Little, Brown, 1988), 186–221. The 1988, 1992, and 1996 estimates are by Alexander; the 2000 estimates are by Candice J. Nelson, "Spending in the 2000 Elections," in *Financing the 2000 Elections,* ed. David J. Magleby (Washington, D.C.: Brookings Institution, 2002).

37. These figures come from the Center for Responsive Politics, www.opensecrets.org/overview/index.php.

38. Federal Election Commission, press releases, March 4, 1993; May 15, 2001; June 18, 2003.

39. Anthony Gierzynski, *Money Rules: Financing Elections in America* (Boulder, Colo.: Westview Press, 2000), 8.

40. Frank J. Sorauf, *Inside Campaign Finance: Myths and Realities* (New Haven, Conn.: Yale University Press, 1992), 187.

41. Bradley A. Smith, *Unfree Speech, The Folly of Campaign Finance Reform* (Princeton, N.J.: Princeton University Press, 2001), 42.

42. Safe incumbents were those rated as safe by *CQ Weekly*, which rates the level of electoral competition in every congressional contest.

43. The fund-raising figures for Senate contests come from the Center for Responsive Politics, www.opensecrets.org.

44. These figures do not include the Minnesota Senate races, which were not decided until June 30, 2009. They also do not include funds spent in Georgia after November 6 for the December 2 runoff between Saxby Chambliss and Jim Martin.

45. Anthony Corrado, "Money and Politics: A History of Federal Campaign Finance Law," in *The New Campaign Finance Sourcebook*, ed. Anthony Corrado, Thomas Mann, Daniel Ortiz, and Trevor Potter (Washington, D.C.: Brookings, 2005). See also Raymond La Raja, *Small Change: Money, Political Parties, and Campaign Finance Reform* (Ann Arbor: University of Michigan Press, 2008).

46. Many states also passed campaign finance reform legislation following Watergate. For an excellent analysis of state campaign regulation, see Michael J. Malbin and Thomas L. Gais, *The Day After Reform: Sobering Campaign Finance Lessons from the American States* (Albany, N.Y.: The Rockefeller Institute Press, 1998). Also see Joel A. Thomas and Gary F. Moncrief, eds., *Campaign Finance in State Legislative Elections* (Washington, D.C.: CQ Press, 1998).

47. Larry J. Sabato and Bruce Larson, *The Party's Just Begun: Shaping Political Parties for America's Future*, 2nd ed. (New York: Longman, 2002), 72.

48. *Buckley v. Valeo*, 424 U.S. 1 (1976). The Court struck down provisions that limited the spending of personal funds by candidates ($35,000 for Senate candidates and $25,000 for House candidates) and those that limited total expenditures. Senate candidates were to be limited to total expenditures of no more than $100,000 or eight cents per eligible voter (whichever is greater) in primaries, and $150,000 or twelve cents per voter (whichever is greater) in general elections. Fund-raising costs of up to 20 percent of the spending limit could be added to these amounts. House candidates were to be limited to no more than $70,000 in primaries and $70,000 in general elections (plus fund-raising costs of up to 20 percent of the spending limit).

49. *Colorado Republican Federal Campaign Committee v. Federal Election Commission*, 518 U.S. 604 (1996).

50. *Nixon v. Shrink Missouri Government PAC*, 528 U.S. 377 (2000).

51. U.S. Congress, Senate, *Congressional Record*, daily ed., 101st Cong., 1st sess., May 11, 1990, S6038.

52. What campaign money buys for challengers is voter recognition. See Gary C. Jacobson, "The Effects of Campaign Spending in Congressional Elections," *American Political Science Review* 72 (June 1978): 469–491; Gary C. Jacobson, "The Effects of Campaign Spending in House Elections: New Evidence for Old Arguments," *American Journal of Political Science* 34 (May 1990): 334–362; and Donald P. Green and Jonathan S. Krasno, "Rebuttal to Jacobson's 'New Evidence for Old Arguments,' " *American Journal of Political Science* 34 (May 1990): 363–372.

53. See Sabato and Larson, *The Party's Just Begun*, 73, 99, n.16. Also see Anthony Corrado, "Party Soft Money," in *Campaign Finance Reform: A Sourcebook*, ed. Anthony Corrado et al. (Washington, D.C.: Brookings, 1997); and Richard Briffault, "Soft Money Reform and the Constitution," *Election Law Journal* 1 (2002): 343–372.

54. Craig B. Holman and Luke P. McLoughlin, *Buying Time 2000: Television Advertising in the 2000 Federal Elections* (New York: Brennan Center for Justice, 2002).

55. *New York Times*, September 8, 1996.

56. Brennan Center for Justice, press release, July 3, 2001.

57. Holman and McLoughlin, *Buying Time 2000.*

58. David Magleby and J. Quin Monson, eds., *The Last Hurrah? Soft Money and Issue Advocacy in the 2002 Elections* (Washington, D.C.: Brookings, 2004).

59. There were also important sublimits. Of the $108,200 an individual could contribute in 2007–2008, $42,700 could go to candidates and $65,500 to parties.

60. Federal Election Commission, "Electioneering Communications," October 2006, www.fec.gov/pages/brochures/electioneering.shtml#Electioneering_ Communications.

61. For an excellent treatment of the Millionaires' Amendment, see Jennifer Steen, "Self-Financed Candidates and the Millionaires' Amendment," in *The Election After Reform: Money, Politics, and the Bipartisan Campaign Reform Act,* ed. Michael Malbin (Lanham, Md.: Rowman and Littlefield, 2006).

62. Glen Justice, "F.E.C. Declines to Curb Independent Fundraisers," *New York Times,* May 14, 2004, A14; John Cochran, "First Big Test of Campaign Finance Law Has Both Sides Girding for Next Round," *CQ Weekly,* May 29, 2004, 1282–3.

63. Center for Responsive Politics, "527 Committee Activity."

64. Marian Currinder, "Campaign Finance: Fundraising and Spending in the 2008 Elections," in *The Elections of 2008,* ed. Michael Nelson (Washington, D.C.: CQ Press, 2009), 167. Michael J. Malbin, "Rethinking the Campaign Finance Agenda," *The Forum* 6, no. 1 (2008).

65. Campaign Finance Institute, "Soft Money Political Spending."

66. *McConnell v. Federal Election Commission,* 540 U.S. 93 (2003).

67. *FEC v. Wisconsin Right To Life,* 551 U.S. 449 (2007).

68. La Raja, *Small Change.*

69. *Davis v. FEC,* 554 U.S. 12 (2008).

70. Michael E. Toner, "The Impact of Federal Election Laws on the 2008 Presidential Election," in *The Year of Obama,* 153.

71. Campaign Finance Institute, press release, "Reality Check: Obama Received About the Same Percentage from Small Donors in 2008 as Bush in 2004," November 24, 2008, www.cfinst.org/pr/prRelease.aspx?ReleaseID=216.

72. Federal Election Commission, press release, May 28, 2009, www.fec.gov/ press/press2009/05282009Party/20090528Party.shtml.

73. Corrado, "Party Finances in the Wake of BCRA."

74. Federal Election Commission data.

75. Corrado, "Party Finances in the Wake of BCRA." In *Colorado Republican Federal Campaign Committee v. FEC,* 518 U.S. 604 (1996) the Supreme Court ruled that the parties have the right to spend without limit on express advocacy—as long as the spending is done independently of their candidates and financed with hard dollars.

76. Federal Election Commission, press release, May 28, 2009; Brian J. Brox, "Show Me The Money: National Party Transfers to State and Local Party Organizations, 1996–2006" (paper presented at the annual meeting of the Midwest Political Science Association, Chicago, Illinois, April 3–6, 2008).

77. Campaign Finance Institute, "Soft Money Political Spending." Also the Center for Responsive Politics at www.opensecrets.org/527s/index.php.

78. James Gimpel, Frances E. Lee, and Shanna Pearson-Merkowitz, "The Check Is in the Mail: Indirect Funding Flows in Congressional Elections," *American Journal of Political Science* 52 (2008): 373–394.

79. See an interesting account, "Don't Look Homeward," in *National Journal,* June 16, 1990, 1458–60.

80. Federal Election Commission, press release, April 24, 2009, www.fec.gov/ press/press2009/20090415PAC/20090424PAC.shtml. The Center for Responsive

Politics, www.opensecrets.org/overview/index.php?cycle=2008&Display=T&
Type=R.

81. See especially the scholarly dialogue between Gary C. Jacobson and Jonathan
S. Krasno and Donald Philip Green assessing the effect of incumbent spending. Don-
ald Philip Green and Jonathan S. Krasno, "Salvation for the Spendthrift Incumbent:
Estimating the Effects of Campaign Spending in House Elections," *American Journal of
Political Science* 32 (November 1988): 884–907; Jonathan S. Krasno and Donald Philip
Green, "Preempting Quality Challengers in House Elections," *Journal of Politics* 50
(November 1988): 920–936; and Gary C. Jacobson, "The Effects of Campaign Spend-
ing in House Elections." *American Journal of Political Science* 34 (May 1990): 334–362.

82. Gary W. Cox and Eric Magar, "How Much Is Majority Status in the U.S. Con-
gress Worth?" *American Political Science Review* 93 (1999): 299–309; and Thomas J.
Rudolph, "Corporate and Labor PAC Contributions in House Elections: Measuring the
Effect of Majority Party Status," *Journal of Politics* 61 (1999):195–206.

83. Federal Election Commission, press release, April 24, 2009, www.fec.gov/
press/press2009/20090415PAC/20090424PAC.shtml.

84. Kevin B. Grier and Michael C. Munger, "Comparing Interest Group Contributions to House and Senate Incumbents, 1980–1986," *Journal of Politics* 55 (1992):
615–643.

85. *Congressional Quarterly Weekly Report*, April 8, 1978, 850–851; and November
11, 1978, 3260–2.

86. Federal Election Commission, press release, April 24, 2009, www.fec.gov/
press/press2009/20090415PAC/20090424PAC.shtml.

87. Currinder, *Money in the House*, 142.

88. See Sabato and Larson, *The Party's Just Begun*, 84–88; Bruce A. Larson, "Incumbent Contributions to the Congressional Campaign Committees, 1990–2000," *Political
Research Quarterly* 57 (March 2004): 155–161.

89. Anthony Corrado, *Creative Campaigning: PACs and the Presidential Selection Process*
(Boulder, Colo.: Westview Press, 1992). *Congressional Quarterly Weekly Report*, August
2, 1986, 1751–4.

90. David R. Mayhew, *Congress: The Electoral Connection* (New Haven: Yale University
Press, 1974), 84.

91. *Wall Street Journal*, September 24, 1986.

92. Campaign Finance Institute, "Soft Money Political Spending"; and Campaign
Finance Institute, press release, "Outside Soft Money Groups Approaching $400 Mil-
lion in Targeted Spending in 2008 Election," October 31, 2008.

93. Herrnson, *Congressional Elections*, 91–95.

94. *Colorado Republican Federal Campaign Committee v. FEC*, 518 u.s. 604 (1996).

95. Federal Election Commission, press release, May 28, 2009.

96. Ibid.

97. Ibid.

98. Incumbents can contribute $2,000 per candidate per election from their prin-
cipal reelection account and $5,000 per candidate per election from a leadership
PAC.

99. These data come from the Center for Responsive Politics, www.opensecrets
.org/overview/cand2cand.php?Cycle=2008&Display=leadpacs.

100. Eric Heberlig, "Congressional Parties, Fundraising, and Committee Ambition,"
Political Research Quarterly 56 (2003): 151–162; Eric Heberlig, Marc J. Hetherington,
Bruce A. Larson, "The Price of Leadership: Campaign Money and the Polarization of
Congressional Parties," *Journal of Politics* 68 (2006): 992–1005; Elizabeth Newlin Car-
ney, "In the Money," *National Journal*, July 10, 2004, 2173; and Sabato and Larson,
The Party's Just Begun, 84–88.

101. Herbert E. Alexander, "Political Parties and the Dollar," *Society* 22 (January/February 1985): 49–58.

102. Federal Election Commission, press release, June 9, 2005.

103. Campaign Finance Institute, "Soft Money Political Spending."

104. BCRA's ban on corporate money to pay for electioneering communications was upheld by the Supreme Court in *McConnell v. Federal Election Commission*, 540 U.S. 93 (2003). Similarly, in *Austin v. Michigan Chamber of Commerce*, 494 U.S. 652 (1990), the Court let stand Michigan's prohibition on independent expenditures made directly from a corporation's treasury (as opposed to its PAC).

105. Allowing unregulated independent spending by nonprofit political groups would comport with a September 2009 federal appeals court decision ruling that the government cannot regulate independent expenditures by nonprofit political groups (in this case, Emily's List). See David D. Kirkpatrick, "Court Backs Outside Groups' Political Spending," *New York Times*, September 19, 2009.

106. Stuart Taylor, "Campaign Money and the Chief Justice," *National Journal*, September 19, 2009.

107. American National Election Study, Cumulative File, 1948–2004.

108. Ibid.

109. Campaign Finance Institute, "Soft Money Political Spending"; and "Outside Soft Money Groups."

110. Federal Election Commission, brochure "Presidential Spending Limits for 2008," www.fec.gov/pages/brochures/pubfund_limits_2008.shtml.

111. Campaign Finance Institute, "Reality Check."

112. Malbin and Gais, *The Day After Reform.*

113. Corrado, "Party Finances in the Wake of BCRA."

114. Diana Dwyre et al., "Committees and Candidates: National Party Finance after BCRA," in *The State of the Parties: The Changing Role of Contemporary Parties,* 5th ed., ed. John Green and Daniel Coffey (Lanham, Md.: Rowman and Littlefield, 2006).

115. Federal Election Commission, press release, May 28, 2009.

116. Toner, "The Impact of Federal Election Laws on the 2008 Presidential Election," in *The Year of Obama.*

117. Seth Gitell, "The Democratic Party Suicide Bill," *Atlantic Monthly*, July–August 2008.

118. Federal Election Commission, press release, December 18, 2002.

119. Alexander, "Political Parties and the Dollar," 49–58.

120. For insight into the reform question, see Michael J. Malbin, "Looking Back at the Future of Campaign Finance Reform: Interest Groups and American Elections," in *Money and Politics in the United States,* 232–270.

5 THE CONGRESSIONAL PARTY AND THE FORMATION OF PUBLIC POLICY

THE TASKS THAT CONFRONT THE MAJOR PARTIES in the United States are formidable. From one perspective, the party is a wide-ranging electoral agency organized to make a credible bid for power. As electoral organizations, the parties recruit candidates, organize campaigns, develop issues, and mobilize voters. Voters get their best glimpse of the workings of parties when they observe the "party in the electorate" during political campaigns. Here and there a party organization is so stunted and devitalized that it cannot make an authentic effort to win office. Where it is not taken seriously, the party finds it difficult to develop and recruit candidates, to gain the attention of the media, and to attract financial contributors. Elections may go by default to the dominant party as the second party struggles merely to stay in business. But throughout most of the country the parties compete on fairly even terms—if not for certain offices or in certain districts, at least for some offices or in a state at large.

From another perspective, the party is a collection of officeholders who in some measure share common values and policy orientations. In the broadest sense, its mission is to take hold of government, identify national problems and priorities, and work for their settlement or achievement. In a narrower sense, the task of the "party in the government" is to consolidate and fulfill promises made to the electorate during the campaign. How it is organized to achieve this aim, and how it does it, is the concern of this chapter. The focus is the party in Congress.

Congressional Elections

In the study of congressional elections, scholars have found ample evidence to support the adage of former House Speaker Thomas P. "Tip" O'Neill Jr. (D-Mass., 1977–1986) that "all politics is local." The two most important variables in the election of members of Congress are, in fact, local political conditions—incumbency status and party affiliation.[1] Although less important, national political conditions, such as economic performance and the popularity of the president, also help determine how well the president's party does in a given year.[2]

Congressional incumbents have numerous advantages in elections. Their offices and staffs are basic units in their campaign organizations; voters are much more likely to recognize the name of an incumbent than that of a challenger; some voters will have benefited from the many services that members regularly perform for their constituents, and the franking privilege permits members to send mail to their constituents at government expense. Of major importance, incumbents ordinarily find it much easier than challengers to raise campaign funds, particularly from interest groups. It is not surprising, then, that incumbents are difficult to defeat. It is rare for less than 90 percent of all House incumbents seeking reelection to be successful; this has happened only twice since 1968—in 1974 and 1992. Typically, the reelection rate surpasses 95 percent. Even in 2006, when twenty-four House Republican incumbents were defeated, the reelection rate was more than 94 percent. And in 2008, another difficult year for the GOP, 90 percent of House Republicans were reelected, and the overall incumbent reelection rate in the House was 95 percent. Although Senate incumbents usually face stronger competition, they also win with great regularity. In 2004, twenty-five of the twenty-six Senate incumbents running for reelection won their races. The reelection rate for senators was 78.6 percent in 2006 and 83.3 percent in 2008.[3]

Party affiliation is a major factor in congressional elections. In the typical state, some districts nearly always elect Democratic legislators, and some districts nearly always elect Republican legislators. There are districts so thoroughly dominated by one party that the second has virtually no chance of winning. With few exceptions, House districts in major cities are securely Democratic, irrespective of the incumbency factor. In some suburban, small-town, and rural districts, Democratic candidates may face insurmountable odds in election after election. Districts do not often switch from one party to the other. In only two elections since 1968—1974 and 1994—did as many as 10 percent of the 435 seats switch party control.[4] Even in 2006 and 2008—elections in which Democrats made noteworthy gains in the House—only 7 percent and 5 percent of seats, respectively, switched party control. Often the percentage is much lower.

Incumbency and party combine to yield a great many one-sided elections, especially in the House. Districts are typically won by a vote of 60 percent or more. In 2008, only 59 of the 435 House races were won by 55 percent of the vote or less.[5] In fact, both parties are accustomed to having a number of House races in which their candidates face no major party opposition.

Although party competition for congressional seats is generally minimal, perceptions of how the president is performing have the potential to unseat more incumbents than usual. In the midst of a still-floundering economy in 1938, Franklin D. Roosevelt's Democratic Party lost a whopping seventy-one seats in the House and six in the Senate. Richard Nixon's Watergate problems cost the Republicans forty-nine House seats and four Senate seats in 1974. An unpopular Bill Clinton saw his party lose fifty-four House and ten Senate seats in 1994; a similarly unpopular George W. Bush saw his party lose thirty-one House seats and six Senate seats in 2006. As Gary Jacobson shows, Bush's low ratings continued to hurt House and Senate Republicans in 2008, even though Bush was not on the ticket.[6] The reason for these big losses is that high-quality challengers, such as people who have previously held elected office, decide to run when conditions are favorable to them. When national conditions are not favorable, such as when an opposing party president is doing well in the polls, they decide to wait.[7] Unfavorable national conditions also tend to produce high retirement rates for the party out of favor. In 2008, the anti-Republican mood led to the retirement of twenty-three GOP House incumbents and five GOP senators, but only three Democratic House incumbents and no Democratic senators.[8] Open-seat races tend to be more competitive than contests in which an incumbent is running, and the Republican retirements in 2008 created substantial opportunities for Democrats to pick up seats.

Even so, large party-oriented changes are less likely to occur today than a generation or more ago. The decline of party competition for congressional seats is one of the most conspicuous features of contemporary American politics. The most compelling explanation is that Democratic and Republican state legislators cooperate to protect each party's incumbents by drawing congressional district lines in such a way as to create as many safe districts as possible. As evidence, fewer than fifty House seats were even considered marginally competitive in 2002, the first election after the census and redistricting, when House seats are most often up for grabs.[9] The influence of redistricting is also evident in the shrinking number of congressional districts that vote for a member of Congress of one party and a presidential candidate of the other. In the 1972 election fully 44 percent of districts split their votes. In 2000 only 20 percent did; by 2004, the percentage had dropped to 14, the lowest since 1944. In 2008 the percentage of split districts rose slightly to 19 percent. Partisanship in the electorate and the "safeness" of districts combine to stifle competitive elections.

David R. Mayhew contends that incumbents have become more skillful in "advertising" their names, in "claiming credit" for federal government programs that benefit their districts, and in "position taking" on issues of concern to their constituents. They also have large and talented staffs to help them cultivate their constituents, and such resources have a significant campaign value.[10] Another study finds that information on the candidates is an important factor. If it is not available on both candidates, voters "are likely to vote for incumbents, whom they already like and may have voted for, faced with challengers they know little, if anything, about."[11] Incumbent advantages in fund-raising, detailed in chapter 4, also help stifle electoral competition.

It is hard to say exactly how public policy is affected by the relatively stable membership of both houses of Congress. Conventional wisdom holds that opportunities for major policy change are limited by a membership that remains largely intact election after election. Alternatively, members today have the luxury of pursuing more ideological ends in Congress, especially in the House. Because their districts are so safe, they feel little pressure to moderate their voting records. Strong ideological tendencies could lead to fundamental changes in a political system that has generally been characterized by its moderation. In yet another interesting perspective, Tracy Sulkin demonstrates that policy change does not necessarily require electoral replacement because incumbents tend to respond legislatively to issues raised by their challengers in the prior election.[12]

In the Senate institutional arrangements favor continuity over change. Only a third of the Senate's seats are up for reelection every two years, guaranteeing a relatively stable membership even when the nation might favor substantial partisan change. Moreover, the Senate's legislative procedures tend to mute the stronger ideological tendencies of the members elected to the chamber since the 1980s. As Bruce Oppenheimer and Marc Hetherington point out, Senate supermajority rules force even an ideologically cohesive majority party to produce policy closer to the minority party's liking than it would under rules (such as in the House) that allowed simple majorities to work their will.[13] Policy change is typically incremental in the American system, even following those rare elections that produce large changes in Congress's membership.

Party Representation in Congress

Figures 5-1 and 5-2 show the representation of the parties in each house over the past seventy-two years, from 1936 to 2008. The broad picture is one of Democratic dominance with brief interludes of Republican control of one or both chambers. Party fortunes changed in 1994, when the Republicans won control of Congress for the first time since the mid-1950s.[14] More important, they held their majorities in both houses for six consecutive elections, the longest period of Republican dominance in Congress since they won the House majority eight consecutive times from 1916 to 1930.[15] The 2002 election is particularly noteworthy because it is one of only three in the last century (along with those of 1902 and 1934) in which the president's party increased its strength in both houses in a midterm election.[16]

Voter frustration with President George W. Bush and his administration allowed Democrats to recapture majority control of both the House and Senate in 2006. Crucial to the Democrats' victory were the public's growing impatience with the war in Iraq, concern with government corruption, and Bush's low popularity.[17]

Figure 5-1 Democratic Strength in Senate Elections: 1936–2008

Number of seats

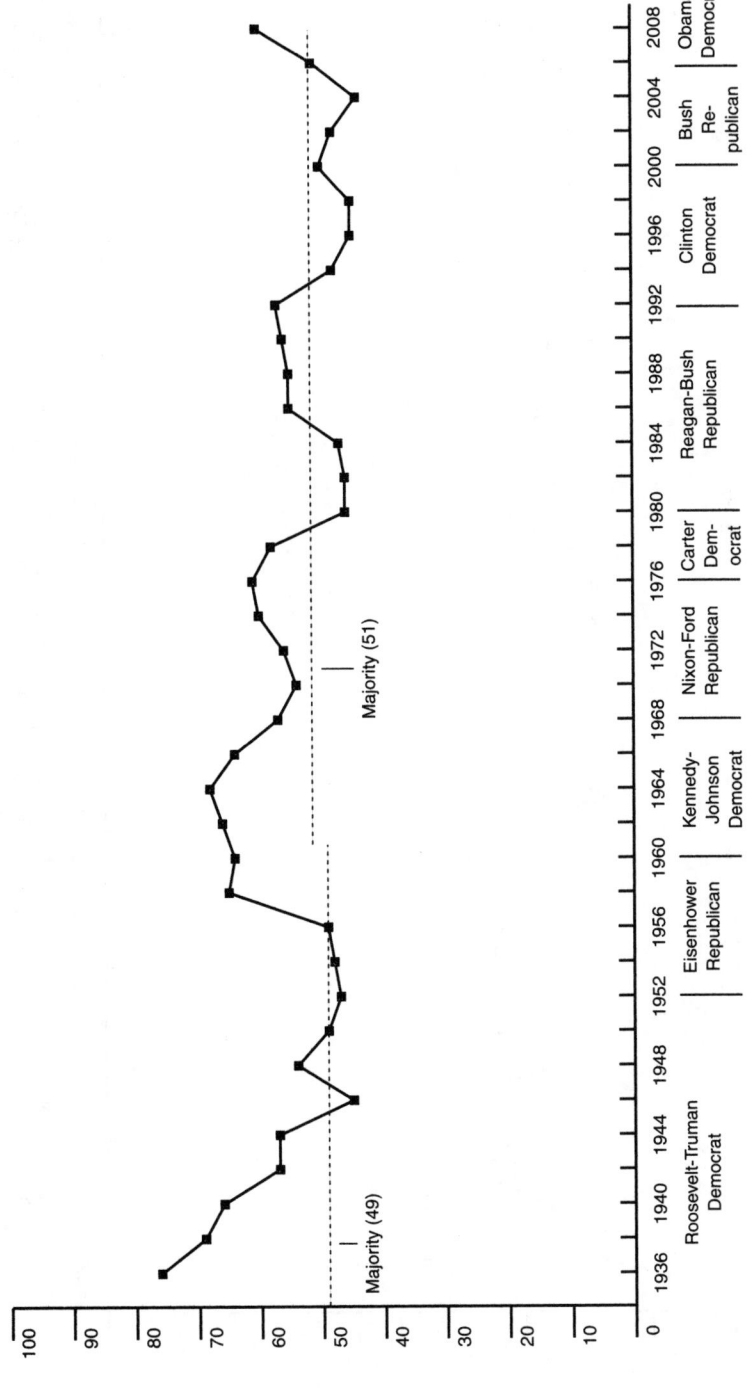

Source: Keith Poole and Howard Rosenthal, DW-Nominate data, publicly available at voteview.com/dwnomin.html.

Figure 5-2 Democratic Strength in House Elections: 1936–2008

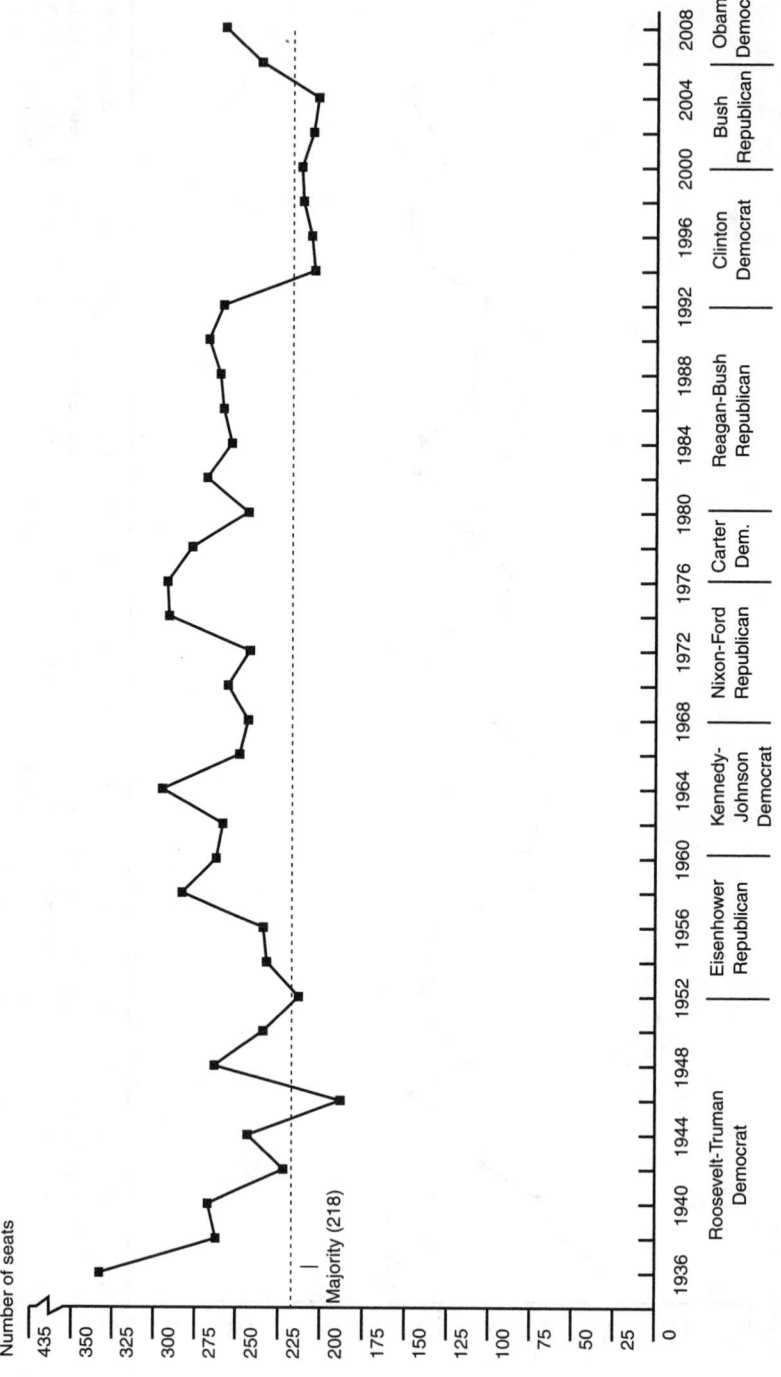

Source: Keith Poole and Howard Rosenthal, DW-Nominate data, publicly available at voteview.com/dwnomin.htm.

In addition, the Bush administration's slow response to the Hurricane Katrina catastrophe in New Orleans allowed Democrats to call into question the priorities and competence of the Republican Party.[18] Continuing frustration with Bush and substantial anxiety about the economy left voters seeking more change in 2008, with Democrats netting twenty-one more seats in the U.S. House and eight additional seats in the U.S. Senate. Both the 2006 and 2008 House elections demonstrate support for Jacobson's claim that a sufficiently powerful partisan tide could help Democrats overcome structural disadvantages in the electoral map.[19]

Do the Parties Differ on Public Policies?

Ordinarily, few surprises occur on election day: Democratic candidates win where they are expected to win, and Republican candidates win where they are expected to win. The public at large may continue to believe that each election poses an opportunity for the outs to replace the ins, but this happens infrequently. The chief threat to an incumbent legislator is a landslide presidential vote for the other party, one so great that congressional candidates on the winning presidential ticket ride into office on the president's coattails. Even such landslides, however, do not disturb the great majority of congressional races.

If party affiliation largely determines who goes to Congress, does it also significantly influence their behavior once in office? The answer for most legislators is yes. Indeed, the main thing to be known about any member is his party—it influences the choice of friends; group memberships; relations with lobbies, other members, and the leadership; and, most important, policy orientations. Even if party cohesion collapses on certain issues that come before Congress, the general proposition that party affiliation is a major explanation of voting behavior remains true. In fact, party is more important in voting behavior today than it has been for decades.[20] Members recognize that there are advantages to going along with the leadership and voting in agreement with their party colleagues. Moreover, especially in the House, majority party leaders can use legislative rules to make it easier for members to support the party's position on the floor.[21]

The proportion of roll call votes in Congress in which the parties are sharply opposed is moderately large, and, of late, is growing larger. The standard that congressional scholars use to measure party unity is the percentage of votes in which a majority of one party votes against the majority of the other party. In the early 1970s, it was not unusual for both houses to have fewer than 40 percent party unity votes, and occasionally the percentage fell to less than 30. Since the 1990s, it has not been unusual for party majorities to be arrayed against each other on 50 percent to 60 percent of roll call votes in both houses.

An analysis by Shawn Zeller of *Congressional Quarterly* concludes that House Democrats in 2007 and 2008 were more unified in their voting behavior than they had been in more than fifty years.[22] This unity can be traced to the changes in the ideological character of the parties. The more liberal eastern wing of the

Republican Party and the more conservative southern wing of the Democratic Party have atrophied since the late 1970s.[23] The congressional parties have become more homogenous and therefore more unified.

What factors promote partisan cleavage? Examining a recent thirty-five-year period, Samuel C. Patterson and Gregory A. Caldeira find that party voting in the House increases significantly when external party conflict is high—in particular, during periods when sharp differences exist between the national parties on central issues of the economy, labor-management questions, and the distribution of wealth. Interparty conflict also escalates when the presidency and the House are controlled by the same party. In the Senate, where party voting is somewhat less common, presidential leadership is also the major factor: when the Senate majority is of the same party as the president, party voting increases.[24]

Scholars have also debated whether changes in party voting are best explained by member adaptation or member replacement. In her research on party voting in the House from 1946 to 1990, Mary Alice Nye finds that the best explanation for shifting levels of partisanship is the changing voting patterns of members who continue from one Congress to the next; that is, these members vote differently in response to the events and circumstances—"period effects"—of a particular session of Congress, and conversion takes place. Nye finds little evidence that changing party support is explained by generational change—newly elected members are either more or less partisan than those they replaced—or by the life-cycle hypothesis that members tend to stray from their party as their tenure increases. The importance of period effects may reflect factors such as party leadership, particularly the role of the Speaker, and the party caucus.[25]

Scholars examining congressional behavior since 1990, however, believe the addition of new members is central to understanding modern party-centric behavior. Keith Poole and Howard Rosenthal demonstrate that the lion's share of change in the preferences of party caucuses can be explained by the influx of new members.[26] Some members adapt; they become either more conservative or more liberal over time, but it is more common to see ideologically extreme members replacing those in the center.

Poole and Rosenthal's findings are reinforced by Sean Theriault, who finds that member replacement explains roughly two-thirds of the party polarization that occurred in the House between 1973 and 2004, with adaptation accounting for the remaining one-third.[27] In addition, Theriault finds that much of the party polarization in the contemporary U.S. Senate is the result of the so-called "Gingrich senators"—GOP senators who had formerly served in the House with Newt Gingrich, the hard-charging Republican leader and eventual Speaker.[28]

Important issues are often at stake when party lines form. In general, Democrats are more likely than Republicans to support expanded health and welfare programs, legislation advantageous to labor and low-income groups, government regulation of business, higher taxes on the wealthy, the use of federal funds for family planning, reductions in the defense budget, federal assistance for cities, and a larger role for the federal government. Republicans, on the other hand, are more likely to favor lower taxes, especially on those with higher incomes, less regulation of business, private solutions to health care issues, and restrictions on abortion rights.

The Parties and Liberal-Labor Legislation

The current policy orientations of the parties in Congress are not distinctly different from those they have held since the middle of the twentieth century. The positions of the parties (and the factions within them) on proposals of interest to the AFL-CIO in the second year of the 110th Congress (2007) are presented in Table 5-1. A member voting in agreement with the AFL-CIO during that session would have supported measures such as the extension of unemployment insurance to laid-off workers, efforts to increase the number of people with health insurance, measures to ensure workplace safety, and legislation to provide workers with overtime pay.

Table 5-1 shows two broad patterns of congressional voting on issues of concern to organized labor. First, Democrats are highly cohesive on this legislation. Although eastern Democrats are slightly more supportive of labor legislation than southern Democrats, southern Democrats are still clearly pro-labor. Among Republicans, those from the East are significantly less hostile toward such legislation than those from other regions, particularly the South. In fact, in the second session of the 110th Congress (2008), 91 percent of southern Republican House members provided less than 25 percent support for labor legislation. A stark regional contrast can also be found among Senate Republicans; 78 percent of southern Republican senators had support scores of 25 percent or less, but only 20 percent of eastern Republican senators had support scores this low. Second, despite certain intraparty divisions, substantial differences between the parties are apparent. Democrats in general give overwhelming support to labor objectives.[29] Republicans are much less supportive, no matter their region. Even conservative southern Democrats are more pro-labor than liberal eastern Republicans.

To assess the policy differences of the congressional parties more generally, it is useful to examine the range of attitudes in the Senate during the first session of the 110th Congress on issues deemed important by the liberal Americans for Democratic Action (ADA) and the conservative American Conservative Union (ACU). (See Figure 5-3.) Select senators are arranged on the diagram according to the percentage of votes they cast in agreement with the positions of each political interest group. Sens. Patty Murray (D-Wash.), Barbara Mikulski (D-Md.), Ted Kennedy (D-Mass.), and Carl Levin (D-Mich.) were the most liberal members of the upper house. At the conservative pole were Sens. Jim DeMint (R-N.C.), John Barrasso (R-Wyo.), Tom Coburn (R-Okla.), and John Kyle (R-Ariz.).

The data in Figure 5-3 reinforce the conclusions reached earlier. Significant differences separate the majorities of the two parties. Nearly all of the Republican senators cluster together in the bottom right-hand corner of the diagram, indicating their agreement with the ACU and disagreement with the ADA. The opposite is true for nearly all of the Democratic senators. The only Democrat who is more

Table 5-1   House and Senate Support for Labor Legislation, by Party and Region, 110th Congress, Second Session (percent pro-labor votes)

	House				Senate			
	0–25%	26–50%	51–75%	76–100%	0–25%	26–50%	51–75%	76–100%
Democrats								
Southern	0	0	8	92	0	0	0	100
Eastern	0	0	0	100	0	0	0	100
Others	0	0	3	97	0	3	0	97
Republicans								
Southern	91	9	0	0	78	22	0	0
Eastern	32	55	13	0	20	20	20	40
Others	83	17	0	0	65	31	4	0

Source: Developed from data in the AFL-CIO 2008 Congressional Scorecards.

Note: House members are ranked by the percentage of votes they cast in accordance with the positions of the AFL-CIO. The South is defined as the eleven states of the Confederacy. The East is defined as the eleven states from Maine in the north to Maryland in the south. Others are those from states not in either the South or East.

conservative than the most liberal Republicans on these two dimensions is Ben Nelson (D-Neb.), and the only Republicans more liberal than the most conservative Democrats (other than Ben Nelson) are Lincoln Chafee (R-R.I.), Arlen Specter (R-Pa.), Susan Collins (R-Maine), and Olympia Snowe (R-Maine). But centrists are a dying breed in Congress. Chafee lost his 2006 reelection bid after narrowly surviving a primary challenge bid from a more conservative Republican candidate. And Specter, facing almost certain defeat by a more conservative Republican in Pennsylvania's 2010 closed primary, bolted the Republican Party in 2009 to join the Democrats.

Democratic presidential candidates typically win the three states represented by these four moderate Republicans, indicating that these states are not particularly conservative. For Republican senators to win reelection in states that tend to vote for Democratic presidential candidates, they must compile moderate voting records. For incumbents who do not, such as New Hampshire's John Sununu—a GOP loyalist in a state trending Democratic—defeat is virtually inevitable. Sununu went down to defeat in 2008, but Collins easily defeated her Democratic rival in neighboring Maine, winning 61 percent of the vote. In addition to Ben Nelson, Sens. Bill Nelson (D-Fla.) and Kent Conrad (D-N.D.) score somewhat more moderate than the rest of the Democratic caucus. Once again, these moderate members come from states typically won by the other party's presidential candidate. Their small number shows the strength of intraparty homogeneity.

Party polarization in Congress is by no means new. In fact, the Congresses of the first decade of the twentieth century were as polarized as any today.[30] But the current polarization developed after a long period of party convergence in the United States. Compare the scatterplot in Figure 5-3 with that in Figure 5-4, which reflects the same analysis using ACU and ADA scores from 1985. A number

Figure 5-3   Support for Positions Held by Americans for Democratic Action (ADA) and by American Conservative Union (ACU) by Selected Senators, 110th Congress, First Session

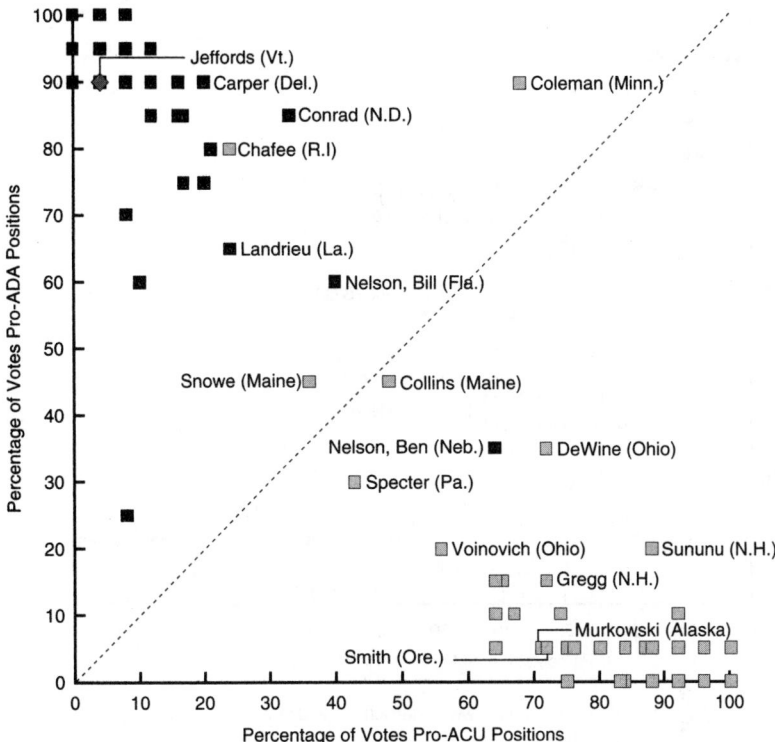

Sources: Developed from data appearing in www.adaction.org and www.conservative.org.

Note: ■ Democrat;   ▨ Republican;   ◆ Independent

of changes are evident, but the most important is the higher level of intraparty heterogeneity in 1985. In stark contrast to the 2007 data, many members had moderate scores, in the forty-point to sixty-point range, from both the ACU and the ADA. Moreover, many Republicans had voting records more liberal than the most conservative Democrats, and many Democrats had more conservative voting records than the most liberal Republicans. If we conducted this analysis for Congresses in the late 1960s and early 1970s, the degree of intraparty heterogeneity and ideological overlap between the parties would be even more pronounced. Relative to Congresses for much of the twentieth century—especially those between the 1930s and 1970s—today's Congress displays an extraordinarily high degree of ideological polarization between the parties.

Figure 5-4   Support for Positions Held by Americans for Democratic Action (ADA) and by American Conservative Union (ACU) by Selected Senators, 99th Congress, First Session

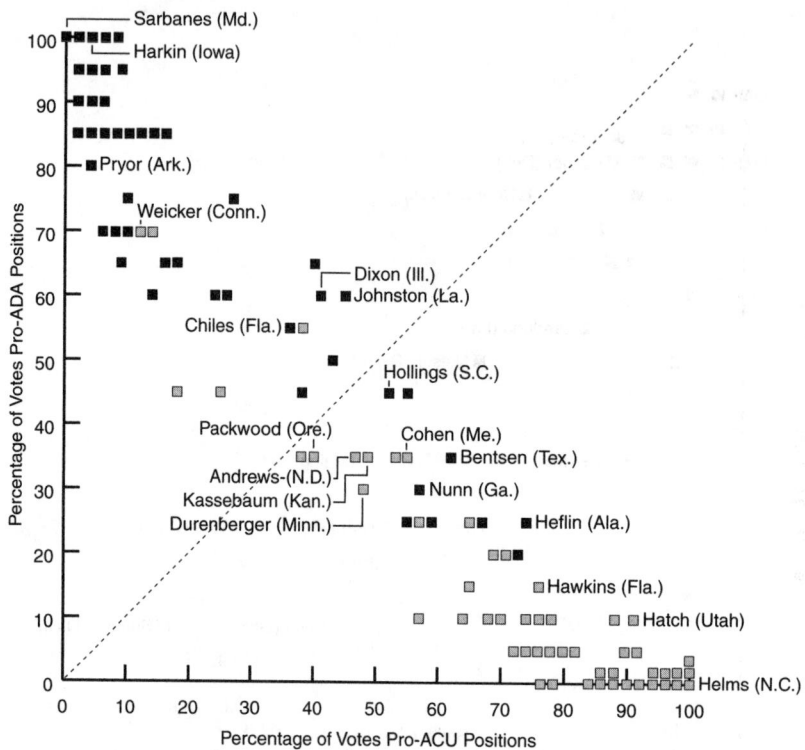

Sources: Developed from data appearing in www.adaction.org and www.conservative.org.

Note: ■ Democrat; ▨ Republican

Moderates are an equally endangered species in the U.S. House. The fate of Rep. Christopher Shays, a moderate House Republican who represented Connecticut's Fourth District from 1987 to 2008, illustrates the shift. With an ADA score of 75 in 2008, Shays was clearly to the left of his House Republican colleagues. In a district that was tilting toward Democrats—Kerry narrowly carried it in 2004—Shays's ideological moderation helped him prevail over strong challenges in 2004 and 2006. Shays's party affiliation, however, tied him to the Republicans and an ideology that was too far to the right of his district (which Obama easily carried in 2008), so even his moderate record was insufficient to save his political career. Shays's loss to Democrat Jim Himes left New England without a single House Republican for the first time since the GOP's founding in 1854 and underscores the demise of centrists in the House.[31]

When partisanship in Congress was weaker, as it was for a good portion of the twentieth century, the formation of bipartisan coalitions was commonplace. The most important was the so-called "conservative coalition"—an informal league of southern Democrats and northern Republicans. The coalition's success rate was impressive. In only two of the thirty-six congressional sessions between 1961 and 1997 did the coalition win fewer than 50 percent of the roll calls on which it appeared. In twenty-seven of the thirty-six sessions during this period, its batting average exceeded 60 percent.[32] In the 1960s and 1970s the conservative coalition would come together on as many as one hundred votes per session, but the rise in intraparty homogeneity has left it in shambles. In fact, the coalition was decisive on only two votes in the 107th Congress (2001–2002), and it has all but disappeared since.[33] By 1998 *Congressional Quarterly,* which conducts widely cited studies of congressional roll call votes, discontinued its analysis of the conservative coalition, pronouncing it no longer relevant.[34]

The Sources of Stronger Parties in Government

What explains the rise in party voting in Congress? David W. Rohde demonstrates that one reason is the realignment of southern politics.[35] Although today the South is perhaps the most ideologically conservative region of the country, the Republican Party was virtually nonexistent there until the 1950s. Holding Republicans responsible for the harsh Reconstruction period following the Civil War, southerners were not inclined toward the party in any way. The Democrats' embrace of civil rights legislation changed this picture. Beginning with Barry Goldwater's campaign in 1964, the South started to vote regularly for Republican presidential candidates. Moreover, when conservative southern Democrats retired from Congress, they were replaced by even more conservative Republicans. If ideology, rather than race, had been the guiding factor in the decades before the civil rights movement, many of these seats would have been won by Republicans long before. Instead, it took until 1994 for the Republicans to win a majority of House seats in the states of the former Confederacy, and this percentage has grown with nearly every succeeding election.

Similarly, since passage of the Voting Rights Act of 1965, African Americans have entered southern state electorates in great numbers, and their participation has driven Democratic incumbents and challengers to adopt more liberal positions on certain domestic policy questions. African American voters in southern Democratic primaries are now in a much better position to influence the behavior and policy stances of Democratic congressional candidates. The behavior of white voters also enters into the mix. Richard Fleisher writes, "In districts with large minority populations and white constituents [who] show a willingness to support progressive Democratic candidates, representatives in Congress respond with liberal voting and party support similar to that of northern Democrats."[36] Stanley P. Berard argues that southern Democrats have become more partisan in their voting behavior in Congress. Three factors have contributed to this new partisanship: the mobilization of African American voters, urbanization, and the rise of Republican electoral competition. In short, these factors have led to the "northernization" of southern Democratic politics.[37]

The redrawing of congressional district boundaries to reflect shifts in population after each census has hardened divisions between the parties. Mapmakers in both parties typically draw district lines to protect as many incumbents as possible, creating districts in which it is almost impossible for a challenger to win. Challengers also have become more ideological over time, which makes their task of unseating an incumbent even harder. A study by Stephen Ansolabehere, James Snyder, and Charles Stewart shows that almost all Republican candidates for Congress in 1996 were more conservative than almost all Democratic candidates; and the ideological gap between Republican and Democratic challengers was often quite large.[38] Ideological differences between the parties are probably even greater today. Under these circumstances, challenger victories are uncommon. Voters in safe Republican districts are unlikely to elect generally liberal Democratic challengers, and voters in safe Democratic districts are unlikely to elect generally conservative Republican challengers.

The result has been what John Aldrich and David Rohde refer to as "conditional party government."[39] According to their theory, parties may pursue strong party-based government characterized by considerable party-line voting, but only when two conditions are met. The first is that differences within the parties must be relatively small. In other words, strong intraparty homogeneity must be present. The second condition is that the parties must disagree sharply on most issues so that moderate members of one party do not perceive that they have much in common with most members of the other party. Put another way, there must be strong interparty heterogeneity.

In the present day, both of these conditions are met, as the results in Table 5-2 confirm with data called DW-NOMINATE scores. These scores, calculated using a complex formula pioneered by Keith Poole and Howard Rosenthal, are generated from members' roll call votes to measure their ideological preferences in such a way that scholars can compare them across Congresses. First note the increase in *intra*party homogeneity. Between the 99th Congress and the 110th Congress, the standard deviation, which measures how spread out a distribution is (in other words, how heterogeneous it is), drops from .182 to .157 among Democrats and from .149 to .147 among Republicans. The smaller standard deviations indicate that intraparty homogeneity is increasing. At the same time, the difference between the parties (the *inter*party heterogeneity) has skyrocketed. In the 99th Congress, it was only .643. In the 110th Congress, however, the distance between the average Republican and the average Democrat had increased to .815. Party polarization has taken hold.

According to the conditional party government thesis, greater party polarization is not only a result of member preferences but also of stronger party leaders. Members of each party endow their respective party leaders with powers to

Table 5-2   Changes in the Homogeneity within House Caucuses and the Distance between House Caucuses, DW-NOMINATE Scores, 99th–110th Congresses

Congress	Democrats		Republicans		Difference in Means
	Mean	Standard Deviation	Mean	Standard Deviation	
99th	−.304	.182	.339	.149	.643
100th	−.303	.180	.340	.157	.643
101st	−.309	.182	.342	.161	.651
102nd	−.309	.182	.350	.155	.659
103rd	−.330	.179	.376	.146	.706
104th	−.360	.172	.403	.155	.763
105th	−.376	.158	.411	.148	.787
106th	−.373	.160	.415	.150	.788
107th	−.378	.154	.421	.152	.799
108th	−.375	.154	.429	.146	.804
109th	−.387	.146	.434	.147	.821
110th	−.364	.157	.451	.147	.815

Source: Keith Poole and Howard Rosenthal, DW-NOMINATE data, publicly available at voteview.com.

advance the policy agenda. When House Democrats became more ideologically unified in the 1970s, they placed the Rules Committee under the control of party leaders and gave the House Democratic Caucus more power to oust recalcitrant committee chairs who stood in the way of party initiatives. The ideologically cohesive Republican Party that won control of the U.S. House in 1994 agreed to several organizational changes (including term limits on committee chairs) designed to enhance Speaker Gingrich's power to push through the GOP agenda. Democrats have maintained many of these changes since winning back control of the House in 2006.[40] The point, as Steven Smith notes in explicating the conditional party government thesis, is that congressional party leaders, endowed with greater powers by their ideologically cohesive party members, polarize the parties "beyond the preferences [members] bring with them into office."[41]

John Aldrich suggests that the changing nature of the parties themselves helps to explain the emergence of today's ideologically polarized parties.[42] When patronage-driven party machines dominated the political scene, winning elections was more important than advancing ideological interests. Government jobs and other spoils went to the winners. As reforms in the political process all but eliminated patronage, Aldrich argues, ideological activists became more important in each party. Using California as a case study, Seth Masket shows the prominence of ideological activists in the informal party organizations that now exercise considerable influence over nominations. Moreover, after the election, these activists press elected officeholders to advance a partisan agenda and threaten wavering lawmakers with a primary challenge. The result is a more partisan legislature.[43]

In addition to changes in the ideological makeup of Congress and the demise of patronage-driven parties, other, more subtle, changes have taken place in Washington and in Congress that likely have contributed to the present situation.

In 2005 Princeton University convened a conference on the causes and consequences of party polarization, where Vin Weber, a former Republican member of
Congress from Minnesota, noted that the 1994 election signaled a massive change
in the culture around the Capitol. The Republicans won the majority in both the
House and the Senate, in part, by running as outsiders who would break the
perceived cycle of corruption that had come to taint the Democrats' forty-year
hold on power in the House. Gingrich, the newly elected Speaker, cautioned his
insurgents against spending too much time in Washington, advising them instead
to tend to their districts. To encourage members to comply, Gingrich in the House
and Majority Leader Trent Lott in the Senate shortened the Washington workweek, conducting business on a tight Tuesday to Thursday schedule. Members
needed to spend only two nights a week in Washington.

The shorter workweek had implications. Because members spent less time on
Capitol Hill, they had fewer opportunities to develop relationships with their colleagues. Relationship-building became particularly challenging across party lines.
Members had little incentive to set up permanent residences in Washington or
bring their families with them. Instead, they tended to stay in dormitories disproportionately occupied by other members of their own party. Former representative David Skaggs (D-Colo.) observed that relationships between spouses, which
often crossed party lines in previous eras, no longer developed.

Journalist Gail Chaddock also noted that political junkets fell out of favor with
the advent of the Republican revolution. Many new Republicans won their seats
by highlighting the amount of taxpayer dollars that Democratic incumbents had
spent going on "official missions" to exotic locales. In practice, however, these
trips were important in that they allowed members of the opposing parties to
meet and develop friendships. Members who served in both the pre- and post-
1994 eras, such as David Price (D-N.C.), pointed to the limited amount of personal contact between members as a principal reason for party polarization. The
message from current and former members was clear: it is much easier to criticize
people in the other party if you are not seeing them (and their spouses) at dinner
the following week.

Members of Congress and scholars alike identify the close partisan division in
Congress as another reason for the strong party discipline and issue polarization
in the institution. When Republicans controlled the House from 1994 to 2006,
they never held more than 232 seats, which meant that a mere 15 defections
would make it impossible to pass legislation if the Democrats voted unanimously
on the other side. Rep. Tom Cole (R-Okla.), previously head staffer on the
National Republican Congressional Committee, suggested that a team mentality
develops in the majority when cooperation from almost all members is necessary
for successful passage of legislation. The caucus can also act as a team around
election time when it needs to protect all of its incumbents to ensure majority
party status. In that sense, the good of the party is more tangible when party
margins are tight.

Party Organization in Congress

Party Conferences

The central agency of each party in each chamber is the conference or caucus.[44] All those elected to Congress automatically become members of their party's caucus. During the early twentieth century, the House majority party caucus was exceptionally powerful, but disillusionment with the caucus set in following World War I, and members came to question its right to bind them to a course of action. By the 1930s the functions of the caucus were limited to the selection of party leaders. After years of somnolence, in 1969 the Democratic caucus began to hold regular monthly meetings to examine proposals for reforming the House. In the early 1970s, the caucus made several modifications to the seniority system, the most important of which provided for secret ballots on nominees for committee chairs. In 1973 it created the Steering and Policy Committee to formulate legislative programs and to participate in the scheduling of legislation for floor consideration.

The power of this renewed and improved Democratic caucus was dramatically demonstrated at the opening of the Ninety-fourth Congress in 1975 when, among other things, the caucus voted to remove three committee chairs from their positions, transferred the power to make committee assignments from the Democratic members of the Ways and Means Committee to the Steering and Policy Committee, and made a number of changes involving nominations and subcommittee procedures. Included in these changes was a provision to empower the Speaker, subject to caucus approval, to nominate the Democratic members of the powerful Rules Committee. A member's allegiance to the party leaders now appears to be the primary criterion for getting a seat on this committee.

As David Rohde points out, in the 1980s Democrats also began using caucus meetings to ensure sufficient representation for differing perspectives within the party and to hold party leaders accountable. Toward the latter goal, in 1985 the Democratic caucus voted to make the party whip—the third-ranking position in the House Democratic leadership—a caucuswide elective post, much like the Speaker and majority leader.[45] (Prior to 1985, the Speaker appointed the party whip.) Barbara Sinclair notes that the value of the caucus as an outlet for participation increased as party leaders clamped down on the number of floor amendments permitted on the House floor. To deliberate on issues, both House party caucuses now also hold annual issue conferences away from Capitol Hill.[46] Caucus meetings appear to promote party cohesion by creating something of a rallying effect. In fact, Richard Forgette finds that attendance at a party caucus meeting before an important floor vote makes a House member more likely to support the party position than his policy preferences alone predict.[47]

When Republicans took control of Congress after the 1994 midterm elections, they further centralized control of the House in the leadership. According to Steven S. Smith and Gerald Gamm, Speaker Gingrich used his standing to pick committee chairs, all of whom were only later endorsed by the party conference, and several subcommittee chairs who were only later appointed by committee chairs. Gingrich even reviewed the appointment of top committee staffers.[48] His successful efforts to centralize power made him the most powerful Speaker in eighty years. Ultimately, however, his imperious style wore thin with the independent-minded rank-and-file members of his party, leading to his ousting from his post after less than four years. Following Gingrich's departure, the trend toward centralization slowed somewhat, although the parties remained far more centralized than they were prior to the 1970s. Indeed, Speaker Nancy Pelosi (D-Calif.) has exercised significant influence on assignments and has retained many of the Republicans' centralizing reforms.[49] Both parties, moreover, remained remarkably unified in their voting behavior.

To be sure, caucus power has the potential to collide with the nagging reality of all legislative politics: the individual member's electoral security, and therefore his primary interest, lies in the constituency. When a party's members are not particularly unified in their policy preferences—as between the 1930s and the 1970s—the attractions of a cohesive party are not nearly so great as the attractions of independence, the opportunities to concentrate on constituency interests and problems. But as members' constituencies have become more polarized, and voting to please one's constituents is the same as voting with one's party colleagues in Congress, an active party caucus more often than not advances a member's political interests.

The Speaker of the House

The most powerful party leader in Congress is the Speaker of the House. In the early twentieth century, the Speaker's powers were almost beyond limit, the House virtually his private domain. It is scarcely an exaggeration to say that legislation the Speaker favored was adopted and that legislation he opposed was defeated. But the despotic rule of Speaker Joseph G. ("Uncle Joe") Cannon (R-Ill., 1903–1911) eventually proved the undoing of this monarchy. In 1910 Democrats and rebellious Republicans formed a coalition to challenge his leadership and succeeded in instituting a number of rule changes that curbed the Speaker's powers. Cannon was removed from membership on the Rules Committee, which he had chaired; his power to appoint and remove members and chairs of standing committees was eliminated; and his power to recognize, or not to recognize, members was curtailed. Although the "revolution of 1910–1911" fundamentally altered the formal powers of the Speaker, it did not render the office impotent. Since then, a succession of Speakers who were disposed to negotiate rather than command has helped to rebuild the powers of the office. What a Speaker like Cannon secured through autocratic rule, today's Speakers secure through persuasion and the astute exploitation of the bargaining advantages inherent in the position.

The Speaker's formal powers are wide-ranging, although not especially significant in and of themselves. The presiding officer of the House, the Speaker announces the order of business, puts questions to a vote, refers bills to committees, rules on points of order, interprets the rules, recognizes members who desire the floor, and appoints members to select committees and conference committees. The Speaker also has the right to vote and enter floor debate, but ordinarily exercises these rights only in the case of major, closely contested issues.

Although difficult to delineate with precision, the informal powers of the Speaker are far more impressive. As the foremost leader of his party in Congress, the Speaker is at the center of critical information and policymaking systems, and no one is in a better position to obtain and disseminate information, shape strategies, or advance or frustrate the careers of members. Perhaps the principal tangible preferment the Speaker can use is the influence he can exert to secure favorable committee assignments for members of the majority party. The Speaker's good will is important to majority-party members anxious to advance in the House.

Writing in 1981, Joseph Cooper and David W. Brady highlighted the limits faced by Speakers. Party leaders, "function less as the commanders of a stable party majority and more as brokers trying to assemble particular majorities behind particular bills."[50] Although today's polarized parties allow leaders to command more, the ultimate failure of the Gingrich speakership illustrates that negotiation remains important. In addition to enhancing his personal role in appointing committee and subcommittee chairs, Gingrich was not shy about punishing those who did not toe his line. He removed Rep. Mark Neumann (R-Wis.) from a plum Appropriations subcommittee to a less desirable post because Neumann had repeatedly voted against the committee leadership. But when a band of junior members mutinied, Gingrich was forced to give Neumann a coveted spot on the Budget Committee to make amends.[51]

Following Gingrich's resignation from the speakership after the Republicans' poor showing in the 1998 midterm elections,[52] his successor, Dennis Hastert (R-Ill.), employed a somewhat softer touch with the party membership. But Hastert did not relinquish power. In fact, as John Aldrich and David Rohde point out, he retained all of the powers given to Gingrich by the House Republican Conference, and he even asked for additional powers. Hastert successfully pushed to have Appropriations Committee subcommittee chairs ratified by the House Republican Steering Committee—a committee on which he enjoyed substantial influence. In choosing committee chairs, he followed Gingrich's practice of violating seniority when a committee's most senior Republican failed to demonstrate sufficient loyalty to the GOP agenda.[53] Hastert was a less public and controversial Speaker than Gingrich, and he understood the importance of both command and negotiation. But no less than Gingrich, he also understood that his job was to facilitate the enactment of the GOP agenda.

Aldrich and Rohde also point out that following the Democrats' takeover of the House in 2006, Speaker Pelosi—the first female Speaker in U.S. history—has proved to be just as aggressive as her Republican predecessors. For example, in pushing through six Democratic legislative priorities in the first one hundred hours of the 110th Congress, Pelosi bypassed committees and brought the legislation to the House floor under highly restrictive rules. House Republicans were completely shut out of the legislative process. Remarkably, Pelosi also forced vaunted chair of the Energy and Commerce Committee, John Dingell (D-Mich.)—long a powerful ally of the automobile industry—to make major concessions on the Democrats' energy bill. "She is a very hands-on Speaker," noted veteran lawmaker Rick Boucher (D-Va.). "She is familiar in detail with the substance of legislation in committees, and she wants to be kept informed. . . . We [at Energy and Commerce] are writing the legislation. But she is setting the agenda."[54] To prevent committee chairs from accumulating too much power, Pelosi retained term limits on chairs enacted by House Republicans in 1994.

The Floor Leaders

In addition to the Speaker, the major figures in the congressional party organizations are the House and Senate floor leaders, who are chosen by party caucuses in their respective chambers. The floor leaders serve as the principal spokespersons for party positions and interests and as intermediaries in both intraparty and interparty negotiations. In the House, the majority party floor leader essentially serves as the Speaker's second-in-command.[55] Minority party floor leaders in both chambers attempt to defeat majority party legislation by holding their own party together and by attracting support from majority party legislators. The floor leaders of the party that holds the presidency also serve as links between the president and his congressional party. Because they must represent both the congressional party and the president, it is not surprising that role conflicts develop. Serving the interests of their congressional party colleagues or perhaps those of their constituents is anything but a guarantee that they will be serving presidential interests.

Floor leaders have a potpourri of informal powers. Their availability, however, does not ensure that they can lead their colleagues or strongly shape the legislative program. By and large, their influence is based on their willingness and talent to exploit these powers steadily and imaginatively in their relations with other members. They can, if they choose:

1. influence the allocation of committee assignments (not only rewarding individual members but also shaping the ideological makeup of the committees);
2. help members advance legislation of particular interest to them;
3. assist members in securing larger appropriations for their committees or subcommittees;
4. play a major role in debate;
5. intercede with the president or executive agencies on behalf of members (perhaps to assist their efforts to secure a federal project in their state or district);

6. make important information available to members;
7. help members secure campaign money from a congressional campaign committee or from the political action committee of an interest group;
8. campaign on behalf of individual members; and
9. focus the attention of the media on the contributions of members.

Much of the influence of floor leaders, like that of the Speaker, is derived from informal powers, in particular from opportunities afforded them to advance or protect the careers of party colleagues. In solving problems for them and helping them further their electoral and legislative goals, floor leaders increase their chances of gaining their party colleagues' support on critical questions. By the same token, floor leaders can in some measure hamper the careers of those members who continually refuse to agree with their views. At the center of an active floor leader's powers is the capacity to manipulate rewards and punishments. Some recent floor leaders, such as former GOP majority leader Tom DeLay (R-Texas)—nicknamed "the Hammer" for his aggressive style—have taken such manipulation to new levels. Over the course of his House career, the House Ethics Committee admonished DeLay three times for employing inappropriate tactics in pursuing the GOP's legislative agenda.[56]

Given the heterogeneous nature of the nation as a whole, floor leaders necessarily face a difficult task, especially in the Senate, where norms and rules empower individual senators at the expense of parties and the rank and file tends to be more independent-minded than in the House. Former Senate majority leader Trent Lott (R-Miss.) likened his job to "putting bullfrogs in a wheelbarrow," and Sen. George Mitchell (D-Maine), one of Lott's predecessors, compared it to "herding cats."[57] The sixty-vote requirement for shutting down filibusters makes the job of a Senate majority leader particularly difficult. Bruce Oppenheimer and Marc Hetherington show that despite increased party polarization over the past thirty years, energy legislation produced by the Senate in the 2000s was quite comparable to that produced by the Senate in the 1970s. The explanation is that without a filibuster-proof majority, policy outcomes necessarily edge closer to the chamber median and away from the party median.[58] Senate majority floor leader Harry Reid (D-Nev.) experienced such challenges first-hand when Democrats regained control of the Senate in 2006. With only a slim fifty-one-seat majority in the 110th Congress (2007–2008), Reid was often thwarted by Senate Republicans and recalcitrant members of his own party. Even with a filibuster-proof majority of sixty Democrats in the 111th Congress (2009–2010), there is no guarantee that Reid can hold together his party on complex legislation that impacts the political interests of many senators.

As a former majority leader of the Senate, Lyndon B. Johnson (D-Texas) once observed, "The only real power available to the leader is the power of persuasion. There is no patronage; no power to discipline; no authority to fire Senators like a President can fire his members of Cabinet."[59] To be persuasive, a leader must know the members well. He must know what they want and what they will settle for, and what concessions they can and cannot make, given their constituencies. In addition, the position requires good lines of communication into the opposition party to pick up support when elements of the majority party appear likely to wander from the fold. Members prefer to support their leader and the party position rather than those of the opposing forces. The task of the leader is to find reasons for them to oppose their own party and the conditions under which they can and will.

The development of a legislative program requires the majority leader to work closely with the leaders in his party, particularly the chairs of the major committees. This is especially true in the House, where committees tend to be more important than they are in the Senate. During the so-called period of committee government (1910–1974), House committee chairs, selected on the basis of seniority, wielded considerable (at times even autocratic) power in the House. As such, majority party leaders had to be acutely sensitive to chairs' interests, adept at recognizing their political problems, and flexible in negotiations with them. Bargaining was the main characteristic of the relationships between the majority leadership and the committee chairs.[60] In the contemporary House, however, majority leaders have amassed considerable clout with committee chairs through the Speaker, who has gained influence over the selection of chairs. Such influence reached new heights under Gingrich and Hastert, who would even bypass the committee process in crafting legislation if they deemed a committee or its chair insufficiently committed to party goals.[61] The Speaker's influence over committees and committee chairs has continued with Pelosi. "We are in a hybrid phase," noted a House Democratic leadership aide. "We don't order the chairmen, but we have told them that they hold their position because of the caucus. . . . The Speaker is the leader of the caucus."[62]

An important function and a major source of power for the majority party leadership in both chambers is the scheduling of bills on the floor. As Tip O'Neill once stated, "The power of the Speaker of the House is the power of scheduling."[63] But scheduling can be fraught with political pitfalls, especially in the Senate, where most legislation is scheduled by unanimous consent agreements.[64] The majority leader who fails to keep lines of communication open, who misjudges the sentiments of members, who neglects to consolidate the majority by winning over undecided members or by propping up wavering members, or who picks the wrong time to call up a bill can easily go down to defeat. Prospective majorities are more tenuous and more easily upset than might be supposed. The effective leader builds a power base by tending to the shop; ordering priorities; having a sense of detail that overlooks nothing; taking account of the demands placed on members; sensing the mood of congressional opinion, especially that of influential members; and exhibiting skill in splicing together the legislative elements necessary to fashion a majority.

For several reasons, party management in the contemporary Congress is more difficult than it was in decades past.[65] First, the adoption of "sunshine" rules in both houses, which place limits on backroom deal-making, has made Congress a more open institution. For the most part, committee and subcommittee meetings are now open to the public, and recorded votes on controversial legislation are now the norm in both chambers. Efforts to make Congress even more open continue. In the 110th Congress, lawmakers passed ethics and lobbying reform measures and brought greater transparency to "earmarks" (federal dollars diverted by incumbents for special projects in their districts and states).[66] Second, the growing power of interest groups, stemming particularly from their campaign contributions, lobbying efforts, and grassroots campaigns, has made members more vulnerable to outside pressures.[67] Third, the extraordinary growth in candidate-centered campaigns means that members elected to Congress have substantial resources and autonomy to act independently of the party when they believe that doing so serves their political interests. Examples of such behavior abound. Despite the efforts of the Democratic Party to present a unified image on prescription drug care legislation in 2003, Democratic senator Edward Kennedy unilaterally chose to work with the Bush administration on the bill.[68] In 2009, three Republican senators—Collins, Snowe, and Specter (before his switch to the Democratic Party)—provided Democratic president Barack Obama with the winning votes to pass his economic stimulus package.[69]

Especially in the U.S. Senate, where norms and rules give party leaders less control over rank-and-file members than in the U.S. House, party leadership can be particularly frustrating. Rarely was this more clear than in 2001, when Sen. Zell Miller (D-Ga.) not only supported but actually cosponsored the tax cut on which Republican George W. Bush had campaigned in 2000. Miller's action badly undercut the efforts by Minority Leader Tom Daschle (D-S.D.) in the evenly split Senate to either defeat, or at least significantly change, the president's initiative. In the end, the tax package that passed included almost everything the president had proposed, thanks in large part to Miller. After the tax vote, Miller remained highly popular in conservative Georgia and, in the ultimate gesture of independence, delivered the keynote address at the 2004 *Republican* National Convention. In stark contrast, fellow Georgia senator Max Cleland, a Democrat who opposed Bush on the tax bill, lost his reelection bid in 2002.

This discussion suggests that the political environment makes it difficult for party leaders to exert control over the behavior of rank-and-file members of their caucus. The leaders have, however, found some innovative techniques to encourage party discipline. Many of these techniques are designed to limit the number of alternatives that rank-and-file members have to vote on and to provide procedural advantages to measures supported by the majority party leadership.[70] Members often are forced to vote for or against a version of a bill managed tightly by the majority leadership. As a consequence, outcomes tend to be closer to the party's median position, which today is significantly to the right of center when Republicans are in the majority and significantly left of center when Democrats are, rather than the chamber median position, which is nearer the ideological center.

The Rules Committee, which exists only in the House, is critical to understanding the increased power of elected leaders. When a bill is approved by one of the House's standing committees, it goes to the Rules Committee to receive a "rule" before it can go to the floor of the House for consideration. A bill's rule, which structures floor debate and determines which amendments are in order, can be critical in determining whether the bill passes. Because the elected party leaders—the Speaker and the floor leaders—dominate the selection of members to the Rules Committee, the leaders can wield tremendous influence over the legislative process in this committee. In fact, the Rules Committee is now completely an arm of the House majority party leadership and has little independence.[71] As with legislation that comes to the floor for a vote, rules must be passed by a majority of House members. Voting against the party leadership on a rule is considered heresy.[72]

Barbara Sinclair identifies a number of changes in how the Rules Committee does business.[73] Restrictive rules, which limit the number of amendments that can be proposed on the floor and the amount of time a bill can be debated, have become far more common. Indeed some controversial bills receive rules that allow for no amendments at all, which ensures that rank-and-file members may vote only on the party leadership's preferred version of a bill. At one time, moderate members of the majority party might break from their party's leadership and, with members of the minority party, craft alternatives to legislation backed by party leadership. Now, leadership is reluctant to provide moderates these opportunities.

Party leadership in the House is also more likely to use so-called king of hill rules to enhance party loyalty in voting. Such a rule allows for votes on several versions of a bill, but the final measure to win a majority (typically the leadership-favored version) is the winning bill—even if other versions received more votes. This practice lets individual members cast votes popular with their constituents, which might insulate them from criticism from their districts, while also supporting the party leadership's measure. Omnibus legislation, which are single bills that contain many (sometimes only tangentially related) provisions, has become common in the present-day House. Rather than allowing rank-and-file members to support the party leadership on certain bills and buck them on others, leadership presents the rank and file with a single choice in one large omnibus bill. If members want to go on record as supporting something that might benefit their constituencies, then they will also have to vote in favor of provisions that they might otherwise have opposed.

It is also worth noting that the ideological profile of floor leaders has changed since the mid-1990s, a condition that may have contributed to greater party polarization in Congress. Conventional wisdom long held that parties choose leaders close to their ideological medians. The logic is straightforward: party members select leaders to advance the party's shared policy goals. Delegating power is inherently risky, because leaders might use their powers to advance policies inconsistent with the party's interests. Roderick Kiewiet and Mathew

McCubbins demonstrate that House leaders (1947–1984) did in fact tend to come from each party's ideological median.[74] In the 108th Congress (2003–2004), however, House Republicans chose Tom DeLay, one of their most conservative members, as majority leader, and House Democrats picked Nancy Pelosi, one of their most liberal members, as minority leader. Moreover, when DeLay was forced to resign the majority leader position in 2005 because of his role in a fund-raising scandal, the Republicans elected Rep. John Boehner (R-Ohio), another conservative ideologue, to replace him. Pelosi was elected Speaker when Democrats won majority control of the House in the 2006 elections, and Boehner was elected the House minority leader.

Eric Heberlig, Bruce Larson, and Marc Hetherington demonstrate that a major reason for the rise of ideologically extreme leaders in the House is their ability to raise campaign funds for the caucus.[75] Campaign money is a critical resource for parties to win and maintain majority control of the House, and ideologically extreme members are better able than moderate members to tap into the ideological donor networks of interest groups. With majority party control nearly always on the line since 1994, the incentive structure of leadership selection has changed for the rank-and-file members. When money was less important and majority status was secure, members could afford to value leaders who specialized in coalition building or legislative management. In today's Congress, however, the insatiable need for money to maintain or win majority control has made fund-raising ability a critical attribute for leaders to possess.

The Whips

The whips are another unit in the party structure of Congress. The whips serve as liaisons between party leaders and the members and mobilize member support on legislation important to the party. The top party whip in each congressional party is selected by a caucuswide vote. Lower-level party whips are selected in each house by the top party leaders and, in some cases, by regional blocs of members within the party. The House Republican whip organization grew to roughly seventy members when the GOP controlled the majority between 1994 and 2006, and the House Democratic whip organization has been even larger. In the 110th Congress (2007–2008) more than one quarter of all House Democrats were whips.[76] The expanding House whip organizations are a component of party leaders' "strategy of inclusion." By providing members with opportunities to participate in crafting party strategy, the organizations give members a stake in the leadership's agenda.[77]

Working to enhance the efforts of the leadership, whips carry out a number of necessary functions. They attempt to learn how members intend to vote on legislation; relay information from party leaders to individual members; work to ensure that a large number of "friendly" members will be present at the time of voting; and attempt to win the support of those party members who are in opposition, or likely to be in opposition, to the leadership. The influence of the Speaker and the majority leader supplement the pressure of the whips.

As described by one chief staff assistant to the majority whip, whips apply "the heavy party loyalty shtick. Then it's more personalities than issues. There are some members who can only be gotten by the Speaker or the majority leader."[78]

The central importance of the whip organization is that it forms a communications link between the party leadership and rank-and-file members. The whips are charged with discovering why members are opposed to certain legislation and how that legislation might be changed to gain their support. The intelligence the whips supply sometimes spells the difference between victory and defeat on a major issue. If the outlook for a bill is unpromising following a "whip check" of members' sentiments, the leadership will often postpone its floor consideration. Whip checks can protect the leadership from embarrassing losses.

There is evidence that the expanded party whip organizations of the contemporary Congress can influence legislative outcomes. Using House Democratic whip counts from the Ninety-second Congress, Barry Burden and Tammy Frisby demonstrate that on sixteen bills, the Democratic whip organization was able to win over several members who initially stated their intention to vote against the party position.[79] In more recent Congresses, the top-down GOP whip operations under DeLay and Roy Blunt (R-Mo.) were especially aggressive.[80] The parties' whip organizations in the Senate can also influence legislative dynamics. A recent study of Senate whip organizations by Erin Bradbury, Ryan Davidson, and C. Lawrence Evans concludes that "whip counts enable majority-party leaders to gauge which alternatives are likely to prevail on the floor; to make adjustments in the timing and content of party initiatives; to signal to rank-and-file members about which initiatives are central to the party agenda; and to persuade wavering members to stay on the partisan reservation."[81]

From a career perspective, the party whip organizations also serve as a training ground for members of Congress who aspire to leadership posts in the party and committee hierarchies. By providing a forum to display one's leadership talents, the whip organization can be a stepping stone for members who seek to advance in the institution.[82] In fact, many of the top elected party leaders— including all of the last eight Speakers—began their assent up the leadership ladder from a lower-level perch in the whip organization.[83] Serving in the party's whip organization may even help members win a plum committee assignment. Representative Price notes that he and several members competing for slots on the powerful Appropriations Committee found whip task forces helpful for cultivating relationships with party leaders.[84]

The Policy Committees

Few proposals for congressional reform have received as much attention as those designed to strengthen the role of political parties in the legislative process. The Joint Committee on the Organization of Congress recommended in its 1946 report that policy committees be created for the purpose of formulating the basic policies of the two parties. Although this provision was later stricken from the reorganization bill, the Senate independently created such committees in 1947. House Republicans established a policy committee in 1949, although it did not become fully active for another decade. Rounding out the list, the rejuvenated House Democratic caucus voted to establish a policy committee in 1973.

The high promise of the policy committees as agencies for enhancing party responsibility for legislative programs has never been realized. Instead, the policy committees mostly assist in various party functions, such as issue research, policy discussion, and communication strategy.

The policy committees vary in their organizational complexity. The most elaborate in the 111th Congress (2009–2010) is the House Republican Policy Committee, which is "comprised of the elected and appointed Republican Leadership; the ranking members of five key committees (Appropriations, Budget, Commerce, Rules, and Ways and Means); Representatives elected from each of the Nation's regions; three Representatives elected by the two newest classes of Members; and at-large members appointed by the Republican Leader." The committee also has several subcommittees "responsible for helping guide the conversation and crafting big ideas in their particular niche."[85] House Democrats no longer operate a policy committee, with Speaker Pelosi preferring instead to conduct such functions through the party's steering committee and a series of issue task forces.[86]

It is not surprising that the policy committees have been unable to function effectively as agencies for the development of overall party programs. An authoritative policy committee would constitute a major threat to the power centers within Congress. Party leaders and committee chairs would undoubtedly find their influence over legislation diminished if the policy committees were to assume a central role in defining party positions. The policy capacity of the committee system would be affected adversely, and many individual members would suffer an erosion of power. If the policy committees had functioned as planned, a major reshuffling of power in Congress would have resulted. To those who hold the keys to congressional power, this is scarcely an appealing idea.

Such limitations do not render the policy committees useless. Both parties require forums for the discussion of issues and for the negotiation of compromises, and for these activities the policy committees are well designed. Moreover, the staffs of the committees have proven to be helpful for individual members seeking research assistance. Most important, the policy committees have served as communications channels between the party leaders and their memberships. As clearinghouses for the exchange of party information and as agencies for the reconciliation of at least some intraparty differences, they have made useful contributions.

Informal Party Groups and Specialized Congressional Caucuses

In addition to the formal party units in Congress, several informal party organizations meet more or less regularly to discuss legislation, strategy, and other questions of common interest. Among these organizations are the Blue Dog

Democrats (conservative), New Democrat Coalition (moderate), Progressive Caucus (Democratic, liberal), Republican Study Committee (conservative), and Wednesday Group (Republican, moderate). Formed to promote the policy positions of a faction within the party, these groups are major sources of information for their members. They focus primarily on the congressional agenda, drafting and introducing legislation and amendments as well as seeking to attract the interest and support of other members and outside forces. Some of these groups have sought to influence the content of party platforms.

Informal party groups compete and cooperate with dozens of other specialized policy caucuses organized to advance particular interests. These relatively narrow-gauge groups are formed around geographic, economic, racial, gender-focused, and other assorted concerns. Included in this far-flung policy network are caucuses such as the Northeast-Midwest Congressional Coalition and the Steel, Coal, Textile, Travel and Tourism, Farm Crisis, Wine, Mushroom, Port, Human Rights, Black, Blue Collar, Hispanic, Sunbelt, Border, Congresswomen's, Rural, Suburban, Crime, Arts, and Drug Enforcement caucuses. Groups such as these, which reflect the diversity of interests in Congress, attempt to influence the policy process through problem identification, member mobilization, and coalition building. They are centers for information exchange.[87] At the same time, they reflect the fragmentation of power in Congress. Indeed, such fragmentation was on display when in 2007 Speaker Pelosi attempted to craft legislation to end the war in Iraq. Pelosi had to sell the leadership bill to the Blue Dog Coalition, which fretted about its inclusion of a timetable for troop withdrawal, and to the Out of Iraq and Progressive caucuses, which claimed that the timetable did not remove troops quickly enough.[88] Whether these groups enhance or inhibit the capacity of party leaders to control the policymaking process is an empirical question. Certainly, they can have clout when they are sufficiently large and united on specific issues. In 2009, the fifty-one Blue Dogs, who are fiscally conservative, pressured the House Democratic leadership into making significant concessions on deficit spending.[89] Whatever their power, it is not likely that these mechanisms of representation will disappear.

Factors Influencing the Legislative Success of Party Leaders

Even in the present period, which is characterized by strong party voting, the cohesiveness of the parties in Congress can never be taken for granted. The importance of constituency pressures, the influence of political interest groups, and the disposition of members to respond to parochial impulses—all, at one time or another, have the potential to erode party unity. In some cases, the leadership can do little to bring refractory members into line. During the George W. Bush presidency, neither Bush nor the Republican leadership could stop Sen. John McCain (R-Ariz.) from sponsoring legislation that the party opposed, such as campaign finance reform or a patient's bill of rights. And party leadership was not a major factor in understanding why McCain took a more conservative turn beginning in 2005. Instead, McCain altered his behavior largely to court conservatives in his bid for the 2008 Republican nomination. Even though ending the Iraq war was a major component of the Democratic Party's 2006 campaign message, in March 2007 House Democrats could barely muster the votes to pass a supplemental spending bill for the war that included a timetable for troop withdrawal. On one of most important pieces of legislation of the 110th Congress, fourteen Democrats—including two members of the Democratic whip organization—defected from the party position.[90]

Several situations may arise that either promote or inhibit the leadership's influence on legislative decisions.[91] First, leadership success is likely to be contingent on a high degree of agreement among the leaders themselves. Ordinarily the Speaker, majority leader, and whip are firm supporters of the party's legislative program; sometimes, however, another leader, such as a committee chair, is not. When unity among the leaders breaks down, prospects for success fall. Second, leadership success in gathering the party together tends to be affected by the nature of the issue under consideration—specifically, whether it is procedural or substantive. On procedural issues (election of the Speaker, adoption of rules, and motions to recommit or to adjourn), party cohesion is ordinarily much higher than on issues that involve substantive policy. And this remains true even in the current period of intense party polarization.[92] Third, the efforts of party leaders are most likely to be successful on issues that are not highly visible to the general public. When issues gain visibility, conflicting pressures emerge, and the leaders must commit greater resources to keep party ranks intact. Fourth, the visibility of the proposed action has a bearing on the inclination of members to follow the leadership. Not all forms of voting are equally noticeable. Roll call votes on final passage of measures are highly conspicuous—the member's "record" on a public question is firmly established at this point. Voting with the leadership on the floor may pose too great a risk, but supporting the leadership in committee, on an amendment, or on a procedural vote is less risky, because these actions are not as easily brought into public focus. Fifth, and perhaps most important, members are most likely to vote with their party when the issue at stake does not upset their constituencies. Party leaders know full well that they cannot count on the support of members who feel that they are constrained by their constituents on a particular issue. In this respect, the more politically homogenous the districts and states held by a party's incumbents are, the easier the party leadership's job is. For incumbents in the current era of partisan polarization, voting the party line may be no different from pleasing constituents back home.[93]

These conditions constitute the background against which leaders try to mold their party into a unit. Party loyalty, it should be emphasized, is more than a veneer. By and large, members prefer to go along with their party colleagues. But they will not queue up in support of their leaders if the conditions appear wrong or if it appears that more is to be lost than gained by following the leadership. In 2002 dozens of Republicans eventually voted in favor of the Bipartisan Campaign Reform Act (BCRA) despite the objections of their party leadership because of the issue's popularity at home. Nor could Republican leaders gin up support in either the House or the Senate for President George W. Bush's Social Security privatiza-tion plan in 2005 because members realized that a majority of their constituents opposed it. When the House voted on Bush's fall 2008 financial emergency bailout package, substantial defections on both sides of the partisan aisle occurred despite the support of House Republican and Democratic leaders.[94] Members guard their careers by taking frequent soundings within their constituencies and among their colleagues and by making careful calculations of the consequences that are likely to flow from their decisions.

National Party Agencies and the Congressional Parties

In theory, the supreme governing body of the party between one national convention and the next is the national committee, which is composed of repre-sentatives from each state. In an ideal world, from the perspective of those who believe in party unity and responsibility, close and continuing relationships would be maintained between the national committees and their fellow party members in Congress. Out of such associations, presumably, would come coher-ent party policies and a heightened sense of responsibility among members of Congress for developing a legislative program consistent with the promises of the party platform. In reality, the tone and mood that dominate relations between the national committees and the congressional parties are as likely to be charac-terized by suspicion as by cooperation. Congressional leaders in particular are little disposed to follow the cues that emanate from the national committees or, for that matter, from any other national party agency.

Not only do national party leaders have a minimal impact on congressional decision making, but also they largely stay out of the process of nominating con-gressional candidates. Occasionally an intrepid president has sought to influence congressional nominations, as Franklin D. Roosevelt did in 1938. As it turned out, nearly all of the lawmakers marked for defeat won easily, much to the cha-grin of the president. Richard Nixon also failed in his efforts to defeat a number of liberal Republicans in 1970. Although a few presidential "purges" have suc-ceeded, most attempts have not. The lesson seems clear: congressional nomina-tions are regarded as local matters, to be decided in terms of local preferences. Even the congressional and senatorial campaign committees tend to stand clear of these battles.[95]

The national party is concerned with the election of members broadly sympa-thetic to its traditional policy orientations and its party platform. Local party organizations and informal partisan networks aim to guarantee their own sur-vival as independent units. Occasional conflict between the two is predictable. The principal consequence of local control over congressional nominations is that all manner of men and women can get elected to Congress. Those who find it easy to accept national party goals may find themselves rubbing elbows with those who are almost wholly out of step with the national party. Recent Con-gresses have been relatively free of such conflict, as ideological activists have gained influence in local nomination contests and nominate candidates who support national party goals.[96]

The President and the Congressional Party

Presidential power appears more awesome at a distance than it does at close range. Although the Constitution awards the president a number of formal powers, such as the power to initiate treaties, to make certain appointments, and to veto legislation, his principal everyday power is simply to persuade. The president who opts for an active role in the legislative process, who attempts to persuade members of Congress to accept his leadership and his programs, encounters certain obstacles in the structure of American government. Foremost among these is the separation of powers or "separated institutions sharing powers."[97] This arrangement not only divides the formal structure of government and creates independent centers of legislative and executive authority, but also it contributes to the fragmentation of the national parties. The perspectives of those elements of the party for whom the president speaks are not necessarily the same as those for whom members of his congressional party speak. Policy that may suit one constituency may not suit another. Indeed, the chances are high that the presidential constituency and the constituencies of individual members of his party in Congress will differ in some important respects, and that makes a certain amount of conflict between the branches inevitable.

Limits on Presidential Influence

For an activist president who hopes to persuade Congress to adopt his programs, the separation of powers is not the only constraint he faces. The limited influence of party leaders on Congress, the insulation and independence of members that stem from the substantial staff and other office resources they enjoy,[98] the relative independence of committees and subcommittees, the difficulty of applying sanctions to wayward legislators, and the parochial cast in congressional perceptions of policy problems all converge to limit presidential influence. Moreover, electoral arrangements and electoral behavior may make executive leadership difficult. Midterm elections are nearly always more damaging to the president's party than they are to the out party.[99] In midterm elections from 1926 to 2006, the president's party gained seats in only three House elections (1934, 1998, and 2002) and in only four Senate elections (1934, 1962, 1970, and 2002). Losses can be severe. The Democrats' losses in 1994 were the worst in any off-year election since 1946. And like the Democrats in 1994, Republicans lost majority control of both the House and Senate in 2006. The president has every reason to believe when these elections roll around that the next two years are almost certain to be difficult.

Finally, the root of the president's legislative difficulties may lie with the voters themselves. An election that produces a president of one party may yield a Congress dominated by the other party or one with a different ideological hue.

Different coalitions form around offices. The coalition that reelected Bill Clinton in 1996, for example, had a much different cast from the one that produced a Republican majority in the House. A disproportionate number of Clinton voters were females, African Americans, Latinos, white Catholics, and people earning less than $50,000 annually. The Republican House majority, by contrast, was elected by a coalition of males, whites, religious right individuals, and people earning more than $50,000 annually. Sixty percent of Clinton voters believed that government "should do more," and 73 percent of the voters who supported Republican House candidates believed that government "should do less." With two different coalitions making claims on the executive and legislative branches, it would be altogether surprising if the relationships at some points were not contentious, conflicted, muddled, or reflective of class concerns.

A measure of the legislative success enjoyed by presidents from 1953 to 2008 is presented in Figure 5-5. This analysis shows how frequently Congress voted in accordance with positions taken by each president during his administration. Lyndon Johnson achieved the highest rate of success of any of these ten presidents; in 1965 his position prevailed 93 percent of the time, and over the course of his presidency he succeeded 81 percent of the time. The major reason for his success was undoubtedly that the Democratic Party controlled both houses by such large margins that even the defections of southern members had minimal impact on outcomes. Ronald Reagan's 82 percent success rate in 1981 ranks among the highest in the preceding thirty years.

George H. W. Bush, whose success rate averaged 51.8 percent over his term, produced the lowest score of any president since 1953. During each of Clinton's first two years in office, when Democrats held a majority in both houses, he had an impressive 86 percent success score. But in his third year in office, following the Republican takeover in the 1994 election, his legislative success rate fell to 36 percent, the lowest score of any president since Congressional Quarterly began its survey in 1953.

George W. Bush had remarkable success in getting his agenda through Congress during his first term. In his first two years, he produced success scores of 87 percent and 88 percent, respectively. Although his success rate fell into the 70s from 2003 through 2005, his overall rate through his first term was second only to Johnson's.[100] One reason for Bush's success was that he took stands on fewer issues than his predecessors. In 2005 Bush took a position on only 46 of the 669 votes taken in the House. By keeping his policy agenda short and focused, Bush was able to win a high proportion of the time. The bipartisanship that developed out of the September 11 terrorist attacks and his overall popularity also contributed to his success, and conditional party government, which has developed with the close partisan split in Congress, helped as well. According to Congressional Quarterly, party voting had reached higher levels in 2003 than at any point during the fifty years CQ had been keeping records.[101] As a result, Republicans in Congress were able to win consistently narrow victories for the president on issues important to him.

Figure 5-5 Presidential Success on Legislative Votes: 1956–2008

Percentage

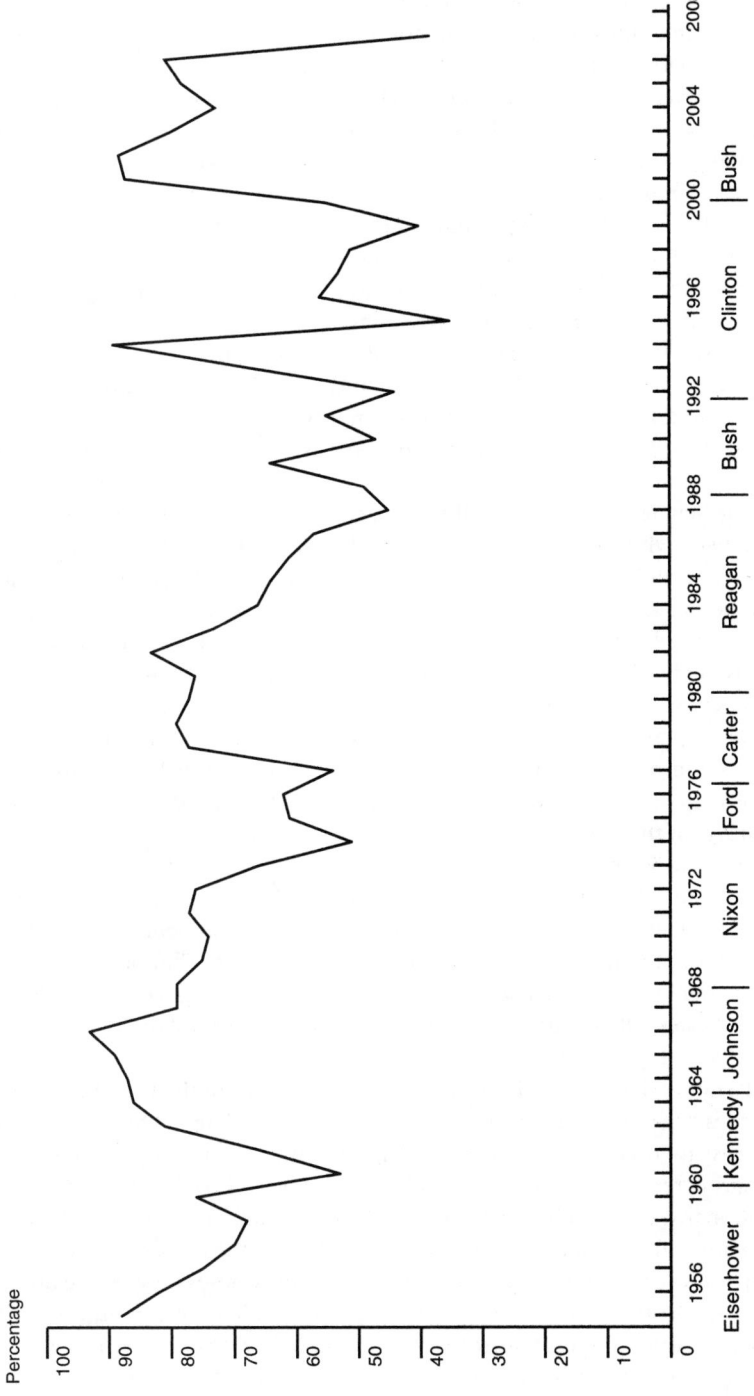

Source: Developed from various issues of *CQ Weekly*.

Although Bush won on 78 percent of the roll call votes on which he took a position in 2005, which is an extraordinarily high percentage—especially five years into a president's term in office—his victories were less clear cut than in previous years. For example, although Congress ultimately approved a Bush-backed energy bill, the final version did not contain certain provisions, such as allowing oil companies to drill in the Arctic National Wildlife Refuge that Bush had championed.[102] Congress also approved an extension of the Patriot Act, which the president sought, but Congress's version did more to protect civil liberties and provided a shorter period of time before another renewal was necessary than the president wanted. Bush experienced similar results in his sixth year, with an 81 percent success rate in 2006. After Democrats won control of the House and Senate in the 2006 elections, Bush's success rate plummeted in 2007 to only 38 percent—identical to Clinton's seventh-year success rate.[103] But during his final year, Bush improved his success rate to 48 percent, a result of his focus on less controversial issues and greater willingness to compromise.[104]

The Senate's moderating influence is critical in determining presidential success. Even with a narrow majority in the House, Republican party leaders could deliver on President Bush's program if they maintained strict party discipline. The potential for Senate members to filibuster makes it harder for a narrow majority to deliver policy results. Ending a filibuster requires sixty votes; Republicans held only fifty-five seats in the 109th Congress (2005–2006). When the president was very popular, as he was early in his presidency, certain Democrats could be persuaded to support his favored initiatives. As his approval ratings dropped into the 30s in 2006, Bush no longer had as much sway. In the end, some of the president's favored provisions had to be negotiated away to gain the approval of the Senate.

When the opposition party controls one or both houses of Congress, presidential influence is constrained even further. Republican presidents understand this nagging reality better than anyone: every Republican president since Eisenhower has confronted it for at least part of his administration. Clinton and Bush, the most recent presidents subject to the challenges of divided government, saw their success rates fall dramatically when their parties lost control of Congress in 1994 and 2006, respectively.

The initiative for generating legislation has shifted to the president in recent decades.[105] So much has been written about the president as chief legislator that it is easy to forget that members of Congress have power in their own right. But Congress remains one of the world's most powerful legislative bodies, and a good many conditions remain inimical to its domination by presidents. The body may adopt what the president proposes but in the process may change the proposal's accent and scope. Sometimes it merely disposes of what the president proposes. Nothing in the president's plans is inviolable. No certainty exists that Congress will share his perceptions or succumb to his influence. The careers of individual legislators are not tightly linked to the president's, except perhaps for those members from marginal districts, and even here the link is firm only when the president's popularity is high.[106] Indeed, some members of Congress have made their careers more secure through the visibility that comes from opposing presidential programs.

Even with a Republican Congress seemingly willing to grant him anything he wanted, George W. Bush was unable to avoid some legislative defeats. In 2004 some Republican senators forced him to accept a tax cut that was considerably smaller than he wanted, and his 2005 legislative proposal to reform Social Security was essentially dead on arrival in Congress.[107] As Joseph Cooper points out, the plebiscitary politics that gave rise to the powerful, modern presidency is a double-edged sword that also imposes limits on presidential power.[108] The worldwide trend toward executive supremacy notwithstanding, Congress remains an independent legislative institution.

The president and Congress get along as well as they do because of one element that the president and some members of Congress have in common: party affiliation. In substantial measure, party provides a frame of reference, an ideological underpinning, a rallying symbol, a structure for voting, and a language for testing and discussing ideas and policies. A member's constituency has never been the only valid criterion for assessing the wisdom of public policies. Legislators prefer to ride along with their party if it is at all possible and if the costs do not loom too large. Moreover, the president and his legislative leaders are not at liberty to strike out in any direction they feel may be immediately popular with the voters. They are constrained by party platforms, by previous policy commitments, by interest group involvement, and by the need to consult with party officials and members at all levels, particularly with those in Congress. Consensus politics is the essence of party processes.

The President and Legislative Leaders

The president and party leaders in Congress can structure their relations with one another in many ways. Typically, when the president and the majority leadership are of the same party and the president assumes the role of chief legislator, relations between the two branches are characterized by cooperation. Within this pattern leaders tend to see themselves as lieutenants of the president, of necessity sensitive to his initiatives and responsible for his programs. During the first six years of George W. Bush's presidency, Republican congressional leaders, often working with slim majorities, pushed forcefully to enact his agenda.[109] By contrast, when the president and the majority in Congress (at least in one house) are of opposing parties (a so-called "truncated majority"), relations between the president and congressional leaders are often characterized by conflict and opposition—sometimes intensely so. Leadership tends to be highly centralized, but legislative successes are usually few in number. This aptly characterizes the relationship between President Clinton and GOP congressional leaders from 1995 to 2001 and between President Bush and Democratic congressional leaders from 2007 to 2009.

The Minority Party in Congress

A classic study by Charles O. Jones identifies a number of political conditions that individually and in combination help to shape the role the minority party plays in mobilizing congressional majorities and influencing public policy. Some of these conditions originate outside Congress; others manifest themselves inside Congress. The principal external forces are the temper of the times, such as the presence of a domestic or international crisis; the relative political strength of the minority party in the electorate; the degree of unity within the parties outside Congress; and the power of the president and his willingness to use the advantages inherent in his office. Conditions within Congress that affect minority party behavior are legislative procedures; the majority party's margin over the minority; the relative effectiveness of majority and minority party leadership; the time the party has been in a minority status, which perhaps contributes to a minority party mentality; and the relative strength of the party in the other house.[110] Although restrictive political conditions depress the range of alternatives available to the minority party, a resourceful minority leadership can occasionally overcome them, enabling the minority party to assume an aggressive, creative role in the legislative process.[111]

In the current period, ideological polarization and narrow partisan margins in the House and Senate have given the minority party strong incentives to remain in continuous campaign mode. Opting for conflict over compromise, minority parties now typically seek to win back control of Congress by blasting majority party initiatives, highlighting wedge issues that divide the majority party, and obstructing majority party legislation in committees and on the chamber floors whenever possible. In the House, especially, the majority party—whether Democratic or Republican—continues to push the minority party into combat mode by using its leverage over the legislative process to deny minority party members any legislative influence.[112]

The Party in Congress: An Assessment

It is as difficult to write about congressional parties with any certainty as it is to pin a butterfly without first netting it. A party is hard to catch in a light that discloses all its qualities or its basic significance. Unquestionably, party is the organizing mechanism of Congress, and Congress cannot function without it. How could Congress assemble itself for work, process the claims made on it, build coalitions, or be held accountable in any fashion without parties as its organizing tools? Moreover, some sessions of Congress are so opaque that the only way to understand what has taken place is to focus on the performance of the majority party. But that is only part of the story. In the critical area of policy formation, majority party control can slip away, to be replaced by enduring biparty alliances or coalitions of expediency. David Mayhew highlights the challenges parties face:

> Modeled in any fashion, the party has its competitors. One is the built-in dissonance supplied by an array of elected officials—presidents, senators, and House members—heaved up by different constituencies at different dates and enjoying fixed terms and

constitutional powers. Another is the complex of incentives, rewards, and penalties that attach to individual politicians as opposed to parties. Individual politicians are in certain ways the natural enemies of the parties and chronic victors over them.[113]

In short, party counts, but not always predictably, and that leads to the uncertainty in assessing the role of the congressional party.

Lately, congressional parties and their leaders appear very strong. But it is important to realize that the strong party discipline that has characterized recent Congresses is as much a function of the people who run for office as it is the powers of the congressional party. The new breed of members comes to Congress with stronger ideological commitments than did their counterparts a generation ago. In many cases, the ideologically minded members of today tend to vote with their leaders no matter whether leaders are offering carrots or sticks. To be sure, leadership power has made the congressional parties more cohesive than they would be otherwise. But the powers enjoyed by contemporary party leaders are themselves granted by, and conditional on, members with strong ideological commitments.[114]

For several reasons, the odds are stacked against the party. First, members of Congress are elected under a variety of conditions: they are elected in constituencies where local party organizations are powerful and where they are weak, where populations are homogenous and where they are heterogeneous, where competition is intense and where it is absent, where the level of voter education is high and where it is low, where income is high and where it is low, where one interest dominates and where many compete. The mix within congressional parties reflects the mix within the nation's constituencies. The result is that the people who make their way to Congress see the world in different ways, stress different values, and pursue different objectives. Even in the current period of polarized parties, some disagreement inevitably lurks within each party.

Second, the salient fact in the lives of legislators is their career. If they fail to protect it, no one else will. Representatives and senators know that their party can do very little to enhance their security in office and, conversely, very little to threaten it. As a member of Congress put it, "If we depended on the party organization to get elected, none of us would be here."[115] Members are on their own. Their reelection depends more on the decisions they make than on those their party makes, more on how they cultivate their constituencies than on how their party cultivates the nation, and more on the credit they are able to claim for desirable government action than on the credit the party can claim.[116] Reelection also depends more on the electoral coalition the members put together or from which they are able to benefit than on the electoral coalition of their party. Although sweeping electoral tides may carry members out of office from time to time, individual members know they cannot do much about such movements. Typical members therefore concentrate on immediate problems. They take their constituencies as they are; if they monitor and defend these interests carefully, they stand a good chance of having a long career in Congress, no matter what hand fate deals to their party.

The growing importance of party independent expenditures in congressional campaigns could potentially increase members' dependence on the party and, accordingly, be reflected in their voting behavior in Congress. But the evidence that members vote one way or another in response to party campaign assistance is mixed at best.[117] In the end, parties are in business to win elections. They spend the bulk of their campaign money in a relatively small number of competitive districts and states, and each prefers the election of its own mavericks to that of loyal members of the opposition. Members' ability to attract interest group contributions, moreover, gives them additional political space in which to maneuver, free from party controls. What those groups extract from the members is another question.

Third, party efforts can be confounded by the fragmentation of power within Congress. In the current period, party leaders, acting as agents of the caucuses, enjoy considerable leverage over committees. But this has not always been true. In fact, the revolt against Speaker Cannon ushered in a long period in which committees and committee leaders possessed considerable power relative to party leaders. During this era of committee government, the chairs, who secured their posts on the basis of seniority, only sometimes worked in harmony with party leaders. Rank-and-file members acting as independent political entrepreneurs also contribute to congressional fragmentation. To be sure, party leaders can make legislative life miserable for party renegades. But even the strong congressional party leaders of the current era have limited influence over its rank-and-file members' primary goal—reelection—especially if a member is electorally secure, which most are. In addition, factions within parties, such as the conservative Blue Dog Democrats, also contribute to the fragmentation of influence in the contemporary Congress.

Fourth, the intricacies of the legislative process make it difficult for the parties to function smoothly and effectively. For the party to maintain firm control, it must create majorities at a number of stages in the legislative process: first in the standing committee, then on the floor, then in the conference committee. Failure to achieve a majority at any stage—and a filibuster-proof majority of sixty on the Senate floor—is likely to scuttle important legislation. Even those bills that do pass through the obstacle course may be so changed as to be scarcely recognizable by their sponsors. In contrast, the opponents of legislation have only one requirement: to splice together a majority at one stage in the decision-making process. Breaking the party leadership at some point in the chain may not require great resources or much imagination. For these reasons, the adoption of a new public policy is immeasurably more difficult than the preservation of an old one. All the advantages, it seems, rest with those legislators bent on protecting existing arrangements. Preserving existing policies may also be an important party goal, as Gary Cox and Mathew McCubbins point out.[118] But it is the enactment of new policies, rather than the preservation of the status quo, that advocates of responsible parties largely have in mind.

Fifth, the congressional party functions as it does because, by and large, it is a microcosm of the party in the electorate, beset by the same internal conflicts.

The American political party is an extraordinary collection of diverse, conflicting interests and individuals brought together for the specific purpose of winning office. The coalition carefully put together to make a bid for power comes under heavy stress once the election is over and candidates have become officeholders. Differences ignored or minimized during the campaign soon come to the surface. Party claims become only one input among many that the members consider in shaping their positions on policy questions. National party objectives may be reconsidered and even discarded as members sort out their own priorities and take account of those interests, whose support may be essential to reelection.

The astonishing fact about the congressional parties is that they perform as well as they do. One reason is the phenomenon of party loyalty—typical members are more comfortable when they vote in league with their party colleagues than when they oppose them. Another is that most members within each party represent constituencies broadly comparable in makeup; in "voting their district" they are likely to be in harmony with the general thrust of their party. A third reason is found in the formal and informal powers of the elected leaders. Leaders can set the agenda and structure choices to facilitate party unity, and members who respond to their leadership may be given assistance in advancing their pet legislation, awarded with an appointment to a prestigious committee, or armed with important information. There are advantages to getting along with the leadership. Lastly, presidential leadership seems to serve as a unifying force for the president's party in Congress. Members may not go along with the president gladly, but many do go along, and even those who do not give his requests more than a second thought.

NOTES

1. For an analysis of the literature on congressional elections, see Gary Jacobson, *The Politics of Congressional Elections,* 7th ed. (New York: Pearson-Longman, 2008); Peverill Squire, "Candidates, Money, and Voters—Assessing the State of Congressional Elections Research," *Political Research Quarterly* 48 (December 1995): 891–917.

2. See, for example, John R. Hibbing and John R. Alford, "Electoral Impact of Economic Conditions: Who Is Held Responsible?" *American Journal of Political Science* 25 (1981): 423–439. For a review, see Richard G. Niemi and Herbert F. Weisberg, *Classics in Voting Behavior* (Washington, D.C.: CQ Press, 1993), especially section IV.

3. These data come from Norman J. Ornstein, Thomas E. Mann, and Michael J. Malbin, *Vital Statistics on Congress, 2001–2002* (Washington, D.C.: American Enterprise Institute, 2002); and various issues of *CQ Weekly.*

4. Ibid.

5. *CQ Weekly,* November 10, 2008, 3043–52. See also Rhodes Cook's Web site: www.rhodescook.com/competition.htm.

6. Gary C. Jacobson, "Congress: The Second Democratic Wave," in *The Elections of 2008,* ed. Michael Nelson (Washington, D.C.: CQ Press, 2009).

7. This theory is articulated by Gary C. Jacobson and Samuel Kernell, *Strategy and Choice in Congressional Elections,* 2nd ed. (New Haven, Conn.: Yale University Press, 1983).

8. The numbers for the House do not include incumbents who left the House to seek U.S. Senate seats.

9. See, for example, Richard Born, "Partisan Intentions and Election Day Realities in the Congressional Redistricting Process," *American Political Science Review* 79 (1985): 305–319; Charles Bullock, "Redistricting and Congressional Stability, 1962–1972," *Journal of Politics* 37 (1975): 569–575; Amihai Glazer, Bernard Grofman, and Marc Robbins, "Partisan and Incumbency Effects of 1970s Congressional Redistricting," *American Journal of Political Science* 30 (1987): 680–707.

10. David R. Mayhew, *Congress: The Electoral Connection* (New Haven, Conn.: Yale University Press, 1974), especially 49–77. See also Kenneth Benoit and Michael Marsh, "The Campaign Value of Incumbency: A New Solution to the Puzzle of Less Effective Incumbent Spending," *American Journal of Political Science* 52 (October 2008): 874–890.

11. Lyn Ragsdale, "Incumbent Popularity, Challenger Invisibility, and Congressional Voters," *Legislative Studies Quarterly* 6 (May 1981): 215. When accused of corruption, House incumbents and challengers are likely to be defeated 25 percent of the time, according to Susan Welch and John R. Hibbing, "The Effects of Charges of Corruption on Voting Behavior in Congressional Elections, 1982–1990," *Journal of Politics* 59 (February 1997): 226–239. Corruption allegations, in fact, are a significant factor in congressional turnover.

12. Tracy Sulkin, *Issue Politics in Congress* (New York: Cambridge University Press, 2005).

13. Bruce I. Oppenheimer and Marc J. Hetherington, "Catch-22: Cloture, Energy Policy, and the Limits of Conditional Party Government," in *Why Not Parties? Party Effects in the U.S. Senate,* ed. Nathan W. Monroe, Jason M. Roberts, and David W. Rohde (Chicago: University of Chicago Press, 2008).

14. Two of these ten additional seats resulted from Democrats switching their party affiliation after the election.

15. In 2000 Republicans won fifty seats in the Senate, which made them the majority party because the vice president (in this case Republican Dick Cheney) is constitutionally allowed to break tie votes. The Democrats took the majority in mid-2001, not because of an election result, but because Sen. James Jeffords of Vermont switched from the Republican Party to independent.

16. Ornstein, Mann, and Malbin, *Vital Statistics on Congress, 2001–2002.*

17. Paul Herrnson and James M. Curry, "Issue Voting in the 2006 Elections for the House of Representatives," in *Congress Reconsidered,* 9th ed., ed. Lawrence C. Dodd and Bruce I. Oppenheimer (Washington, D.C.: CQ Press, 2009).

18. James W. Ceaser, Andrew E. Busch, and John J. Pitney, *Epic Journey: The 2008 Elections and American Politics* (Lanham, Md.: Rowman and Littlefield, 2009), 41–43.

19. Gary Jacobson, *The Politics of Congressional Elections,* 7th ed. (New York: Pearson-Longman, 2008), 209.

20. Keith T. Poole and Howard Rosenthal, "D-NOMINATE after Ten Years: A Comparative Update to *Congress: A Political Economic History of Roll-Call Voting,*" *Legislative Studies Quarterly* 26 (February 2001): 5–29.

21. Gary Cox and Mathew McCubbins, *Setting the Agenda: Responsible Party Government in the House* (New York: Cambridge University Press, 2005); Steven S. Smith, *Party Influence in Congress* (New York: Cambridge University Press, 2007); Barbara Sinclair, "Do Parties Matter?" in *Party, Process, and Political Change in Congress: New Perspectives on the History of Congress,* ed. David Brady and Mathew McCubbins (Stanford, Calif.: Stanford University Press, 2002).

22. Shawn Zeller, "Parties Dig in Deep on a Fractured Hill," *CQ Weekly,* December 15, 2008, 3332.

23. For excellent discussions of these changes and their effects, see Nicol Rae, *The Decline and Fall of the Liberal Republicans* (New York: Oxford University Press, 1991); and David W. Rohde, *Parties and Leaders in the Postreform House* (Chicago: University of Chicago Press, 1991).

24. Samuel C. Patterson and Gregory A. Caldeira, "Party Voting in the United States Congress," *British Journal of Political Science* 18 (January 1988): 111–131. The authors employ the "majority versus majority" concept of a party vote.

25. Mary Alice Nye, "Party Support in the House of Representatives: Generational Replacement, Seniority, or Member Conversion," *American Politics Quarterly* 22 (April 1994): 175–189.

26. Keith Poole and Howard Rosenthal, *Congress: A Political-Economic History of Roll Call Voting* (New York: Oxford University Press, 1997).

27. Sean M. Theriault, "Party Polarization in the U.S. Congress: Member Replacement and Member Adaptation," *Party Politics* 12 (July 2006): 483–503.

28. Sean M. Theriault, *Party Polarization in Congress* (New York: Cambridge University Press, 2008).

29. See an interesting study of the strong relationship between organized labor and congressional Democrats by Taylor E. Dark, "Organized Labor and the Congressional Democrats: Reconsidering the 1980s," *Political Science Quarterly* 111 (Spring 1996): 83–104.

30. Theriault, *Party Polarization in Congress.*

31. Tim Storey and Edward Smith, "Election 2008: History Making," *State Legislatures,* December 2008, 16.

32. Ornstein, Mann, and Malbin, *Vital Statistics on Congress, 2001–2002.*

33. *Congressional Quarterly Weekly Report,* December 15, 2002.

34. Stephen Gettinger, "R.I.P. to a Conservative Force," *Congressional Quarterly Weekly Report,* January 9, 1999, 82.

35. Rohde, *Parties and Leaders in the Postreform House.*

36. Richard Fleisher, "Explaining the Change in Roll-Call Behavior of Southern Democrats," *Journal of Politics* 55 (May 1993): 327–341.

37. See Stanley P. Berard, *Southern Democrats in the U.S. House of Representatives* (Norman: University of Oklahoma Press, 2001), especially chapters 5 and 6.

38. Stephen Ansolabehere, James Snyder, and Charles Stewart, "Candidate Positioning in U.S. House Elections," *American Journal of Political Science* 45 (January 2001): 136–159.

39. John H. Aldrich and David W. Rohde, "The Logic of Conditional Party Government: Revisiting the Electoral Connection," in *Congress Reconsidered,* 7th ed., ed. Lawrence C. Dodd and Bruce I. Oppenheimer (Washington, D.C.: CQ Press, 2001).

40. Kathryn Pearson and Eric Schickler, "The Transition to Democratic Leadership in the House," in *Congress Reconsidered,* 9th ed.

41. Smith, *Party Influence in Congress,* 120.

42. John H. Aldrich, *Why Parties? The Origin and Transformation of Political Parties in America* (Chicago: University of Chicago Press, 1995).

43. Seth Masket, *No Middle Ground: How Informal Party Organizations Control Nominations and Polarize Legislatures* (Ann Arbor: University of Michigan Press, 2009), 9.

44. Congressional Democrats call this entity the caucus; congressional Republicans call it the conference. For ease of exposition, we use the term caucus in the following discussion.

45. Rohde, *Parties and Leaders in the Postreform House.*

46. Barbara Sinclair, *Party Wars: Polarization and the Politics of National Policymaking* (Norman: University of Oklahoma Press, 2006), 103–104, 134.

47. Richard Forgette, "Party Caucuses and Coordination: Assessing Caucus Activity and Party Effects," *Legislative Studies Quarterly* 29 (August 2004): 407–430.

48. Steven S. Smith and Gerald Gamm, "The Dynamics of Party Government in Congress," in *Congress Reconsidered*, 7th ed., 245–268.

49. Pearson and Schickler, "The Transition to Democratic Leadership in the House."

50. Joseph Cooper and David W. Brady, "Institutional Context and Leadership Style: The House from Cannon to Rayburn," *American Political Science Review* 75 (June 1981): 417.

51. For a more complete treatment of the relationship between Neumann and Gingrich, see Larry J. Sabato and Bruce Larson, *The Party's Just Begun: Shaping Political Parties for America's Future,* 2nd ed. (New York: Longman, 2002).

52. Gingrich's role in the 1998 debacle is interesting. Benjamin Highton demonstrates that Gingrich's lack of popularity was decisive in understanding why the Republicans lost seats in a midterm election. See Benjamin Highton, "Bill Clinton, Newt Gingrich, and the 1998 Congressional Elections," *Public Opinion Quarterly* 66 (Spring 2002): 1–17.

53. John Aldrich and David W. Rohde, "Congressional Committees in a Continuing Partisan Era," in *Congress Reconsidered*, 9th ed.

54. "I have never seen a Speaker take such an active and forceful role on policy," added House Democrat Henry Waxman (D-Calif.). Richard Cohen, "Power Surge," *National Journal,* July 21, 2007, 23.

55. Roger Davidson, Walter Oleszek, and Frances E. Lee, *Congress and its Members,* 11th ed. (Washington, D.C.: CQ Press, 2008), 168.

56. Susan Ferrechio Smith, with Alan K. Ota, "Delay's Third Ethics Rebuke Threatens Potential Rise to Speaker," *Congressional Quarterly Weekly Report,* October 9, 2004, 2369–71.

57. *Congressional Quarterly Weekly Report,* January 4, 2003.

58. Oppenheimer and Hetherington, "Catch-22."

59. "Leadership: An Interview with Senate Leader Lyndon Johnson," *U.S. News and World Report,* June 27, 1960, 88. Also see Ralph K. Huitt, "Democratic Party Leadership in the Senate," *American Political Science Review* 55 (June 1961): 333–344.

60. Julian E. Zelizer, *On Capitol Hill, The Struggle to Reform Congress and its Consequences, 1948–2000* (New York: Cambridge University Press, 2004); Aldrich and Rohde, "Congressional Committees in a Continuing Partisan Era."

61. Sinclair, *Party Wars,* 153–154.

62. Cohen, "Power Surge."

63. Davidson, Oleszek, and Lee, *Congress and its Members,* 182. The original source of the quote is U.S. Congress, *Congressional Record,* daily edition, 98th Cong., 1st sess., November 15, 1983, H9856.

64. Barbara Sinclair, *Unorthodox Lawmaking: New Legislative Processes in the U.S. Congress,* 3rd ed. (Washington, D.C.: CQ Press, 2007), 51.

65. Zelizer, *On Capitol Hill.*

66. Thomas E. Mann and Norman J. Ornstein, "Is Congress Still the Broken Branch?" in *Congress Reconsidered*, 9th ed.

67. Barbara Sinclair, *The Transformation of the U.S. Senate* (Baltimore: Johns Hopkins University Press, 1989), especially chapter 4.

68. Sinclair, *Party Wars,* 229.

69. Paul M. Krawzak and Joseph J. Schatz, "Senate Clears Stimulus Package Without a Vote to Spare," CQ Politics, February 15, 2009, www.cqpolitics.com/wmspage .cfm?docID=news-000003046178.

70. Barbara Sinclair, "Do Parties Matter?"

71. Aldrich and Rohde, "Congressional Committees in a Continuing Partisan Era."

72. Sinclair, *Party Wars*, 166.

73. Barbara Sinclair, *Unorthodox Lawmaking: New Legislative Processes in the U.S. Congress*, 2nd ed. (Washington, D.C.: CQ Press, 2000).

74. D. Roderick Kiewiet and Mathew McCubbins, *The Logic of Delegation: Congressional Parties and the Appropriations Process* (Chicago: University of Chicago Press, 1991).

75. Eric Heberlig, Marc Hetherington, and Bruce Larson, "Redistributing Campaign Money and the Polarization of Congressional Leadership," *Journal of Politics* 68 (November 2006): 989–1002.

76. Sinclair, *Party Wars*, 134; C. Lawrence Evans and Clair E. Grandy, "The Whip Systems in Congress," in *Congress Reconsidered*, 9th ed.

77. Sinclair, *Party Wars*, 96–102. David Price, *The Congressional Experience*, 2nd ed. (Boulder, Colo.: Westview Press, 2000).

78. *Congressional Quarterly Weekly Report*, May 27, 1978, 1304.

79. Barry Burden and Tammy Frisby, "Preferences, Partisanship, and Whip Activity in the U.S. House," *Legislative Studies Quarterly* 29 (2004): 569–590.

80. Evans and Grandy, "The Whip Systems of Congress."

81. Erin Bradbury, Ryan Davidson, and C. Lawrence Evans, "The Senate Whip System: An Exploration," in *Why Not Parties?* 97.

82. David Canon, "The Institutionalization of Leadership in the U.S. Congress," *Legislative Studies Quarterly* XIV (1989): 415–443; John Hibbing, *Congressional Careers: Contours of Life in the U.S. House of Representatives* (Chapel Hill: University of North Carolina Press, 1991), 61–62.

83. Evans and Grandy, "The Whip Systems in Congress," 191.

84. Price, *The Congressional Experience*, 173.

85. House Republican Policy Committee Web site, www.republicanhousepolicy.com.

86. Davidson, Oleszek, and Lee, *Congress and its Members*, 187; Sinclair, *Party Wars*, 135.

87. Among the studies to consult on this subject are Susan Webb Hammond, "Congressional Caucuses in the 104th Congress," in *Congress Reconsidered*, 6th ed., ed. Lawrence C. Dodd and Bruce I. Oppenheimer (Washington, D.C.: CQ Press, 1997), 274–292; Arthur H. Miller and Thomas E. Mann, "Mobilization of Liberal Strength in the House, 1955–1970: The Democratic Study Group," *American Political Science Review* 68 (June 1974): 667–681.

88. John M. Donnelly and Tim Starks, "Iraq Timetable Gains Momentum," *CQ Weekly*, March 12, 2007, 746.

89. David Clarke, "Budget Moves on Hard Party Lines," *CQ Weekly*, May 4, 2009, 1036.

90. Lirial Higa and John M. Donnelly, "Supplemental Squeaks Through," *CQ Weekly*, March 26, 2007, 894–896.

91. See Lewis A. Froman Jr. and Randall B. Ripley, "Conditions for Party Leadership: The Case of the House Democrats," *American Political Science Review* 59 (March 1965): 52–63.

92. Theriault, *Party Polarization in Congress*.

93. Ibid.

94. Bruce A. Larson, "The 2008 Congressional and Gubernatorial Contests," in Larry J. Sabato, *The Year of Obama: How Barack Obama Won the White House* (New York: Pearson-Longman, 2009).

95. Jacobsen, *The Politics of Congressional Elections*, 7th ed.

96.   Masket, *No Middle Ground*.

97.   Richard E. Neustadt, *Presidential Power: The Politics of Leadership* (New York: Wiley, 1960).

98.   See a particularly instructive discussion of the insulation of members from party and committee controls in Burdett A. Loomis, *The New American Politician: Ambition, Entrepreneurship, and the Changing Face of Political Life* (New York: Basic Books, 1988), chapter 6.

99.   For a study that finds, contrary to conventional wisdom, that presidential campaigning in midterm Senate elections helps candidates in close races, particularly through the mobilization of voters, see Jeffrey E. Cohen, Michael A. Krassa, and John A. Hamman, "The Impact of Presidential Campaigning on Midterm U.S. Senate Elections," *American Political Science Review* 85 (March 1991): 165–178.

100.   Joseph J. Schatz, "Presidential Support Vote Study: With a Deft and Light Touch, Bush Finds Ways to Win," *Congressional Quarterly Weekly Report*, December 11, 2004, 2900–5.

101.   Isiah J. Poole, "Presidential Support: Two Steps Up, One Step Down," *CQ Weekly*, January 9, 2006, 81.

102.   Ibid.

103.   Clea Benson, "Presidential Support: The Power of No," *CQ Weekly*, January 14, 2008, 132.

104.   Richard Rubin, "2008 Vote Studies: Presidential Support: An Unpopular Lame Duck Prevails," *CQ Weekly*, December 15, 2008, 3322.

105.   Joseph Cooper, "From Congressional to Presidential Preeminence: Power and Politics in Late Nineteenth-Century America and Today," in *Congress Reconsidered*, 9th ed.

106.   Evidence suggests that a member's support for the president's policy proposals is influenced by how well the president ran in his district. See George C. Edwards III, "Presidential Electoral Performance as a Source of Presidential Power," *American Journal of Political Science* 22 (February 1978): 152–168. For a study that finds that the president's coattails significantly help his party's Senate candidates (covering 1972 to 1988), see James E. Campbell and Joe A. Sumners, "Presidential Coattails in Senate Elections," *American Political Science Review* 84 (June 1990): 513–524.

107.   Sinclair, *Party Wars*, 229.

108.   Cooper, "From Congressional to Presidential Preeminence."

109.   Sinclair, *Party Wars*, especially chapter 7.

110.   Charles O. Jones, *The Minority Party in Congress* (Boston: Little, Brown, 1970), especially 9–24.

111.   Ibid., 19–24, and chapters 4–8. Jones identifies eight strategies open to the minority party in the overall task of building majorities in Congress: support of the majority party by contributing votes and possibly leadership, inconsequential opposition, withdrawal, cooperation, innovation, consequential partisan opposition, consequential constructive opposition, and participation (this strategy representing a situation in which the minority party controls the White House and therefore is required to participate in constructing majorities). Strategies may vary within a single session of Congress and from one stage of the legislative process to the next.

112.   Sinclair, *Unorthodox Lawmaking*; Rohde, *Parties and Leaders in the Postreform House*; William F. Connolly and John Pitney, *Congress's Permanent Minority?* (Lanham, Md.: Rowman and Littlefield, 1994).

113.   David Mayhew, *Parties and Policies: How the American Government Works* (New Haven, Conn.: Yale University Press, 2008), 3.

114.   Rohde, *Parties and Leaders in the Postreform House*.

115. Charles L. Clapp, *The Congressman: His Work as He Sees It* (Washington, D.C.: Brookings Institution, 1963), 30–31.

116. For an analysis of the "credit claiming" activities of members, see Mayhew, *Congress: The Electoral Connection,* 52–61. The basic assumption of this remarkable little book is that reelection to Congress is the singular goal of members, and its relentless pursuit steadily influences not only their behavior but also the structure and functioning of the institution itself.

117. A few studies suggest that party financial assistance has a subtle effect. See Kevin M. Leyden and Stephen A. Borrelli, "An Investment in Goodwill: Party Contributions and Party Unity Among U.S. House Members in the 1980s," *American Politics Quarterly* 22 (1994): 421–452; David C. W. Parker, *The Power of Money in Congressional Campaigns, 1880–2006* (Norman: University of Oklahoma Press, 2008). Parker also demonstrates that party financial assistance can induce candidates in close races to run on party-developed issue agendas. Other studies, however, demonstrate either little or no effect. See Richard Clucus, "Party Contributions and the Influence of Campaign Committee Chairs on Roll-Call Voting," *Legislative Studies Quarterly* 22 (1997): 179–194; and David M. Cantor and Paul S. Herrnson, "Party Campaign Activity and Party Unity in the U.S. House of Representatives," *Legislative Studies Quarterly* 22 (August 1997): 393–415.

118. Gary Cox and Mathew McCubbins, *Setting the Agenda: Responsible Party Government in the U.S. House of Representatives* (New York: Cambridge University Press, 2005), 5.

6 PARTY IDENTIFICATION, PARTISANSHIP, AND ELECTIONS

IN THE MID-1950S RESEARCHERS at the University of Michigan undertook the second large-scale academic study of the political attitudes of ordinary American citizens.[1] The result of their research, *The American Voter*, was the most significant book about political behavior published in the last fifty years. The most important political opinion held by individuals, the study discovered, was their party identification. Generations of research have confirmed that the psychological attachment of individuals to one or the other of the major parties (or the absence of such an attachment) reveals more about their political attitudes and behaviors than any other single opinion.

By contemporary standards, this finding may not seem particularly exceptional—that is, that people who think of themselves as Republicans tend to vote Republican and those who think of themselves as Democrats tend to vote Democratic. At the time, however, it was an extraordinary observation because the conventional wisdom about voting behavior revolved around social group identification, such as race, religion, social class, and the like.[2] The social groups with which people identify are important in influencing their voting decisions, but parties are even more important. They organize how most people think about politics.

In addition, party identification explains more than simply how people are likely to vote. It often shapes what policy attitudes they have, how they interpret new political information, and how they evaluate their political leaders. In short, parties influence in major ways how ordinary people interact with the political world.

199

The Origins of Party Identification

More than any other group or factor, the party provides cues to voters and gives shape and meaning to elections. Some voters reject party labels, choosing instead to be independent. Even though the importance of independents cannot be minimized, especially in presidential elections, their consistent impact on politics is less than that of party members. The reason is partly a matter of numbers: about 60 percent of voters classify themselves as members of one or the other of the two major parties, and another 30 percent lean toward one of them.

Where does the choice of party (or no party) come from? Most research suggests that party identification is learned early in life and that parents are influential in its development. If a child grows up in a household where Republicans are held in high esteem and Democrats are derided, the child will typically grow up to be a Republican. In that sense, people are born into a party, much as they are born into a religion. As evidence, the National Election Study (NES) last asked people in 1992 if they recalled their parents' party identification. Of those who could recall, fully 87 percent said that both parents identified with the same party. Of those who said both their parents were Democrats, 59 percent identified themselves as Democrats, with 29 percent independent and 13 percent Republican. Among respondents who said both their parents were Republicans, the results were a mirror image: 59 percent of them identified as Republicans, 29 percent as independent, and 12 percent Democrats. From very early in life, most people develop an attachment to a party, not unlike that to a sports team. Moreover, this association tends to grow stronger through the life cycle. Once someone decides that he is a Republican, he usually remains a Republican, and his identification tends to grow stronger over time. By the time a person reaches his mid-thirties, conversion from one party to another is vanishingly rare.[3]

Although the concept of party identification was an important innovation by the Michigan research group, social groups—the paradigm that party identification replaced—are still important in understanding which party people choose. Donald Green, Bradley Palmquist, and Eric Schickler articulate a remarkably cogent theory of how social group identification informs partisan identification. They demonstrate that over many decades people have connected the two major parties with a remarkably consistent set of social groups. In the 1950s people saw the Democrats as the party of "common people," the "working class," "poor people," and "labor unions." In contrast, Americans saw the Republican Party as the party of "big business," the "upper class," and "capitalists." The same stereotypes about the parties still hold today, but with added groups: people connect the Democratic Party with racial minorities and the Republican Party with religious conservatives.

Green, Palmquist, and Schickler use data from the 1996 NES to provide further evidence for their theory. That year, respondents were given a list of social groups and asked to which they felt particularly close. "Of those who felt close to business people but not minority or working-class groups, 62.1 percent identify as Republicans and 15.3 percent as Democrats. Of those with the converse pattern of group affinities, 65.7 percent are Democrats, and 6.5 percent are Republicans."[4] In other words, people can use their own group identifications to inform their party identification, which also explains why younger people tend to experience more change in their party identification than older people. Before the age of thirty, people's lives are in a state of flux, and their social group identifications are more likely to change. After thirty, social group identities are stronger, leading to less fluctuation in party identification.

In addition, people acquire significant information about politics through informal learning, which reinforces their social group identifications with parties. If you identify yourself as part of a group, you most likely have people in your life who share that group identification, which then affects political identification. Labor families, for example, are well aware that the Democratic Party has been more responsive to their concerns than has the Republican Party. That view is likely to be reinforced by conversation with other union members and by union leaders, who tell members who their political friends are and who their enemies are. Being part of the business elite would provide a socialization experience that would likely move people toward the Republicans. The GOP has most often followed a policy course that is friendlier to business than has the Democratic Party, and knowledge of the parties' differing responses to business is reinforced through contact between group members. Specifically, business people tend to be involved with organizations, political or civic, with which other business people are involved. And, just like people in labor unions tend to live in proximity to other people in labor unions, business people tend to live in neighborhoods with other business people. Neighborhood gatherings will, then, have the effect of bringing like-minded people together in ways that may reinforce orientations toward the parties.

Religious institutions can be powerful socializing agents, especially those, such as evangelical churches, that take strong stands on political issues. If a church leader or authority figure makes a connection between the nature of one's faith and politics, it can be particularly powerful. To that end, scholars have observed over time that people from different religious denominations tend to identify disproportionately with different political parties. Because social justice and religious tolerance are important to the Jewish faith and because the Democratic Party has been more attuned to these concerns, Jews are more likely to identify as Democrats. Similarly, because evangelical Protestant churches take conservative positions on social issues such as abortion and gay rights, and the Republican Party is more in tune with these positions, evangelicals are, by and large, Republicans. The members who gather once or twice a week with each other in the congregation will reinforce to each other the messages that they received from religious elites.

Early political experiences also bear on party identification.[5] People who grew up in the shadow of the Great Depression, which was blamed on Republicans, tend to be less Republican than the population as a whole. Their early experiences included both Republican failures with the economy and the Democratic successes with the New Deal. Those who came of age politically during Democrat Jimmy Carter's failures in the late 1970s and Republican Ronald Reagan's successes in the 1980s are more likely to be Republicans. The first indications of this Republican generation were found in the high percentage of young people who voted for Reagan in the early 1980s. In that light, it bears watching whether the 2000s might be another period in which early life experiences provide a partisan tilt to the electorate. Barack Obama won an overwhelming 69 percent of the vote from people under age thirty in 2008. An unpopular war in Iraq and the Republican Party's conservatism on social issues brought many young voters to the Democratic candidate's side.

Although party identification usually takes hold early in life, it can be changed. A person's intense interest in a particular issue can affect his party identification. Someone who grew up in a Republican household but developed an intense prochoice position on abortion may shift to the Democratic Party or become an independent. Issues take on greater importance to people as they enter their twenties.[6] In addition, vote choice and party identification are not the same thing, and regularly voting for candidates of the opposite party may alter party identification.[7] Consistently voting for Republican presidential candidates by southern Democrats eventually moved them to identify as Republicans. It is also possible for the social group identifications of the parties to change. Green, Palmquist, and Schickler demonstrate that in the late 1980s and early 1990s young southerners started to identify with the Republican Party more than their parents did, with the rise of Newt Gingrich of Georgia (House Speaker), Tom DeLay of Texas (House majority leader), and from Mississippi, Haley Barbour (head of the Republican National Committee) and Trent Lott (Senate majority leader).[8]

The Effects of Party Identification

Party identification is by far the most stable political attitude, which means that it typically influences other opinions and behaviors rather than being influenced by them.[9] Certain issues, such as abortion, can affect a person's party identification, but usually it is party identification that affects his opinions about political issues.

For most people, party provides a useful shortcut for understanding a complicated political world. People have neither the time nor the desire to learn everything they should know about politics; party helps them find their way around, albeit with less than perfect information. Public opinion research shows that most Americans know very little about politics and government.[10] If asked to identify the chief justice of the United States, fewer than 10 percent of respondents regularly answer correctly. Usually only about one-half can identify which party holds a majority in the House of Representatives. About 10 percent cannot identify the vice president by name. The uncomfortable truth is that many Americans barely have any opinions about the issues of the day.

As a result, most people use their attachment to party to decide where they stand. Most Americans do not follow politics closely enough to have a well-formed opinion on tax policy, for example, but they can use information presented in the mass media to see how political elites analyze tax issues. They might find that Republicans in Congress favor deep tax cuts that benefit upper income groups and that Democrats support smaller cuts that reward persons with lower incomes. Partisans use this information to form their own positions.

Because ordinary Americans use partisan cues, public opinion typically follows elite opinion. Consider the question of racial integration in the 1950s and 1960s. The Democratic Party's decision to embrace civil rights for African Americans was not the result of an enormous shift in the percentage of people favoring this policy course. Rather, the shift occurred only after the Democratic Party took up the issue and signaled its legitimacy.[11] Some southerners abandoned their Democratic identification, but more Americans changed their opinions on racial integration than changed their partisanship. In general, the decisions of party leaders drive the opinions of partisans, not the other way around. Partisans tend to align their views with those of their party leaders. Thomas Carsey and Geoff Layman demonstrate that most people change their issue positions to match their existing partisanship because they do not tend to have particularly strong feelings about issues. The only people who change their partisanship because of their preference on a given issue know both of the parties' positions on the issue and think the issue is very important—a relatively small group indeed.[12]

The level of agreement that partisans have with their party on a range of different issues is reasonably impressive. The parties in Washington have staked out clear ideologies, with Republicans decidedly conservative and Democrats decidedly liberal. Most partisans reflect these differences. Based on data from the 2008 NES, only 3 percent of Republicans classified themselves as liberal, while fully 74 percent identified themselves as conservative. (The other 23 percent either identified themselves as moderates or said they did not know.) Among Democrats, the differences are not as sharp, but that is because the word "liberal" has developed a negative connotation for some after decades of pejorative usage by conservatives. Even so, 40 percent of self-identified Democrats described themselves as ideologically liberal, while only 12 percent said they were conservative. (The remaining 48 percent claimed they were moderate or said they did not know.)

An important dividing line between the parties' ideological approach to governance is how many services the government ought to provide. Democratic elites usually promise more, and Republican elites make limited government a centerpiece of their ideology. When asked whether the government "should provide more services than it does now, fewer services than it does now, or about the same number of services as it does now," 54 percent of self-identified Democrats in the electorate said more services and only 12 percent said fewer. In stark contrast, only 21 percent of self-identified Republicans in the electorate wanted more government services compared with 40 percent who wanted fewer. The differences were even greater when people were asked whether they favored or opposed "the U.S. government paying for all necessary medical care for all Americans." Among Republicans, 23 percent favored it, 68 percent opposed it, and 9 percent expressed no opinion. Democrats, however, overwhelmingly supported more government involvement in health care: 71 percent favored it, 18 percent opposed it, and 12 percent had no opinion. Although Congress never passed George W. Bush's initiative to allow people to invest their Social Security taxes into stocks and bonds, the legislation would have shifted a significant amount of responsibility for paying for seniors' retirement from the government to the private sector. Republican partisans were more supportive of this idea (48 percent in favor, 25 percent opposed, and 28 percent expressing no opinion) than Democrats (26 percent in favor, 46 percent opposed, and 28 percent expressing no opinion).

Partisans are deeply divided on social issues. Consider preferences about gay adoption, one of today's hot button issues. About 60 percent of Democrats favor allowing same-sex couples to adopt children, while only 35 percent of Republicans do. Access to guns also divides partisans. In 2008 only about a third of Republicans thought it ought to be more difficult for people to purchase guns, while 62 percent thought it should remain the same, and 5 percent thought it should be easier. Fifty-seven percent of Democrats thought buying a gun should be more difficult, 41 percent thought it should remain the same, and only 2 percent thought it should be easier. On abortion, two-thirds of Democrats fall into the NES's two prochoice categories. In contrast, a little over half of Republicans fall into the NES's two pro-life categories.

On some issues, Republicans and Democrats actually agree, with the major difference between them a matter of degree. According to the 2008 NES, more than half of Democrats (58 percent) supported the death penalty, and 85 percent of Republicans did. This finding probably explains why anti–death penalty Democrats running for office try to obscure, or even change, their position. Indeed, when Obama first sought elected office in 1996, he said he was against the death penalty. When he ran for the U.S. Senate in 2004, he said he was not against the death penalty but supported a moratorium on its use until more study could be conducted on whether it was carried out fairly. Finally, when he ran for president in 2008, he supported the death penalty for the most heinous crimes. That *both* Republicans and Democrats support capital punishment provides at least one explanation for Obama's changing position.

On some issues, however, a relatively high percentage of partisans do not agree with their party's stand. The Republican Party does not favor a universal health care system in which the government plays a central role, but about a quarter of Republicans in the electorate still favor it. Democrats in Congress took a hard line against the Bush administration's proposals to privatize Social Security, but the data show that a quarter of Democrats in the electorate expressed support for it. Part of the reason for this slippage between the mass and elite levels is ignorance of where the parties stand on issues. Partisans who follow politics closely are almost always more in step with the issue positions of their party in government. If everyone followed politics closely, the correspondence between the elite position on an issue and the mass position on that issue would be closer. But even more of the slippage is due to legitimate disagreement, and campaigns capable of exploiting differences in preferences between party leaders running for office and their partisans may be able to attract these voters to their candidates.

In addition to shaping issue preferences, party identification also acts as an important perceptual screen for incoming political information. Indeed, partisanship can even be sufficiently powerful that it can cause people to reach erroneous conclusions about political information. Gary Jacobson notes this tendency regarding information about the justification for the Iraq War. Although the intelligence community had discredited reports that Saddam Hussein had links to al Qaeda, 44 percent of Republicans still thought such links existed, but only 25 percent of Democrats believed this to be true. Similarly, although American troops and weapons inspectors did not find weapons of mass destruction in Iraq after the invasion, a survey conducted by Polimetrix in October 2006 revealed that 50 percent of Republicans, compared with 8 percent of Democrats, believed such weapons had been found. It is not that only Republicans who misperceive reality. Larry Bartels shows that during the Reagan years, Democrats were more likely than Republicans to say that the economy had gotten worse or much worse over the past year, even though the economy had become demonstrably better. Partisans have a tendency to believe what they want to believe.

Watching exactly the same news broadcast, Republicans and Democrats can often take away completely different impressions. How important people think the morality of political leaders to be seems to depend on the party affiliation of the transgressor. As evidence grew that Bill Clinton had carried on an affair in the Oval Office with a young intern, Monica Lewinsky, Republicans became outraged and called for his removal from office. In contrast, many Democrats supported the president even more intensely, believing that the affair had little or no relevance to his ability to conduct the presidency. When it came to light during the last week of the 2000 presidential campaign that George W. Bush had been arrested for drunk driving in the mid-1970s, Republicans dismissed his misdeed as old news. But the same Democrats who in 1998 had claimed that Clinton's improprieties were irrelevant spoke quite differently about Bush's misconduct. Both Bush and Obama have admitted to using illegal drugs when they were young. Democrats in 2000 sought to make this an issue when it involved Bush, and Republicans cried foul. The reverse was the case when the situation involved Obama in 2008. Party elites presented these views through the mass media, and partisans in the electorate lined up their opinions accordingly.

In the 1990s Democrats did not seem particularly troubled that their presidential candidate, Bill Clinton, lacked heroic military service. In fact, documents released during the 1992 presidential campaign suggested that Clinton had worked to avoid service during the Vietnam era. In contrast, Republicans who backed decorated World War II-era war heroes George H. W. Bush in 1992 and Bob Dole in 1996 were outraged. In 2004 the tables were turned. Democrats trumpeted John Kerry's valor in the Vietnam War and criticized George W. Bush's decision to join the National Guard, which for many people in the 1960s was akin to avoiding service. Republicans seemed unconcerned that in addition to joining the guard rather than choosing active duty, Bush apparently did not complete his guard service before he went to graduate school. Issues of military service and the ability to lead the armed forces were again front and center in the 2008 election because of the stark contrast in the candidates' backgrounds. Republican John McCain came from a military family and served heroically in Vietnam. He was captured by the enemy early in his service there and endured years of torture. Several times he refused an earlier release than the men captured before him, demonstrating valor under the worst of conditions. Obama never served in the military. In September, a *USA Today*-Gallup poll found that only 5 percent of Republicans thought that Obama would be better than McCain at handling terrorism and the situation in Iraq. Indeed, only 19 percent of Republicans thought that Obama could handle the responsibilities of commander in chief at all. Democrats saw the world differently: more than three-fourths thought Obama would be better than McCain at handling terrorism and the situation in Iraq, and 86 percent thought he was up to the responsibilities of commander in chief.

The hotly contested 2000 presidential election also provides evidence of the importance of party identification as a perceptual screen. In assessing the election's outcome, Republicans tended to highlight that George W. Bush had received more legal votes in Florida than had Al Gore. Democrats highlighted that thousands more voters in Florida intended to vote for Gore than for Bush, but that poorly designed ballots and racial discrimination had distorted or invalidated their votes and cost Gore the election. Survey data taken by the Gallup Organization paints a highly partisan picture of the Florida controversy. More than 90 percent of Republicans criticized Gore's legal efforts in Florida, and more than 80 percent of Democrats approved of them.[13] Democrats and Republicans developed vastly different opinions about a seemingly objective outcome (who won a presidential election), even though they received basically the same information from the mass media. This case suggests that party identification matters a great deal in shaping opinions.

The perceptual screen of party identification also affects a range of other opinions, including estimates of how well the president is doing his job. In fact, in the history of polling no president has produced larger differences in job approval between Republicans and Democrats than George W. Bush. According to a poll by *USA Today* in conjunction with the Gallup Organization taken as Bush left office in January 2009, 78 percent of Republicans approved of his job performance compared with only 6 percent of Democrats, an astonishing seventy-two–percentage point difference. Although Clinton was a polarizing figure, especially during his impeachment trial, the difference between Republicans and Democrats in assessing his job performance never exceeded sixty percentage points. Under Presidents Reagan and George H. W. Bush, the differences averaged about fifty percentage points, and from the 1950s to the 1970s, the differences hovered around thirty percentage points.[14]

The list of attitudes that party identification affects is impressive. When a Republican is in the White House, Democratic partisans always view the economy as worse than their Republican counterparts do, and vice versa. In evaluating the personal characteristics of political candidates, Republican partisans always rate the competence, character, and attractiveness of Republican candidates more favorably than do Democrats, and vice versa. Moreover, attitudes that were once somewhat immune to party differences now show massive differences by party, indicating that partisanship in the electorate is stronger than in decades past. Not too long ago, partisanship had little impact on whether people supported American participation in foreign wars. Whether a person was a Republican or a Democrat told us little about whether he or she favored the Korean War in the 1950s or the Vietnam War in the 1960s. The Iraq war is a different story. Republicans have been overwhelmingly supportive; Democrats, in contrast, overwhelmingly have supported withdrawal.[15] In short, party identification structures the political world of partisans more thoroughly than any other attitude or set of attitudes.

The Distribution of Party Identification

To understand partisanship and its intensity, the NES regularly asks a random sample of Americans a set of questions beginning with:

Generally speaking, do you usually think of yourself as a Republican, Democrat, an independent, or what?

Tracking responses to this question over time reveals what appears to be an extraordinary change in identification. (See Figure 6-1.) In the early 1950s, when the NES began asking this question, 47 percent of Americans classified themselves as Democrats, 28 percent as Republicans, and 23 percent as independents. By 1984, the percentage of Democrats had dropped by about ten points, the percentage of independents had increased by about the same amount, and the percentage of Republicans remained steady. Based on this apparent dealignment from the parties, scholars published books with titles such as *The Decline of American Political Parties*.[16] In 2008 fully 40 percent of Americans chose the independent label rather than the label of one of the major parties, tied with 2000 (and statistically the same as 2004) as the highest percentage of independents ever recorded by the NES surveys.

That the high water mark for partisan independence seems to have occurred in the 2000s is strange given the partisan contentiousness of all three presidential campaigns, not to mention the partisan polarization of Congress that was discussed in chapter 5. In fact, an examination of the responses to the other two

Figure 6-1 The Distribution of Party Identification in the Electorate: 1952–2008

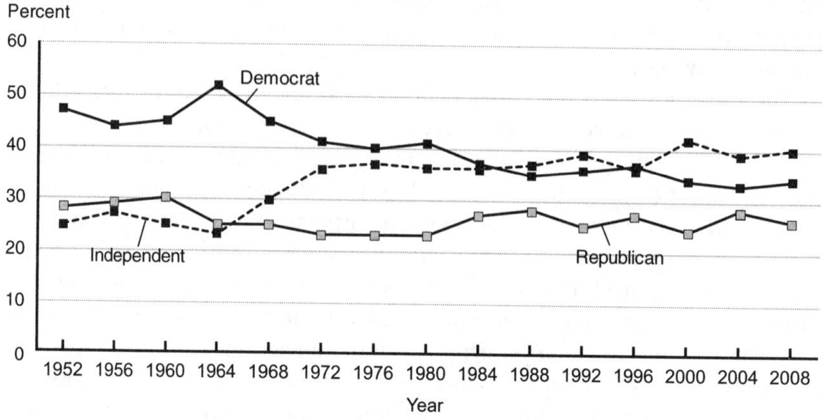

Source: American National Election Study, Cumulative File, 1948–2008.

party identification questions asked by the NES reveals a much different picture of contemporary party identification:

> If a person answers that he is a Republican or Democrat to the first question, he is asked, "Would you call yourself a strong or a not very strong Republican/Democrat?"
>
> If a person answers that he is an independent to the first question, he is asked, "Do you think of yourself as close to the Republican or Democratic Party?"

Public opinion researchers usually combine the responses to these questions to form a seven-point scale, ranging from strong Democrat on one end to strong Republican on the other, with pure independent at the midpoint. Those who fail to fit into any of these categories are labeled apoliticals, a group that has never been larger than a percentage point or two. The data showing the seven-point party identification scale from 1952 to 2008 appear in Table 6-1.

The scale creates three partisan categories for each party: strong partisans, weak partisans, and independents who lean in a partisan direction. Bruce Keith and his coauthors observe that people who call themselves independent but lean toward one of the parties (partisan leaners) behave politically in a manner that is at least as partisan, if not more partisan, than those who are weak partisans.[17] The only group that behaves as if it is truly disconnected from the parties and the political system is the pure independents. After a surge in the 1970s, the percentage of pure independents is basically the same today as it was in the 1960s. In other words, people today are not nearly as disconnected from the parties as scholars and commentators previously had argued.

The findings of this study suggest that to assess partisan alignment and dealignment, the three partisan categories should be combined. When that is done, the distribution of Republicans, Democrats, and independents in 2008 looks almost exactly the same as it did in 1960, an intensely partisan year. (See Figure 6-2.)

Table 6-1   Party Identification, Selected Presidential Years: 1952–2008

Party Identification	1952	1964	1980	1984	1988	1992	1996	2000	2004	2008
Strong Dem.	22%	27%	18%	18%	17%	18%	19%	19%	17%	19%
Weak Dem.	25	25	23	22	18	18	20	15	16	15
Ind. Dem.	10	9	11	10	12	14	14	15	17	17
Ind. Ind.	6	8	13	6	11	12	8	12	10	11
Ind. Rep.	7	6	10	13	13	12	11	13	12	12
Weak Rep.	14	14	14	15	14	14	15	12	12	13
Strong Rep.	14	11	9	14	14	11	13	12	16	13
Apolitical	3	1	2	2	1	1	1	1	0	0

Source: Center for Political Studies, University of Michigan; 2008 data: American National Election Study.

Note: Columns may not add to 100 because of rounding.

Figure 6-2   The Distribution of Party Identification in the Electorate, Leaders Included as Partisans: 1952–2008

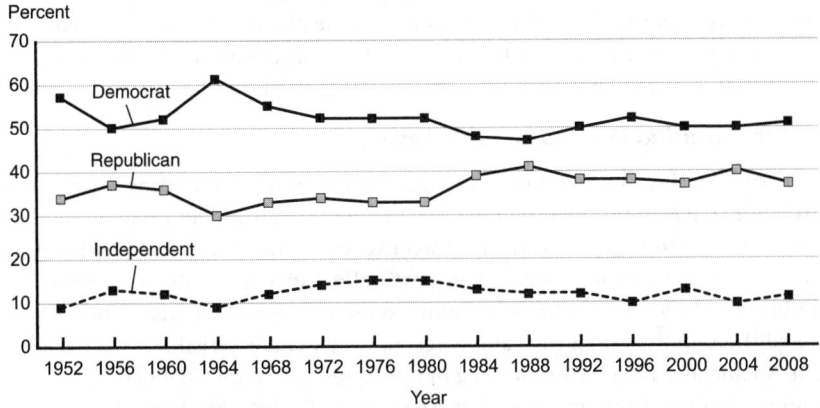

Source: American National Election Study, Cumulative File, 1948–2008.

In 1960, 52 percent of Americans were classified as Democrats, 37 percent as Republicans, and 12 percent as independents. In 2008 the percentages were 51, 38, and 11—statistically indistinguishable from those in 1960. In this interpretation, the data point to a relatively marked increase in political independence in the 1970s that was, in fact, short lived. It should also be noted that the relatively large Democratic identification advantage in the 1960s shrank from the 1980s through the early 2000s. This decrease is largely the result of the evolution of the South from Democratic to strongly Republican.[18] In 2008, however, the Democratic advantage widened again.

To examine the durable changes in the strength of party identification, it is useful to fold the scale at its midpoint. Table 6-2 shows that the percentage of strong partisans has declined noticeably since the early 1960s, but that this percentage has begun to recover. When John F. Kennedy defeated Richard Nixon

Table 6-2   Strength of Partisanship, Selected Presidential Years: 1952–2008

	1952	1964	1976	1988	1992	1996	2000	2004	2008
Ind. or apolitical	9%	9%	15%	12%	13%	10%	13%	10%	11%
Leaning partisan	17	15	22	25	27	26	28	29	29
Weak partisan	39	38	39	32	32	34	27	28	28
Strong partisan	35	38	24	31	29	30	31	33	32

Source: American National Election Study, 2008 Series, and Cumulative File, 1948–2004.

in 1960, 36 percent of Americans identified themselves as strong partisans. By 1976 this figure had dropped by a third, to 24 percent. In 2008 the percentage of strong partisans increased to 32 percent, which is not much less than the 36 percent in the three presidential election years from 1952 through 1960. The biggest decline over time is in weak partisans, whose numbers held in the high thirties from the 1950s to the early 1980s. The percentage of weak partisans dropped into the high twenties in the first three presidential election years of the twenty-first century. By contrast, the percentage of partisan leaners more than doubled since the late 1950s and early 1960s.[19] Because weak and leaning partisans behave somewhat the same, however, this change has limited significance.

Party Identification and Voting Behavior

Party identification data raise the question of why Republicans tend to win presidential elections when Democrats consistently outnumber them in the electorate. Since 1968 Republicans have won seven of the eleven presidential elections. Obviously, factors other than party affect election outcomes. Even the authors of *The American Voter,* who centered their analysis on party identification, noted the importance of the candidates' personal characteristics in vote choice. The Michigan scholars were writing in the 1950s, when the Democrats' identification advantage was greatest, but Republican Dwight Eisenhower won two terms by comfortable margins, undoubtedly helped by his status as a war hero. Since then, the Republicans often have fielded more attractive presidential candidates than the Democrats, including Ronald Reagan, perhaps the most charismatic president of the last several decades. Virtually all analyses of the 2000 election stressed George W. Bush's likeability advantage over Gore, and he maintained this trait advantage over John Kerry in 2004.[20]

Differences between Republican and Democratic identifiers also help account for Republican presidential successes. First, Republicans are more loyal to their candidates than are Democrats. In 2004, 89 percent of self-identified Democrats voted for Kerry, and 93 percent of self-identified Republicans voted for Bush.[21] And, even in 2008, a losing year, Republicans were as loyal to McCain (90 percent reporting having voted for him) as Democrats were to Obama (89 percent reported having voted for him).

In addition to voting more loyally, Republicans are more likely than Democrats to vote. Numerous studies have shown that citizens who are better educated and have higher incomes are more likely to vote than those with limited education and lower incomes. In other words, higher socioeconomic status (SES) encourages turnout; lower SES discourages it. Because upper-SES persons tend to vote Republican and lower-SES persons tend to vote Democratic, it is not surprising to find that in the 2008 election, 90 percent of Republicans reported voting as contrasted with 84 percent of Democrats. Both figures are inflated, however, because many people say they vote when they actually do not. (Voter turnout in 2008 was only about 57 percent of the voting-age population.) Although Obama's 2008 victory resulted in part from the mobilization of greater numbers of Democrats than usual, more important to his success was his appeal with nonpartisans and the nonideological.

In sum, Republicans over the last several decades have been able to overcome the Democrats' party identification advantage because they vote more loyally for their candidates and turn out in (slightly) higher numbers. In addition, Republicans, with their limited-government philosophy, have profited from their ability to field better candidates and from the general antigovernment sentiment that followed the end of Lyndon Johnson's burst of liberal public policy (the Great Society), the military's failure in Vietnam, the Watergate crisis, and the series of failures in the Carter administration. The financial crisis that gripped the nation in the final months of the Bush administration, however, has caused Americans to think that more government regulation of the private sector might be warranted. In addition, the Bush administration's feeble efforts to aid Gulf Coast residents during and after Hurricane Katrina in 2005 may have significantly undermined the Republicans' narrative that limited government is always the best alternative. Certainly the elections of a Democratic Congress in 2006 and 2008 and a Democratic president in 2008 suggest the winds of partisan change may be blowing.

Gender and Religion Gaps in Party Identification

For years, the most striking change in party identification was the movement of white southerners away from the Democratic Party that began in the 1960s. They turned to the Republicans when they became disillusioned with the liberal thrust of the national Democratic Party, particularly its position on civil rights.

Another dramatic development is the difference in party identification of men and women, as shown in Figure 6-3. As recently as 1976, men and women identified with the parties in basically the same numbers, but in 1980 a gender gap in party identification started to develop. In 2008 data from the NES show that men were six percentage points more Republican than women, and that women were nine points more Democratic than men. This difference manifests itself in voting behavior. In 2000 the Voter News Service (VNS) exit poll found that 54 percent of women voted for Gore, compared with 43 percent for Bush, and 53 percent of men voted for Bush, compared with 43 percent for Gore. The eleven-point gender difference in the vote for the Democratic candidate is close to the fourteen-point difference recorded in 1996, the largest gap between

Figure 6-3   Gender Gap in Party Identification: 1976–2008

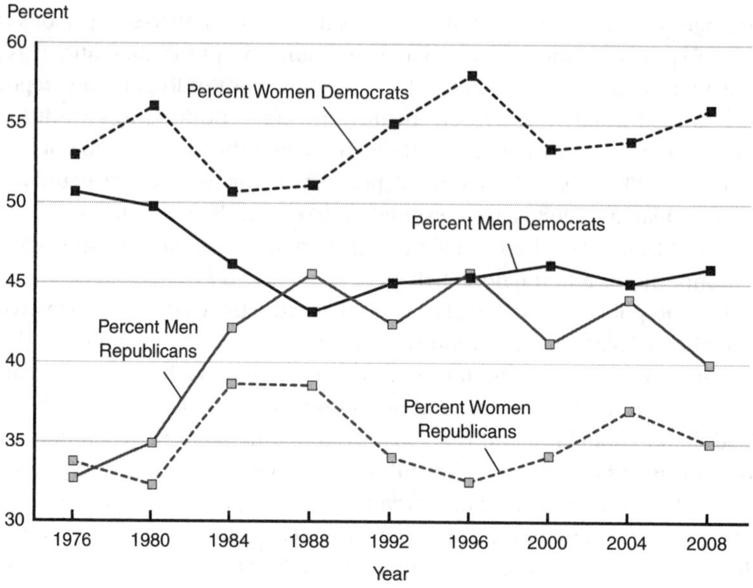

Source: American National Election Study, Cumulative File, 1948–2008.

the sexes recorded in the survey era.[22] With security concerns at the forefront of the 2004 campaign, the gender gap eased to some degree. But, even so, women still favored Kerry by three percentage points, and men favored Bush by eleven. And in 2008, with men and women both moving in a Democratic direction, Obama enjoyed a twelve-point edge among women but ran even with McCain (49 percent to 48 percent) among men.

Although popular analysis tends to focus on women in discussions of the gender gap, most of the change in attitudes occurred among men.[23] In 2004, 53 percent of women identified themselves as Democrats, about the same percentage as in 1976. The attitudes of men, by contrast, have changed a great deal. In 1976, 51 percent of men identified themselves as Democrats, but only 45 percent did so in 2004. The percentage of male Republicans increased dramatically, from 33 percent to 44 percent. The usual stability that characterizes partisan attitudes makes this change of eleven percentage points nothing short of extraordinary. In comparing 2008 with 2004, however, it appears that men and women both are moving toward the Democrats and away from the Republicans. Fully 56 percent of women either identified with or leaned toward the Democrats, three points higher than four years before. Although the percentage of male Democrats did not increase appreciably in 2008 relative to 2004, the percentage of male Republicans dropped from 44 percent to 40 percent. Most of the disaffected Republican men appear to have moved into the independent category, which is sometimes an indication of a future change in partisanship.

Figure 6-4   Religious Participation Gap in Party Identification: 1976–2008

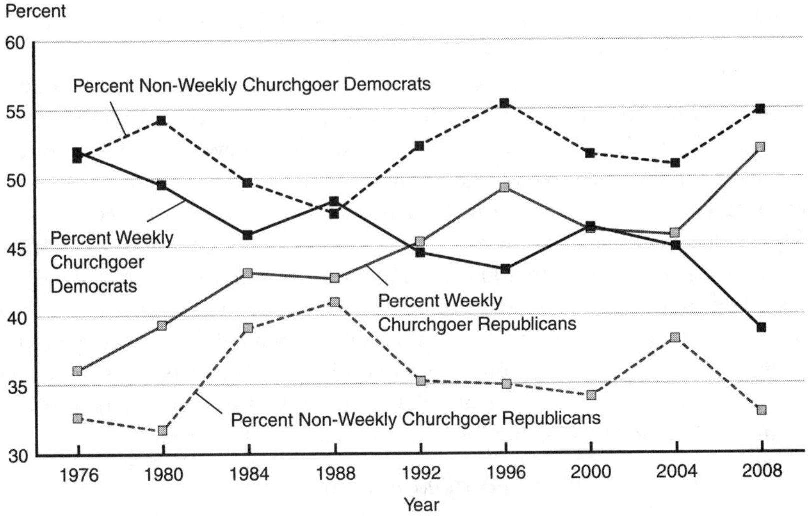

Percent

Source: American National Election Study, Cumulative File, 1948–2008.

Karen Kaufmann and John Petrocik find that the gender gap results from disparities in policy attitudes, particularly on social welfare issues, and in the weight that men and women assign to these issues. Men tend to be more conservative than women on issues such as spending for the poor and for minorities, and they are also more likely to favor a smaller government role in creating jobs and providing health care. In addition, men tend to place greater emphasis on these issues than women typically do.[24]

In addition to the growing chasm between men and women voters, a major division has developed between those who attend church regularly and those who attend infrequently or not at all. Specifically, those who attend church at least once a week have become stalwarts of the Republican Party; those who attend church less often or not at all are now disproportionately Democratic. The trend over time appears in Figure 6-4. According to NES data, church attendance and party identification were basically unrelated in the 1970s. The gap began to show up in the 1980s, with the election of Reagan, who was closely identified with the Reverend Jerry Falwell and the Christian Right movement. The gap disappeared in 1988, but reappeared and became wider in succeeding presidential election years. In 1996 the percentage of regular church attendees who identified as Democrats had dropped to 43 percent, and the percentage of less-regular churchgoers who identified as Democrats increased to 55 percent—a twelve percentage point difference. By 2008 that gap had grown to sixteen percentage points (55 percent versus 39 percent). The gap is even more pronounced on the Republican side. In 2008, 52 percent of regular churchgoers identified as Republicans compared with 33 percent of less-regular churchgoers, a difference of twenty percentage points. These differences are even more stark if the analysis is limited to white survey respondents; 64 percent of whites who called themselves weekly churchgoers either identified with or leaned toward the Republican Party.

This cleavage is clearly an important feature of American politics today. Indeed, religious participation now has a greater impact on party identification than traditional factors such as region and social class. Religion's new importance is due in part to the "family values" campaigns waged by Republican candidates over the last two decades and to the Republican Party's antiabortion position. Moreover, it also helps explain the change in the voting behavior of Catholics, formerly stalwarts of the Democratic coalition. In 2000 and 2004 white Catholics cast more votes for Bush than they did for Gore and for Kerry, respectively, with a particularly large thirteen-point gap evident in 2004.[25] Although Obama did better than Kerry did among white Catholics, the group still provided a plurality of its votes to McCain in 2008. Religious denomination aside, the centrality of religion in a person's life significantly influences whether he is a Republican or a Democrat.

Evidence of the Growing Importance of Party

Since the 1980s the conventional wisdom among political scientists was that party meant relatively little to American voters. The Michigan studies provided evidence that it was very strong in the electorate in the 1950s but declined after the political upheavals of the 1960s and 1970s. Rather than viewing one party positively and the other negatively, as strong partisans do, people tended to view both parties in more neutral terms.[26] Parties became less able to structure voting behavior, particularly at the congressional level.[27] During that period, the political system also became more media driven. Television, in particular, created an increasingly candidate-centered world, and voters became less likely to organize their thoughts about politics in party terms and images. From the late 1960s through the early 1980s, ample evidence points to party decline in the electorate.

This trend began to reverse after Reagan was elected. Ordinary people once more began to rely on party to form their opinions and to make voting decisions—a trend that continues today. The NES surveys illustrate the point. The surveys ask people what they like and dislike about the major parties, allowing up to five likes and five dislikes about each party. Individuals who provide few responses obviously are not thinking about politics in terms of parties. If respondents provide numerous likes and dislikes, however, their answers may indicate that parties are doing more to inform their thinking. Figure 6-5 demonstrates that parties are more salient today than they were in the 1970s and 1980s.[28] In fact, the mean number of responses to the likes/dislikes questions in 2004 was higher than any year since 1968. The parties-in-decline thesis is applicable to the 1970s and early 1980s, but it no longer applies today.[29]

This resurgence in party is, however, somewhat puzzling. If today's political world is more media-driven and candidate-centered than ever, why has party made a comeback? Mass opinion does not change without cause. When it does

Figure 6-5   Mean Total Number of Likes and Dislikes about the Parties: 1952–2004

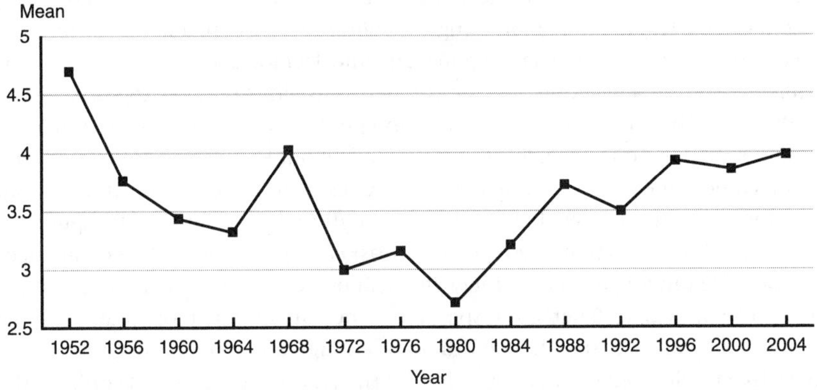

Source: American National Election Study, Cumulative File, 1948–2004.

shift, it usually does so in response to changes in the information environment provided by political elites. In 1966 V. O. Key Jr. put it this way: "[T]he voice of the people is but an echo chamber. The output of an echo chamber bears an inevitable and invariable relation to the input." [30] In other words, when politicians provide party-oriented cues, the public is likely to respond in a party-centric manner. They are unlikely to do so otherwise. [31]

The changes in Congress described in chapter 5 are important for understanding the resurgence of party among ordinary Americans. The growing ideological divide between the parties in the legislature has had an impact on the public. Today, Americans are much better at placing the Democrats to the ideological left of Republicans than they were in the past. In addition, the public is more likely than it was a generation ago to perceive important policy and ideological differences. [32] Nothing explains the increase in partisan thinking and behavior in the electorate better than does the upturn in partisan behavior in Congress. As political elites exhibited sharper party differences between them, the masses began to reflect these differences. [33]

Why should the parties' pronounced ideological polarization at the congressional level produce more partisan behavior among ordinary Americans? If the parties did not differ in basic respects, it would not matter who ran the government because policy outcomes would be roughly the same. But, in a political world informed by significant cleavage between the parties, who wins and who loses really matters. Greater partisan differences in Washington have created a more partisan public.

Is the American Public Polarized?

Chapter 5 demonstrated that Congress was polarized by party. In the 108th Congress (2003–2004), every Republican House member was more conservative than every Democratic member. The only exception was Ralph Hall (D-Texas), but he switched parties and was elected to the 109th Congress (2005–2006) as a Republican. Party differences in Congress continue to widen, and for the foreseeable future, overlap between Republicans and Democrats in the House seems unlikely. The 2004 electoral map for president was almost exactly the same as the 2000 map, which caused many pundits and political scientists to suggest that the public is similarly polarized. Some analysts talk about Republican "red states" and Democratic "blue states" as if their respective residents have nothing in common.

Morris Fiorina has challenged the conventional wisdom that the public is polarized.[34] He notes that when people are asked to place themselves on an ideological scale ranging from extremely liberal at one end to extremely conservative at the other, nearly 50 percent respond that they are either "moderate," "middle of the road," or that "they haven't thought enough about it," hardly a picture of polarized public opinion. Rather, claims Fiorina, it is the choices that confront the public at election time that are polarized. Indeed, although he campaigned as a "compassionate conservative" in 2000, suggesting a moderate stance on issues, George W. Bush was actually a very conservative president. And John Kerry, his 2004 opponent, is one of the most liberal members of the Senate by most measures. Fiorina marshals an impressive amount of data to suggest that (1) people in Republican red states are not much different from people living in Democratic blue states in their political thinking; (2) Democrats and Republicans are somewhat more divided than they used to be, but the differences are still not that large; (3) attitudes toward abortion, supposedly one of the most polarizing issues on the political agenda, have remained fairly constant over time; and (4) that Americans are much less hostile toward homosexuality than ever before, which suggests moderation rather than polarization on another hot button social issue. Fiorina concludes that polarization is confined to a small core of activists in each party and that a vast number of Americans are politically moderate.

Fiorina's argument is compelling on many levels. He is right that Americans' positions on issues have not become more extreme over time. Instead, their positions tend to echo their parties, and today the Republican Party's positions on issues are likely be conservative, and the Democratic Party's positions are likely to be liberal, which has increased the difference in issue preferences between the average Democrat and the average Republican. But it does not mean that either Republicans or Democrats are more likely to take extreme positions on issues than they were a generation ago.

Still, Fiorina's argument does have certain limitations. Not all red states are uniformly red, and not all blue states are uniformly blue. Pennsylvania is a blue state that Obama won by ten points in 2008. The state also has substantial heterogeneity. Its two major population centers—Philadelphia and Pittsburgh—provide Democrats strong support, but the area between these metropolitan areas is reliably Republican. James Carville, the political consultant who masterminded Bill Clinton's election in 1992, aptly described the state as "Philadelphia and Pittsburgh with Alabama in between." Consistent with Carville's observation, Pennsylvania's congressional delegation in the 110th Congress included Democrats Robert Brady and Chaka Fattah, two of the more liberal members of the House, and Republicans Joe Pitts and Bill Shuster, two of the more conservative. Many other states are similarly split. Arizona's congressional delegation includes Jeff Flake and Trent Franks, two of the five most conservative members of the House, and Raúl Grijalva, one of the twenty most liberal. These representatives illustrate the polarization between residents of different parts of states. Republicans from red congressional districts and Democrats from blue congressional districts have very different preferences.[35]

In addition, Alan Abramowitz and Kyle Saunders argue that even if most Americans do not express the most polarized positions available on measures of political attitudes, the nation's electorate is further apart on the issues today than in years past. They find that Democrats are increasingly likely to think of themselves as liberal and Republicans are increasingly likely to think of themselves as conservative. In fact, when asked to place themselves on a scale from "extremely liberal" at one end and "extremely conservative" at the other, with "moderate, middle of the road" in the center, the average distance between Republicans and Democrats has more than doubled since 1972.[36] John Evans and Lisa Nunn note that although Americans have not become more polarized on abortion over time, they are still more divided on this issue than on almost any other. In other words, even if the public's preferences on abortion are no longer moving apart, they are already relatively far apart.[37]

Views about homosexuality might be considered in the same way. The opinions of experts and elites have made homosexuality more acceptable to Americans than it was a generation ago.[38] Prior to 1974 the American Psychiatric Association (APA) still classified homosexuality as "deviant" behavior. When the APA changed its stance on the matter, attitudes about homosexuals began a gradual evolution. Even so, the concept of homosexuality was so unpopular that political leaders never endorsed gay rights. In 1988 the NES asked a sample of the electorate to rate "gay men and lesbians" on a "feeling thermometer" between 0 and 100 degrees. The average score was 29 degrees, with 35 percent of Americans providing a score of 0. By 2008, this score had vaulted to 49 degrees, with only 13 percent of those sampled giving a score of 0. Yet relative to other groups, homosexuals are still unpopular. In 2008 the only groups that produced a lower average feeling thermometer score were "illegal immigrants" and "atheists." Contrasted with the recent past, however, Fiorina is right: Americans' views are now more moderate toward homosexuality.

Oddly, this moderation has actually increased the potential for polarization in American politics. With feelings about homosexuals so negative in the 1980s, there was little or no sustained discussion of gay marriage, gay adoption, or even gays in the military. Certainly, neither party adopted the gay rights position on any of these issues until years later. Because political leaders rarely talked about gay rights, they did not affect how people thought about them politically. As people's feelings about homosexuality have grown more positive, and gay rights have reached the issue agenda, people are now more divided on this issue than they are on all others. Even though feelings have moderated, the gays and lesbians feeling thermometer in 2008 still produces by far the largest standard deviation (spread) of any of the feeling thermometers now used by the NES. For more than any other group, feelings about homosexuals are closer to 0 and 100 or, to put it another way, polarized. The result is a more polarized electorate when gay rights issues enter the political dialogue.

Moreover, sociologist James Davison Hunter argues that the present divide in American politics is about more than just the issue positions Fiorina examines. He believes polarization is about worldviews, the beliefs that people have about right and wrong. Specifically, Hunter distinguishes between the "progressives," who believe that authority to decide what is right or wrong rests with people, and the "orthodox," who believe that authority is transcendent.[39] Liberals and Democrats are more relativist in their approach, placing greater emphasis on people to determine what might be evolving moral values in a society. Conservatives and Republicans often embrace "traditional family values" in their campaigns, which suggests that they believe that values, particularly traditional conceptions of right and wrong, ought to remain steadfast in response to a changing world. The long and the short of it is that religious observance and worldview have become important lines of political cleavage in both campaigns and electoral behavior.

Decades of social science research suggest that a good way to understand people's worldviews is to ask them questions about rearing children. In 1992 the NES began to ask the following:

> Although there are a number of qualities that people feel that children should have, every person thinks that some are more important than others. I am going to read you pairs of desirable qualities. Please tell me which one you think is more important for a child to have. The pairs of attributes are the following:

1) INDEPENDENCE OR RESPECT FOR ELDERS
2) OBEDIENCE OR SELF-RELIANCE
3) CURIOSITY OR GOOD MANNERS
4) BEING CONSIDERATE OR WELL BEHAVED

The orthodox and tradition-minded ought to favor children who are respectful of elders, obedient, well mannered, and well behaved. Those who are more progressive and relativist ought to favor children who are independent, self-reliant, curious, and considerate. In 1992 Republicans and Democrats did not differ in their responses to these questions. By 2004, however, they diverged dramatically in their responses—and not because people's worldviews changed. Rather, people began to sort themselves into parties along these lines. Among whites, Republicans provided an average of 2.20 orthodox responses, compared with an average of 1.66 for Democrats, a 27 percent difference. Democrats, meanwhile, provided an average of 1.88 progressive responses compared with 1.38 among

Republicans, a 35 percent difference. And the difference in progressive responses widened even further in 2008.

The mobilization of fundamentalist Christians by the Republican Party helps to explain this phenomenon. Fundamentalists tend to believe in a literal interpretation of the Bible, and nothing divides orthodox views from progressive views more deeply than a belief in biblical inerrancy. In 2008 those who believed "the Bible is the actual word of God and is to be taken literally, word for word" provided an average of 2.68 orthodox responses and only 0.67 progressive responses, and those who believed that "the Bible is a book written by men and is not the word of God" provided an average of 1.48 orthodox responses and 2.04 progressive responses.

It is also noteworthy that the worldview revealed by the child-rearing preferences tends to undergird people's preferences on several of the most highly contested issues in American political life—morals, race, and national defense. On these hot button topics, the average Republican and the average Democrat differ by increasingly large amounts. Since the 1980s the NES has asked a battery of four questions to tap what it calls moral traditionalism. Respondents are asked their level of agreement or disagreement with a set of statements, including "the newer lifestyles are contributing to the breakdown of our society," "the country would have many fewer problems if there were more emphasis on traditional family ties," and "the world is always changing and we should adjust our view of moral behavior to those changes." Figure 6-6 tracks the percentage difference among nonblacks between self-identified Democrats and self-identified Republicans over time. In 1986 the average difference between Republicans and Democrats was

Figure 6-6 Differences between the Average Republican and Average Democrat on Several Hot Button Dimensions, White Respondents Only: 1988–2008

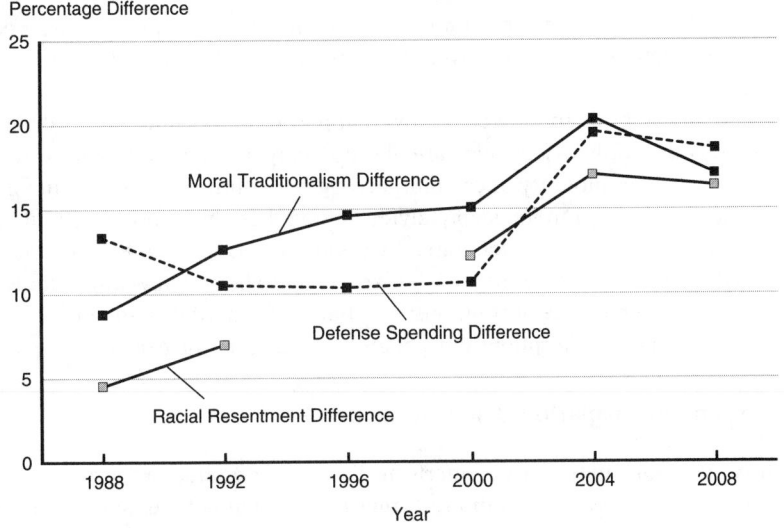

Percentage Difference

only four percentage points, barely statistically significant. Ten years later it had grown to fifteen percentage points, and by 2004 it was twenty-three points. This percentage narrowed a bit in 2008, but the average Republican and average Democrat still differed by seventeen percentage points on moral traditionalism, a wide gulf indeed.

Another cleavage that divides white Democrats from white Republicans is race. Figure 6-6 also graphs how far apart the average white Republican and average white Democrat are on a set of questions used by the NES called racial resentment. Specifically, the survey asks people their level of agreement or disagreement with the following items: "Irish, Italians, Jewish and many other minorities overcame prejudice and worked their way up. Blacks should do the same without any special favors"; "Generations of slavery and discrimination have created conditions that make it difficult for blacks to work their way out of the lower class"; "Over the past few years, blacks have gotten less than they deserve"; and "It's really a matter of some people not trying hard enough; if blacks would only try harder they could be just as well off as whites." The gap between white Republicans and white Democrats in racial resentment increased gradually between 1988 and 2000, from a barely statistically significant 4.5 percentage points to about 12 percentage points. The difference then surged in 2004 to 17 percentage points and remained there in 2008. This pattern of change is curious because race has recently come to play a less central role in electoral politics.

The last line in Figure 6-6 traces the distance over time between the average Republican and the average Democrat on defense spending. The difference for defense spending was larger in the late 1980s than for either moral traditionalism or racial resentment. With the demise of the Soviet Union, party differences decreased to about ten percentage points from 1992 to 2000. Since then, however, how much people want to spend on defense has become a particularly sharp dividing line between partisans. In 2004 and 2008, the difference between the average Republican and the average Democrat was about twenty percentage points.

The reason for this analysis is to show that partisans are more sharply divided on matters that ordinary people care about deeply. People are bound to have strong feelings on morality, race, and keeping the country safe from enemies. With the party system more deeply divided along these lines, no one should be surprised that the intensity generated by politics has increased. People may be able to disagree civilly about how high taxes ought to be and how much government should spend on education, but it is harder for parties to disagree civilly when fundamental conceptions of right and wrong enter the debate.

Voting and Participation: The Diminished Electorate

It is an unfortunate fact of American life that for a large proportion of the population politics carries no interest, registers no significance, and excites no demands. A vast array of evidence shows that the political role of the typical citizen is that of spectator, occasionally aroused by political events but more often inattentive to them. Whether greatly interested and active citizens are necessary to have strong and responsible political institutions is by no means clear. No neat or simple formula exists for assessing public support for political institutions. Does the presence of a large nonvoting population reflect substantial disillusionment with the political system and its processes, or does it reflect a general satisfaction with the state of things? The answer is elusive.

Whatever the consequences of low or modest turnouts to the vitality of a democratic political system, it is obvious that some American citizens use their political resources far more than others. Their political involvement is reflected not only in their voting habits but also in their participation in politics in various other ways. They may attempt to persuade other voters to support their candidates or party, make campaign contributions, or devote time and energy to political campaigns. The net result of differential rates of participation is that some citizens gain access to political decision makers and influence their decisions, and others are all but excluded from the political process.

Who Participates?

The act of voting is an appropriate point of departure for exploring the political involvement of American citizens, but it is only one form of participation. A comprehensive survey of political participation in the United States by Sidney Verba and Norman H. Nie shows the range and dimensions of citizen activities in politics. (See Table 6-3.) Several findings should be emphasized. Perhaps of most importance, the only political activity in which a majority of eligible American citizens participate is voting in presidential elections. Voting regularly in local elections follows as a rather distant second. The survey reveals that as a particular

Table 6-3   A Profile of the Political Activity of American Citizens

Form of Activity	Percentage of Citizens
Report regularly voting in presidential elections	72
Report always voting in local elections	47
Acting in at least one organization involved in community problems	32
Have worked with others in trying to solve some community problems	30
Have attempted to persuade others to vote as they were	28
Have ever actively worked for a party or candidates during an election	26
Have ever contacted a local government official about some issue or problem	20
Have attended at least one political meeting or rally in last three years	19
Have ever contacted a state or national government official about some issue or problem	18
Have ever formed a group or organization to attempt to solve some local community problem	14
Have ever given money to a party or candidate during an election campaign	13
Presently a member of a political club or organization	8

political activity requires more time, initiative, and involvement of the citizen—working to solve a community problem, attempting to persuade others how to vote, working for a party or candidate, or contributing to political campaigns—participation levels drop even lower.

The impression that the data most deeply conveys is that a relatively small group of citizens performs most of the political activities of the nation. Yet, to some extent, the data underrepresent the political activity of citizens, because those citizens who perform one political act are not necessarily the same as those who perform another act. Verba and Nie indicate that less than one-third of their sample reported engaging in no political activities (other than voting).[40]

The evidence indicates that people do not get involved randomly in politics. Instead, there is a hierarchy of political involvement.[41] (See Figure 6-7.) Individuals who are politically active engage in a wide variety of political acts. A major characteristic of their participation is that it tends to be cumulative. The active members of a political party are likely to solicit political funds, contribute time and money to campaigns, attend meetings, and so on. Individuals who

Figure 6-7   Hierarchy of Political Involvement

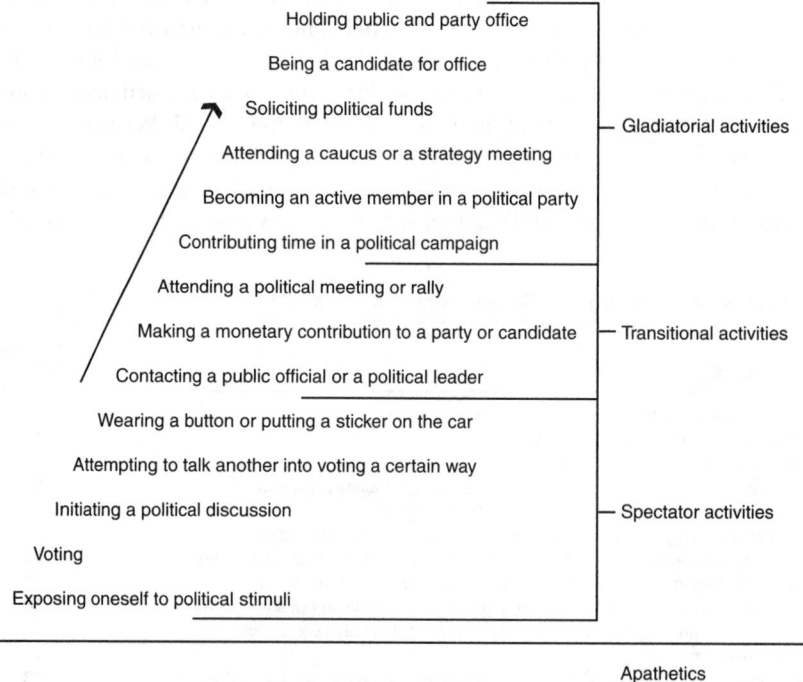

Source: Lester W. Milbraith, *Political Participation: How and Why Do People Get Involved in Politics.* Copyright © 1965 by Houghton Mifflin Company. Used with permission.

are minimally involved in politics typically take part only in limited activities, such as those grouped near the base of the hierarchy. At the very bottom are those persons who stand on the outskirts of the political world, scarcely aware of the political forces that play on them or of the opportunities open to them to use their resources, including the vote, to gain political objectives.

Some portion of the explanation for the passivity of American citizens may lie with the parties and candidates themselves: neither is particularly active in clearing the way for popular participation. Traditionally, only a small proportion of citizens were contacted by workers for the parties or by candidate organization workers in an effort to win their vote, although some evidence suggests that this is changing. During the 1992 election campaign, only 12 percent of the public reported having been contacted by someone from the Democratic Party, and only 10 percent by someone from the Republican Party. In 2008, however, 32 percent reported having been contacted by the Democrats, and 24 percent by the Republicans.[42]

Several social, demographic, and political variables are related to the act of voting. The data in Table 6-4 provide a profile of those citizens more likely to turn out for elections and those who are less likely. Some of the characteristics are closely related—for example, a high income,[43] a high occupational status, and a college education. But the high rate of participation by citizens of higher socioeconomic status is not simply a function of status. The explanation lies in the civic orientations linked to upper-class status. Upper-class citizens are more likely than other citizens to belong to organizations and to participate in the activities of these organizations, more likely to possess the resources and skills to be effective in politics, and more likely to be attentive to political problems and to feel efficacious in dealing with them.[44]

Table 6-4 A Profile of the More Active and Less Active Citizenry

More Likely to Vote	Less Likely to Vote
High income	Low income
High occupational status	Low occupational status
College education	Grade school or high school education
Older	Young
White	Black and Hispanic
Resident in competitive party environment	Resident in noncompetitive party environment
Union member	Nonunion member
Homeowner	Renter
Married	Single, separated, divorced, widowed
Government employees	Private workers
Jews	Protestants and Catholics
Strong partisan	Independent

Sources: These findings were drawn from a large number of studies of the American electorate. For wide-ranging analyses, see Lester W. Milbrath, *Political Participation* (Chicago: Rand McNally, 1965); Raymond E. Wolfinger and Steven J. Rosenstone, *Who Votes?* (New Haven: Yale University Press, 1980); M. Margaret Conway, *Political Participation in the United States*, 2d ed. (Washington, D.C.: CQ Press, 1991); and Paul R. Abramson, John H. Aldrich, and David W. Rohde, *Change and Continuity in the 2004 Elections* (Washington D.C.: CQ Press, 2006).

Table 6-5   Education and Voting Turnout in Presidential Elections

Education Level	Percentage Voting						
	1980	1984	1988	1992	2000	2004	2008
Grade school	58.6	58.0	50.0	54.8	49.1	52.1	52
High school	65.4	66.3	59.2	65.4	62.9	71.2	71
College	82.6	85.5	85.1	88.1	84.8	90.3	91

Source: Adapted from M. Margaret Conway, *Political Participation in the United States,* 2nd ed. (Washington, D.C.: CQ Press, 1991), 22 (updated). As Conway pointed out, individuals who are more highly educated are also more likely to overreport voting.

Socioeconomic status aside, the number of demographic factors strongly predictive of turnout is smaller today. The participation rates of people who live in rural or urban areas are about equal, and men and women vote at about the same rate. Turnout is rising faster in the South than it is in the North, so regional differences are no longer as pronounced as they once were. A noticeable decline in voting by the middle-aged has occurred in concert with higher levels of voting among the elderly. As a result, the only age group that votes at a significantly different rate from the others is younger voters, who are much less participatory. Although youth turnout in 2008 was markedly higher than in previous years, the same was true of other age groups, meaning that young people still lagged behind. In addition, Republican efforts to mobilize evangelical Christians have narrowed the voting turnout differences that used to exist between Catholics and Protestants. Among religious groups, Jews remain by far the most participatory.

It should be stressed that the variables are not of equal importance. The best indicators of voting participation are those that reflect socioeconomic status: education, income, and occupation. (See Table 6-5.)

Scholars who study electoral behavior contend that education is the predominant influence on turnout.[45] Its importance is said to derive from its ability to inculcate a sense of civic duty; increase political efficacy, which is a disposition of a person to see his own participation in politics as important and effective; enhance political awareness; and make registration easier. Robert A. Jackson finds that education's impact on registration is especially important: "Advanced schooling cultivates skills and interests that make the hurdle of registration easier to overcome, which, in turn, elevates voting odds."[46]

Citizens who show enthusiasm for voting and who participate regularly in elections can be distinguished by their psychological makeup as well as by their social and economic backgrounds. The prospect that persons will vote is influenced by the intensity of their partisan preferences: the more substantial their commitments to a party, the stronger the probability that they will vote. Those who have strong partisan preferences and who perceive the election as close are virtually certain to vote.[47] Voters are more likely than nonvoters to perceive major differences between the parties' positions on public policy questions such as Medicare, taxes, and the national deficit.[48] Voters can also be distinguished by other indices of psychological involvement in political affairs. Survey research data show them to be more interested in campaigns and more concerned with election outcomes.[49] They are also more likely than nonvoters to possess a strong sense of political efficacy. Finally, in contrast to nonvoters, voters are more likely to accept the norm that voting is a civic obligation. In sum, the evidence suggests that psychological involvement—marked by interest in elections, concern over their outcome, a sense of political efficacy, and a sense of civic duty—increases the probability that a person will pay the costs in time and energy that voting requires.

The most provocative questions concerning participation are those for which empirical evidence is in shortest supply. Does who votes matter? Does it affect public policy outcomes? How do parties play into this equation? When parties do contact voters, the individuals most likely to be reached are those with high socioeconomic status—in particular, those with a college education, a professional or business background, and a high income. That the well off are mobilized rather than those who are not means that office-seekers will be more inclined to confront the problems of the former group rather than the latter.

There is systematic evidence suggesting that the pattern of participation matters. Kim Quaile Hill and Jan E. Leighley found that where poor people have higher levels of turnout, welfare benefits are higher.[50] Steven Rosenstone and John Mark Hansen find a similar connection between African American participation and public policy designed to help this group.[51] It is not much of a reach to believe that economically advantaged elements in American society generally have a much stronger claim than inactive citizens on the attention and dispositions of their representatives. Indeed, Larry Bartels provides compelling evidence that the impact of voting among the well off relative to that of the poor and middle classes is so great that it helps explain most of the significant growth in income inequality since the 1980s.[52] Legislators pay more attention to the people with means. In short, who votes almost certainly matters and does so profoundly.

Atrophy of the Electorate

Turnout was high in presidential elections during the last quarter of the nineteenth century. In the election of 1876, for example, more than 85 percent of eligible voters cast ballots. (See Figure 6-8.) Beginning around 1900, however, a sharp decline in voting set in, reaching its nadir of 44 percent in 1920. A moderate increase in turnout occurred during the next several decades, with participation hovering around 60 percent during the 1950s and 1960s. Beginning with the 1960 election, turnout dropped in most elections, falling to less than 50 percent of the voting-age population in 1996. Since then, however, voter turnout has risen from slightly more than 50 percent in 2000 to more than 55 percent in 2004 and nearly 57 percent in 2008.

Voter turnout is lower in nonpresidential elections. In off-year congressional elections from 1950 to 1970, turnout ranged between 41 percent and 45 percent of eligible voters, but a marked downturn occurred thereafter. In 1974 turnout

Figure 6-8   Percentage of Voting-Age Population Casting Votes for the Office of President: 1856–2008

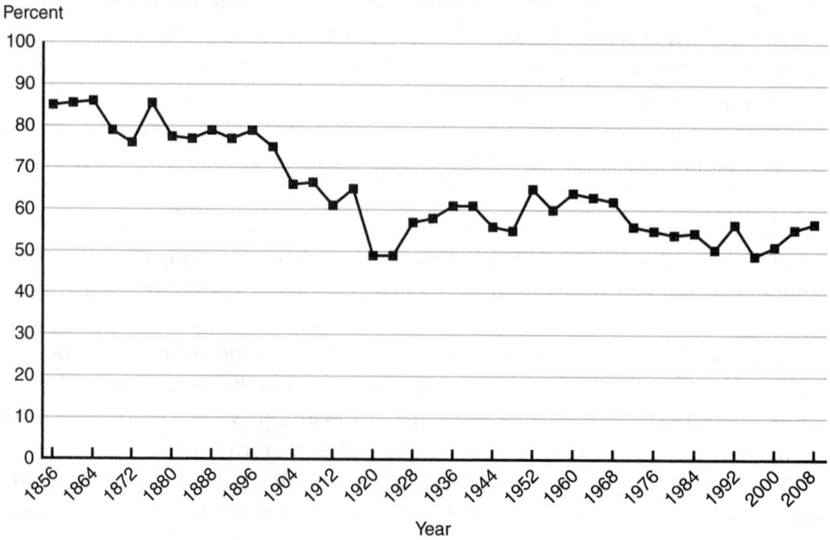

Source: Developed from data in Paul Allen Beck, "The Electoral Cycle and Patterns of American Politics," *British Journal of Political Science* 9 (April 1979): 134 (as updated).

dropped to 38.1 percent, and it has not reached the 40 percent mark since. When people perceive that times are bad, as with the severe economic downturn in 1982 and the extreme anger directed at Clinton's policies in 1994, a few more voters may participate. But, even then, current off-year voting rates do not approach those of the 1950s and 1960s. Only 38.8 percent of eligible voters participated in the ground-breaking victory by the Republicans in 1994, and only 37.1 percent participated when the Democrats regained majorities in the House and Senate in 2006.

Turnout in state and local elections is more of the same story of citizen indifference. An analysis of voting for the office of governor supports three main generalizations. First, the states differ sharply in their turnout patterns. As a rule, higher voter participation rates occur in New England, the Midwest, the Great Plains, and the Rocky Mountain states. Many southern states and western states, including Arizona, Nevada, and New Mexico, usually vote at low rates. Second, those states that elect governors in presidential years (about one-fifth of the total) nearly always have higher turnouts than those in which gubernatorial elections occur in off years. Third, notwithstanding major variations among the states, overall citizen performance is disappointing. The average turnout in off-year gubernatorial elections hovers around 40 percent, and in some southern states it fails to reach even 30 percent.

The low point in participation usually occurs in primary elections: a total primary vote of only 20 percent to 25 percent of the eligible electorate is not unusual. Primary turnout is highest in states in which primaries are open, the parties are most competitive, presidential primaries coincide with other primaries, and the electorate is more highly educated. There is some evidence that the closeness of an election race stimulates turnout and that incumbency diminishes it. Ultimately, each state has a different mix of these factors and therefore vary in turnout rates.

Causes of the Early Twentieth-Century Decline

It is a major and uncomfortable fact of American political life that a great many citizens—that is, nearly half of the eligible electorate even in presidential years—are almost wholly detached from the political system and the processes through which its leadership is selected. As this was not always the case, it is important to understand what caused the decline in voter participation. To answer this question, it is best to divide the decline into its two eras. The steepest took place in the early twentieth century, in the wake of the Progressive movement. The second, more gradual decline took place after 1960.

Major changes in the rules for elections were the most salient reason for turnout decline in the early twentieth century. Before the Progressive movement took hold, voter registration was not widely used. People could simply show up to vote, receive a ballot from a party representative, and register their preferences at the ballot box. Indeed, there is strong evidence that the nearly 90 percent turnouts in the late 1800s were, at least in part, the result of fraud. In many counties, people voted "both early and often," which inflated turnout. Some counties recorded more votes than the number of residents. During the early twentieth century, states began to tighten registration laws, making voting more difficult. Some states adopted provisions that required voters to register annually in person, and voters' names were purged from the registration rolls if they failed to vote within a particular period. Voters were required to reside within a state at least a year (and sometimes two) before becoming eligible to register. As voting rules became more stringent, fewer people voted, either legally or illegally.

In addition to registration laws, other election devices caused turnout to drop. In the southern states, limitations placed on African American political participation in the late 1890s drastically reduced turnout. A variety of legal abridgments and strategies, buttressed by social and economic sanctions of all kinds, effectively disenfranchised all but the most persistent and resourceful African American citizens. The ingenuity of southern white politicians during this era can scarcely be exaggerated. Poll taxes, literacy tests, "understanding-the-Constitution" tests, white primaries,[53] strict residency and registration requirements, discriminatory registration administration, and outright intimidation were consciously employed by dominant elites to maintain a white electorate and therefore to settle political questions exclusively among whites.

Another contributing factor to lower turnout rates might seem counterintuitive at first. The expansion of the franchise allowed women to vote beginning in 1920, but large numbers of women were indifferent to their new right and did not use it immediately. Although the size of the eligible electorate doubled with the inclusion of women, the turnout rate dropped because they voted at much lower rates than men. The first two presidential years during which women could vote, 1920 and 1924, had among the lowest overall turnouts of the century. As women acquired political expertise—a strong predictor of voting—their participation increased accordingly.[54]

Another reason for the contraction of the active electorate stems from the advent of one-party politics and the resultant drop in party competition throughout large sections of the country. Democratic domination of the South began shortly after the post–Civil War Reconstruction governments were terminated. The election of 1896, one of the most decisive in American history, culminated in the virtual disappearance of the Republican Party from the South and in a precipitate drop in Democratic strength in the North.

The smothering effect of a noncompetitive environment on participation can be seen in election turnouts following the realignment of the 1890s. Between 1884 and 1904, turnout in Virginia dropped 57 percent; in Mississippi, 51 percent; and in Louisiana, 50 percent. Part of the explanation for these drop-offs is the exclusion of African Americans, but one-party politics also had a decisive impact. The drop in participation was too large to be accounted for only by the disappearance of black voters. Moreover, the impact of the new sectionalism was not confined exclusively to the South. Despite their growing populations, some fourteen northern states had smaller turnouts in 1904 than in 1896.[55] If the outcome of an election is predictable, voters have little incentive to invest the time, energy, and other costs that voting requires.

Causes of the Contemporary Decline (and Resurgence) in Turnout

The reasons for turnout decline after 1960 are both similar to those of the early twentieth century and also quite different. One analogous development is that a major expansion of the electorate occurred. After 1971 the number of potential voters increased when the voting age was lowered from twenty-one to eighteen. Although nearly half of eighteen-to-twenty-year-olds voted in 1972, when the Vietnam War was still raging and many young people were serving in the military, only 31 percent of this group voted in the 1996 presidential election.[56] Younger voters have the lowest participation rate of any group in American society bar none. Just as the inclusion of women to the franchise raised the number of eligible voters, but not participation, the addition of another relatively indifferent group caused the turnout rate to drop.

In addition, the drop in the number of strong partisans since John F. Kennedy was elected president has contributed to turnout decline. Strong partisans vote at significantly higher rates than do less enthusiastic partisans. In 2008 the NES found that 70 percent of partisan leaners, the fastest growing group among the partisan categories, said that they voted, as contrasted with 91 percent of strong partisans. A loss of strong partisans translates into a loss of voters. This evidence is also consistent with the increase in turnout that occurred from 2000 to 2008, given that the percentage of strong partisans rose over this period.

Steven Rosenstone and John Mark Hansen identify another party factor to explain the decline in turnout between 1960 and 1988.[57] They demonstrate that the diminished efforts of party organizations and social movements to mobilize voters were responsible for more than half of the decline. The parties were once labor-intensive organizations. At election time, party workers would go door-to-door contacting other partisans to urge them to vote and sometimes offering them rides to the polls (and maybe even a few dollars). Alan Gerber and Donald Green show that this type of personal campaigning is better at stimulating turnout than devices such as direct mail or telemarketing.[58] The new capital-intensive parties put more stock in television advertising than face-to-face work to turn out the vote. When parties do contact potential voters, they usually seek out those from middle- and upper-income brackets to solicit contributions as well as urge them to vote. As a result, those with the fewest resources—the same people who need party mobilization efforts the most—are the least likely to be contacted and the least likely to vote.

Parties and interest groups have, however, once again begun to work harder at the ground game. Higher turnouts in 2004 and 2008 were due in part to get-out-the-vote efforts, with the Obama campaign particularly invested in motivating lower-income voters. Efforts by both political parties and the so-called 527 and 501(c) groups (see chapter 4) were unprecedented by contemporary standards. In 2004 Republicans budgeted $125 million for get-out-the-vote drives, about three times the amount they allocated in 2000. Democrats doubled their investment in 2004 relative to 2000—to $60 million.[59] The parties, especially Democrats, made even more extensive efforts for the 2008 elections. According to one account, the Democratic Party and the Obama campaign operated some 770 field offices largely devoted to mobilizing voters.[60] Scores of groups also engaged in get-out-the-vote activities. In 2004 America Coming Together, a Democratic-allied 527 committee funded by George Soros, spent more than $100 million on voter mobilization alone, and labor unions contributed nearly $50 million to stimulate turnout.[61] In 2008 America Votes, another Democrat-oriented 527 group, spent roughly $17 million organizing voter contact efforts among some forty different groups, and the National Rifle Association's 501(c) committee, which supports Republicans, spent several million dollars registering and getting gun owners to the polls.[62] The increase in the number of states offering early voting means that parties and groups must begin their voter mobilization efforts earlier.[63]

A sense of political efficacy is also related to participation. Those individuals who feel that they do not have a say in government are less likely to vote than those who feel that they do. In 1960 only 27 percent of Americans agreed with the statement, "People like me don't have any say about what the government does." By 2008, 44 percent of respondents agreed with the statement. Only 25 percent of Americans agreed that "public officials don't care about what people like me think" in 1960, but by 2008 that percentage had more than doubled to 57 percent.[64]

A central explanation for nonvoting therefore is the public's attitude toward politics and political institutions. Participation has declined because people believe that their votes will not make much difference and that elected officials are unresponsive to the public. The overall decline in the strength of voters' party identification has also contributed to the decline of electoral participation. Indifference, alienation, and declining party loyalty combine to cut the turnout rate in elections. Frequent elections also discourage turnout, particularly among the peripheral electorate—those people who easily lapse into nonvoting unless party and campaign organizations make a special effort to motivate them.

Recently, however, Michael McDonald and Samuel Popkin have persuasively argued that the decline in turnout since the 1960s is due in large part from the difficulties in measuring the size of the eligible electorate.[65] Specifically, the United States has experienced a large increase in the percentage of noncitizen immigrants and people serving prison sentences, and neither group is eligible to vote. When McDonald and Popkin divide the total number of voters in an election by the total number of *eligible* voters, as opposed to the total number of Americans who are of voting age, contemporary turnout rates are not sharply different from those of the 1960s. Substituting the voting-eligible population for the voting-age population as the denominator to figure out the turnout rate, McDonald finds that it was 61.7 percent in 2008. This result is lower, but not by much, than turnout in 1960 and 1964, the highest turnout rates of the second half of the twentieth century. Moreover, this adjusted turnout rate in 2008 is actually somewhat higher than the turnout rate in 1956 and about the same as that in 1968.

Although there is much merit to this argument, it is still the case that changes in U.S. demographics should have brought a sizable *increase* in turnout over the period in question. As noted earlier, no other factor is more closely associated with the turnout decision than education, and education levels have risen markedly since 1960, when the average American had about nine years of schooling. By 2008 that average was more than thirteen years.[66] Other things being equal, turnout should have gone up dramatically over the period in question. It is apparent that several of the factors shown here have offset the effect of increasing education.

The Nation's Response to Declining Voter Turnout

The low voter turnout in the United States makes it an outlier among democracies. As Table 6-6 shows, turnout in other democratic countries averages about 80 percent of the eligible electorate, compared with 50 to 60 percent in U.S. presidential elections. A study by G. Bingham Powell Jr. suggests that voter participation in the United States, as compared to the rest of the democratic

Table 6-6   Turnout in National Elections: 1945–2008

Country	National Parliamentary	Presidential
Australia (26)	94.5%	
Belgium (20)	92.4	
Luxembourg (13)	89.9	
Austria (20)	89.6	(11) 89.1%
Iceland (19)	89.1	(6) 81.1
Malta (16)	89.0	
Italy (17)	88.9	
New Zealand (22)	86.5	
Netherlands (19)	86.3	
Denmark (25)	86.0	
Sweden (19)	85.5	
Germany (16)	84.5	
Norway (16)	80.2	
Greece (18)	79.4	
Israel (17)	77.0	
Finland (18)	75.9	(10) 74.0
Spain (11)	75.7	
United Kingdom (17)	74.4	
France (17)	74.0	(8) 82.1
Portugal (12)	72.8	(7) 68.2
Ireland (17)	72.3	(6) 57.6
Japan (24)	70.1	
Canada (21)	68.8	
Switzerland (16)	55.4	
United States (32)	44.7	(16) 55.7

Source: Paul R. Abramson, John H. Aldrich, and David W. Rohde, *Change and Continuity in the 2008 Elections* (Washington, D.C.: CQ Press, 2010).

Note: Numbers in parentheses are the number of parliamentary or presidential elections. For all countries with bicameral legislatures, we report turnout for the lower house. For all countries except the United States, we calculate turnout based on voter registration lists. For the United States turnout is based upon the voting-age population.

world, is largely the result of institutional factors such as voluntary registration (as opposed to automatic registration common in other nations), low levels of competition in many electoral districts, and weak linkages between parties and social groups, which makes the parties' task of voter mobilization more difficult. To approach the turnout levels of other democracies, Powell argues, the United States would need to adopt automatic registration laws and change the structure of party competition to mobilize lower-class voters.[67] Without question, changing registration laws would be easier to accomplish than changing party character and party competition.[68]

Turnout has remained relatively low, however, despite major changes that have greatly relaxed registration laws. Poll taxes and literacy tests were eliminated by the Voting Rights Act of 1965 and the subsequent court cases that forced states to comply with it. Periodic registration gave way virtually everywhere to permanent registration. As a result of an act passed by Congress in 1970, the residency requirement for federal elections is now limited to a maximum of thirty days before the election; moreover, for other elections, only a handful of states have closing dates earlier than thirty days. In about one-third of the states, registration is possible up to twenty days before the election. Idaho, Maine, Minnesota, New Hampshire, and Wisconsin permit voters to register and vote on election day, and North Dakota and Wyoming have no registration laws at all. Although turnout rates in these states in the 2008 election were all among the top fifteen, with the exception of Idaho,[69] high turnout characterized these states even before they liberalized their voting laws. Such laws do not ensure that turnout will remain uniformly high. Turnout dropped in Minnesota by five percentage points between 1996 and 2000, even though the state continued to have same-day registration. Although less restrictive laws can enhance turnout, they are by no means magic bullets.

Another effort to expand the ranks of voters occurred in 1993, when Democratic majorities in Congress, with the help of a handful of moderate Republicans in the Senate, adopted the National Voter Registration Act, popularly known as the "motor voter" law. Effective since 1995, the law provides that states must permit citizens eighteen years of age or older to register to vote when they apply for or renew a driver's license. It also requires states to permit registration by mail and to make registration forms available at state and federal agencies that administer programs dealing with public assistance, disability benefits, and armed forces recruitment. Millions of new voters have been added to the rolls under this law, but its effects on turnout and election outcomes have been less than impressive. In fact, turnout rates in both 1996 and 2000—the first two elections after the adoption of the motor voter law—were significantly lower than in the election before its passage. One study shows that class differences in participation were even greater after passage of the law than before.[70] It is also true that the percentage of registered voters relative to the size of the eligible electorate also increased, so more people *could have* voted had they wished. Moreover, it is impossible to know how many people would have stayed home had it not been for the new law. Turnout might have been even lower than the 48 percent achieved in 1996. Still, it is clear that the motor voter law has not been a panacea.[71]

Reforms to raise turnout typically fall short of expectations, although some are more successful than others. Although many blame the choice of Tuesday for federal elections (instead of weekends or voting holidays as in Europe), it is not clear that changing the day would make much of a difference. Texas has liberal registration laws by national standards and allows early voting; people can cast their ballots between seventeen days and four days before election day. And their polling stations are housed in convenient locations, so that Texans can vote in places that they might otherwise visit as part of their workaday life, such as the grocery store. Despite the relative ease of voting, not to mention that their former governor was a presidential candidate, only 45.3 percent of Texans voted in 2004, ranking the state ahead of only Hawaii in turnout. The low rate occurred in 2008 as well.

Paul Gronke, Eva Galanes-Rosenbaum, and Peter Miller provide an exhaustive account of different early voting options that some states have adopted and their effect on voter participation.[72] Allowing voters to cast ballots by mail, as Oregon does, has led to the largest bump in voter turnout, about five percentage points. Eric Oliver has shown that allowing people to cast absentee ballots for reasons other than being infirm or away from the voting precinct (as might be the case for college students or people in the military) leads to small but statistically significant growth turnout.[73] Robert Stein shows that the same is true of early voting practices such as those in Texas.[74] Again, however, the effects are quite small in a substantive sense.

In short, with the exception of voting by mail in Oregon, the liberalization of the country's voting laws has not affected turnout very much. As Curtis Gans, director of the Committee for the Study of the American Electorate, notes, the best explanation for declining participation is declining motivation.[75] California may or may not be a special case, but a 1990 poll by the *Los Angeles Times* found that the main reason people in that state fail to vote is that they are too busy doing other things to bother. This reason was given by an extraordinary 35 percent of the respondents.[76] The next most frequent explanation, cited by 8 percent, was a lack of interest in politics. For many citizens, "voting simply isn't worth the effort."[77] Even as parties have boosted their efforts at voter mobilization during the last few election cycles, and states have liberalized registration and voting requirements, increases in turnout have been relatively modest. Absent a large crisis or other galvanizing event, it is hard to imagine what would cause American voters to go to the polls in numbers comparable to those in Great Britain or Germany.

NOTES

1. Angus Campbell, Philip Converse, Warren Miller, and Donald Stokes, *The American Voter* (New York: Wiley, 1960). The first large-scale academic survey work was done by scholars at Columbia University. These efforts produced *The People's Choice: How the Voter Makes Up His Mind in a Presidential Campaign*, by Paul F. Lazarsfeld, Bernard Berelson, and Hazel Gaudet (New York: Duell, Sloan, and Pearce, 1944); and *Voting: A Study of Opinion Formation in a Presidential Campaign*, by Bernard Berelson, Paul F. Lazarsfeld, and William N. McPhee (Chicago: University of Chicago Press, 1954).

2. Berelson, Lazarsfeld, and McPhee, *Voting*.

3. Donald Green, Bradley Palmquist, and Eric Schickler, *Partisan Hearts and Minds: Political Parties and the Social Identities of Voters* (New Haven, Conn.: Yale University Press, 2002).

4. Ibid., 10.

5. For an excellent recent treatment of the importance of political events, see David O. Sears and Nicholas A. Valentino, "Politics Matters: Political Events as Catalysts for Pre-adult Socialization," *American Political Science Review* 91 (March 1997): 45–66.

6. M. Kent Jennings and Richard G. Niemi, "The Transmission of Political Values from Parent to Child," *American Political Science Review* 62 (March 1968): 169–184.

7. Charles H. Franklin and John E. Jackson, "The Dynamics of Party Identification," *American Political Science Review* 85 (December 1983): 957–973.

8. Green, Palmquist, and Schickler, *Partisan Hearts and Minds,* 13.

9. Campbell et al., *The American Voter.* Also see Jon Krosnick, "The Stability of Political Preferences: Comparisons of Symbolic and Nonsymbolic Attitudes," *American Journal of Political Science* 35 (August 1991): 547–576.

10. See, for example, Michael X. Delli Carpini and Scott Keeter, *What Americans Know About Politics and Why It Matters* (New Haven, Conn.: Yale University Press, 1996); and Stephen Earl Bennet, "Americans' Knowledge of Ideology, 1980–1992," *American Politics Quarterly* 69 (September 1995): 476–490.

11. Howard Schuman, Charlotte Steeh, Lawrence Bobo, and Maria Krysan, *Racial Attitudes in America: Trends and Interpretations,* rev. ed. (Cambridge, Mass.: Harvard University Press, 1997).

12. Thomas M. Carsey and Geoffrey C. Layman, "Changing Sides or Changing Minds? Party Identification and Policy Preferences in the American Electorate," *American Journal of Political Science* 50 (2006): 464–477.

13. Gallup Poll, news release, December 6, 2000.

14. Matthew Dowd, "The Politics of Polarization," *Washington Post,* December 16, 2002, A25.

15. Gary C. Jacobson, *A Divider, Not a Uniter: George W. Bush and the American People* (New York: Pearson-Longman, 2007).

16. Martin P. Wattenberg, *The Decline of American Political Parties* (Cambridge, Mass.: Harvard University Press, 1988).

17. Bruce Keith et al., *The Myth of the Independent Voter* (Berkeley: University of California Press, 1992).

18. Green, Palmquist, and Schickler, *Partisan Hearts and Minds.*

19. For an excellent discussion of the sources of partisan independence, see Steven Greene, "The Psychological Sources of Partisan-Leaning Independence," *American Politics Quarterly* 28 (October 2000): 511–537.

20. See Gerald M. Pomper, *The Election of 2000: Reports and Interpretations* (New York: Chatham House Publishers, 2001).

21. VNS does not distinguish between leaning partisans and pure independents. If it did, data from the NES suggests that the Republicans' party loyalty advantage in 2000 would have been even starker. NES data show that 79 percent of leaning Republicans voted for Bush compared with only 72 percent of leaning Democrats voting for Gore.

22. Karen M. Kaufmann and John R. Petrocik, "The Changing Politics of American Men: Understanding the Sources of the Gender Gap," *American Journal of Political Science* 43 (July 1999): 864–887.

23. Also see Warren E. Miller and J. Merrill Shanks, *The New American Voter* (Cambridge, Mass.: Harvard University Press, 1996).

24. It is also worth noting that not all scholars agree with this explanation. Margaret C. Trevor argues that pre-adult socialization explains the gender differences. Specifically, she finds that women were less inclined than men to shed their parents' party identification for the independent label when they were adolescents and young adults. Because most parents of this generation were Democrats, greater loyalty to their parents' party identification explains why women are more likely to be Democrats than men. See Margaret C. Trevor, "Political Socialization, Party Identification, and the Gender Gap," *Public Opinion Quarterly* 63 (Spring 1999): 62–89.

25. See the Voter News Service exit poll.

26. See Martin P. Wattenberg, *The Decline of American Political Parties, 1952–1996* (Cambridge, Mass.: Harvard University Press, 1998).

27. Morris P. Fiorina, *Retrospective Voting in American National Elections* (New Haven, Conn.: Yale University Press, 1981).

28. This figure originally appeared in Marc J. Hetherington, "Resurgent Mass Partisanship: The Role of Elite Polarization," *American Political Science Review* 95 (September 2001): 619–631.

29. Also see Larry M. Bartels, "Partisanship and Voting Behavior, 1952–1996," *American Journal of Political Science* 44 (January 2000): 35–50.

30. V. O. Key Jr., *The Responsible Electorate: Rationality in Presidential Voting 1936–1960* (Cambridge, Mass.: Harvard University Press, 1966).

31. See Benjamin I. Page and Robert Shapiro, *The Rational Public* (Chicago: University of Chicago Press, 1992); Richard A. Brody, *Assessing the President: The Media, Elite Opinion, and Public Support* (Stanford, Calif.: Stanford University Press, 1991); and John Zaller, *The Nature and Origins of Mass Opinion* (New York: Cambridge University Press, 1992).

32. See Hetherington, "Resurgent Mass Partisanship" for a detailed analysis.

33. Marc J. Hetherington, "Putting Polarization in Perspective," *British Journal of Political Science* 39: 413–448.

34. Morris Fiorina, *Culture War? The Myth of a Polarized America* (New York: Pearson, 2005).

35. Hetherington, "Putting Polarization in Perspective."

36. Alan Abramowitz and Kyle Saunders, "Why Can't We All Get Along," *The Forum* 3, no. 2 (July 2005).

37. John H. Evans and Lisa M. Nunn, "Deeper Culture Wars Issues," *The Forum* 3, no. 2 (July 2005).

38. John Zaller, *The Nature and Origins of Mass Opinion.*

39. James Davison Hunter, *Culture Wars: The Struggle to Define America* (New York, Basic Books, 1991).

40. The findings of these paragraphs are drawn from Sidney Verba and Norman H. Nie, *Participation in America: Political Democracy and Social Equality* (New York: Harper and Row, 1972), 25–43.

41. Lester W. Milbrath, *Political Participation* (Chicago: Rand McNally, 1965), 17–21. The holding that political participation involves a hierarchy of political acts—under which the citizen who performs a difficult political act, such as forming an organization to solve a local community problem, is virtually certain to perform less demanding acts—can be overstated. See Verba and Nie, *Participation in America,* especially chapters 2 and 3. Their general position is that "the citizenry is not divided simply into more or less active citizens. Rather there are many types of activists engaging in different acts, with different motives, and different consequences." Quotation on page 45.

42. American National Election Study, 2004.

43. Although the turnout of the highest-income group exceeds that of the lowest-income group by about twenty percentage points in the typical presidential election, there has been little change in socioeconomic class bias in the electorate since 1964. The only exception was in 1988 (Bush vs. Dukakis), when class bias in turnout did increase. See Jan E. Leighley and Jonathan Nagler, "Socioeconomic Class Bias in Turnout, 1964–1988: The Voters Remain the Same," *American Political Science Review* 86 (September 1992): 725–736.

44. See Verba and Nie, *Participation in America,* 133–137.

45. See Jan E. Leighley and Jonathan Nagler, "Individual and Systemic Influences on Turnout: Who Votes? 1984," *Journal of Politics* 54 (August 1992): 718–740.

46. Robert A. Jackson, "Clarifying the Relationship between Education and Turnout," *American Politics Quarterly* 23 (July 1995): 279–299.

47. In information-poor environments, such as House elections, voters tend to rely on prior beliefs concerning the closeness of elections in making their decisions on

whether to vote. Stephen P. Nicholson and Ross A. Miller, "Prior Beliefs and Voter Turnout in the 1986 and 1988 Congressional Elections," *Political Research Quarterly* 50 (March 1997): 199–213.

48. Mellman Group and Wirthlin Worldwide, *Analysis of a Survey on Nonvoting* (Washington, D.C.: League of Women Voters, 1996), 25.

49. For a study that finds that voters with high levels of information are more likely to rely on issues in deciding how to vote than voters who have moderate or low levels of information, see David Moon, "What You Use Still Depends on What You Have: Information Effects in Presidential Elections, 1972–1988," *American Politics Quarterly* 20 (October 1992): 427–441.

50. Kim Quaile Hill and Jan E. Leighley, "The Policy Consequences of Class Bias in State Electorates," *American Journal of Political Science* 36 (May 1992): 351–365.

51. Steven Rosenstone and John Mark Hansen, *Mobilization, Participation, and Democracy in America* (New York: Macmillan, 1993).

52. Larry M. Bartels, *Unequal Democracy: The Political Economy of the New Gilded Age* (Princeton, N.J.: Princeton University Press, 2008).

53. The white primary in southern states resulted from the exclusion of African Americans from membership in the Democratic Party, which was held to be a private organization. Because the real election at this time in most southern states occurred in the Democratic primaries, African Americans had little opportunity to make their influence felt. After many years of litigation, the Supreme Court in 1944 held that the white primary was in violation of the Fifteenth Amendment. The Court's position in *Smith v. Allwright* was that the primary is an integral part of the election process and that political parties are engaged in a public, not a private, function in holding primary elections. After the white primary was held unconstitutional, southern states developed literacy and understanding tests, along with discriminatory registration systems, to bar black access to the polls.

54. Michael X. Delli Carpini and Scott Keeter, *What Americans Know about Politics and Why It Matters*; and Sidney Verba, Kay Lehman Schlozman, and Henry E. Brady, *Voice and Equality: Civic Voluntarism in American Politics* (Cambridge, Mass.: Harvard University Press, 1995).

55. E. E. Schattschneider, *The Semisovereign People* (New York: Holt, Rinehart and Winston, 1975), 84.

56. Federal Election Commission archives turnout data; see www.fec.gov.

57. Rosenstone and Hansen, *Mobilization, Participation, and Democracy in America.*

58. Alan S. Gerber and Donald P. Green. "The Effects of Personal Canvassing, Telephone Calls, and Direct Mail on Voter Turnout: A Field Experiment," *American Political Science Review* 94 (2000): 653–664.

59. Paul R. Abramson, John H. Aldrich, and David W. Rohde, *Change and Continuity in the 2004 Elections* (Washington D.C.: CQ Press, 2006), 45.

60. T. W. Farnam and Brad Haynes, "Democrats Far Outspend Republicans on Field Operations, Staff Expenditures," *Wall Street Journal*, November 3, 2008. Cited in Michael E. Toner, "The Impact of Federal Election Laws on the 2008 Presidential Elections," in *The Year of Obama: How Barack Obama Won the White House*, ed. Larry J. Sabato (Pearson-Longman, 2009), 154.

61. Abramson, Aldrich, and Rohde, *Change and Continuity in the 2004 Elections.*

62. Campaign Finance Institute, press release, "Soft Money Political Spending by 501 (c) Nonprofits Tripled in the 2008 Election," February 25, 2009; Peter Stone, "Taking Aim," *National Journal*, September 13, 2008, www.nationaljournal.com/njmagazine/ks_20080913_2513.php.

63. Greg Giroux, "Early Voting, Underway in Ohio and Elsewhere, Scrambles Campaign Logic," *CQ Politics*, October 1, 2008, www.cqpolitics.com; Toner, "The Impact of Federal Election Laws on the 2008 Presidential Elections," 161.

64. These data are taken from the American National Election Study's Cumulative File, 1948–2004. The percentage was even higher in the mid-1990s.

65. Michael P. McDonald and Samuel L. Popkin, "The Myth of the Vanishing Voter," *American Political Science Review* 95 (December 2001): 963–975.

66. See Robert D. Putnam, *Bowling Alone, The Collapse and Revival of American Community* (New York: Simon and Schuster, 2000).

67. G. Bingham Powell Jr., "American Voter Turnout in Comparative Perspective," *American Political Science Review* 80 (March 1986): 17–43.

68. Why do close elections increase turnout? One explanation is that ordinary citizens are more likely to participate in close elections because they believe their vote will make a difference. A second possibility is that turnout increases because the closeness of any election prompts elites (candidates and their financial supporters) to focus on getting voters to the polls. A study by Gary W. Cox and Michael C. Munger finds that closeness of elections affects behavior at both mass and elite levels; see "Closeness, Expenditures, and Turnout in the 1982 U.S. Elections," *American Political Science Review* 83 (March 1989): 217–231. Also see Kenneth D. Wald, "The Closeness-Turnout Hypothesis: A Reconsideration," *American Politics Quarterly* 13 (July 1985): 273–296. Along the same line, Priscilla L. Southwell finds that shifts in economic performance can have a mobilizing effect on turnout, particularly among less-privileged individuals and groups, in "Economic Salience and Differential Abstention in Presidential Elections," *American Politics Quarterly* 24 (April 1996): 221–236.

69. Mark J. Fenster, "The Impact of Allowing Day of Registration Voting on Turnout in U.S. Elections from 1960 to 1992," *American Politics Quarterly* 22 (January 1994): 74–87. Fenster estimated that if all states permitted day-of-registration voting, turnout would increase by 5 percent.

70. Michael D. Martinez and David Hill, "Did Motor Voter Work?" *American Politics Quarterly* 27 (July 1999): 296–315.

71. Also see Benjamin Highton, "Easy Registration and Turnout," *Journal of Politics* 59 (May 1997): 565–575. Highton argues that motor voter will have a marginal effect on turnout.

72. Paul Gronke, Eva Galanes-Rosenbaum, and Peter A. Miller, "Early Voting and Turnout," *PS: Political Science and Politics* 40 (October 2007): 639–645.

73. J. Eric Oliver, "The Effects of Eligibility Restrictions and Party Activity on Absentee Voting and Overall Turnout," *American Journal of Political Science* 40 (1996): 498–514.

74. Robert Stein, "Early Voting," *Public Opinion Quarterly* 62 (1998): 57–69.

75. Curtis B. Gans, "A Rejoinder to Piven and Cloward," *Political Science* 23 (June 1990): 176–178.

76. *Pittsburgh Press,* July 9, 1990.

77. Richard A. Brody, "The Puzzle of Political Participation in America," in *The New American Political System,* ed. Anthony King (Washington, D.C.: American Enterprise Institute for Public Policy Research, 1978), 306.

7 THE AMERICAN PARTY SYSTEM: PROBLEMS AND PERSPECTIVES

EXTOLLING THE VIRTUES OF THE AMERICAN PARTY system is something of an anomaly in popular commentary and scholarship. A few scholars have found merit in the party system, particularly in its contributions to unifying the nation, fostering political stability, reconciling social conflict, aggregating interests, and institutionalizing popular control of government. But the broad thrust in evaluations of this basic political institution has been heavily critical. American parties, various authors contend, are dominated by special interests, are unable to deal imaginatively with public problems, are beset by a confusion of purposes, are ineffective because of their internal divisions, are short on discipline and cohesion, are insufficiently responsive to popular claims and aspirations, and are deficient as instruments for assuming and achieving responsibility in government. And although critics in the mid-twentieth century argued that American parties were too much alike in their programs to afford voters a meaningful choice, critics now pillory the parties for being too polarized.

The Doctrine of Responsible Parties

The major grounds for popular distress over the parties may be simply that most Americans are in some measure suspicious of politicians and their organizations. The criticism of scholars, meanwhile, has focused mainly on the lack of party responsibility in government. The most comprehensive statement on behalf of the doctrine of party responsibility is found in a report by the Committee on Political Parties of the American Political Science Association (APSA), "Toward a More Responsible Two-Party System," published in 1950. This classic document in political science argues that what is required is a party system that is "democratic, responsible, and effective." In the words of the committee:

> Party responsibility means the responsibility of both parties to the general public, as enforced in elections. Party responsibility to the public, enforced in elections, implies that there be more than one party, for the public can hold a party responsible only if it has a choice. . . . When the parties lack the capacity to define their actions in terms of policies, they turn irresponsible because the electoral choice between the parties becomes devoid of meaning. . . . An effective party system requires, first, that the parties are able to bring forth programs to which they commit themselves and, second, that the parties possess sufficient internal cohesion to carry out these programs.[1]

Two major presumptions underlie the doctrine of responsible parties. The first is that the essence of democracy is to be found in popular control over government rather than in popular participation in the immediate tasks of government. A nation such as the United States is far too large and its government too complex for most citizens to become actively involved in its decision-making processes. But this condition does not rule out popular control over government. And the direction of government can be controlled by the people only as long as they are consulted on public matters and possess the power to replace one set of rulers with another—the "opposition." The party, in this view, becomes the instrument through which the public—or, more precisely, a majority of the public—can decide who will run the government and for what purposes. Government by responsible parties is therefore an expression of majority rule.

The second tenet in this theory holds that popular control over government requires that the public be given a choice between competing, unified parties capable of assuming collective responsibility to the public for the actions of government. A responsible party system would make three contributions. One, it "would enable the people to choose effectively a general program, a general direction for government to take, as embodied in a set of leaders committed to that program." Two, it would help to "energize and activate" public opinion. Three, it would increase the prospects for popular control by substituting the collective responsibility of an organized group, the party, for the individual responsibility assumed, more or less adequately, by individual officeholders.[2]

The goal of advocates of party responsibility is to place the parties at the creative center of policymaking in the United States. Voters would choose between two disciplined and cohesive parties, each distinguished by relatively clear and consistent programs and policy orientations. Responsibility would be enforced through elections. Parties would be retained or removed from power depending on their performance and the attractiveness of their programs. Collective responsibility for the conduct of government would displace the individual responsibility of officeholders. Such are the characteristics of the model party system.

How well responsible parties would mesh with the American political system is another matter.[3] Critics have contended that disciplined parties might contribute to an erosion of consensus, to heightened conflict between social classes, to the formation of splinter parties (and perhaps to a full-blown multiple-party system), and to the breakdown of federalism. Moreover, the voting behavior and attitudes of the American people would have to change markedly to accommodate the model of centralized parties, because many voters focus more on candidates than on parties or issues. The indifference of the public to the idea of programmatic parties would appear to be a major obstacle to rationalizing the party system along the lines of the responsible parties model.

The responsible parties model proposed by the Committee on Political Parties is worth examining because, even in the current era of partisan polarization, it presents a contrast to the contemporary party system. Although parties are significantly more disciplined and programmatic than they were at the time of the committee report, the environment in which U.S. parties must operate will always produce institutions that are looser and more inchoate than their counterparts in Europe. The party leader in the British government, the prime minister, can see his government disbanded if he fails to retain the support of his party members in Parliament on party-supported initiatives. In the United States, members of the House and Senate regularly buck the party if they believe a party initiative will play badly at home. Experience with the more disciplined parties that American politics has produced since the 1980s has caused some observers to question the wisdom of the committee report. To examine their doubts, we detail some of the report's recommendations on national party organizations and platforms, intraparty democracy, congressional party organization, nominations and elections, the degree to which American parties have adopted these recommendations, and the degree to which these reforms, when adopted, have produced the expected outcomes.

National Party Organizations and Platforms

The national party organizations envisioned by the committee would be very different from those existing today. The national convention, for example, would be composed of not more than five hundred or six hundred members, more than half of whom would be elected by party voters. Ex officio members drawn from the ranks of the national committee, state party chairs, and congressional leaders, along with certain prominent party leaders outside the party organizations, would make up the balance of the convention membership. Instead of meeting every four years, the convention would assemble regularly at least once every two years and perhaps in special meetings. Reduced in size, more representative of the actual strength of the party in individual states, and meeting more frequently and for longer periods, the new convention would gain effectiveness as a deliberative body for the development of party policy and as a more representative assembly for reconciling the interests of various elements within the party.

The most far-reaching proposal for restructuring national party organization involves the creation of a party council of perhaps fifty members, composed of representatives from units such as the national committee, the congressional parties, the state committees, and the party's governors. Meeting regularly and often, the party council would examine problems of party management, prepare a preliminary draft of the party platform for submission to the national convention, interpret the platform adopted by the convention, screen and recommend candidates for congressional offices, consider possible presidential candidates, and advise appropriate party organs such as the national convention or national committee "with respect to conspicuous departures from general party decisions by state or local party organizations." Empowered in this fashion, the party council would represent a firm break with familiar and conventional arrangements that contribute to the dispersion of party authority and the elusiveness of party policy. The council's task would be to blend the interests of national, congressional, and state organizations to foster the development of an authentic national party, one capable of fashioning and implementing coherent strategies and policies.

The report holds that party platforms are deficient on a number of counts. At times the platform "may be intentionally written in an ambiguous manner so as to attract voters of any persuasion and to offend as few voters as possible." State party platforms frequently espouse principles and policies in conflict with those of the national party. Congressional candidates and members of Congress may feel little obligation to support platform planks. No agency exists to interpret and apply the platform in the years between conventions. Substantial confusion and difference of opinion exist over the authority of a platform—that is, whether party candidates are bound to observe the commitments made in the adoption of the platform.

To put new life back into the party platform, the report recommends that it should be written every two years to take account of developing issues and to link it to congressional campaigns in off-year elections; that it should "emphasize general party principles and national issues" that "should be regarded as binding commitments on all candidates and officeholders of the party, national, state and local"; that state and local platforms "should be expected to conform to the national platform on matters of general party principle or on national policies"; and that the party council should take an active role in the platform-making process, both in preparing tentative drafts of the document in advance of the convention and in interpreting and applying the platform between conventions. In sum, the report argues that at present, party platforms and the way they are formulated and implemented are inimical to the development of strong and responsible parties.

The APSA report on responsible parties anticipated a potpourri of reforms made by the national parties that were consistent with its overall thrust. Among them were the reassertion of the national convention's authority over the national committee, the selection of convention delegates by direct vote of the rank and file, the allocation of national committee members on the basis of the actual strength of the party within the areas they represent, the use of closed primaries for the selection of convention delegates, and the provision for holding a national party conference between national conventions (which Democrats did from 1974 to 1982).[4] Still, it is not clear that any of these changes led directly to a reinvigoration of party organizations. Today, party organizations are stronger than in the decades after the APSA report, but they derive their strength from an ability to raise money, not from the quality or cohesiveness of their ideas. Moreover, partisans today tend to agree with each other on the issues, but not because of the party platforms, which tend to become invisible after the party conventions.

Intraparty Democracy

The achievement of a system of responsible parties demands more than the good intentions of the public and of party leaders. It requires widespread and meaningful political participation by grassroots members of the party, democratic party processes, and an accountable leadership. According to the report:

> Capacity for internal agreement, democratically arrived at, is a critical test for a party. It is a critical test because when there is no such capacity, there is no capacity for positive action, and hence the party becomes a hollow pretense. It is a test which can be met only if the party machinery affords the membership an opportunity to set the course of the party and to control those who speak for it. The test can be met fully only where the membership accepts responsibility for creative participation in shaping the party's program.

The task of developing an active party membership capable of creative participation in the affairs of the party is not easy. Organizational changes at both the summit and the base of the party hierarchy are required:

> A national convention, broadly and directly representative of the rank and file of the party and meeting at least biennially, is essential to promote a sense of identity with the party throughout the membership as well as to settle internal differences fairly, harmoniously, and democratically.

At the grassroots level, local party groups need to be developed that will meet frequently to generate and discuss ideas concerning national issues and the national party program. The emergence and development of local, issue-oriented party groups can be facilitated by national party agencies engaged in education and publicity and willing to undertake the function of disseminating information and research findings.

A new concept of party membership is required—one that emphasizes "allegiance to a common program" rather than mere support of party candidates in elections. In accordance with the concept of party advanced in the opening chapter of the report, such an emphasis would track more closely with ideological rather than electoral definitions. Its development might take this form:

> The existence of a national program, drafted at frequent intervals by a party convention both broadly representative and enjoying prestige, should make a great difference. It would prompt those who identify themselves as Republicans and Democrats to think in terms of support of that program, rather than in terms of personalities, patronage, and local matters. . . . Once machinery is established which gives the party member and his representative a share in framing the party's objectives, once there are safeguards against internal dictation by a few in positions of influence,

members and representatives will feel readier to assume an obligation to support the program. Membership defined in these terms does not ask for mindless discipline enforced from above. It generates the self-discipline which stems from free identification with aims one helps to define.

If there is one place where parties have changed in ways envisioned by the APSA report, it is in the realm of intraparty democracy. No feature of the reform movement of the Democratic Party, beginning with the guidelines of the McGovern-Fraser Commission (the Commission on Party Structure and Delegate Selection), stands out more sharply than the commitment to make the party internally democratic and more responsive to its grassroots. Commenting on the overall process by which delegates were selected to the 1968 convention, the McGovern-Fraser Commission observed that "meaningful participation of Democratic voters in the choice of their presidential nominee was often difficult or costly, sometimes completely illusory, and, in not a few instances, impossible." The commission found evidence of inconsistent rules governing delegate selection; imposition of binding instructions that forced Democrats to vote against their preferred presidential candidate; procedural irregularities such as secret caucuses, closed slate-making, and proxy voting; excessive filing fees for entering primaries; and underrepresentation of women, minorities, and youth among the delegates.

In response, the Democratic Party adopted a series of guidelines to regulate the selection of delegates for future conventions. The initial step required the state parties to adopt a comprehensive set of rules governing the delegate-selection process to which all rank-and-file Democrats would have access. Not only were these rules to make clear how all party members could participate in the process, but also they were to be designed to facilitate "maximum participation." In addition, certain procedural safeguards were specified. Proxy voting and the use of the unit rule were outlawed. Party committee meetings held for the purpose of selecting convention delegates were required to establish a quorum of no fewer than 40 percent of the members. Mandatory assessments of convention delegates were prohibited. Adequate public notice of all party meetings called to consider delegate selection was required, as were rules to provide for uniform times and dates of meetings.

The commission had enjoined state parties to seek a broad base of support. Therefore, the national party required standards eliminating all forms of discrimination against minority group members in the delegate-selection process. To overcome the effects of past discrimination, moreover, each state was expected to include in its delegation African Americans, women, and young people in numbers roughly proportionate to their presence in the state population.

The national party adopted a number of specific requirements for delegate selection. Delegates must be selected in a "timely manner" (within the calendar year in which the convention is held); alternates must be selected in the same manner as delegates; delegates must be apportioned within the state on the basis of a formula that gives equal weight to population and to Democratic strength; and at least 75 percent of the delegates must be selected at the congressional district level or lower (in states using the convention system). The number of delegates to be selected by a party state committee was limited to 10 percent of the total delegation.

One of the most remarkable aspects of this unprecedented action by the national Democratic Party was the response of the state parties. They accepted the guidelines, altered or abandoned a variety of age-old practices and state laws, and selected their delegations through procedures more open than anyone thought possible. With "maximum participation" in mind, in 1972 they produced a convention whose composition—with its emphasis on demographic representation—was vastly different from any previous one.[5] Whether for good or ill, the Democratic Party accepted the main tenets of intraparty democracy.[6]

No evidence exists, however, that party democratization has contributed to the development of a more responsible party system. Instead, the reverse is probably true: the greater the degree of intraparty democracy, the harder it is to develop a coherent program of party policy.[7] Indeed, Stephen Ansolabehere and his colleagues show that following the introduction of primary elections as a means for nominating congressional candidates in a state, the party loyalty of the state's congressional representatives typically declined.[8]

Congressional Party Organization

In the judgment of the APSA report, one of the most vexing problems in the effort to develop more responsible parties was the performance of the congressional parties. The proliferation of leadership committees in Congress, the weakness of the caucus (or conference), the independence of congressional committees, and the seniority system combined to limit possibilities for the parties to develop consistent and coherent legislative records. Seeking to tighten up congressional party organization, the APSA report made several recommendations.

First, it called on each party in both the Senate and the House to consolidate its various leadership groups, such as policy committees, committees on committees, and the House Rules Committee, into a single leadership group. This group's functions would be to manage legislative party affairs, submit policy proposals to the membership, draw up slates of committee assignments, and assume responsibility for scheduling legislation.

Second, the party caucuses should meet more often and their decisions should be binding on legislation involving the party's principles and programs. Members of Congress who ignore a caucus decision "should not expect to receive the same consideration in the assignment of committee posts or in the apportionment of patronage as those who have been loyal to party principles." In other words, the APSA report called on leaders to punish the rank and file for failing to support the party's program.

Third, the seniority system should be made to work in harmony with the party's responsibility for a legislative program. The report stated:

> The problem is not one of abolishing seniority and then finding an alternative. It is one of mobilizing the power through which the party leadership can successfully use the seniority principle rather than have the seniority principle dominate Congress. . . . Advancement within a committee on the basis of seniority makes sense, other things being equal. But it is not playing the game fairly for party members who oppose the commitments in their party's platform to rely on seniority to carry them into committee chairmanships. Party leaders have compelling reason to prevent such a member from becoming chairman—and they are entirely free so to exert their influence.

Fourth, the APSA report urged the congressional parties to give party leaders responsibility for making committee assignments. "Personal competence and party loyalty should be valued more highly than seniority in assigning members to such major committees as those dealing with fiscal policy and foreign affairs." At the same time, according to the report, the party caucus should review committee assignments at intervals of no more than two years.

Fifth, the APSA report called on party leaders to take over the function of scheduling legislation for floor consideration. In particular, it argued that the power of the House Rules Committee over legislative scheduling should be vested in the party leadership committee. If the party could not control the flow of legislation to the floor and shape the agenda, there is little chance that it would control legislative output, which is the essence of responsible party performance in Congress.

Beginning in the 1970s, many congressional reforms similar to those outlined by the APSA report actually came to pass, particularly in the House. Rooted in changes in the Democratic Party's electoral coalition, the initial reforms were pushed by a growing bloc of House Democratic liberals frustrated by the party's southern conservative wing, which had a lock on committee and agenda power. The changes were impressive. Long dormant, the Democratic caucus became a more influential force in the House, particularly in controlling committee assignments and in shaping rules and procedures. At the opening of the Ninety-fourth Congress (1975–1976), the caucus removed three committee chairs from their positions, increased party control over the committee assignment process, brought the Rules Committee more firmly under the leadership of the Speaker, and established a requirement that the chairs of the appropriations subcommittees be ratified by the caucus. These were not stylized or marginal alterations; rather, they were systematically conceived efforts to reshape the power structure of Congress by diminishing the influence of senior leaders—who had often been out of step with a majority of the party—and augmenting the power of the party caucus and the leadership. Further demonstrations of caucus power occurred in the 1980s. At the opening of the Ninety-eighth Congress (1983–1984), the Democratic caucus voted to remove a southern party member from the Budget Committee because he had been influential in fashioning President Ronald Reagan's budget strategy in the preceding Congress.

The power of party leadership grew again after the GOP takeover of the House in the 1994 midterm elections. Supported by a victorious cohesive party in the 104th Congress (1995–1996), Speaker Newt Gingrich ignored seniority in the selection of several committee chairs; named new members to the party's committee on committees, which centralized party control over assignments; directed an overhaul of the committee system that cut committee staffs and eliminated three standing committees; altered a variety of House procedures; and moved a "Contract with America" policy agenda through the House in the first one hundred days of the session. The party-strengthening measures pushed through by Gingrich outlasted his speakership, and his successor, Dennis Hastert (1999–2006), continued to exploit the extensive powers enjoyed by majority party leaders in the contemporary House. Hastert was assisted in these efforts by Tom Delay (R-Texas), an aggressive party whip who became majority leader.[9] Between 2000 and 2006 House Republican leaders used their leverage to enforce strict party discipline on President George W. Bush's legislative initiatives. Following the Democratic Party's takeover of the House in 2006, Speaker Nancy Pelosi remained committed to the strong party model. She reined in committee chairs, bypassed committees when it served Democratic caucus goals, and brought legislation to the House floor under highly restrictive rules.[10]

These party-strengthening reforms clearly have moved Congress closer to the responsible party model envisioned by the APSA report. Indeed, the contemporary congressional parties are sharply polarized on many issues, and party loyalty on roll call votes is higher than it has been in decades. Yet it may be going too far to characterize these trends as genuine responsible party government. As Morris Fiorina points out, even the remarkably disciplined and unified Republican government between 2000 and 2006 did not entirely conform to the model. Although publicly committed to smaller government and freer markets, the GOP nevertheless pushed through tariff protections for the U.S. steel industry, significant agricultural subsidies for U.S. farmers, a transportation bill loaded with pork, and, in the Medicare Prescription Drug and Modernization Act of 2003, the largest expansion of any federal entitlement program since the passage of Medicare in 1965. On other issues, moreover, the GOP held firm to its core principles but offered only symbolic gestures, such as a proposed constitutional amendment to ban gay marriage that had little chance of passing.[11] As an opposition party, Democrats also failed to adhere fully to the responsible party government model, with Senate Democrats even helping Republicans pass Bush's signature tax cut in 2001. Parties conforming more closely to the responsible party government model would have rejected such convergence.

Genuine party responsibility is likely made more difficult by the intense competition for control of Congress that has characterized the post-1994 period. Waging a nearly permanent campaign for majority control of the House and Senate, even the ideologically polarized congressional parties of the current era find it tempting to abandon their principles on certain issues if doing so ensures winning the handful of seats on which party control hinges. Ironically, although the ideological divergence between the parties has raised the value of majority status for each party,[12] the parties seem willing to sacrifice at least some of their ideological commitments to secure a majority.

Incumbent electoral security also conspires against responsible party government. With the battle for majority control focusing on a relatively small number of competitive seats in each chamber, most individual incumbents remain electorally invincible, leaving voters little opportunity to hold them accountable for their party's failures. Even though more turnover than usual took place in the 2008 House elections, fewer than 15 percent of the contests were decided by less than ten percentage points, a benchmark for a marginally competitive district. Short of experiencing a major disaster—including serious, dramatic, and highly publicized policy failures—the safeness of incumbents' seats makes it wholly improbable that many will lose their next election. Tidal elections, such as 1974, 1994, and 2006, tend to be rare, and big-time legislative mistakes by a party are only seldom followed by big-time electoral punishment of the party's incumbents.

Many other features of the U.S. system work against responsible party government in Congress. Senate rules, which give significant prerogatives to individual senators, severely limit the ability of Senate party leaders to push through the party's legislative program. (See chapter 5.) Moreover, when the government is divided, even the most disciplined congressional party can be undermined by a strong opposition party president. But perhaps most important, congressional incumbents have the resources, inclination, and electoral autonomy to distance themselves from their party's failures. Indeed, such was the case when congressional Republicans, led by Speaker Gingrich, shut down the government while trying to force President Bill Clinton to adopt the 1995 GOP budget. With much of the public blaming Republicans for the debacle, and with GOP incumbents anxious about the 1996 election, many House Republicans simply abandoned the Speaker, sought accommodation with the president on a variety of policy fronts, forgot about the "contract," and focused on securing benefits for their districts. In the United States, leader-centered party government will always be hampered by members' strong instincts for self-preservation.

It is also not clear that fully responsible congressional parties, even if they did exist, would yield more effective and productive government than the less-centralized parties that have often organized Congress. Although congressional parties are closer to the responsible party model today than they were when the APSA committee crafted its report, the result has not been uniformly pleasing to political scientists or citizens concerned about effective governance. As Fiorina speculates, the ideological purists, whose numbers are growing in both parties, seem less likely to consider evidence about public policy that is inconsistent with their ideological commitments.[13] Along similar lines, Thomas Mann and Norman Ornstein argue that legislative quality suffers when the House majority party systematically excludes the minority party from lawmaking efforts.[14] Finally, analyzing congressional productivity between 1947 and 2000, Sarah Binder finds that Congresses with lower levels of ideological polarization succeeded in passing significantly more of the nation's agenda than did Congresses with higher levels of polarization. "Despite the faith of responsible party advocates in disciplined and cohesive political parties," concludes Binder, "the results suggest instead that policy change is *less* likely when the parties stand for different policy agendas." [15]

Nominations and Elections

The report's recommendations for changing nomination and election procedures fit comfortably within its overall political formula for strengthening the American party system. It endorses the direct primary—"a useful weapon in the arsenal of intraparty democracy"—while expressing preference for the closed rather than the open version. The open primary is incompatible with the idea of a responsible party system because permitting voters to shift from one party to the other between primaries subverts the concept of membership as the foundation of party organization. Pre-primary meetings of party committees should be held for the purpose of proposing and endorsing candidates in primary elections. Delegates to the national conventions should be selected by the direct vote of party members instead of by state conventions. Local party groups should meet prior to the convention to discuss potential candidates and platform planks.

The report suggests three major changes in the election system. First, the Electoral College should be changed to give "all sections of the country a real voice in electing the president and the vice-president" and to help develop a two-party system in areas now dominated by one party. Second, the term of members of the House of Representatives should be extended from two to four years, with coinciding election of House members and the president. If this constitutional change were made, prospects would be improved for harmonizing executive and legislative power through the party. Third, the report recommends giving parties greater flexibility in raising and spending campaign money and for the government to provide assistance to the parties in the form of free mailing and radio time. Only the last recommendation has found its way into the reform movement. And the effects of public financing on party responsibility have been a bit of a mixed bag at best.

In sum, many of the reforms that have been introduced in the party structure and in Congress are consistent with the recommendations of the APSA report. They touch far more than the outer edges of the party and congressional systems. Nevertheless, one should not expect that responsible party government is around the corner—that these reforms will somehow result in the institutionalization of a durable, highly centralized, and disciplined party system. Obstacles throughout the political environment make change of this magnitude all but impossible.

Trends in American Politics

Election to office in the United States is dominated by the two major parties. The vast majority of aspirants for public office carry on their campaigns under the banner of either one or the other. Party affiliation is so decisive for election outcomes that it may be the most important fact to be known about a candidate. Virtually everywhere, save in nonpartisan environments, the trappings of party—symbols, sponsorship, slogans, buttons, and literature—are in evidence. The parties and their candidates collect money, spend money, and incur campaign deficits on a scale that dwarfs their budgets of only a generation ago. Party bureaucracies are larger than in the past. More than two-thirds of U.S. citizens continue to see themselves as Democrats or Republicans, however imperfectly they may comprehend their party's program or the performance of its representatives. Party-based voting decisions are common in numerous jurisdictions.

Despite this degree of loyalty, major problems confront the party system, many of which are the outgrowth of a political system designed to stymie the aggregation of power, exactly the job that parties were created to accomplish. That said, parties have proven to be remarkably sophisticated organizations capable of overcoming many of the challenges presented by the political environment. Although many recent trends have put the parties on the defensive, parties have responded well to many of these challenges.

Party Organizations Adjust to a Loss of Power

Voters may still classify themselves as Democrats or Republicans, but at virtually every point in the recruitment and election of public officials, the formal party organizations have suffered an erosion of power. One main reason is the direct primary. "He who can make the nominations is the owner of the party," E. E. Schattschneider wrote many years ago, and his observation is still correct.[16] Given that unendorsed candidates may defeat party nominees in primaries, one may wonder whether, in some elections and in some jurisdictions, anyone except the candidates really owns the parties. To be sure, informal party networks maintain strong control over nominations in some jurisdictions.[17] But these organizations usually lie outside of the legal party framework, tend to be controlled by officeholders and activists rather than by formal party leaders, and are likely to be less durable than regular party organizations. Either way, a party that cannot control its nominations may find it difficult to achieve unity once it has won office and is faced with the implementation of its platform. Candidates who defeat the organization may see little reason to subscribe to party tenets, defend party interests, or follow party leaders. Not only does the primary contribute to the fragmentation of party unity in office, but also it divides the party at large:

> Primaries often pit party leaders against party leaders, party voters against party voters, often opening deep and unhealing party wounds. They also dissipate party financial and personal resources. Party leadership usually finds that it has no choice but to take sides in a primary battle, the alternative being the possible triumph of the weaker candidate.[18]

An observer viewing the changes in the nomination process in the early 1980s would have noted that the situation was most dire for parties on the presidential level. Compared with the party boss system in place before the McGovern-Fraser reforms, the proliferation of primaries and the opening up of caucuses introduced a participatory system that undermined the role of party leaders and organizations in the presidential nominating process. The typical national convention became a party conclave in name only. As Byron Shafer observed, the democratic reforms "restricted, and often removed, the regular party from the mechanics of presidential selection." [19]

Worse yet, the Democratic Party, which had done the most to democratize the nomination process, consistently chose weak candidates. Both George McGovern in 1972 and Walter Mondale in 1984 were swept away in landslides, and Jimmy Carter barely defeated Gerald Ford in 1976, despite Ford's extremely unpopular pardon of Richard Nixon. Of these three candidates, it is likely that only Mondale would have received the nomination under the traditional leader-dominated system.

With the perspective afforded by thirty years of experience with McGovern-Fraser, however, it is clear that the parties have adjusted well to their new environment, at least at the presidential level. As Marty Cohen and his coauthors show, although bosses no longer meet in smoke-filled rooms to decide their party's nominee, the present system provides results close to those that the old system very likely would have produced. Today, once party leaders agree on the most electable candidate, they publicly endorse him in advance of the primary season. These endorsements, in turn, increase public support for the candidate.[20] As such support increases, so too does the candidate's fund-raising power, which, in turn, makes him a more formidable candidate. Although party leadership support does not ensure a candidate's nomination, the track record since 1980 has been remarkable. McGovern's nomination in 1972 and Carter's in 1976 were unexpected, but there have been few such surprises since then. Since 1980 the front-runner for the nomination in the months leading up to the first caucuses and primaries has almost always won the nomination, with a few exceptions. Howard Dean entered the 2004 primary season as the Democratic front-runner despite tepid support within the Democratic Party establishment, and his campaign collapsed partly because of a concerted effort among party regulars to defeat him.[21] In 2008 both parties' establishments had difficulty coalescing around a candidate: Democrats were split over whether Hillary Clinton or Barack Obama should be the party's standard-bearer, and Republicans were divided over several candidates. When the party establishments cannot reach a consensus, as in 2008, primary voters and caucus-goers are left to make the decision.

That party insiders can sometimes coalesce around a candidate of their choice does not mean that parties today wield the same kind of power they did early in the twentieth century. They do not. The great urban machines of generations past have practically disappeared. Employing an intricate system of rewards and incentives, the machines once dominated the political process—controlling access to power, political careers, and, most important, votes. Their decline has been accompanied by the growing independence within the electorate and among politicians. Moreover, electoral party organization is not an integral part of the political lives of today's self-reliant candidates. Many members of Congress, for example, have created their own political action committees (PACs) for electoral purposes. Virtually all of them not only campaign continuously, using all the resources of their office, but also have their own campaign operations, including staff aides assigned to the district and reelection treasuries. John McCartney quotes a field representative of a California member of Congress:

> I'm never through campaigning—except for one evening every two years. Election night there's no campaign. We have a victory party, I drink a lot of champagne, and I go home and go to bed. Next morning I begin campaigning all over again.[22]

Candidate-centeredness is particularly evident below the presidential level. Ambitious, issue-oriented, and media-conscious, the "new model" members of Congress exploit the resources of their office to the hilt in gaining publicity, advertising their names, and strengthening their reelection base. Some years before he became Speaker, Thomas S. Foley (D-Wash.) commented on the new style of politician in Congress: "At worst, these guys say in effect, 'It doesn't matter. I am my own party,' [and] they emphasize their personal qualities."[23]

The classic functions of party are recruitment, nomination, and campaigning,[24] but today's parties no longer dominate any of these activities. American politics in the media age is very much candidate-centered, although candidates no doubt spend substantial time and energy seeking the endorsements of party insiders.[25] Still, for many offices, major and minor, candidates are on their own much of the time in making the decisions that count. Party leaders can encourage some candidate decisions and discourage others, but rarely do they possess sufficient formal power to tell candidates when to run, how to run, what to believe, what to say, or (once in office) how to vote.

Candidates may tolerate party nudging on some matters because they welcome money, technical assistance, and services—resources that have become more available with the proliferation of party money.[26] But it is unmistakably the candidates who decide what to make of their party membership and party connections both in and out of government. And party leaders and committees can often do little about it. In jurisdictions where American parties have more than ordinary importance, they are essentially facilitators, helping candidates who wear their label to do better what generally they would do in any case.

Campaign Management: Image Makers and Technical Experts

American party organizations no longer dominate the process of winning political support for the candidates who run under their labels. The role of party organizations in campaigns has declined as professional management firms, pollsters, and media specialists—stirred by the prospects of new accounts and greater profits—have arrived on the political scene. To be sure, the parties continue to raise and spend money, to staff their headquarters with salaried personnel and volunteers, and to seek to turn out the vote on election day. And in a handful of targeted races each year, their presence can be quite strong. What they do matters, but much less so than in the past, when they routinely underwrote the bulk of candidate campaigns.

The center of most major political campaigns now lies primarily in the decisions and activities of individual candidates and in their use of consultants, campaign management firms, and the mass media. Public opinion surveys are needed to pinpoint important issues, to locate sources of support and opposition, and to learn how voters appraise the qualities of the candidate. Electronic data processing is useful in the analysis of voting behavior and for the simulation of campaign decisions. Candidates with sufficient financial resources can avail themselves of specialists of all kinds: in public relations, advertising, fund-raising, communications, and financial counseling. They can hire experts in filmmaking, speechwriting, speech coaching, voter registration, direct mail, computer information services, time buying (for radio and television), voter analysis, get-out-the-vote drives, campaign strategy, and "spinning" (interpreting) events and voter behavior. Fewer and fewer matters are left to chance or to the vicissitudes of party administration. The parties can, however, still enjoy influence by helping candidates assemble their campaign teams, and nearly all consultants are partisans who work exclusively with one party's candidates. In the most competitive contests, moreover, the parties may run their own independent or parallel campaigns to attack opposition party candidates.[27]

Campaign consulting is a lucrative industry. Top guns can make upwards of $1 million a year in consulting fees alone. A recent American University study suggests that more than 20 percent of consultants make more than $200,000 a year.[28] In addition, practitioners have become bona fide celebrities. James Carville and Paul Begala, the Democratic consultants who engineered Bill Clinton's 1992 victory, have written best-selling books and still appear regularly on national news programs. On the Republican side, Karl Rove was perhaps more feared by Democrats than any candidate for office. The architect of George W. Bush's two presidential election victories, Rove was often portrayed as more instrumental to Bush's success than Bush himself, which earned him the nickname "Bush's Brain." After leaving the White House, Rove became a senior commentator on Fox News and contributes a regular column to *Newsweek* magazine. The newest star consultants on the scene, David Axelrod and David Plouffe, were the chief strategists for Barack Obama's 2008 innovative presidential campaign. Continuing the trend of top consultants moving from the campaign into the administration, Axelrod became a senior adviser to President Obama. In general, consultants whose candidates upset a favored opponent or win an overwhelming victory are celebrated by politicians and the media alike. They are hot commodities, and candidates vie to purchase their services. The right consultant often appears to be the key to victory.

The coming of age of the mass media, technocracy, and the techniques of mass persuasion has had a marked impact on the political system.[29] The new politics is dominated by image makers and technical experts—organizations and individuals who know what people want in their candidates and how to give it to them. Consider these views and prognoses for an issueless pseudopolitics:

> It is not surprising . . . that politicians and advertising men should have discovered one another. And, once they recognized that the citizen did not so much vote for a candidate as make a psychological purchase of him, not surprising that they began to work together. . . . Advertising agencies have tried openly to sell Presidents since 1952. When Dwight Eisenhower ran for reelection in 1956, the agency of Batton, Barton, Durstine and Osborn, which had been on a retainer throughout his first four years, accepted his campaign as a regular account. Leonard Hall, the national Republican chairman, said: "You sell your candidates and your programs the way a business sells its products." [30]

> Day-by-day campaign reports spin on through regular newscasts and special reports. The candidates make their progress through engineered crowds, taking part in manufactured pseudo events, thrusting and parrying charges, projecting as much as they can, with the help of makeup and technology, the qualities of youth, experience, sincerity, popularity, alertness, wisdom, and vigor. And television follows them, hungry for material that is new and sensational. The new campaign strategists also generate films that are like syrupy documentaries: special profiles of candidates, homey, bathed in soft light, resonant with stirring music, creating personality images such as few mortals could emulate. [31]

> [Party] organizations find themselves increasingly dependent on management and consultant personnel, pollsters, and image-makers. The professional campaigners, instead of being the handmaidens of our major political parties, are independent factors in American elections. Parties turn to professional technicians for advice on how to restructure their organizations, for information about their clienteles, for fund-raising, and for recruiting new members. Candidates, winning nominations in primaries with the aid of professional campaigners rather than that of political parties, are increasingly independent of partisan controls. The old politics does not rest well beside the new technology. [32]

> If we get the visual that we want, it doesn't matter as much what words the networks use in commenting on it. [33]

> If you're not on television, you don't exist. [34]

> No matter what happens, the national political parties of the future will no longer be the same as in the past. Television has made the voter's home the campaign amphitheater, and opinion surveys have made it his polling booth. From this perspective, he has little regard for or need of a political party, at least as we have known it, to show him how to release the lever on Election Day. [35]

The heightened importance of campaign professionals, and the partial eclipse of party, carries significant normative implications. Voters can hold parties at least somewhat accountable for their actions in office. If a party adopts a policy that voters do not like, it can be punished in the next election. Consultants cannot be held similarly accountable.[36] Once they help elect a candidate, their job is done; but being associated with a win may be critical to landing the next consulting job. Their calculations, therefore, are more likely to be based on electoral consider-ations than on anything involving governance.

Rarely has this dichotomy been more evident than in September 2002, when Congress debated a war resolution that would allow President George W. Bush to use military force in Iraq. Working for Democratic members of Congress facing reelection in November, consultants advised the need to act swiftly on the war resolution in order to focus on domestic issues where Democrats had an advan-tage with voters. This advice seemed to be given with little regard for the pro-found consequences of war. For consultants, the issue was the best way to win the coming election, irrespective of policy implications.

The Effort to Strengthen Party Organization

Although the centrifugal force of candidate-centered, mass media–dominated politics has eroded the dominant role of formal party organizations in the politi-cal process, party organizations have actually been strengthened in certain respects. Evidence of professionalization and organizational strength appears in the growth of permanent and professional party staffs at both national and state committee levels. The national committee's functions have been broadened and diversified, as the committee has shifted from an exclusive preoccupation with presidential matters. Both parties' national committees have become heavily involved in a range of party-building activities that include efforts to promote party fortunes in state and local election campaigns. The capacity of the national parties to raise funds, particularly through direct mail and the Internet, has improved dramatically—in this respect, the Republican Party has led the way, but the Democrats have been gaining ground. On the Democratic side, national party authority has been substantially enlarged through the development of rules for state party participation in national nominating conventions. Although the Democratic Party has increased the legal authority of its national organization, the importance of the national Republican apparatus has stemmed from suc-cessful fund-raising that enables it to offer extensive services to state party organizations and candidates.[37]

The strength of state party organizations is partly a function of the party-building activities of the national party organization, leading to greater national-state party integration. The organizational strength of state parties appears in the form of services to candidates, staff size and complexity, newsletters and other communications, voter mobilization programs, public opinion polling, candidate recruitment, issue leadership, and money contributions to candidates. Many state Republican Party organizations score high on these indicators, and Demo-cratic state organizations tend to be weaker than their Republican counterparts.[38] Nevertheless, the Democratic National Committee seems to have had more success than the Republican National Committee in adding to the capabilities of its state party organizations, as any addition of resources can make a weak organization more effective. For the most part, national-state party integration (or influence) has been a one-way street, because most state parties rank low in the degree to which they are involved in (and therefore influence) national committee affairs.[39]

The huge sums of soft money given to the parties from the mid-1990s until it was outlawed in 2002, and the parties' ability to replace it with hard money, have enabled them to become more professional. At the national level, their financial strength never has been greater. Staff development has been impressive. Through their staffs, the parties have become sophisticated in the use of modern campaign technologies that involve computers, electronic mail, television, marketing, advertising, survey research, data processing, and direct mail solicitations. Moreover, influence generally flows from the national level downward, a pattern distinctly different from the state-dominated party structure of the past.[40] It is possible, however, that the new rules governing the regulation of soft money under the 2002 Bipartisan Campaign Finance Act (BCRA) may weaken national party influence over state parties (and national-state party integration more generally), because the law makes it more difficult for national parties to work with state parties that raise soft money.[41] Certainly the national parties transferred fewer dollars to their state affiliates in 2004 and 2008 than they did in 2000, the last presidential election in the pre-BCRA period.

The question is whether the structural changes and other developments have arrested the parties' downward slide and strengthened their capacity to function as parties. How well do parties groom and recruit candidates, control nominations, manage campaign resources (money, manpower, expertise), elect candidates and control a range of offices simultaneously, mobilize voters, stimulate competition, maintain effective coalitions, and inhibit factional conflict? How well do parties illuminate issues and fashion policy alternatives, represent and integrate group interests, make public policy, enforce discipline, provide public instruction, win public acceptance and loyalty, and provide voters with a means for keeping government accountable? Exactly what a resurgence of the parties would consist of is hard to say, but it would seem to require them to conduct these activities, or at least most of them, reasonably well.

The actual record is a mixed bag. By the mid- to late twentieth century, the conventional scholarly view of parties as organizations was that they were in a "precipitous decline."[42] Candidates and incumbents were dominating the electoral system. Party coalitions, the quintessence of American parties, had atrophied. Control over nominations, the sine qua non of strong parties, as Schattschneider and others have argued, was thin and insubstantial at all levels.[43] Divided government was often the norm in nation and state. The influence of the media and interest groups in important phases of politics had never been greater; in the presidential selection process, the media, it was believed, had simply supplanted the parties.[44]

But parties have clearly regained some of the influence they were thought to have lost, and more recent scholarly work on parties documents a significant role for them in recruitment, nominations, and campaigning.[45] The parties' greater ability to raise money has made them more important players than they were just a decade ago. With hundreds of millions of dollars in campaign money available in each election cycle, the parties' opportunity to provide services to candidates has improved markedly. Moreover, party get-out-the-vote efforts have taken on an unprecedented scope, with 43 percent of Americans reporting that they were contacted by one of the major parties before the 2008 election—more than double the 1992 number. In fact, this percentage of party contacts is the highest reported since the National Election Study (NES) started asking this question in 1952. In addition, congressional parties have grown into disciplined organizations over the last two decades, maintaining party-line voting on most of the issues that traditionally divide the parties. The partisan polarization in Washington has also contributed to ordinary Americans now identifying with parties more strongly than they have in generations. At the same time, however, at least some of the new research describing contemporary party influence has required scholars to broaden their conceptualization of parties to include a wider array of party players, group leaders, fund-raisers, and policy activists. Party influence, then, is at least partly a function of how one conceptualizes and defines party.[46]

An Era of Party and Governmental Reform

Ordinarily, changes in American politics do not come easily. No democratic political system anywhere rivals the American system for the number of opportunities to prevent or delay the resolution of public problems or the adoption of new forms and practices. American politics is slow politics. Nevertheless, many large-scale reforms have found their way into the party structure, into Congress, and into public policies that shape and regulate the political process. In the main, these changes took shape and were adopted when the political system was in substantial disarray. In the midst of an unpopular war, challenged on all sides, President Lyndon Johnson withdrew from the presidential election campaign of 1968; Robert F. Kennedy was assassinated; the 1968 Democratic National Convention, meeting in Chicago, was an ordeal of rancor, tumult, and rioting. And then came the Watergate affair—an assault on the political process itself. Public alienation from the political system, which had been building for years, reached a high point. The stage was set for reform. Those who brought it about owed their success to their ability to seize on unusual and transitory circumstances to develop new ways of carrying on political business.

From almost any perspective, the changes were remarkable. More reforms were adopted between 1968 and 1974 than at any time since the early nineteenth century.[47] The power of national party agencies to set standards for state party participation in national nominating conventions was established—and the Supreme Court added its imprimatur to this development. The first national party charter was adopted by the Democrats. At the state level, presidential primary laws were passed to broaden political participation, and caucus-convention systems were opened up, contributing to the democratization of the nominating process.

Nor was Congress immune to change. The seniority system was modified by providing for secret caucus ballots on nominees for committee chairs, a move that increased the responsiveness of these leaders to fellow party members. Committee power itself was dispersed as subcommittees and their chairs won new measures of authority. The filibuster rule was revised, making it easier for a Senate majority to assert itself. The party caucus took on new roles and new vigor. To reduce the influence of private money and big contributors in political campaigns, the Federal Election Campaign Act was adopted, with its provision for public financing of presidential campaigns. In sum, numerous new choices and opportunities were presented to politicians and the public alike.

For the most part, the party reforms of the modern period were designed to democratize political institutions and processes. Concretely, reformers set out to reduce the power of elites (that is, party leaders or "bosses") and to augment the power of ordinary citizens. And they were successful, at least on the surface. But, as Nelson W. Polsby has shown, the reforms led to numerous unanticipated consequences, particularly on the Democratic side: state party organizations were weakened; party elites lost influence to media elites; candidate organizations came to dominate the presidential selection process; and the national convention fell under the sway of candidate enthusiasts and interest group delegates as its role in the presidential nominating process shifted from candidate selection to candidate ratification.[48] These changes are truly momentous.

In evaluating the party reforms, it is easy to lose sight of their relationship to the strength of American parties. As David B. Truman observed, the McGovern-Fraser Commission reforms "could not have been accomplished over the opposition of alert and vigorous state parties. The commission staff exploited the limitations and weaknesses of the state parties; they did not cause them." [49] The reforms, in other words, weakened an institution already in more than a little trouble.

Party reform, therefore, is not the same as party strengthening. A more open political process does not necessarily contribute to greater participation by the public or to popular acceptance of the parties. A demographically representative national convention, a central objective of the Democratic reforms, did not immediately lead to the selection of candidates who could best represent the party, unify it, or be elected. The public financing of presidential election campaigns has not by any means solved the problem of money in politics, as the spiraling costs of elections and the growing power of interest group campaign money show. Indeed, George W. Bush in 2000 and 2004, John Kerry in 2004, and Barack Obama in 2008 proved that candidates often do better when they refuse public money, and the rules attached to it, in favor of personal fund-raising efforts. Bush, Kerry, and Obama raised far more money and could spend it with greater flexibility than they would have had they accepted federal campaign funds.

The reform of the party system must therefore be taken with a grain of salt. American parties are to an important extent the dependent variable in the scheme of politics, more the products of their environment than the architects of it. The only system of government the parties have known is Madisonian, marked by division of power and made to order for weak parties. Federalism, the separation of powers, and all manner of structural arrangements and election laws (such as the direct primary, candidate-oriented campaign regulations, single-member legislative districts, nonconcurrent terms for executive and legislature, nonpartisan elections, and staggered elections) militate against the development of strong parties. Parties today are stronger by American standards, but the political environment will never allow them to match the strength of European parties. And by diminishing party control over the presidential nominating process, the reforms weakened the only national institution fully empowered to represent the party's constituent elements. The massive use of television for political campaigns; the power of special interest groups; and the arrival on the scene of experts in public relations, media, survey, computer, and fund-raising also have contributed to the current candidate-centered system that emphasizes personality over party and, frequently, style over substance. Reinvigorated American parties have not altered these trends. Contemporary party campaigns are now run by the same kinds of consultants who run candidate campaigns. Most party campaign efforts are designed not to bolster the party *per se* but to help the party's candidates succeed in a candidate-centered environment.

The Escalation of Interest Group Activity

The growth in the number and influence of interest groups is one of the major developments in American politics. For the most part, scholars have reasoned that the explosion of interest group activity since the 1960s has contributed to the weakening of the parties.[50] According to conventional wisdom, interest groups and parties compete for the same political space. When legislators are more concerned with satisfying interest group claims than with supporting party positions and leaders, the vitality of legislative party organizations is sapped. When party lines collapse, collective responsibility for decisions is diminished, and individual members are pressured by groups intent on getting their way. As Rep. David R. Obey (D-Wis.) said, "It's a lot more difficult to say no to anybody because so many people have well-oiled mimeograph machines."[51] Or, in the grimly blunt words of the late senator Edward M. Kennedy (D-Mass.): "We have the best Congress money can buy. Congress is awash in contributions from special interests that expect something in return."[52]

The main controversy over interest groups has centered on their gifts to candidates for office and their spending in election campaigns more generally. In 2008 PAC contributions to congressional campaigns reached $404 million. PAC money accounted for nearly one-third of receipts for all House candidates and just short of one-fifth for all Senate candidates; as usual, incumbents claimed the lion's share (79 percent).[53] Scores of 527 and 501(c) groups also spent millions of dollars in the 2008 elections.

Surveys find that a large portion of the public perceives campaign financing to be a corrupt system—one in which legislators are bought and forced to compromise their independence to satisfy interest group claims. Fairly or not, such perceptions are fueled by stories such as those pointing out that Sen. Max Baucus (D-Mont.), chair of the Senate Finance Committee in the 111th Congress and a major architect of health care reform legislation, is one of the leading recipients of campaign contributions from the health care industry.[54] Although systematic evidence of such favoritism is not as clear as most citizens believe or as the media portray, the issue remained sufficiently hot that Congress passed, and President Bush signed, major campaign finance reform legislation in 2002. Even so, many observers view the reforms with skepticism, and the Federal Election Commission did much to water them down before they took effect.

Another dimension of the interest group problem is that of single-issue groups.[55] Their issue is *the* issue; their position is the one on which legislators are to be judged. The compromises that occur naturally to practical politicians seldom carry much weight with the leaders of single-issue groups: members are either for or against issues such as gun control, abortion rights, tax reductions, gay marriage, and government-funded health care. Legislators do not find it easy to hide from such groups, especially because decision-making processes have opened up as a result of the reform wave of the 1970s and because technological advances have made it easier for groups to communicate directly with members' constituents. Shortly before he was defeated for reelection in 1978, a northern Democratic senator observed:

> The single-interest constituencies have just about destroyed politics as I knew it. They've made it miserable to be in office—or to run for office—and left me feeling it's hardly worth the struggle to survive.[56]

The "special cause" quality of much of contemporary politics is also reflected in these comments by a leading official in Minnesota's Democratic Party:

> Frankly, there are very few of us in the party leadership now whose primary goal is the election of candidates committed to a broad liberal agenda. Most of the people in control are there to advance their own special causes. From the time we spend on it, you would think the most important problem in the world is whether there should be speedboats on six lakes in northern Minnesota.[57]

Several scholars, however, have called into question the proposition that parties and interest groups compete for power. According to these scholars, the current interest group system is itself polarizing along partisan lines, with many groups sorting themselves into one of the two party camps. In some cases, as Barbara Sinclair shows, interest group preference for a party is the result of party pressure, such as the GOP's K Street Project, begun by Grover Norquist, the founder of Americans for Tax Reform, and former GOP leader Tom DeLay to cajole interest groups to hire Republican lobbyists and to contribute more campaign money to Republican candidates. In other cases, a group may simply find one of the parties overly hostile to its interests.[58] Either way, as Morris Fiorina writes, "Modern parties and their associated groups now overlap so closely that it is often hard to make the distinction between a party activist and an issue activist."[59]

Although the relationship between parties and interest groups is no doubt dynamic, the arrival of narrow-issue politics has changed the American political landscape. Pragmatic politics has been diminished and compromise has declined as a way of doing business. In forming their positions on certain high stakes issues, members see a reduced margin for error. A wrong vote can cost them electoral support and produce new challenges to their reelection. And in not a few cases members believe they are faced with a no-win situation in which a vote on either side of a controversial, high-visibility issue appears likely to damage their electoral security.

The Nationalization of Politics

So unobtrusively has the change come about that a great many American citizens are unaware of the extent to which sectional political alignments have been replaced by a national political alignment. From the latter part of the nineteenth century until the 1970s, the main obstacle to the nationalization of politics was the strength of the Democratic Party in the South. Presidential, congressional, state, and local offices were won, as a matter of course, by Democrats. Today, Republicans dominate presidential elections in the South. In 1992 the Republicans won eight southern states, even though the Democrats offered an all-southern ticket in Bill Clinton (Arkansas) and Al Gore (Tennessee). In 2000 and 2004 Democratic presidential candidates failed to carry a single state in the South.

Republican gains in southern congressional elections have been particularly impressive. The Republican statewide percentage of the vote for representatives has grown more or less steadily since the 1950s. Back then, the Republican Party rarely even nominated candidates for the House of Representatives in the Deep South. After the 2004 election, 60 percent of the southern House members and 80 percent of the southern Senate members were Republicans. In short, a strong breeze of Republicanism has been coursing through southern electorates.

The movement from parochial to national politics has not been limited to the South. No matter what its history of party allegiance and voting, no state is wholly secure from incursions by the minority party. One-party political systems have especially dwindled below the presidential level where the parties have developed strong regional bases: "It is probably safe to say that in national and state-wide politics we are in the time of the most intense, evenly-spaced, two-party competitiveness of the last 100 years," says Frank J. Sorauf.[60]

Ironically, the increase in the national strength of both parties can serve as a challenge to party responsibility. State-level candidates often distance themselves from the positions of the national party to appeal to their state's particular constituency. In his efforts to win votes in rural southwestern Virginia in 2001, Democratic gubernatorial candidate Mark Warner trumpeted his support for gun rights, a position in conflict with the gun control message advocated by the national Democratic Party. In his 2002 reelection campaign Senator Baucus stressed his agreement with President Bush on a range of issues of concern to Montana, his decidedly conservative state. Mark Pryor, a successful Arkansas senatorial candidate in 2002 ran an advertisement that said, "Unlike some Democrats in Washington, I believe in strengthening the military," a winning position in his conservative southern state.[61] When party policy and constituency interest collide, constituency nearly always wins.

The sources for the growing nationalization of American politics are both numerous and varied. Social changes, rather than conscious party efforts to extend their spheres of influence, have provided the principal thrust for the new shape given to American party politics. Among the most important have been the emergence and extraordinary development of the mass media in political communications. Through the electronic media, national political figures can be created virtually overnight, national issues can be carried to the most remote and inaccessible community, and new styles and trends can become a matter of common knowledge in a matter of days or weeks. Insulation, old loyalties, and established patterns are difficult to maintain in the face of contemporary political communications.

For all their importance to the changes under way, however, the electronic media have not by themselves transformed the face of American politics. Changes in technology, the diversification of the economic bases of the states, the growth of an affluent society, the higher educational attainments of voters, the mobility of the population, the migration of African American citizens to the North, the enfranchisement of African American citizens in the South, the illumination of massive nationwide problems, the growth of vast urban conglomerations, and the assimilation of immigrant groups have all contributed to the erosion of internal barriers and parochialism and, consequently, to the strengthening of national political patterns. Whatever the complete explanation for this phenomenon, one thing is clear: the forces for the nationalization of politics are far more powerful than those for localism and sectionalism. A changing party system is the inevitable result.

The Polarization of Activists and Congress on the Issues

Political parties in the United States are often criticized for being Tweedledum and Tweedledee—so similar that even attentive voters can miss the alternatives they present. This criticism has limited merit. Consider the ideology and policy attitudes of Democratic and Republican elites, the delegates to the 2008 party conventions. (See Figure 7-1.) Seventy-two percent of the Republican delegates described themselves as conservatives, as contrasted with a mere 3 percent of the Democratic delegates. At the other ideological pole, the differences are also striking: liberals made up 43 percent of the Democratic delegates but were completely absent from the Republican delegation.[62]

Figure 7-1   The Ideology of Democratic and Republican National Convention Delegates, 2008, Contrasted with the Ideology of Rank-and-File Democrats and Republicans

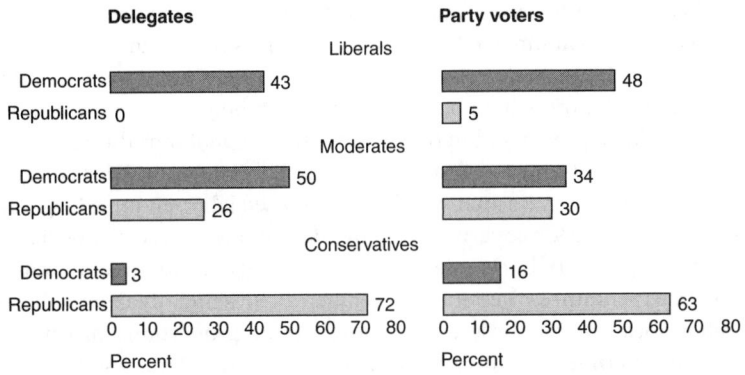

Source: CBS News/*New York Times* Poll, August 24, 2008.

Differences in ideological perception and in political philosophy translate into differences in public policy views and on the proper role of government. Democratic delegates to the last several party conventions have been much more likely than their Republican counterparts to agree with the following propositions: affirmative action programs should be continued; laws to protect racial minorities are necessary; government should do more to regulate the environment and the safety practices of business and do more to solve the nation's problems; and a nationwide ban on assault weapons should be instituted. In addition, Democratic delegates have been much more likely to be prochoice than Republican delegates, and Republican delegates were much more likely to believe that organized prayer should be permitted in public schools. The differences between the activists of the two parties are important and unmistakable: one set is clearly liberal, the other clearly conservative.[63]

The differences between party activists are often enormous. When convention delegates were asked in 2008 whether government should do more to solve national problems or whether the government was doing too many things better left to business and individuals, 83 percent of Democratic delegates thought government should do more compared with only 3 percent of Republican delegates. In contrast, fully 91 percent of Republican delegates thought the government was doing too many things already, compared with just 9 percent of Democratic delegates. When asked whether "providing health care coverage, even if it means raising taxes for some Americans" was desirable, 94 percent of Democratic delegates agreed, but only 7 percent of Republican delegates did. When asked whether government should do more to promote traditional values, 48 percent of Republicans said yes, but only 12 percent of Democrats did.

Differences are particularly stark on foreign policy. Eighty percent of Republican delegates believed the United States "did the right thing" in taking military action in Iraq, compared with only 2 percent of Democratic delegates. By a difference of 96 percent to 36 percent, Republican delegates were more inclined to think the results of the troop surge in Iraq was "making the situation in Iraq better." The *New York Times*/CBS News delegate survey in 2004 found that 79 percent of Democrats believed it "extremely important" to work through the United Nations to solve international problems, but only 7 percent of Republicans thought so.

Party conflict in Congress also occurs along liberal-conservative lines. Over the years most Democratic members have supported labor-endorsed legislation, measures to provide for government regulation of business, social welfare bills of great variety, civil rights legislation, federal aid to education, and limitations on defense expenditures. Republican members have generally favored business over labor, social welfare programs of more modest proportions, private action rather than government involvement, state rather than federal responsibility for domestic programs, the interests of higher-income groups over those of lower-income groups, and a greater emphasis on national defense. When viewing the economy, party members typically focus on different problems: Republicans are more concerned about inflation, Democrats more concerned about unemployment.[64] Those who believe that there is not "a dime's worth of difference" between the parties have not paid much attention to the preferences of the parties' congressional members on contemporary issues involving labor, business, social welfare, civil rights, and contentious social issues, including abortion and the death penalty.

Clearly, the parties' weaknesses have not clouded the ideological differences between their leaders. Meaningful differences separate the parties in Congress (or at least the vast majority of the two parties). Even larger differences divide the parties' national convention delegates. Quite plainly, Democratic and Republican Party elites do not evaluate problems in the same light. Nor are they attracted to the same solutions.

Differences between the parties can also be examined from the perspective of the public. The survey data in Table 7-1 show the internal differences within the electoral parties as well as the broad differences between them. Obviously, neither party is monolithic, in the sense that its members share a common set of beliefs. On certain issues, such as teaching creationism in public schools and raising the minimum wage, certain Democratic and Republican subgroups share the same political space. Nevertheless, in their attitudes toward social issues and social justice issues, most Democratic partisans are easily distinguished from most Republican partisans. Democrats are more supportive of gay marriage, abortion rights, government-sponsored health care, and an increase in the minimum wage. Republicans, in contrast, are more supportive of private Social Security accounts and displaying the Ten Commandments in public buildings. Divisions within Republican clusters are less serious than those found on the Democratic side, although the "enterprisers" (mostly affluent, well educated, suburban whites)

Table 7-1   Party in the Electorate: The Views of Democratic and Republican Voters on Major Social and Economic Issues: 2005

Position	Democratic Groups			Republican Groups	
	Liberals	Disad. Dems.	Cons. Dems	Enterprisers	Social Cons.
Favor gay marriage	80%	37%	19%	8%	12%
Favor changing laws to make it more difficult for a woman to get an abortion	10	22	37	54	54
Favor conducting stem cell research	84	60	57	38	40
Favor displaying 10 Commandments in gov't buildings	35	84	82	89	92
Favor teaching creationism along with evolution	49	50	46	83	62
Favor gov't health insurance for all (even if taxes go up)	90	65	73	23	59
Favor raising the minimum wage	94	95	94	46	79
Favor allowing immigrants to work in US temporarily	58	30	43	71	44
Favor allowing drilling in Arctic Wildlife Refuge	14	30	46	92	71
Favor allowing private accounts in Social Security	28	17	36	88	56

Source: Developed from data in *Pew Research Center for the People and the Press: Beyond Red vs. Blue,* May 10, 2005.

Note: Liberals—largest voting bloc in the typology, affluent, well educated, highly secular; Disadvantaged Democrats—many minority voters, heavily female, poorly educated, highly pessimistic about the future; Conservative Democrats—religious, socially conservative, more moderate on foreign policy, older; Enterprisers—affluent, well educated, white, suburban, probusiness, antigovernment, tolerant on personal freedom issues; Social conservatives—middle-aged, middle income, white, disproportionately southern, suburban, small cities and rural areas, regular churchgoers, anticommunist, prodefense.

are often more conservative than the rest of the party on economic issues. The position of liberals (well educated, affluent, secular) within the Democratic Party is particularly problematic when compared with other types of Democrats, especially on social issues such as gay marriage, where 80 percent of liberals support it, compared with only 19 percent of conservative Democrats. The point is that the parties do stand for something in the minds of many voters.

Further evidence points to the public's sensitivity concerning party differences. Survey data presented in Table 7-2 show the public's perceptions of the ideologies of the parties. In 2008, 66 percent of respondents correctly perceived the Democrats as left of center, and 69 percent correctly perceived the Republicans as right of center. The general public may miss some of the fine points, but most voters are essentially accurate in their appraisals of the Democratic Party as liberal and the Republican Party as conservative. This perception of liberal-conservative differences between the parties is a classic distinction in American politics. It is salient for many voters, helping them to organize political information, interpret political conflict, and evaluate candidates.

Table 7-2 The Public's Perception of Party Ideologies during the 2008 Presidential Campaign

Question: We hear a lot of talk these days about liberals and conservatives. Here is a 7-point scale on which the political views that people might hold are arranged from extremely liberal to extremely conservative. Where would you place the Democratic Party on this scale? The Republican Party?

	Democratic	Republican
Extremely liberal	14%	3%
Liberal	34	6
Slightly liberal	18	7
Middle of road	16	14
Slightly conservative	9	18
Conservative	6	34
Extremely conservative	3	17

Source: 2008 National Election Study, Center for Political Studies, University of Michigan.

The Decline and Resurgence of Partisanship

For decades, advocates of strong parties lamented the decline in partisanship in the electorate. Without strong parties and clear cues for voters, they contended, ordinary people for whom politics is a minor concern would be unable to hold officeholders accountable for their actions. Indeed, evidence drawn from the period immediately after the party reform movement was clear. For many voters, party no longer carried much weight. A much greater percentage of Americans eschewed partisan labels in favor of political independence than in previous decades. As a result, third party or independent presidential candidates drew more votes than usual. Even among those who voted for major party candidates, split-ticket voting reached an apex. Droves of Democrats crossed party lines to create landslide winners of Republican presidential aspirants, such as Richard Nixon in 1972 and Ronald Reagan in 1980 and 1984, while at the same time maintaining a Democratic House of Representatives.

Candidate-centered voting has major ramifications for the control of government, as can be seen in an examination of the vote for presidential and congressional candidates within congressional districts. Table 7-3 includes data on the number and percentage of congressional districts won by the presidential candidate of one party and the congressional candidate of the other party from 1920 to 2008. The data depict a significant increase in split elections for these offices, followed by a reversal of this trend. A high point was reached in 1972, when 44 percent of all House districts split their results, due largely to the voters' rejection of George McGovern, the Democratic presidential nominee. The proportion of split results was almost as high in 1984 as voters chose President Reagan and Democratic House candidates. Especially from the late 1960s through the early 1980s, party provided less structure to voting than it had in the past.[65]

The trend toward politically independent behavior has reversed, and in 2000 only 20 percent of districts provided split-ticket outcomes. Of the 228 congressional districts carried by George W. Bush, only 40 were carried by Democratic

Table 7-3   Congressional Districts with Split Election Results: 1920–2008

Year and Party of the Winning Presidential Candidate	Number of Districts	Number of Districts with Split Results	Percentage
1920 R	344	11	3.2%
1924 R	356	42	11.8
1928 R	359	68	18.9
1932 D	355	50	14.1
1936 D	361	51	14.1
1940 D	362	53	14.6
1944 D	367	41	11.2
1948 D	422	90	21.3
1952 R	435	84	19.3
1956 R	435	130	29.9
1960 D	437	114	26.1
1964 D	435	145	33.3
1968 R	435	141	32.4
1972 R	435	193	44.4
1976 D	435	124	28.5
1980 R	435	141	32.4
1984 R	435	191	43.9
1988 R	435	148	34.0
1992 D	435	101	23.2
1996 D	435	111	25.5
2000 R	435	87	20.0
2004 R	435	58	13.3
2008 D	435	83	19.1
Total	9,453	2,257	23.9

Source: Milton C. Cummings Jr., *Congressmen and the Electorate* (New York: Free Press, 1966), 32 (as updated).

Note: R = Republican; D = Democrat. Presidential returns for some congressional districts were not available between 1920 and 1948.

House candidates; Republican candidates won only 47 of the 207 congressional districts carried by Al Gore. In 2004 the trend toward more partisan voting continued, with 13.6 percent split results. Forty-one of the fifty-eight "misfits" were carried by Democratic congressional candidates and Bush. The 2004 election produced the smallest number of split results since 1944. Although there were more split results in 2008 (a total of eighty-three) than in 2004, the percentage was still low by historical standards. Together, the presidential elections of 2000, 2004, and 2008 produced 20 percent or fewer split outcomes. The last time that happened was between 1936 and 1944.

The incidence of landslide elections also provides clues as to the strength of partisanship in the electorate. An election is considered a landslide if the winning candidate receives 55 percent or more of the two-party vote. Landslides occur because numerous partisans desert their party. In the sixteen presidential elections between 1836 and 1896, only one was a landslide, but three occurred between 1964 and 1984. In 1972 fully one-third of Democrats voted for the Republican presidential nominee, Richard Nixon.

No landslides have occurred since 1984, even when one or the other party has chosen a candidate who generated little enthusiasm. Party ties have come to shape voter decisions and diminished the likelihood of one party winning an overwhelming victory. Overall, the present era resembles that of the Civil War and its aftermath (1860–1892), which was distinguished by consistently competitive presidential elections. At the electoral level, as in Congress, it is clear that party identification is significantly stronger today than it was in the 1970s and early 1980s.

Visceral Issues Drive Mass Party Differences

Since the 1930s differing beliefs about how large the government ought to be and how many services it ought to provide have dominated party conflict. Democrats have favored a more generous safety net than have Republicans in areas such as education, health care, and programs for the elderly. Because they want fewer government programs, Republicans have generally favored lower taxes than the Democrats. In addition, the Democrats have tended to support the interests of the labor movement when it has been in conflict with big business, while the Republicans have tended to support business interests.

Although these divisions have not gone away, Geoff Layman and Tom Carsey demonstrate that party conflict has extended into new realms.[66] These conflicts have tended to be in areas where fundamental understandings of right and wrong are at stake—issues such as gay rights, national security, and the protection of civil liberties. The newer disagreements, in that sense, are more visceral because opponents have difficulty finding common ground on them. Partisans will tend to have an easier time compromising on how big the federal government's role in education ought to be than on whether gays and lesbians should be allowed to marry.

Americans have been sorting themselves into the appropriate parties based on these visceral issues, making them an important and potentially polarizing line of party conflict. As evidence, consider data collected in 2003 and 2007 by the Pew Foundation. For all the items, people were read a series of statements and asked whether they agreed or disagreed. Table 7-4 presents the results broken down by party. The top half of the table includes items that are visceral in nature. The bottom half includes issues of decades-long conflict between the parties, mostly about the size of government. The first two columns in the table present the percentage difference in preference between self-identified Republicans and Democrats in each of the years. The last column is the difference between the years. A positive number in the last column indicates that party differences grew between 2003 and 2007, and a negative number indicates that they shrank. Because African Americans are generally conservative on visceral issues but still identify with the liberal party (suggesting that these issues are not important in informing their party identification), the analysis here is confined to nonblack respondents.

On the visceral issues, the last column reveals a growing chasm. Given the short time frame, moreover, the large numbers are quite significant. Of the

Table 7-4 Gaps between Partisans on Visceral vs. Traditional Issues, 2003 and 2007 (nonblack respondents)

	Percentage Gaps in 2003	Percentage Gaps in 2007	Difference between 2003 and 2007
Visceral Values and Preferences			
School boards should fire gay teachers	16	21	5
Police should be able to search known drug dealer without court order	1	18	17
Have old-fashioned values about family and marriage	20	20	0
There are clear guidelines about good and evil	12	19	7
Free speech should not extend to neo-Nazis and other extremists	7	12	5
Books with dangerous ideas should be banned from school libraries	4	9	5
Concerned government is gathering too much info about people like me	21	25	4
Newcomers threaten traditional American customs	11	20	9
Improve position of blacks even providing preferences	28	25	-3
Should do more to restrict people coming into the country	8	13	5
Discrimination against blacks is rare	7	15	8
Hasn't been much improvement in the position of blacks in U.S.	28	25	-3
Best way to ensure peace is through strength	29	35	6
Willing to fight for country, whether it is right or wrong	17	25	8
Average Gap	14.9	20.1	5.2
Traditional Values and Preferences			
Businesses strike fair balance between profits and public interest	17	20	3
Too much power concentrated in a few big companies	24	21	-3
Businesses make too much profit	28	22	-6
Unions are necessary to protect working people	24	26	2
Often worry about the chances of nuclear war	16	7	-9
Today rich are getting richer, poor getting poorer	36	35	-1
I often don't have enough money to make ends meet	17	18	1
I think the tax system is unfair to people like me	8	12	4
Poor have become too dependent on government assistance programs	23	27	4
Government must take care of those who can't care for themselves	22	23	1
Government should help more needy people even if it means more debt	32	36	4
Government should guarantee all enough to eat and place to sleep	36	36	0
Government regulation of business does more harm than good	17	3	-14
Federal government should run *only* things that can't be run at local level	16	4	-12
Average Gap	22.5	20.6	-1.9

Source: Pew Research Center for the People and the Press Values Study, 1987–2007.

fourteen items, ten produced increases in the difference between Republicans and Democrats of five or more percentage points. This is generally true on the concerns about sexual orientation, immigration, civil liberties, and a preference for the use of force. We should add that not all the differences grew, with matters involving African Americans generally holding steady. In most cases, however, mass party differences sharpened on these visceral issues.

For preferences and values that have traditionally divided the parties, the story is quite different. Of these fourteen items, none of the differences increased by as much as five percentage points, although three items came close. When differences between 2003 and 2007 were large, all suggested a narrowing rather than a widening. Self-identified Republicans and Democrats in 2007 were much closer together on fears about nuclear war, government regulation of business, and the federal government's role in policymaking. The latter two items, which saw double digit decreases between 2003 and 2007, are particularly central to understanding the traditional New Deal difference between the parties.

Overall, the average difference on the fourteen more visceral issues increased from about fifteen points in 2003 to about twenty points in 2007, roughly a five percentage point change. For the traditional issues, the average difference across all issues held relatively steady, dropping from about 22.5 points to about 20.5, a statistically insignificant change. In 2007 Republicans and Democrats were about as divided on the visceral issues as they were on the traditional issues. In 2003 the cleavage was significantly deeper on the traditional issues than on visceral issues.

The same pattern of results holds for one the most divisive of cultural issues of the day—gay marriage. Starting in October 2004, various survey organizations have asked people to place themselves in one of three categories: supporting the legality of gay marriage, supporting civil unions, or opposing both. An October 2004 *Los Angeles Times* survey found that, among nonblacks, Republicans were twenty-two percentage points less likely to support legal gay marriage than Democrats and twenty percentage points more likely to oppose both gay marriage and civil unions. By April 2005, according to a survey taken by ABC News and the *Washington Post*, those differences had both grown to twenty-four percentage points. In March 2007 *Newsweek*, in conjunction with Princeton Research Associates, found that Republicans were fully thirty-one percentage points less likely to support gay marriage and twenty-nine percentage points more likely to oppose both gay marriage and civil unions. To put it another way, party differences on the question of same-sex marriage deepened by nine percentage points between late 2004, in the midst of a presidential election that highlighted the issue, and early 2007—a remarkable change in a short time.

Racial Polarization in Voting

The division of the races along party lines, which is grounded in economic and social policies as well as the parties' differing positions on the struggle for civil rights, is one of the outstanding facts of contemporary American politics.[67] Historically, the great divide in racial voting took root in the 1960s, beginning with a massive shift by African Americans in 1964 and continuing with a sizable shift by whites in 1968. Basically, this is what happened: under the leadership of

Table 7-5 Racial and Ethnic Polarization in Voting in Presidential Elections: 1960–2008

	1960	1964	1968	1972	1976	1980	1984	1988	1992	1996	2000	2004	2008
Percentage of electorate voting Democratic	50	61	43	38	50	41	41	46	43	49	49	48	53
Percentage of whites voting Democratic	49	59	38	32	46	36	34	41	40	43	43	41	45
Percentage of blacks voting Democratic	68	94	85	87	85	86	87	82	82	84	90	88	95
Percentage of Latinos voting Democratic	—	—	—	—	—	—	—	—	62	72	62	53	67
Racial differential 1: percentage-point difference between black and white Democratic vote	19	35	47	55	39	50	53	41	42	41	47	47	50
Racial differential 2: percentage-point difference between Latino and white Democratic vote	—	—	—	—	—	—	—	—	22	29	19	12	22

Sources: Developed from data in Gallup Report, November 1988, 6–7; Gallup Poll Monthly, November 1992, 9; 1996, 2000, 2004, 2008 national exit poll of Voter News Service.

President Johnson, a bipartisan majority in Congress passed the Civil Rights Act of 1964, the most significant civil rights legislation since Reconstruction. Shortly thereafter, the Republican National Convention chose Sen. Barry Goldwater of Arizona as its presidential nominee. Goldwater was a militant conservative, an exponent of states' rights, and one of the main opponents of the 1964 act. With the lines clearly drawn, African Americans voted overwhelmingly (94 percent) for Johnson. (See Table 7-5.) Of the six states Goldwater carried, five were in the Deep South, where his states' rights/civil rights stance undoubtedly was attractive to white voters. Following Johnson's landslide victory, a top-heavy Democratic Congress passed the Voting Rights Act of 1965. This landmark legislation paved the way for African Americans to enter fully into the nation's political life, but alienated white voters, especially in the South.

By 1968, as a result of movement by white voters, black-white voting divisions intensified; 85 percent of African Americans, but only 38 percent of whites, voted Democratic. With a southerner, Jimmy Carter, at the head of the ticket in 1976, more whites (but less than a majority) voted Democratic than in either of the previous two elections. But this election was merely a blip—a modest exception to the trend. Today, there are no signs that racial cleavages are ebbing, and the current split is quite sharp. In 2000 African Americans increased their support for the Democratic candidate, to 90 percent, compared with 8 percent for the Republican. Whites, on the other hand, voted 54 percent to 42 percent Republican. With the first African American standard-bearer, Barack Obama, atop the Democratic ticket, African American support for the party increased to 95 percent in 2008. Whites provided Obama with only 45 percent of their ballots.

As Latinos have become a larger percentage of American voters, observers are taking note of the voting behavior of this group. Exit polls indicate that Latinos are a Democratic-leaning group. Making up only 3 percent of voters in 1992, Latinos provided 62 percent of their votes to Bill Clinton, 22 percentage points higher than his support from whites. Clinton did even better with Latinos relative to whites in 1996, with the difference between white and Latino voting behavior reaching its maximum of 29 percent. George W. Bush made inroads with Latinos in 2000 and 2004, the result of a concerted effort by the former Texas governor to woo them, but Obama dominated John McCain with this group in 2008. Only 45 percent of whites voted for Obama, but fully 66 percent of Latinos did, reestablishing the twenty-plus point difference in voting behavior between whites and Latinos. This development is important because Latinos are now a larger minority than African Americans. In 2004 Bush won all the desert Southwest states, where the Latino population is generally large. In 2008, with the help of strong Latino support, Obama won all of them except Arizona, McCain's home state. As the United States becomes more racially diverse, Republicans will be hard pressed to win elections without increasing their support from racial and ethnic minorities.

Table 7-6 Popular Trust in Government: 1972–2008

Question: How much of the time do you think you can trust the government in Washington to do what is right—just about always, most of the time, or only some of the time?

Response	1972	1976	1980	1984	1988	1992	1996	2000	2004	2008
Always	5%	3%	2%	4%	4%	3%	3%	4%	4%	5%
Most of the time	48	30	23	40	37	26	26	40	43	25
Some or none of the time	45	63	73	54	58	70	69	55	53	70
Don't know	2	3	2	2	1	1	2	1	0	0

Source: National Election Study, Center for Political Studies, University of Michigan.

The Public's Declining Confidence in Political Institutions

The confidence of the American public in its political institutions is substantially lower today than it was in the 1960s, a change with important consequences. Although the public's feelings about government have often been largely ignored, the surge in public spiritedness following the September 11, 2001, attacks on New York City and the Pentagon placed a spotlight on these attitudes for a time.

It is important to note that popular disillusionment concerning politics and political institutions did not start with Watergate. The trend began in the mid- to late 1960s and ran steadily through the 1970s. (See Table 7-6.) The disclosures of criminal activities by White House officials and Nixon's role in the cover-up merely accentuated it.

No simple explanation exists for the decline of trust in government. Many factors have been at work, probably the most important of which center on public dissatisfaction with policy outcomes such as the Vietnam War and the government's inability to solve certain social and economic problems, which led to the urban unrest and riots of the 1960s.[68] In addition, the media's steady preoccupation with negative news about policies that go awry and with skewering politicians, especially the president, have helped to maintain the public's negative feelings about Washington and politics in general.[69]

For at least a short while, all this changed. After the 2001 terrorist attacks, trust in political institutions surged to a level not seen since the mid-1960s. Some commentators suggested that this was a watershed time for government revitalization. The surge, however, proved short lived. (See Figure 7-2.) Within three months, the percentage of people saying that they trusted the government in Washington to do what was right all or most of the time had dropped by fifteen percentage points. By July 2002, less than a year after the attacks, trust in government had dropped below the level it had been when Bill Clinton left office. In a word, people began to think about the political system in terms of a prolonged slump in the stock market, a softening economy, and a rash of corporate scandals, which caused their evaluations of government to sour.

Figure 7-2 Changes in Trust in Government: 2000–2002

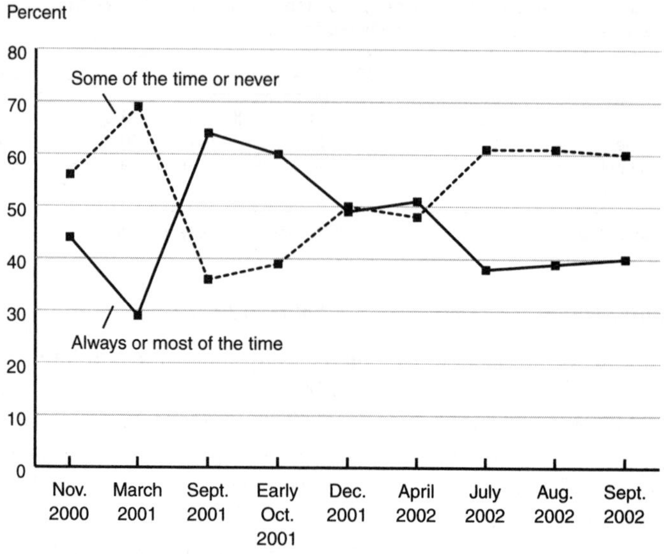

Percent

Source: Data compiled by authors.

Why was trust in government so much higher in the 1950s and 1960s than it is today? With Americans perceiving a constant threat from the Soviet Union in the decades after World War II, most tended to evaluate the government in terms of its ability to deal with foreign crises. Because only government can deal with such problems and because institutions like the military were very popular, feelings about government tended to be positive. Starting in the late 1960s, however, people began to think about government in terms of its ability to deal with domestic problems, such as race relations and poverty. Government agencies tasked with these responsibilities were less popular and their efforts were often not obviously successful. In general, the American public trusts the federal government more when evaluating it in terms of its performance on international issues than on domestic issues.[70]

Since the mid-1970s more than 60 percent of people have said that "government is pretty much run by a few big interests looking out for themselves." More than half of those surveyed contend that "public officials don't care much what people like me think." (See Figure 7-3.) And since then at least 60 percent of the public also has thought that the government wastes "a lot" of money.

The consequences of the public's negative feelings toward government are hard to measure in a precise way. It is known, however, that almost no difference is found between voters and nonvoters in the level of their distrust of government, so distrust does not bear on turnout.[71] Nevertheless, there is considerable evidence that those who distrust the government are less likely to vote for an

Figure 7-3 Evidence of Public Alienation from Government

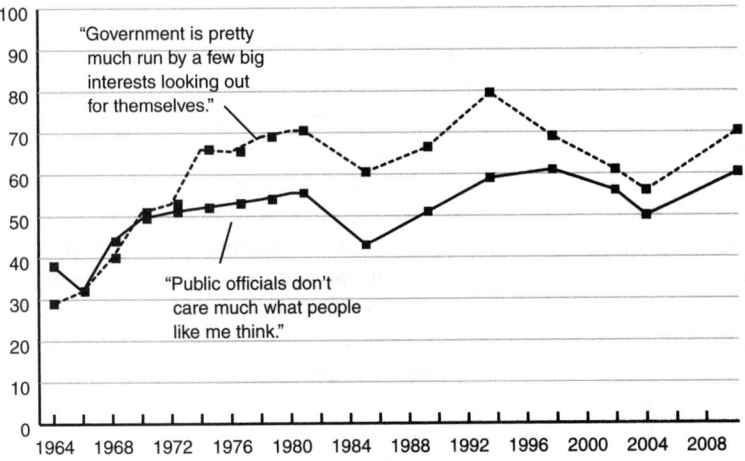

Source: Data drawn from National Election Study, Center for Political Studies, University of Michigan.

incumbent president and more likely to support a third party candidate than those who trust the government. As a consequence, the incumbent party's presidential candidate lost six of the eleven elections between 1968 and 2008, the worst record for incumbents since the early to mid-1800s, and Ross Perot secured historically large percentages of the vote in 1992 and 1996. Presidential approval ratings are, generally speaking, no longer as high today as they were in the 1950s and 1960s, and declining political trust helps account for that fact.

In addition, political distrust has a major impact on how much the public wants the government to do. Those who are distrustful are less supportive of government programs, especially those directed toward African Americans and the poor, than those who trust the government.[72] Indeed, the demise of the Clinton administration's efforts to provide universal health insurance was largely the result of people's negative feelings about government. Americans looked askance at the prospect of an incompetent government, as they saw it, administering a large new bureaucracy.[73] Similarly, in 2009 negative sentiments about government (aided by GOP rhetoric) likely underlay some of the public's reservations about a "public option" in the Democratic health care reform proposals. It is worth noting, however, that 55 percent of the Pew survey respondents favored a public option, a surprisingly strong number, given the intensity of the GOP campaign waged against it.[74]

Declining trust in government has undoubtedly affected the relative success of the parties over the last political generation. The Democratic Party has traditionally favored using the government to level the economic playing field, while the Republican Party has generally opposed this notion. Given popular suspicions of government, it is not surprising that the Republicans have often dominated national politics since 1968, winning the presidency in seven of eleven elections. The party's small government philosophy obviously is attractive to a public distrustful of government. The 2008 election suggests that people will embrace the idea of more government regulation even if they do not trust it very much, provided they distrust banks and big business even less.

Declining trust is not immutable. Changes in political leadership, reorientations in government policies leading to amelioration or resolution of nagging problems, successful new policy ventures, and the more complete fulfillment of popular expectations could strengthen trust in government.[75] That political trust increased markedly between 1994 and 2000 suggests that sustained economic growth and public satisfaction with political leadership can bring about positive change. The quick drop in trust after its post–September 11 high, however, shows that gains can be fleeting in a political environment in which cynicism is never far below the surface and where a mood of disenchantment and disconnection is commonly present.

Prospects for the Parties

The American party system has been shaped more by custom and environment than by intent. Often, the major parties have been loose and disorderly coalitions, heavily decentralized, lacking in unity and discipline, preoccupied with winning office, and no more than erratically responsible for the conduct of government and the formation of public policy. Even during periods of party polarization, the two parties find it hard to resist edging toward the ideological center when election season is at hand. Genuine responsible party government does not come easily or naturally in the American setting.

There is, however, another side to parties. They have performed at least as well as the parties of other democratic nations—and perhaps far better. Democratic politics requires the maintenance of a predictable legal system; institutionalized arrangements for popular control of government and the mobilization of majorities; methods and arenas for the illumination, crystallization, and reconciliation of conflict; and the means for endowing leaders and policies with legitimacy. To each of these requirements the parties have contributed steadily and often in major ways.[76]

A truism of American politics is that it is difficult to cut free from familiar institutions. Old practices die hard. Conventional arrangements hang on and on. Change arrives incrementally and unnoticed. Most Americans are habituated to pragmatic electoral parties, and the parties themselves are accustomed to the environment in which they function. It would seem that prospects for the development of a system of responsible parties are thin at best. But the matter deserves a closer look.

On many counts the parties have lost ground since the era of reform in the late 1960s and early 1970s. The formal electoral party organizations have been weakened. Their control over the nominating process, once a virtual monopoly, has gradually slipped away. Primary battles for major offices occur frequently, and the regular party organization's candidate (if there is one) is by no means assured victory. Although the parties have responded favorably to some of these challenges, they have nowhere near the same control they enjoyed generations ago. The power of local party leaders has probably never been weaker than it is today. The media, public relations consultants, campaign management firms, interest groups, and informal partisan networks are now as much a part of campaigns as the formal party organizations—at least when important offices are at stake. So-called "independent candidates" can be quite successful; indeed, the widespread support for Perot in 1992 was a wake-up call for both major parties.

The sum of these developments is that American parties compete within the political process but do not dominate it. In some jurisdictions they are all but invisible. A great deal of contemporary politics lies outside the parties and beyond their control. Most troubling of all is that many voters profess deep skepticism of parties, politicians, and government. Even though the parties have made certain gains since the 1980s, the prospects remain dim for the development of a full-blown responsible party system. Too many obstacles—constitutional, political, and otherwise—stand in the way. But this is not to say that responsible party performance in government is unattainable. How parties govern is not dependent on the strength and vitality of the electoral party organizations or on the way individuals are elected to office. The party-in-the-government, it is worth remembering, is both different from the party-in-the-electorate and at least partly independent of it.

The essence of a responsible party system is not to be found in party councils, closed primaries, demographically representative national conventions, off-year party conventions, government financing of elections, or intraparty democracy. Instead, the key to a responsible party system is for parties *to design and take responsibility for a program of public policy.* Such responsibility first requires a strong measure of internal cohesion within the party-in-the-government in order to adopt its program and, second, an electorate sufficiently sensitive to party accomplishments and failures that it can hold the parties, especially the one in power, accountable for their records. At times, neither requirement can be met to any degree; at other times, American political institutions function in a manner largely consonant with the responsible party model.

A responsible party system at the national level demands a particular kind of Congress—one in which power is centralized rather than dispersed. Over long stretches of time, Congress has not been organized to permit the parties *qua* parties to govern. The seniority system, the independence of committees and their chairs, the filibuster, the weaknesses present in elected party positions and agencies, and the unrepresentativeness of Congress itself have made it difficult for party majorities to assert themselves and to act in the name of the party. But these barriers to party majority building have been notably diminished in the past two decades.

Every so often the congressional party comes fully alive. Consider the first session of the Eighty-ninth Congress (1965)—"the most dramatic illustration in a generation of the capacity of the president and the Congress to work together on important issues of public policy":

> In part a mopping up operation on an agenda fashioned at least in spirit by the New Deal, the work of the 89th Congress cut new paths through the frontier of qualitative issues: a beautification bill, a bill to create federal support for the arts and humanities, vast increases in federal aid to education. . . . [The] policy leadership and the legislative skill of President Johnson found a ready and supportive response from a strengthened partisan leadership and a substantial, presidentially oriented Democratic majority in both houses. A decade of incremental structural changes in the locus of power in both houses eased the President's task of consent-building and of legislative implementation. Yet Congress was far from being just a rubber stamp. On some issues the President met resounding defeat. On many issues, presidential recommendations were modified by excisions or additions—reflecting the power of particular committee chairmen, group interests, and bureaucratic pressures at odds with presidential perspectives.
>
> [The lessons of the Eighty-ninth Congress] proved that vigorous presidential leadership and sizable partisan majorities in both houses of the same partisan persuasion as the President could act in reasonable consonance, and with dispatch, in fashioning creative answers to major problems. The nation's voters could pin responsibility upon a national party for the legislative output. If that partisan majority erred in judgment, it could at least be held accountable in ensuing congressional and presidential elections.[77]

Party responsibility came to the fore again in the Ninety-seventh Congress (1981–1982). President Reagan was the beneficiary of the highest party support scores received by any president in the preceding three decades. During the first session, Senate Republicans voted in agreement with the president 80 percent of the time, and House Republicans 68 percent of the time.[78] At session end, Republicans could reasonably claim that their party had moved the nation in a new direction, greatly reducing federal regulations in several areas. Consonant with the responsible party model, the performance of the Reagan administration was the overriding issue in the off-year election of 1982, in which Republicans lost twenty-six seats in the House while holding Democrats to a standoff in Senate races. From the perspective of the president, these were halcyon days, but they passed quickly. Conflict between the branches intensified, the president's legislative successes declined, and the legislature reasserted itself during the latter stages of the Reagan administration, particularly during the 100th Congress (1987–1988).

Government by party was conspicuously absent during the succeeding administration of George H. W. Bush. His domestic agenda was limited, and the Democrats controlled Congress. Conflict between the parties increased in both houses during Bush's term, reaching a near record level in his last year in office. His success rate in Congress in 1992 was the lowest of any president in forty years. Few administration bills were passed, confrontations were frequent, and the president vetoed a number of major Democratic bills. Low public opinion ratings further undermined the president's position. Toward the end of the Bush administration, "gridlock" vied with "morass" to become the most fashionable term to describe the state of Washington politics.

Control of the presidency and both houses of Congress by the Democrats in 1993 provided the first opportunity for authentic majority-party policy leadership in more than a decade. But getting the Democratic Party to stick together was not easy. President Clinton's major initiatives in his first year, including his deficit-reduction plan, were threatened by liberal-conservative conflict within his own party as well as by the concerted opposition of Republicans in both chambers. One after another presidential initiative became a hostage to intraparty bargaining and deal cutting. Conflict between the parties was also at unusually high levels during the first three years of Clinton's presidency, particularly in 1995, following the Republicans' off-year capture of both houses of Congress. More than 70 percent of all recorded floor votes were *party votes*—votes in which a majority of one party voted against a majority of the other party.[79]

With the Democrats holding the presidency and the Republicans in control of Congress, little was accomplished. The government itself was shut down on two occasions, and the Republicans received most of the blame for these debacles. As the 1996 election approached and apprehension increased, both parties muted their partisanship, adopted more centrist positions, and cooperated to pass a number of major bills on issues ranging from welfare reform to the minimum wage. Voters responded to the bipartisanship by reelecting Clinton by a comfortable margin (but short of a majority) and returning a (narrowed) Republican majority to Congress.

The period between 2000 and 2006 offered another opportunity for responsible party government when the Republicans captured and maintained both the presidency and Congress. In some respects, the GOP adhered to the responsible party model by passing the large tax cuts George W. Bush promised in his campaign. But, as noted earlier, the GOP also passed several legislative measures inconsistent with their public commitment to freer markets and smaller government. And on other important issues, such as Social Security reform and immigration, the party lacked the internal cohesion to act.

The 2008 elections produced a unified Democratic government and another opportunity for responsible party government. It will not come easily. The Democratic Party expanded its House and Senate majorities, but the party's membership also became more ideologically diverse, with the election of moderate members who won in formerly Republican districts. The diversity may make it more difficult for leaders to hold the party together.[80] Moreover, the magnitude of the problems facing the nation is daunting. Bringing the war in Iraq to a sensible close, providing security in Afghanistan, reforming health care, fixing Social Security, halting climate change, reining in mountainous budget deficits, and keeping the nation safe from terrorist attacks are only a sample of the challenges facing Democrats.

The conditions must be right for responsible party government to move forward: a partisan majority in general ideological agreement (or an effective majority, such as the Republican-led conservative coalition in the House during the Ninety-seventh Congress) and a vigorous president are essential. A long or innovative policy agenda also may be required. In any case, under the right circumstances, the deadlocks in American politics can be broken and the political system can function vigorously and with a high degree of cooperation between the branches of government. Party responsibility can thrive even if unrecognized and unlabeled. The evidence suggests that the first requirement for government by responsible parties—a fairly high degree of internal party agreement on policy—can, at least occasionally, be met.

Indeed, the election of Democrat Barack Obama as president and the expansion of Democratic majorities in the House and Senate in 2008 makes party rule once again a lively prospect. As has been shown repeatedly throughout this book, the parties at the beginning of the twenty-first century are very distinct ideologically. Party-line voting in Congress is at a historic high point, and Democrats today have a fairly well-defined agenda, which includes reforming health care, re-regulating the nation's financial markets, moving to a greener economy, implementing a more progressive tax code (and slowing the growth of income inequality more generally), and practicing a more multilateral foreign policy. In all these areas, Republicans have a different vision.

The clear differences between the parties do not complete the picture, however. The second requirement of responsible party government—an electorate attuned to party performance in government—has not come to pass. This is the point at which the system of responsible parties tends to break down. As Donald Stokes and Warren Miller wrote in 1966:

> What the public knows about the legislative records of the parties and of individual congressional candidates is a principal reason for the departure of American practice from an idealized conception of party government. . . . The electorate sees very little altogether of what goes on in the national legislature. Few judgments of legislative performance are associated with the parties, and much of the public is unaware even of which party has control of Congress. . . . Many of those who have commented on the lack of party discipline in Congress have assumed that the Congressman votes against his party because he is forced to by the demands of one of several hundred constituencies of a superlatively heterogeneous nation. In some cases, the Representative may subvert the proposals of his party because his constituency demands it. But a more reasonable interpretation over a broader range of issues is that the Congressman fails to see these proposals as part of a program on which the party—and he himself—will be judged at the polls, because he knows the constituency isn't looking.[81]

Although voters today are better able to perceive differences between the parties than voters of a generation ago, their knowledge is still quite limited and fragmented. The first requirement of voters in a responsible party model is for them to know which party holds a majority of seats in Congress so they can hold the appropriate side responsible for successes and failures. According to data from the 2008 National Election Study, however, only 40 percent of Americans knew that the Democrats held the majority in the House before the election, a percentage comparable with decades past.[82] Only 33 percent knew the Democrats controlled the Senate. Moreover, this percentage is probably inflated by a fair number of people who simply guess which party is in control.

Experiments with forms of party responsibility, like fashion, will perhaps always possess a probationary quality—tried, neglected, forgotten, and rediscovered. The tone and mood of such a system will appear on occasion, but without the public's either anticipating it or recognizing it when it arrives. More generally, however, the party system is likely to resemble, at least in broad lines, the model to which Americans are adjusted and inured: the parties situated precariously atop the political process, threatened and thwarted by a variety of competitors, only partly able to control their own nominations or to elect "their" nominees, active in fits and starts and often in hiding, beset by factional rifts, shunned or dismissed by countless voters (including many new ones), and moderately irresponsible. From the vantage point of both outsiders and insiders, the party system will sometimes appear, to the extent that it registers at all, in disarray. And often it *is* in disarray, but not to a point that either promises or ensures its enfeeblement and disintegration.

NOTES

1. Committee on Political Parties of the American Political Science Association, "Toward a More Responsible Two-Party System," *American Political Science Review* 44, no. 3, part 2, Supplement (September 1950): 1, 2, 22.

2. Donald E. Stokes and Warren E. Miller, "Party Government and the Saliency of Congress," in *Elections and the Political Order,* ed. Angus Campbell (New York: Wiley, 1966), 209–211.

3. For excellent analyses of party responsibility, see Austin Ranney, "Toward a More Responsible Two-Party System: A Commentary," *American Political Science Review* 45 (June 1951): 488–499; T. William Goodman, "How Much Political Party Centralization Do We Want?" *Journal of Politics* 13 (November 1951): 536–561.

4. In addition, certain major recommendations of the report were met through action by the federal government. A number of barriers to voting were eliminated as a result of the passage of the Voting Rights Act of 1965 and the adoption of the Twenty-sixth Amendment to the Constitution in 1971.

5. The price of these reforms was high. Delegates of the new-enthusiast variety were far more numerous than party professionals. Moreover, these delegates were more liberal than the general run of Democrats, and fewer delegates belonging to labor unions were present than usual. In some respects the new rules produced a most unrepresentative convention. The candidate it nominated, George McGovern, was

overwhelmingly defeated in the election—a result due in part to the defection of party moderates and conservatives. Ironically, although it was expected that the quota system for African Americans, women, and youth would increase support among these groups in the election, nothing of the sort occurred. African Americans and youths supported the 1972 Democratic presidential candidate in about the same proportion as they did the 1968 candidate. Support among women voters declined notably. See Austin Ranney, *Curing the Mischiefs of Faction: Party Reform in America* (Berkeley: University of California Press, 1975), 153–156, 206–208.

6. According to "Toward a More Responsible Two-Party System," to achieve a system of responsible parties, "The internal processes of the parties must be democratic, the party members must have an opportunity to participate in intraparty business, and the leaders must be accountable to the party." Quote on page 23.

7. See the analysis by Kenneth Janda, "Primrose Paths to Political Reform: 'Reforming' versus Strengthening American Parties," in *Paths to Political Reform,* ed. William J. Crotty (Lexington, Mass.: Heath, 1980), especially 319–327.

8. Stephen Ansolabehere, Shigeo Hirano, and James M. Snyder Jr., "What Did the Direct Primary Do to Party Loyalty in Congress?" in *Party, Process, and Political Change in Congress,* vol. 2: *Further New Perspectives on the History of Congress,* ed. David W. Brady and Mathew D. McCubbins (Stanford, Calif.: Stanford University Press, 2007).

9. John Aldrich and David W. Rohde, "Congressional Committees in a Continuing Partisan Era," in *Congress Reconsidered,* 9th ed., ed. Lawrence C. Dodd and Bruce I. Oppenheimer (Washington, D.C.: CQ Press, 2009).

10. Ibid.; Richard Cohen, "Power Surge," *National Journal,* July 21, 2007, 23.

11. Morris Fiorina, "Parties as Problem Solvers," in *Promoting the General Welfare: New Perspectives on Government Performance,* ed. Alan S. Gerber and Eric M. Patashnik (Washington, D.C.: Brookings, 2006).

12. Ibid.

13. Ibid.

14. Thomas E. Mann and Norman J. Ornstein, *The Broken Branch: How Congress Is Failing America and How to Get It Back on Track* (New York: Oxford University Press, 2006).

15. Emphasis in the original. Sarah Binder, "Elections, Parties, and Governance," in *The Legislative Branch,* ed. Paul Quirk and Sarah Binder (New York: Oxford University Press, 2005). See also Sarah Binder, *Stalemate: The Causes and Consequences of Legislative Gridlock* (Washington, D.C.: Brookings, 2003).

16. E. E. Schattschneider, *Party Government* (New York: Holt, Rinehart and Winston, 1942), 64.

17. Seth Masket, *No Middle Ground: How Informal Party Organizations Control Nominations and Polarize Legislatures* (Ann Arbor: University of Michigan, 2009).

18. Frank J. Sorauf, *Political Parties in the American System* (Boston: Little, Brown, 1964), 102.

19. Byron E. Shafer, *Quiet Revolution: The Struggle for the Democratic Party and the Shaping of Post-Reform Politics* (New York: Russell Sage Foundation, 1983), 529.

20. See the outstanding book by Marty Cohen, David Karol, Hans Noel, and John Zaller, *The Party Decides: Presidential Nominations Before and After Reforms* (Chicago: University of Chicago Press, 2009).

21. An earlier possible exception is Gary Hart, who was the Democratic front-runner for the 1988 election after his stronger than expected showing in 1984. Hart all but disqualified himself after an extramarital affair came to light in 1987.

22. This quotation appears in Burdett A. Loomis, *The New American Politician: Ambition, Entrepreneurship, and the Changing Face of Political Life* (New York: Basic Books, 1988), 187.

23. Ibid., 10.

24. David B. Truman, "Party Reform, Party Atrophy, and Constitutional Change: Some Reflections," *Political Science Quarterly* 99 (Winter 1984–1985): 167.

25. Cohen et al., *The Party Decides*; Masket, *No Middle Ground*.

26. David C. W. Parker, *The Power of Money in Congressional Campaigns, 1880–2006* (Norman: University of Oklahoma Press, 2008).

27. Paul S. Herrnson, *Congressional Elections: Campaigning at Home and in Washington*, 5th ed. (Washington, D.C.: CQ Press, 2008).

28. Susan B. Glasser, "Hired Guns Fuel Fundraising Race," *Washington Post*, April 30, 2000.

29. See an analysis by Benjamin Ginsberg, "Money and Power: The New Political Economy of American Elections," in *The Political Economy*, ed. Thomas Ferguson and Joel Rogers (Armonk, N.Y.: M. E. Sharpe, 1984), 163–179.

30. Joe McGinniss, *The Selling of the President* (New York: Trident Press/Simon and Schuster, 1968), 27.

31. Robert MacNeil, *The People Machine: The Influence of Television on American Politics* (New York: Harper and Row, 1968), xvii.

32. Dan Nimmo, *The Political Persuaders: The Techniques of Modern Election Campaigns* (Englewood Cliffs, N.J.: Prentice Hall, 1970), 197.

33. Comment by a Bush adviser quoted in *Time*, November 14, 1988, 66.

34. An unnamed gubernatorial candidate quoted by Barbara G. Salmore and Stephen A. Salmore, *Candidates, Parties, and Campaigns* (Washington, D.C.: CQ Press, 1989), 139.

35. Harold Mendelsohn and Irving Crespi, *Polls, Television, and the New Politics* (Scranton, Pa.: Chandler, 1970), 310–311.

36. David Menefee-Libey, *The Triumph of Campaign-Centered Politics* (New York: Chatham House, Seven Bridges Press, LLC, 2000).

37. Cornelius P. Cotter and John F. Bibby, "Institutional Development of Parties and the Thesis of Party Decline," *Political Science Quarterly* 95 (Spring 1980): 1–27. For a close analysis of the services made available to congressional candidates by national party committees, especially those of the Republican Party, see Paul S. Herrnson, "Do Parties Make a Difference? The Role of Party Organizations in Congressional Elections," *Journal of Politics* 48 (August 1986): 589–615.

38. John Aldrich, "Southern Parties in State and Nation," *Journal of Politics* 62 (August 2000): 643–670.

39. Robert J. Huckshorn, James L. Gibson, Cornelius P. Cotter, and John F. Bibby, "Party Integration and Party Organizational Strength," *Journal of Politics* 48 (November 1986): 976–991.

40. For the development of these and cognate themes that point to a political rebirth of the American party system, see Xandra Kayden and Eddie Mahe Jr., *The Party Goes On: The Persistence of the Two-Party System in the United States* (New York: Basic Books, 1985).

41. Raymond J. La Raja, "State Political Parties after BCRA," in *Life after Reform: When the Bipartisan Campaign Reform Act Meets Politics*, ed., Michael J. Malbin (Lanham, Md.: Rowman and Littlefield, 2003), 101–137.

42. Byron E. Shafer, "The Democratic Party Salvation Industry," *Public Opinion* 8 (June/July 1985): 47. For a finding that local parties did not become less active and less organized during this current era, see James L. Gibson, Cornelius P. Cotter, John F. Bibby, and Robert J. Huckshorn, "Whither the Local Parties? A Cross-Sectional and Longitudinal Analysis of the Strength of Party Organizations," *American Journal of Political Science* 29 (February 1985): 139–160. In addition, see Barbara C. Burrell, "Local Political Party Committees, Task Performance and Organizational Vitality," *Western Political Quarterly* 39 (March 1986): 48–66.

43. Schattschneider, *Party Government*, 64ff.

44. Thomas Patterson, *Out of Order* (New York: Knopf, 1994).

45. On recruitment, see Kira Sanbonmatsu, *Where Women Run: Gender and Party in the American States* (Ann Arbor: University of Michigan Press, 2006); on nominations, see Cohen et al., *The Party Decides*, and Masket, *No Middle Ground*; on party campaigning, see Parker, *The Power of Money*.

46. Cohen et al., *The Party Decides*; Masket, *No Middle Ground*.

47. Ranney, *Curing the Mischiefs of Faction*, 3.

48. For an elaboration of these themes, see Nelson W. Polsby, *Consequences of Party Reform* (Oxford: Oxford University Press, 1983), especially chapter 2.

49. Truman, "Party Reform, Party Atrophy, and Constitutional Change," 169.

50. Fiorina, "Parties as Problem Solvers."

51. *Time*, January 29, 1979, 12.

52. *U.S. News and World Report*, January 29, 1979, 24.

53. Federal Election Commission, press release, April 25, 2009.

54. Dan Eggen, "Industry Cash Flowed to Drafters of Reform: Key Senator Baucus Is a Leading Recipient," *Washington Post*, July 21, 2009.

55. See a discussion of single-issue and ideological PACs in William J. Crotty and Gary C. Jacobson, *American Parties in Decline* (Boston: Little, Brown, 1980), 117–155.

56. *Washington Post*, September 13, 1978. The comment was made by Sen. Wendell R. Anderson (D-Minn.) to columnist David S. Broder.

57. *Washington Post*, September 13, 1978.

58. Barbara Sinclair, *Party Wars: Polarization and the Politics of National Policymaking* (Norman: University of Oklahoma Press, 2006), especially chapter 9.

59. Fiorina, "Parties as Problem Solvers," 249. Some scholars have cast doubt on whether this arrangement would be long term. Allen J .Cigler and Burdett Loomis, "Organized Interests, Political Parties, and Representation: James Madison, Tom Delay, and the Soul of American Politics," in *Interest Group Politics*, 7th ed., ed. Allen J .Cigler and Burdett Loomis (Washington, D.C.: CQ Press, 2007).

60. Frank J. Sorauf, *Party Politics in America* (Boston: Little, Brown, 1980), 48.

61. "Hutchinson Struggling to Keep Arkansas Senate Seat for GOP," *Washington Post*, October 28, 2002.

62. These data on the 2008 national convention delegates are drawn from the *New York Times*, August 24, 2008.

63. For a study of party-switching among county-level activists in the 1988 presidential campaign, see John A. Clark, John M. Bruce, John H. Kessel, and William G. Jacoby, "I'd Rather Switch Than Fight: Lifelong Democrats and Converts to Republicanism among Campaign Activists," *American Journal of Political Science* 35 (August 1991): 577–597. See also John M. Bruce, John A. Clark, and John H. Kessel, "Advocacy Politics in Presidential Parties," *American Political Science Review* 85 (December 1991): 1089–1105.

64. Concerning this point, see Edward R. Tufte, *Political Control of the Economy* (Princeton, N.J.: Princeton University Press, 1978), especially chapter 4. See a study of presidential elections from 1948 through 1984 that finds that the *state of the economy* is an even better predictor of election outcomes than the *candidates' popularity* (or the voters' relative liking of them). Robert S. Erickson, "Economic Conditions and the Presidential Vote," *American Political Science Review* 83 (June 1989): 567–573.

65. For good evidence that Republican Party activists in the South are substantially more conservative than their Democratic counterparts, see Harold D. Clarke, Frank B. Feigert, and Marianne C. Stewart, "Different Contents, Similar Packages: The

Domestic Political Beliefs of Southern Local Party Activists," *Political Research Quarterly* 48 (March 1995): 151–167.

66. Geoffrey C. Layman and Thomas C. Carsey, "Party Polarization and Conflict Extension in the American Electorate," *American Journal of Political Science* 46 (October 2002): 786–802.

67. For analysis of the voting patterns of African Americans and whites, as well as other groups, see Harold W. Stanley and Richard G. Niemi, "Partisanship and Group Support, 1952–1988," *American Politics Quarterly* 19 (April 1991): 189–210; Harold W. Stanley, William T. Bianco, and Richard G. Niemi, "Partisanship and Group Support over Time: A Multivariate Analysis," *American Political Science Review* 80 (September 1986): 970–976; and Edward G. Carmines and James A. Stimson, "Racial Issues and the Structure of Mass Belief Systems," *Journal of Politics* 44 (February 1982): 2–20.

68. See, for example, Arthur H. Miller, "Political Issues and Trust in Government, 1964–70," *American Political Science Review* 68 (September 1974): 989–1001; Jack Citrin, "Comment: The Political Relevance of Trust in Government," *American Political Science Review* 68 (September 1974), 973–988; Marc J. Hetherington, "The Political Relevance of Political Trust," *American Political Science Review* 92 (December 1998): 791–808.

69. See, for example, Joseph A. Cappella and Kathleen Hall Jamieson, *The Spiral of Cynicism: The Press and the Public Good* (New York: Oxford University Press, 1997).

70. Marc J. Hetherington and Thomas J. Rudolph, "Priming, Performance, and the Dynamics of Political Trust," *Journal of Politics* 70 (May 2008): 498–512.

71. See Citrin, "Comment."

72. Marc J. Hetherington, *Why Trust Matters: Declining Political Trust and the Demise of American Liberalism* (Princeton, N.J.: Princeton University Press, 2005).

73. Haynes Johnson and David S. Broder, *The System: The American Way of Politics at the Breaking Point* (Boston: Little, Brown, 1996); Theda Skocpol, *Boomerang: Clinton's Health Security Effort and the Turn against Government in U.S. Politics* (New York: W. W. Norton, 1996).

74. Pew Research Center for the People and the Press, "Mixed Views of Economic Policies and Health Care Reform Persist; Support for Health Care Principles, Opposition to Package," October 8, 2009, http://people-press.org/report/551/.

75. See Jack Citrin and Donald Philip Green, "Presidential Leadership and the Resurgence of Trust in Government," *British Journal of Political Science* 16 (October 1986): 431–453.

76. To explore the literature that defends the American party system, see in particular Herbert Agar, *The Price of Union* (Boston: Houghton Mifflin, 1950); Pendleton Herring, *The Politics of Democracy* (New York: Norton, 1940); Arthur N. Holcombe, *Our More Perfect Union* (Cambridge, Mass.: Harvard University Press, 1950); and Edward C. Banfield, "In Defense of the American Party System," in *Political Parties, U.S.A.*, ed. Robert A. Goldwin (Chicago: Rand McNally, 1964), 21–39.

77. Stephen K. Bailey, *Congress in the Seventies* (New York: St. Martin's Press, 1970), 102–103. Among the other major accomplishments of the first session of the Eighty-ninth Congress were the passage of bills to provide for medical care for the aged under Social Security, aid to depressed areas, the protection of voting rights, federal scholarships, the Teacher Corps, immigration reform, and a variety of programs to launch the "war on poverty."

78. *Congressional Quarterly Weekly Report,* January 2, 1982, 20–21.

79. *Congressional Quarterly Weekly Report,* December 21, 1996, 3432.

80. On the positive side, as Bruce Oppenheimer notes, congressional Democrats of the 111th Congress are less ideologically diverse than in the 103rd Congress (1993–1994), when the party had a difficult time governing. Bruce Oppenheimer, "Barack Obama, Bill Clinton, and the Democratic Congressional Majority," *Extensions: A Journal of the Carl Albert Congressional Research and Studies Center* (Spring 2009): 11–15.

81. Donald E. Stokes and Warren E. Miller, "Party Government and the Saliency of Congress," in *Elections and the Political Order*, 209–211.

82. Data taken from the 2004 American National Election Study. Only 51 percent knew the Republicans held the majority in the Senate.

INDEX

*Figures, notes, and tables are indicated
with f, n, and t following the page number.*